$16.10

Elite Deviance

Elite Deviance

Second Edition

David R. Simon
University of North Florida

D. Stanley Eitzen
Colorado State University

Allyn and Bacon, Inc.
Boston　London　Sydney　Toronto

To Craig Finney, counselor and friend, who also knows the meaning of oppression.

David R. Simon

To my wife and children: Florine, Keith, Mike, and Kelly.

D. Stanley Eitzen

Series Editor: Judy Shaw
Production Administrator: Jane Schulman
Editorial/Production Services: Susan Freese
Cover Coordinator: Linda K. Dickinson

Library of Congress Cataloging in Publication Data
Simon, David R., 1944–
   Elite deviance.
   Includes bibliographical references and index.
   1. White collar crimes—United States. 2. Deviant behavior.
3. Elite (Social sciences)—United States. I. Eitzen, D. Stanley
II. Title
HV663.S47 1986   364.1'68'0973   85-18660
ISBN 0-205-08673-X

Printed in the United States of America
10 9 8 7 6 5 4 3 2 1   90 89 88 87 86

Contents

Preface

As we complete this second edition of *Elite Deviance*, Ronald Reagan has just begun his second term as president. His first term has been popularly characterized as a return to old-fashioned patriotism and a restoration of confidence in business and government. The public mood is optimistic as President Reagan and a conservative Congress have moved to get government off the backs of the business sector and out of the sponsorship of social programs.

Lest we forget—and that is one goal of this book—deviance among political and business elites is as prevalent today as it has ever been. At the government level, corruption and unethical behavior are relatively commonplace, even among the president's own staff. Some forty-five members of the Reagan administration have either resigned from office or are under serious investigation for wrongdoing. And in foreign policy, this administration continues to support regimes that violate elementary human rights on a large scale, insisting that such support is democratic.

Among corporate interests, crimes and incidents of unethical behavior have continued unabated during the Reagan years—from Union Carbide's tribulations in India and West Virginia to General Dynamics' and General Electric's scandalous defense contracts to corporate efforts to weaken the Foreign Corrupt Practices Act. Little has changed regarding institutionalized patterns of elite deviance, and with good reason: The structural factors that constitute the core of elite deviance remain unchanged.

Throughout the chapters that follow, we stress that the contemporary crises facing the United States are not aberrations of individual personalities. Rather, their causes are structural. They stem directly from the nature of the U.S. political economy. The profit motive, the ever-present stimulus of advertising on mass consumption, the massive military establishment, and the global nature of the economy of late capitalism have all contributed to a situation in which deviant behavior by elites is a necessary ingredient in maintaining this system of wealth and power as we know it.

Most Americans are woefully unaware of the nature of the political economy of capitalism and its role in causing deviance on the part of elites. Even when confronted with a political-economy approach to analyzing deviance, most people tend to become fatalistic regarding the chances for changing such mammoth entities as our governmental and economic systems. This problem is magnified when people are unaware of political ideology and the antagonisms that are built into the very fabric of our capitalist society. And social scientists tend to exacerbate the problem by failing to point to the structured sources of societal crises and solutions that require fundamental structural changes.

This book addresses the following concerns: (1) declining public confidence caused by revelations of elite wrongdoing and economic crises; (2) the lack of social-scientific knowledge regarding elite deviance; and (3) the need to suggest solutions for the crises of contemporary politics and economics.

THE ORGANIZATION OF THIS BOOK

Chapter 1 addresses the problem of defining *elite deviance*. In doing so, we review the representative forms of wrongdoing by wealthy and powerful individuals and organizations that are encompassed by the concept *elite deviance*. Chapter 2 discusses the *higher immorality* as an aspect of the U.S. elite, a sort of systemic violation of the laws and ethics of business and politics. This includes everything from the hiring of prostitutes to close business agreements to the hiring of members of criminal syndicates to gain a business or political advantage. In addition, the term refers to special advantages that business executives receive from government, including tax breaks and subsidies, as well as special salary arrangements that bypass tax laws. The term also applies to the violation of antitrust laws. Hence, it covers a host of illegal and unethical practices.

Chapters 3 and 4 are devoted exclusively to economic deviance. Specifically, Chapter 3 details the problems generated by the monopolistic structure of the economy, including price fixing, price gouging, deceptive advertising, and fraud. Chapter 4 discusses the more dangerous aspects of corporate deviance, including hazardous products, pollutions, dangerous working conditions, and resource waste.

Chapter 5 examines the international dimensions of corporate and political deviance. We will discuss the United States' defense policy, including defense contracting and arms sales, the bribery and product dumping of multinational corporations, and violations of human rights as they relate to U.S. foreign policy and the questionable practices of multinational corporations.

Chapters 6 and 7 deal exclusively with various dimensions of political deviance. Chapter 6 focuses on the types of political corruption that have characterized the history of U.S. domestic politics. Chapter 7 explores political repression in the United States, including the bias of the criminal justice system, as well as the abuses of power perpetrated by such agencies as the FBI, the CIA, and the Internal Revenue Service.

We believe that scientific objectivity and questions about values are interrelated and cannot, therefore, be divorced from each other. To this end, Chapter 8 offers a theory of elite deviance, relating the various elements of social structure and social character responsible for causing much of the deviance described in this book. The theoretical propositions we advance are both measurable in the scientific sense and moral in the humanistic sense that they address harm to both society and its citizens. We have prepared this chapter because the field of corporate or white-collar elite deviance remains quite new and has barely moved beyond the stage of classifying various examples upon which a theory could be based. Chapter 8 represents our effort to both summarize and synthesize extant empirical examples and theoretical viewpoints in order to begin the construction of a coherent theory of elite deviance.

The Epilogue grew out of our mutual experiences with students. Often students become fatalistic about resolving social problems that relate to the distribution of wealth and power in the United States. Our conviction is that the United States is democratic in form and that meaningful solutions to the problem of elite deviance can come through democratic processes. We do not believe that the necessary changes will be easy, but we insist that they are worth struggling to attain. The Epilogue describes one plan for making significant changes in the economic system. We feel that this proposal will eliminate or at least minimize the forms of elite deviance discussed in this book. We invite the reader to consider this plan seriously and to think of other alternatives that might be effective in diminishing elite deviance.

ACKNOWLEDGEMENTS

As with any text, ours has benefitted from the contributions of a number of colleagues, friends, and reviewers. Among them are Gil Geis (University of California—Irvine) and Randall Stokes (University of Massachusetts—Amherst), who served as constructive critics of this new edition.

David Simon thanks Rhona Mazer and Otis Johnson of the University of North Florida and Robert Dunn of California State University at Hayward for their comments regarding Chapter 8. He also thanks his colleagues at the Alcohol Research Group, School of Public Health, University of California, Berkeley—Mark Temple, Walter Clark, Robin Room, and Rob McBride.

Stan Eitzen thanks his colleague, T. R. Young, and several former and current students—Bill Flint, Dean Purdy, and Doug Timmer—for their contributions to his theoretical understanding of crimes by the powerful.

CHAPTER 1

The Nature
of Elite Deviance

ELITE DEVIANCE
AND THE CRISIS OF CONFIDENCE

In late 1983, pollster Lou Harris asked a representative sample of U.S. adults about the accuracy of the predictions made in *1984*, George Orwell's famous novel about a futuristic, government-dominated, totalitarian society based on repression of civil liberties via torture, spying, propaganda, and war. To a majority of those sampled, *1984* seemed more like fact than fiction. Indeed, 69 percent of those polled felt that the society described in *1984* was at least somewhat similar to contemporary U.S. society. Specifically:

- 88 percent believed that computerized records are vulnerable to outside tampering and favor strict federal laws to guard privacy;
- 70 percent thought it likely that the federal government would use information to intimidate groups it views as enemies;
- 67 percent felt that the government would use closed-circuit television to document individuals involved in compromising acts;
- 58 percent thought it likely that the government would use confidential information to take away individual privacy, freedom, and liberty; and
- 84 percent felt that the government could easily assemble a file on any individual, containing such personal information as credit and employment histories, as well as records of personal telephone calls, past residences, buying habits, and trips.[1]

Two weeks earlier, Harris had polled U.S. adults concerning another theme in Orwell's vision--war. Nearly 90 percent of those polled feared that the world could plunge into nuclear war in the near future. Moreover, 57 percent feared that such a war would develop between the United States and the Soviet Union if U.S. policymakers decided to place nuclear missiles in Western Europe. Two-thirds of those polled favored banning the production, storage, and use of such weapons in every country that already possesses them.[2]

These polls reflect the profound doubt Americans feel about government and the policies of those who govern. Unfortunately, this mistrust is by no means confined to the government. A Gallup poll in July 1983 asked U.S. adults about the honesty and ethical standards they

1

associated with a variety of professional occupations. Namely, those polled were instructed to indicate which occupations were characterized by "very high" or "high" standards. The following professions fared poorly, receiving positive ratings from less than 20 percent of those surveyed:

Stockbrokers	19 percent
Business executives	18 percent
U.S. senators	16 percent
U.S. congresspersons	14 percent
Realtors	13 percent
Insurance salespersons	13 percent
Labor union leaders	12 percent
Advertising executives	9 percent
Car salespersons[3]	6 percent

In addition, less than 40 percent felt that TV newspersons, funeral directors, journalists, lawyers, and bankers possess "very high" or "high" standards.

Another Gallup poll in October 1983 asked U.S. adults to rate their confidence in institutions. Less than 40 percent of those polled expressed a "great deal" or "quite a lot" of confidence in the following U.S. institutions:

Public schools	39 percent
Newspapers	38 percent
Congress	28 percent
Big business	28 percent
Organized labor	26 percent
Television media[4]	25 percent

These polls reflect the crisis of confidence in society that Americans have experienced since the late 1960s. This distrust is spread across a number of major governmental and business institutions. And, contrary to popular belief, the level of distrust has actually increased since 1980.[5]

Numerous incidents between 1967 and today have served to elevate public concern regarding the behavior of the nation's most powerful and wealthy individuals and organizations. Let's review some representative cases, beginning with those from the political arena.

Political Events Leading to Public Cynicism

Politicians and governmental agencies have been involved in a number of incidents that have contributed to a deep public distrust of government. Most significant was the conduct of the government during the Vietnam War (1964-1975). The Pentagon Papers, investigative reporting, and leaks from within the government had the effect of turning public opinion against the war and the government. A number of governmental transgressions were revealed, including the manipulation of Congress by President Johnson with the Gulf of Tonkin incident; the indictment of high-ranking officers for war crimes similar to those committed by the Germans and Japanese during World War II; the deliberate destruction of civilian targets by U.S. forces; intelligence agency suppression of information regarding enemy troop strength and sympathizers in South Vietnam; falsified reports by American field commanders regarding the destruction of enemy targets; the spraying of more than five million acres of South Vietnam with defoliating chemicals; the execution of more than 40,000 so-called enemy agents by the CIA under the Phoenix Program (most without trial); and unauthorized bombing raids against North Vietnam.[6] From early 1969 until May 1970, President Nixon assured the U.S. people that the neutrality of Cambodia was being respected. Yet Nixon had secretly ordered the bombing of so-called enemy sanctuaries in that country during that period. He was able to keep the bombings secret through the use of a double-entry bookkeeping system arranged between the White House and the Defense Department.

In 1975, governmental investigations revealed that the CIA had violated its charter by engaging in domestic intelligence, opening the mail of U.S. citizens and spying on congresspersons and newspaper reporters. Moreover, this organization plotted the assassinations of a number of foreign political officials.[7] Most significant, the Senate Intelligence Committee revealed that every U.S. president from Eisenhower to Nixon had lied to the American people about the activities of the CIA.

Public confidence in government was also lowered when it became known that every president since Franklin Roosevelt had used the FBI for political and sometimes illegal purposes. After J. Edgar Hoover's death, we found out how the Bureau had been used by its longtime chief to silence his and the Bureau's critics. Hoover had also involved the Bureau in a number of illegal acts to defeat or neutralize those domestic groups that he thought were subversive.

The Watergate scandal, which brought down the Nixon administration, was also a most significant contributor to low public confidence in government. The litany of illegal acts by governmental officials and/or their agents in Watergate included: securing illegal campaign contributions, dirty tricks to discredit political opponents, burglary, bribery, perjury, wiretapping, harassment of administration opponents with tax audits, and the like.

By 1975, when the above revelations became public and just after the end of the Watergate scandal, public confidence in government was understandably low. One poll revealed that 68 percent of Americans believe that the government regularly lies to them.[8]

Between 1941 and 1971, there were fifteen criminal prosecutions against members of Congress, about one every two years. Between 1972 and 1982, there were twenty-nine such prosecutions, about three per year —a fivefold increase. One journalist remarked that the arrest rate among members of the 95th Congress was higher than that for unemployed black males in Detroit![9]

The effect of these developments is hardly surprising. In 1980, law professor Arthur S. Miller declared that, in 1978, two years after President Carter's election, distrust of government was actually higher than it was during the Watergate period. Nearly two-thirds of voting-age Americans expressed distrust in government, and 70 percent expressed distrust in Congress. Thus, despite the removal of corrupt figures from office, trust in government has not increased. The result, claims Miller,

may be a permanent erosion of political trust and the eventual "undermining of the respect citizens have for political institutions themselves."[10]

The Reagan administration has done virtually nothing to increase
public confidence in the ethical conduct of government officials. Indeed,
between January 1981 and April 1984, forty-five members of President
Reagan's administration resigned under clouds of ethical or criminal
wrongdoing or as topics of congressional investigations or criticism.
Table 1-1 presents some representative cases of what became known in
the 1984 presidential campaign as the "sleaze factor."

Scandals within the Economic Sphere

The public's sagging confidence in major U.S. institutions extends
beyond government. Increasingly, big business has come to be viewed
with distrust and cynicism. Indeed, by 1979, big business tied with
Congress as "least trusted" from a list of ten major institutions.[11] Let's
review some of the incidents that have contributed to these negative
feelings.

Since the 1960s, when Ralph Nader launched the consumer
movement, consumer unhappiness with the quality of goods and services
provided by business has grown dramatically. By 1978, it was estimated
that the federal government alone received about ten million consumer
complaints annually.[12] Some corporations have willfully marketed
products known to be dangerous. There are numerous examples of this
problem, the most notorious being the marketing of the Pinto by the Ford
Motor Company. Ford knew that this car had a defective gasoline tank
that would ignite even in low-speed rear-end collisions, yet the company
continued its sales. Ironically and tragically, Ford continued to sell this
defective and dangerous car even though the problem could have been
solved for a cost of $11 per vehicle.[13]

In 1978, the Senate revealed that, between 1945 and 1976,
approximately 350 U.S. corporations admitted to making bribes of some
$750 million to officials of foreign governments. Many of these compa-
nies made such payments without informing their stockholders.[14] Moreover, the Watergate investigation revealed that over 300 corporations
illegally contributed to President Nixon's 1972 reelection campaign.[15] No
corporate executives were sent to prison for their involvement in concealing or making such payments.

Another problem that has turned the public against business is the
relatively high incidence of fraud. Fraud in the business community takes
many forms. For example, General Motors substituted Chevrolet engines
in thousands of its new Oldsmobiles, without informing customers of the
switch.[16] Advertising is also full of examples of fraudulent claims for
products. And the stock market has been manipulated to defraud clients.
The largest case of this nature surfaced in 1975 when officials of the
Equity Life Insurance Company were indicted for manipulating the price
of shares by literally inventing thousands of nonexistent insurance policies. Between $2 and $3 billion was lost by thousands of investors.
Equity's chairman, along with several other company officials, were
convicted of the crime but received suspended sentences or prison terms
that varied from only two to eight years.[17]

By 1982, it was estimated that price fixing among corporations costs the consumer $60 billion per year. In addition, between 1970 and 1980, 117 of 1,043 major corporations (11 percent) had committed at least one serious criminal offense, including twenty-eight cases of bribery, kickback, or illegal rebates; twenty-one cases of illegal campaign contri- butions; eleven cases of fraud; and five cases of tax evasion. In all, fifty executives were sent to jail, and thirteen fines were levied in excess of $550,000 (ranging to a high of $4 million).[18]

Again, what is the effect of these developments? An early 1980s survey by *Fortune* magazine of Americans with incomes over $25,000 revealed that slightly over half of the respondents believed that big business was becoming a threat to the American way of life.[19]

Perhaps the largest energizer of negative feelings toward big business has been the realization that corporations are guilty of what we might call "chemical crimes." Through their dumping of waste products into the air, water, and land fills, or through the production of products that pollute unneccessarily, businesses have assaulted the public with dangerous implications for the health of present and future generations. Of the many examples of this chemical assault, we will describe one in some detail--Love Canal.

From 1942 to 1953, the Hooker Chemical Company dumped more than 20,000 tons of toxic chemical waste into the Love Canal near Niagara Falls, New York. After Hooker sold the dump site to the Board of Education in 1953 for one dollar, an elementary school and playground were built on the site, followed by a housing development. For at least twenty years prior to 1977, toxic chemicals had been seeping through to the land surface. However, in 1977, highly toxic black sludge began seeping into the cellars of the school and nearby residences. Tests showed the presence of eighty-two chemicals in the air, water, and soil of Love Canal, among them, twelve known carcinogens, including dioxin, one of the deadliest substances ever synthesized. There is evidence that Hooker Chemical knew of the problem as far back as 1958 but chose not to warn local health officials of any potential problems because cleanup costs would have increased from $4 to $50 million.

Knowledge of the existence of toxic chemicals in the area caused a financial hardship for the residents. Once word of the contamination got out, their homes became worthless. But much more important, tests revealed that the inhabitants of this area had disproportionately high rates of birth defects, miscarriages, chromosomal abnormalities, liver disorders, respiratory and urinary disease, epilepsy, and suicide. In one neighborhood a few blocks from the Love Canal, a survey by the homeowner's association revealed that only one of the fifteen pregnancies begun in 1979 ended in the birth of a healthy baby--four ended in miscarriages, two babies were stillborn, and nine others were born deformed.[20]

Today, it is now clear: Love Canal is merely the tip of the United States' waste iceberg. In fact:

- The Environmental Protection Agency has estimated that 90 percent of the United States' toxic waste is illegally disposed of, that one-fifth of the drinking water systems in the United States are contaminated, and that 13,000 community water systems are below federal standards.
- In 1982, the U.S. Office of Technology Assessment studied 17,000 lakes in a twenty-seven-state area. The results showed that 3,000

Table 1-1
Elite Deviance and the Reagan Administration

Richard V. Allen, White House National Security Adviser—resigned in 1982 after it was disclosed he received $1,000 in cash and three wristwatches from a Japanese newsman.

Frederic André, commissioner of the Interstate Commerce Commission—said in 1982 he saw nothing wrong with trucking companies conspiring to fix prices or with a convicted felon's operating a trucking business from jail.

Malcolm Baldridge, Secretary of Commerce—spent $15,272 on office furnishings.

Donald Bogard, president of the Legal Services Corporation—contracted for the government to pay for his membership in a private club and for his trips home to Indianapolis and to provide him severance pay.

Charles M. Butler III, Federal Energy Regulatory Commission chairman—recused himself from past cases involving former law clients, but not new cases.

Anne M. Burford, Environmental Protection Agency administrator—resigned after disclosures that E.P.A. showed persistent favoritism to industrial polluters.

Robert Burford, director of the Interior Department's Bureau of Land Management—obtained a waiver from regulations allowing him to own an interest in grazing land administered by his bureau.

Carlos C. Campbell, Assistant Secretary of Commerce for Economic Development—resigned amid allegations he awarded grants to firms with questionable credentials, some operated by personal friends.

Joseph Canzeri, White House assistant to the President—resigned following disclosures that he had billed both the government and the Republican National Committee for expenses and that he had received large loans at favorable rates to buy a Washington home.

Gerald Carmen, General Services administration—failed to list a $425,000 low-interest government loan on a financial disclosure form; allegedly placed family members and friends in government jobs.

William J. Casey, Director of the Central Intelligence Agency—traded oil and computer stocks worth $3 million in 1982 despite his access to sensitive financial intelligence; refused (until 1983) to place holdings in blind trust; allegedly (he denied it) handled documents purloined from Jimmy Carter's White House.

Michael J. Connolly, general counsel, Equal Employment Opportunity Commission—resigned amid allegations he conspired to end an E.E.O.C. investigation of a company represented by his brother.

Michael Deaver, White House deputy chief of staff—used his White House position to promote a diet book he wrote and deferred royalty payments to escape provisions of the Ethics in Government Act. Like Mr. Meese, received a loan arranged by California accountant John McKean, who won appointment as a governor of the U.S. Postal Service.

Raymond J. Donovan, Secretary of Labor—accused of ties to union corruption and organized crime; was investigated by a special prosecutor who found evidence to support the charges, but not enough to seek an indictment.

Guy W. Fiske, Deputy Secretary of Commerce—resigned in 1983 after allegations he negotiated the sale of weather satellites to the COMSAT Corporation at the same time he was seeking a job with COMSAT.

Robert Funkhouser, E.P.A. director of international activities—resigned after allegations that he helped the Dow Chemical Company influence trade talks on toxic chemicals.

William Harvey, chairman of Legal Services Corporation—collected $25,000 in consulting fees from the government over an eleven-month period.

Reverend Sam Hart, U.S. Civil Rights Commission nominee—nomination withdrawn after disclosures he failed to pay local taxes, defaulted on a federal small business loan, and was delinquent on a state loan repayment.

Arthur Hull Hayes, Food and Drug Administration administrator—billed the government for trips paid for by businesses and trade associations, accepted speaking fees from private groups with interests before the F.D.A.

William S. Heffelfinger, Assistant Secretary of Energy—accused of falsifying his resume, deceiving federal investigators, and violating civil service merit protection regulations.

J. Lynn Helms, Federal Aviation administrator—resigned after allegations he operated a business that took over small companies and bled them of assets.

John Hernandez, deputy E.P.A. director—resigned after allegations he invited Dow Chemical Company to "edit" a draft of a report on dioxin contamination near the

Table 1-1 (continued)

company's plant in Midland, Michigan.

Donald Hovde, Undersecretary of Housing and Urban Development—took trips to Puerto Rico and Italy paid for by builders and realtors, repaid $3,000 after charges he used government chauffeurs for private travel.

Max C. Hugel, Deputy Director, C.I.A.—resigned after allegations he engaged in fraudulent stock dealings before taking office.

Rita Lavelle, chief of toxic waste cleanup, E.P.A.—fired after allegations of favoritism to polluters, convicted of perjury before Congress.

Dennis E. LeBlanc, associate administrator of the Commerce Department's National Telecommunications and Information Administration—took $58,500 annual government salary on "detail" to the President's California ranch to chop wood and clear brush.

Leslie Lenkowski, nominated to be deputy director of U.S. Information Agency—accused in Congressional staff report of lying to Congress about responsibility for a "blacklist" of persons barred from speaking abroad for U.S.I.A.

John Lehman, Secretary of the Navy—accused of failing to fully divest himself of his defense consulting firm, the Abingdon Corporation.

James L. Malone, Assistant Secretary of State—accused by the Senate Foreign Relations Committee of lobbying for a former client, the Taiwan Power Company, before the Export-Import Bank.

William E. McCann, ambassador to Ireland—nomination withdrawn after allegations he was involved in shady business deals and had connections to organized crime.

John McElderry, Denver regional administrator, Department of Health and Human Services—resigned after allegations he used his federal position to promote and sell Amway products.

Robert Nimmo, administrator of the Veterans Administration—resigned after disclosures he spent $54,183 redecorating his office, misused charter aircraft, and used government cars for personal affairs.

William Olsen, board member of the Legal Services Corporation—collected $19,721 in consulting fees in 1982.

Richard N. Perle, Assistant Secretary of Defense—urged the Secretary of the Army in 1982 to buy weapons from an Israeli firm that had paid him $50,000 in consulting fees prior to his joining the government.

Thomas Reed, Deputy National Security Adviser—resigned after disclosures that he engaged in insider stock trading.

Armand Reiser, counselor to the Department of Energy—resigned after disclosures he failed to reveal $106,000 in earnings from five energy-related companies.

James W. Sanderson, nominated as assistant administrator at E.P.A.—nomination withdrawn after disclosures he represented companies regulated by E.P.A. while consulting for the agency.

Emanuel J. Savas, Assistant Secretary of HUD—resigned after allegations he used HUD employees to work on a private book and charged the government for private travel.

Bill J. Sloan, California regional director, HUD—reprimanded and forced to pay back $6,800 he charged the government for private travel and meals.

William French Smith, Attorney General—took advantage of an impermissible tax shelter after being nominated and accepted $50,000 severance pay from a company on whose board he served.

Nancy H. Stoats, chairman, Consumer Product Safety Commission—spent $10,000 in government funds to redecorate her office.

Paul Thayer, Deputy Secretary of Defense—resigned amid S.E.C. charges he leaked inside stock information while serving on boards of three corporations.

James Watt, Secretary of the Interior—resigned after uttering slurs against minorities and the handicapped and after offending even conservative environmental groups with his favoritism toward energy interests.

Charles Z. Wick, director of the U.S.I.A.—secretly taped telephone conversations and lied to reporters about doing so, gave jobs to eight children and other relatives and friends of high-ranking Administration officials, was forced to pay back the government for security devices installed in his private home.

lakes had already been damaged by acid rain and that 9,000 others were in danger of being damaged. Of the 117,000 miles of rivers and streams surveyed, 25,000 had acid rain damage, and 49,000 additional miles were at risk.[21]

• By 1985, the EPA had recognized 19,000 hazardous waste dump sites. Eight hundred of these sites had been placed on a priority list, but only ten had been cleaned up.[22]

Among the most damning and damaging recent environmental scandals involves the herbicide dioxin. Between 1962 and 1970, the U.S. government purchased 12.8 million gallons of dioxin containing Agent Orange, which was used in the defoliation program in Vietnam. The chief supplier of the dioxin was Dow Chemical, who has always claimed that human beings suffer no ill effects from dioxin, save for a possible skin disease. By the late 1970s, however, returning Vietnam veterans, who were exposed to Agent Orange during the war, were reporting a variety of what they believed were dioxin-related maladies, including soft-tissue cancers, birth defects in offspring, genetic damage, and shortened life spans. The chemical companies involved refused to acknowledge any ill effects from dioxin exposure. So, in 1978, a class action law suit was filed on behalf of the 20,000 veterans exposed to Agent Orange in Vietnam.

During the course of the trial, internal Dow documents, which were ordered to be released by one of the judges, revealed that the chemical firms involved had known about the ill effects caused by dioxin as far back as 1965 but had withheld such information from the U.S. Army, who purchased dioxin for its Vietnam defoliation program. It was also learned that Dow workers had contracted skin diseases from dioxin exposure as early as the 1930s and that the U.S. Army knew that dioxin exposure could result in death as far back as 1959.

In 1984, 20,000 Vietnam veterans were tentatively awarded $128 million in damages. Love Canal residents had also filed lawsuits over dioxin exposure and its link to birth defects. Moreover, in 1983, the federal government purchased outright the entire town of Times Beach, Missouri, when it was learned that the homes there had become exposed to dioxin. It was also revealed in 1983 that, despite a Carter administration effort to ban the use of dioxin in the United States as a weed killer in rice fields, range lands, and industrial areas, Dow Chemical met with Reagan EPA officials Anne Burford and Rita Lavelle at Dow's Midland, Michigan, plant to oppose the proposed dioxin ban. Reportedly, Dow's effort was successful. A congressional subcommittee on Energy and Commerce, meeting in Chicago in March 1983, heard testimony from local EPA inspectors that they had been ordered by their superiors in Washington to change an important report on dioxin to comply with Dow's wishes.[23]

The list of acts involved the United States' most powerful political and business organizations and their leaders could be extended almost indefinitely. Similarly, scores of additional opinion polls registering mounting public distrust, cynicism, and alienation regarding the United States' most powerful economic and political institutions and the individuals who head them could be discussed. What is most important for our purposes, however, is what these incidents have in common. The characteristics they share comprise what we call *elite deviance*. These characteristics include:

1. The acts are committed by persons from the highest strata of society: members of the upper and upper-middle classes. Some of the deeds mentioned above were committed by the heads of corporate and governmental organizations; others were committed by their employees on behalf of the employers.

2. Some of the acts are crimes in that they violate criminal statutes and carry penalties such as fines and imprisonment.[24] Other acts violate administrative or civil law, which may also involve punishment. Included are acts of commission, as well as acts of omission.[25] Other acts, such as U.S. presidents lying to the public about the Vietnam War, although not illegal, are regarded by most Americans as unethical or immoral (i.e., deviant). Thus, elite deviance may be either criminal or noncriminal in nature.

3. Some of the actions described above were committed by elites themselves for personal gain (e.g., congresspersons who accepted bribes), or they were committed by the elites or their employees for purposes of enhancing the power, profitability, or influence of the organizations involved (e.g., when corporations made bribes overseas for the purpose of securing business deals).

4. The acts were committed with relatively little risk. When and if the elites were apprehended, the punishments inflicted were in general quite lenient compared to those given common street criminals.[26]

5. Some of the incidents posed great danger to the public's safety, health, and financial well-being.

6. In many cases, the elites in charge of the organizations mentioned were able to conceal their illegal or unethical actions for years before they became public knowledge (e.g., Hooker Chemical's dumping of poison chemicals and the presidential misuses of the FBI and CIA). Yet the actions mentioned were quite compatible with the goals of such organizations (i.e., the maintenance or enhancement of the organization's power and/or profitability).[27]

These features of elite deviance also involve important issues relative to: (1) composition and power of the U.S. elite, (2) specific types of acts regarded as deviant, (3) causes of elite deviance, and (4) consequences of elite deviance for society. These issues are central to the understanding of elite deviance. Their discussion constitutes the remainder of this chapter.

THE COMPOSITION AND NATURE OF U.S. ELITES

The word *elite* refers to "groups of persons who in any society hold positions of eminence. More specifically, it denotes persons who are eminent in a particular field--especially the governing minority and the circles from which the governing minority is recruited."[28] Such positions of eminence are distinguished from mainstream society by their rewards.[29]   These rewards generally involve the greatest amount of authority (political power) and/or material gain (wealth and/or income). Virtually all of the world's nations (modern industrial democracies, communist countries, and developing nations) are governed by elites. What distinguishes these nations from each other, in part, are the differences in the strata of society from which elites are recruited, as well as the degree of wealth and power concentrated in elite hands. There are also vast differences among the nations of the world regarding the degree of public scrutiny to which elite decisions are subject.

The social structure of the contemporary United States is characterized by a heavy concentration of elite wealth and power. In the United States, elites possess not only great riches and the ability to make decisions that affect the conduct of nonelites (political power), but they also exert a great deal of control over such resources as

> [e]ducation, prestige, status, skills of leadership, information, knowledge of political processes, ability to communicate, and organization. [Moreover,] elites (in America) are drawn disproportionately from . . . society's upper classes, which are made up of those persons . . . who own or control a disproportionate share of the societal institutions--industry, commerce, finance, education, the military, communications, civic affairs, and law.[30]

One recent study concludes that there are 5,416 positions within the nation's most powerful economic, governmental, military, media, legal, civic, and educational institutions. These positions constitute a few ten-thousandths of one percent of the population.[31]   Yet, the amount of resources controlled by this elite of power is immense. Consider these data for the early 1980s:

- In industry, 100 out of 200,000 corporations control 55 percent of all industrial assets. The largest 500 industrial corporations control three-quarters of manufacturing assets. The largest 800 corporations employ one of every five workers in the civilian labor force.[32]
- In transportation and utilities, fifty out of 67,000 companies control two-thirds of the assets in the airline, railroad, communications, electricity, and gas industries.[33]
- In banking, fifty out of 17,700 banks control 61.3 percent of all banking asssets.   Three of these banks--Bank America, Citicorp, and Chase Manhattan--control almost 20 percent of such assets.
- In insurance, fifty out of 1,890 firms control 75 percent of all insurance assets. Two insurance companies--Prudential and Metropolitan Life--control nearly one-quarter of such assets.[34]
- In the mass media, a mere fifty corporations are in control. Twenty companies own half of the 61 million newspapers sold daily in the United States, and another twenty companies receive over one-half of the revenues from the 61,000 U.S. magazines published. Three firms control most of the revenues and audiences in television, while ten control radio, eleven control book publishing, and four control movies.[35]

The Economic Elite

One basis of this great concentration of power and resources stems from the wealth possessed by the elite; that is, from its economic power. Such wealth is owned by relatively few individuals in families and corporations. Regarding the wealth owned by individuals, consider that only 55,400 adults have $1 million or more in corporate stock, and only 73,500 adults have $200,000 or more in bonds and debt holdings. In addition, one-twentieth of 1 percent of adults own 20 percent of all corporate stock, two-thirds of the worth of all state and local bonds, and two-fifths of all bonds and notes. And the richest 1 percent own one-seventh of all real estate and one-seventh of all cash.[36]

Summing up, two important points emerge. First, the nation's wealth is centralized with the richest 1 percent of the population owning about 25 percent of the entire population's net worth. Even this figure belies the real concentration of wealth, since one-half of 1 percent own 20 percent. Second, and contrary to popular belief, the amount the wealthy own has remained stable over the years.

> Since the end of World War II, there has been no change in their (the wealthy) share of the nation's wealth; it has been constant in every year studied, at roughly five-year intervals, since 1945. The richest 1 percent own a quarter, and the top half of 1 percent own a fifth, of the combined market worth of everything owned by every American. Remarkably, economic historians who have culled manuscript census reports on the past century report that on the eve of the Civil War the rich had the same cut of the total: the top 1 percent owned 24 percent in 1860 and 24.9 percent in 1969 (the latest year thoroughly studied). Through all the tumultuous changes since then--the Civil War and the emancipation of the slaves, the Populist and Progressive movements, the Great Depression, the New Deal, progressive taxation, the mass organization of industrial workers, and World Wars I and II--this class has held on to everything it had. They owned America then and they own it now.[37]

Collectively, economic power is centralized in relatively few major corporations and financial institutions.

> Out of the 2 million or so corporations, some 200 nonfinancial companies account for 80 percent of all resources used in manufacturing; 60 percent of all assets--three-fifths of all buildings, equipment, and land are owned by nonfinancial companies.[38]

One recent Federal Trade Commission study demonstrated that the 200 corporations in manufacturing control assets as large as those controlled by the largest 1,000 corporations in 1941.[39] One study of the 250 largest U.S. corporations found that all but a handful (seventeen) had at least one of their chief executives sitting on the board of at least one additional corporation in the top 250. Some of them even held seats on competing companies, a practice that has been illegal since 1914 with the passage of the Clayton Antitrust Act. Moreover, even people who serve on the board of directors of one company may serve as an executive of another company. This situation has been found to exist for over 250 directors of the top 500 corporations.[40]

More important than such interlocks is the shared ownership that characterizes U.S. corporate capitalism. Such ownership is concentrated among large banks and wealthy families. Out of the 14,000 commercial banks in the United States, 100 control one-half of all bank deposits.[41] Many of these banks administer trust funds of wealthy individuals or other sources of capital with which they purchase stock. The largest forty-nine such banks (as of the mid-1960s) held at least 5 percent of the stock (often enough to gain a seat on the board) of 147 of the nation's largest 500 companies. In all, these 49 banks held 768 directorships, influencing 286 of the nation's 500 largest industrial corporations.[42]

As of 1978, one large New York bank, Morgan Guarantee Trust, was the single largest stockholder in fifty-six of the largest 122 U.S. corporations.[43] And to link things thoroughly, the nation's largest banks (and other financial institutions) own large chunks of each other. Thus, "the largest owner of J. P. Morgan and Co. are Citibank and Chase Manhattan. Morgan and Citibank are the largest shareholders in Bank America Corporation. And if we add Manufacturers Hanover, Chemical Bank and Bankers Trust to the picture, the same pattern continues."[44] These banks are owned by wealthy families (e.g., the Rockefellers, the Morgans, the Mellons), whose concern for the workings of the profit system stretches over the corporate order.

What all these facts mean is that the largest 500 or so manufacturing firms and some fifty financial institutions, controlling two-thirds of all business income and half of the nation's bank deposits, are interlocked by directorships and controlled by less than one-half of 1 percent of the population. Thus, U.S. corporate assets reside in a few hands. More specifically, half of all the assets in industry, banking, insurance, utilities, transportation, telecommunications, and the mass media are controlled by a mere 4,500 individual presidents and directors.[45]

This concentration allows a very small corporate community to exercise power over one-third of the nation's gross national product and considerable indirect influence over the remainder of the nation's goods and services. This is true because:

> Corporate leaders can invest money where and when they choose; expand, close, or move their factories and offices at a moment's notice; and hire, promote, and fire employees as they see fit. These powers give them direct influence over the great majority of Americans who are dependent upon wages and salaries for their incomes. They also give the corporate rich indirect influence over elected and appointed officials, for the growth and stability of a city, state, or the country as a whole can be jeopardized by a lack of business confidence in government.[46]

The Political Elite

Aside from the economic elite, the nation also possesses a *political elite*. The political elite, to a significant extent, overlaps with, yet is independent from, the economic elite. The corporate managers, owners (superrich individuals and families), and directors are, for the most part, member of the United States' national upper class. Membership in the upper class of U.S. society is typically measured by such indicators as (1) having one's name in the *Social Register* (an exclusive list of influential persons published in major U.S. cities and containing the names of about 138,000 persons); (2) attendance at elite private secondary schools and universities; (3) membership in exclusive social clubs and annual attendance at upper-class vacation retreats (e.g., Bohemian Grove, Pacific Union Club, Knickerbocker Club); and, of course, (4) seats on boards of the largest, interlocked corporations.[47]

The political elite differs from the corporate or economic elite in that it includes persons occupying "key federal government positions in the executive (presidential), judicial (the Supreme Court and lesser federal courts), and legislative (congressional) branches (and) . . . the top command positions in the Army, Navy, Air Force, and Marines."[48] Numerous studies reveal that the political elite is composed of persons from both the upper-middle class (e.g., lawyers, small-business people, doctors, farmers, educators, and other professionals) and the upper class. The upper class tends to dominate the federal branch of the government, while upper-middle-class professionals make up the preponderance of the legislative branch. A study of presidential cabinets from McKinley's to Nixon's, examining the degree to which cabinet heads were recruited from the ranks of big business, indicated that, from 1897 to 1973, big business supplied from 60 percent (under McKinley) to 95.7 percent (under Nixon) of presidential cabinet members.[49]

On the other hand, the 96th Congress (which opened in January 1979) was composed of 270 lawyers, 156 bankers and/or business people, sixty-four educators, and seven doctors. The 1978 Senate had eighteen millionaires and eighty-two members with net worths between $500,000 and $1 million.[50] Thus, while the Senate is made up of more affluent members, the House of Representatives is largely composed of slightly less affluent, upper-middle-class persons.

While it is true that economic power and state or government power are interlinked, they are not related in a conspiratorial fashion. This is an important point, because a number of people who have written on the subjects of elite power and political corruption do believe in conspiracies. Some members of the radical right in the United States believe that, not only is the country run by a secret clique of wealthy capitalists, but that such a clique is plotting with the Soviets to lead the nation to communism.[51] A second distorted view of the elite has been put forth by certain muckraking journalists, who hold that, while the state and the upper class are relatively independent, certain "moral and legal lapses in this independence" occur.[52] This view purports that the business class gets what it desires from government by engaging in all manner of corruption, excessive lobbying, and other forms of illegal or unethical behavior.

The view expressed in this book is that the conspiratorial view of elite behavior is simplistic. Even though conspiracies do occur from time to time--and always will--such explanations do a disservice to the complex nature of elite power and elite deviance.

The conspiratorial view of the elite is unrealistic for a number of reasons. First, not only are the elite somewhat diverse as to class backgrounds, but they are ideologically diverse, as well. That is, political opinions among elites range from conservative to social democrat. Although it is true that the elites agree on the basic rules of politics (i.e., free elections, the court system, and the rule of law) and believe in the capitalist economic system, they disagree considerably about such issues as the power of business, civil rights, welfare, foreign policy, and so on.[53]

Second, elites do not control the federal government because they do not possess a monopoly of political power. The structure of capitalist society is such that elite rule is faced with economic and other crises (e.g., inflation, unemployment, war, racism), which lead nonelite interests to demand changes consistent with their interests (e.g., unemployment benefits in periods of high unemployment). As William Chambliss has concluded, "The persistence of and importance of the conflicts resolved through law necessarily create occasions where well-organized groups representing (nonelite) class interests manage to effect important legislation."[54]

Third, the conspiratorial view relating to elites dominating the state through corruption masks some of the most important unethical patterns that characterize much of elite deviance. For example, during the hearings regarding his appointment as vice-president in the mid-1970s, Nelson Rockefeller was questioned about his gift-giving habits but was not held "accountable for the shootings at Attica (prison) or . . . for the involvement of Chase Manhattan (bank) in the repressive system of South African racism."[55]

Likewise, the right wing's conspiratorial view of a capitalist elite plotting to lead the nation into communism hides much of the unethical behavior of corporations that results as a consequence of the structure of corporate capitalism itself. As mentioned, about one-third of the economy is dominated by corporate giants. Such giantism means that, in many manufacturing and financial industries (e.g., cereals, soups, autos, and tires), a handful of firms (often four or less) accounts for over half the market in a particular industry or service. Such situations are often characterized by artificially high prices due, not to secret price-fixing conspiracies, but to a practice known as price leadership. This results when one firm decides to raise prices on a given product and is then copied by the other major firms in the same field. One Federal Trade Commission economist estimated that such "monopolistic price distortions cost the economy $87 billion every year"[56] in inflated prices, and that was in the mid-1970s. This and other unethical practices considered in detail in this volume are not accounted for by conspiratorial views of the economy and government and the linkages between them.

Our position is that it is more fruitful to consider deviance within the context of the relationships between business and governmental organizations, the functions performed by government, as well as the internal organizational structure of both the corporate and political organizations that constitute the elite sectors of society. In sum, we concur with Michael Parenti's view that "elite power is principally systemic and legitimating rather than conspiratorial and secretive."[57]

ECONOMY-STATE LINKAGES
AND THE FUNCTIONS OF GOVERNMENT

To understand the interrelationships between the economy and the state is to comprehend how elites attempt to formulate and implement public policy. These interrelationships are based on connections among corporations, large law firms that represent large corporations, elite colleges and universities, the mass media, private philanthropic foundations, major research organizations (think tanks), political parties, and the executive and legislative brances of the federal government. Key examples of these interlocks of monies, personnel, and policies are pictured in Figure 1-1.

Aside from the major corporations and the federal government, the rest of the organizations are included for several reasons:

1. The twelve universities and colleges listed control 50 percent of all educational endowment funds and include some 656 corporate and other elites as their presidents and trustees. Moreover, only fifty foundations out of 12,000 control 40 percent of all foundation assets.[58] The officers of such foundations often have experience in elite corporations, educational institutions, and/or government.

2. The elite civic associations bring together elites from the corporate, educational, legal, and governmental worlds. Such organizations have been described as "central coordinating mechanisms in national policy making."[59] Such organizations issue public position papers and investigative reports on matters of domestic and foreign policy. Membership in one or more of these organizations is sometimes a prerequisite to a high-ranking post within the executive branch of the federal government.

For example, the majority of the Carter cabinet (including Jimmy Carter himself), served on the Trilateral Commission prior to assuming office. The Commission was formed by David Rockefeller, chairman of the board of the Chase Manhattan Bank; heir to the Exxon fortune; graduate of Harvard; member of the board of directors of B. F. Goodrich, Rockefeller Bros., Inc., and Equitable Life Insurance; and trustee of Harvard. Rockefeller is also the chairman of the Council of Foreign Relations. Almost all recent secretaries of state, including Cyrus Vance and Henry Kissinger, have been CFR members.[60]

3. The mass media is concentrated in that there are three major televison and radio networks--NBC, ABC, and CBS. These networks are also multinational corporations, who own or are owned by other corporations. CBS, for example, owns Holt, Rinehart, and Winston, a publishing firm. NBC is owned by RCA, a major manufacturer of appliances and weapons systems components. Controlling shares in the three televison networks are owned by five New York commercial banks--Chase Manhattan, Morgan Guaranty, Citibank, Bankers Trust, and the Bank of New York.[61]

Figure 1-1
The Capitalist Elite—Links among the Ruling Elite

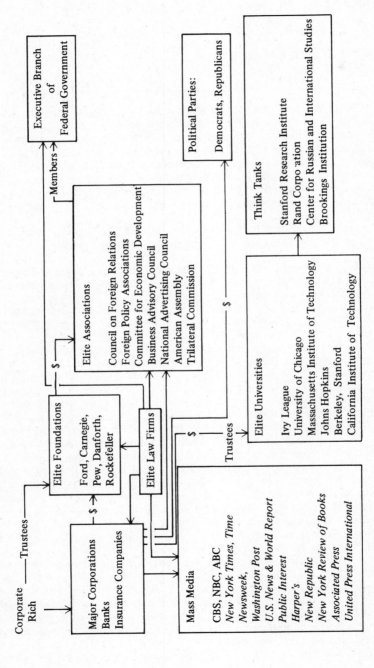

Source: Adapted from G. William Domhoff, "State and Ruling Class in Corporate America," *The Insurgent Sociologist* 4 (Spring 1974), 9. By permission of G. William Domhoff and *The Insurgent Sociologist.*

The media also includes major wire services, Associated Press and United Press International, from which most national and international news makes its way into U.S. radio, television, and newspapers. Regarding newspapers and news weeklies, the *New York Times*, the *Washington Post, Time, Newsweek* (owned by by the *Washington Post*), and *U.S. News and World Report* are regarded as the most influential publications in their field.[62]

Moreover, the major sponsors of television programs on the three networks are other large corporations. The media tends to portray deviant behavior as violent behavior that is perpetrated by powerless and poor nonelites. As one recent study concludes, the crime reported in television news and news magazines includes kidnappings and particularly gruesome murders. "Ordinary people who carry out nonviolent crimes or violate the mores rarely appear in national news."[63] On the other hand,

> the economically powerful, such as officers of large corporations and holders of great wealth, are filmed or written about rarely, and then usually for reasons having little to do with their economic power--primarily when they are involved in some conflict with the federal government or are having legal difficulties.[64]

Overall, the media function to portray crime and deviance as a problem created by nonelites and to describe corporate capitalism as a system characterized by competition, freedom, and, while flawed, the best of all existing worlds. As a *Time* magazine profile recently put it:

> Plainly capitalism is not working well enough. But there is no evidence to show the fault is in the system--or that there is a better alternative. . . . For all its obvious blemishes and needed reforms, capitalism still holds out the most creative and dynamic force that any civilization has ever discovered: the power of the free ambitious individual.[65]

Such propagandistic exercises are also characteristic of numerous television commercials and public service announcements (often prepared by the elite National Advertising Council) that insist that the oil companies are "working to keep your trust" or that our "economics quotients" (knowledge about the U.S. economic system) could stand improvement. Thus, one overall function of the mass media is to ensure the continuation and growth of the system of corporate capitalism.

4. Twenty-eight super law firms do much of the legal work for the corporations, mass media, and educational and civic foundations. In addition, senior lawyers in such firms often fill posts on various foundations and civic and educational institutions and from time to time assume various posts within the executive branch of the federal government. A good example of one such superlawyer is Paul Warnke, President Carter's chief negotiator in the Strategic Arms Limitation Talks (SALT). Warnke is also a member of the Trilateral Commission, a director of the Council on Foreign Relations, a former assistant secretary of defense, and partner in a Washington law firm that includes former Defense Secretary Clark Clifford.[66]

5. Finally, there is a host of elite-related think tanks, which are primarily research institutes. In general, these operations receive monies from both public and private sources, depending on the type of research they do. For example, about 5 percent of the Defense Department's Research and Development budget in the 1960s and early 1970s went to such research organizations.[67]

Think tanks perform a very wide variety of research tasks. For instance, throughout the 1960s and 1970s, The Rand Corporation and the Stanford Research Institute (owned by Stanford University until 1970) performed many tasks for the Pentagon, including everything from language training of military personnel to feasibility studies regarding the use of nuclear, chemical, and biological weapons. Such institutes were heavily involved in research on various aspects of guerrilla and counter-guerrilla warfare in both Southeast Asia and other portions of the Third World during this period.

Other think tanks, such as the American Enterprise Institute, are more closely allied with the business arm of the American power elite. The American Enterprise Institute is allied with the conservative wing of the Republican Party and Southern Democrats. Its activities primarily involve studies, the end products of which are policy proposals aimed at enhancing the profitability and power of its corporate clients.[68]

The American Enterprise Institute and other think tanks also prepare studies for influential big-business lobby groups, such as the National Association of Manufacturers and the United States Chamber of Commerce.

In short, think tanks provide valuable research aid in achieving the policy aims of elites, both inside and outside of government.

Figure 1-1 depicts the structures that supply personnel, money, and policy to the federal government but does not describe the processes used by or the benefits sought by elites from the state. Such means and benefits are important in that, when they are abused, they constitute forms of elite deviance. These benefits will be discussed in following sections.

Lobbying

The principle of majority rule is sometimes violated by special interests, which, by deals, propaganda, and the financial support of political candidates, attempt to deflect the political process for their own benefit. Individuals, families, corporations, and various organizations use a variety of means to obtain numerous benefits from congressional committees, regulatory agencies, and executive bureaucracies. To accomplish their goals, lobbyists for the special interests,

> along with the slick brochures, expert testimonies, and technical reports, . . . still have the slush fund, the kickback, the stock award, the high paying job offer from industry, the lavish parties and prostitutes, the meals, transportation, housing and vacation accommodations, and the many other hustling enticements of money.[69]

The existence of lobbyists does not ensure that the national interests will be served or that the concern of all groups will be heard. Who, for example, speaks for the interests of schoolchildren, minority groups, the poor, the mentally retarded, renters, migrant workers--in short, for the relatively powerless? And if there is a voice for these people, does it match the clout of lobbyists backed by the fantastic financial resources of the elite?

In fairness, it must be stressed that the success of such lobbies is not ensured:

> Big economic interests don't always win. The cargo preference bill was defeated. So was the 1979 sugar quota. The Consumer Cooperative Bank bill passed the House by one vote and became law. Sometimes scandal or the weight of evidence can push Congress in the right direction. And it must be noted that when a congressman from Michigan votes to bail out Chrysler, or a congressman from Wisconsin votes for dairy price supports, he is also voting to benefit his own constituents. This may not favor the public interest, but it is predictable politics, not personal corruption.
>
> . . . To receive money from an interest doesn't mean a member of Congress is controlled, per se. There are indentured politicians and there are principled conservatives--the former virtually auction their souls to the highest bidder while the latter may truly believe that the government shouldn't be forcing pharmaceutical firms to pre-market-test their drugs.[70]

Nevertheless, corporate lobbies usually do exert a significant influence.

The Financing of Political Campaigns

Perhaps one of the most elite-dominated and undemocratic features (at least in its consequences) of the U.S. political system is a result of the manner in which campaigns are financed. Political campaigns are expensive, with statewide campaigns sometimes costing hundreds of thousands of dollars and a national campaign running into the millions. These monies are raised from contributions. For example, Nixon received $47.5 million from ninety-five persons for his 1972 campaign (including $2 million from W. Clement Stone, an insurance executive). Such contributions are given for a number of reasons, including the hope of future favors or payoffs for past benefits. In the 1978 election campaign, for example, the American Medical Association (AMA) contributed $1.79 million to congressional campaigns. Following the election, a House committee voted by a one-vote margin to kill hospital cost-containment legislation that would have saved $27 billion through 1982. Interestingly, the AMA had donated money to the campaigns of all committee members, but those voting the pro-AMA position of that legislation received an average of $4,482, while those voting against the AMA received only $1,007.[71] Thus, the passage of favorable laws or the defeat of unfavorable ones may directly result from the finances of special interests. So, too, may the special interests receive beneficial governmental rulings and the maintenance of tax loopholes. Since these investments pay off, it is only rational for the special interests to donate to the candidates of both parties to ensure that their interests are served. The result is that the wealthy have power while the less well-to-do and certainly the poor have little influence on office holders.[72]

By law, corporations cannot directly contribute any of their funds to political parties or candidates. However, because corporations apparently find that political contributions help them, many have contributed to political campaigns illegally. This can be done either by giving money to employees, who in turn make individual contributions, or by forcing employees to contribute to a party or candidate as a condition of employment. Watergate showed that many companies engaged in fraudulent bookkeeping practices to cover up their political expenditures. For example, Minnesota Mining and Manufacturing Company (3M) gave $634,000 to political candidates between 1963 and 1969. To achieve such a fund, officials from the company made payments for nonexisting insurance premiums and for foreign legal services never rendered. On a larger scale, Gulf Oil contributed over $12 million to politicians from 1959 to 1972. These monies were provided to state and local officials (e.g., $75,000 yearly in Pennsylvania) and to Republicans and Democrats alike nationally. Presidents Nixon and Johnson were recipients, as were Republican Senators Hugh Scott and Howard Baker and Democratic Senators Hubert Humphrey and Henry Jackson. Typically, these funds were channeled through a Gulf subsidiary in the Bahamas and given in cash to the politicians by couriers to avoid detection.[73]

To counter the potential and real abuses of large contributors, the 1976 presidential campaign was partially financed from public funds (about $20 million was allocated to each of the two major candidates). Congress, however, refused to provide such a law for its members or potential members. As a result, the monies contributed to congressional candidates rose sharply. In 1978, the total gifts from all reporting interest groups to candidates for Congress was $35 million, compared to $22.6 million in 1976 and only $12.5 million in 1974.

The most-discussed phenomenon in campaign financing today is undoubtedly the political action committee, or PAC.

> PACs are "non-party", "multicandidate" political committees that maintain a separate, segregated fund for political contributions: "non-party" because they are set up by interest groups, "multicandidate" because they distribute their largesse to at least five candidates ("political contributions" only; no charity to be mixed in here).[74]

While some PACs are established by a host of single-issue groups, such as the National Rifle Association, environmental, or antiabortion causes, the vast majority of PAC money stems from corporate interests. Thus, in the 1981-1982 congressional campaign, corporate PACs spent $50 million of the $83 million given to candidates, a tenfold increase over the amount given to candidates in 1972. Seven million dollars of that money (over 7 percent) came from oil and gas interests. The chairs of the House and Senate Energy Committees received funds from thirty-four and thirty-seven energy PACs, respectively.[75]

PAC money is now far and away the largest source of congressional campaign funds, with business PAC contributions favoring Republicans over Democrats by a ratio of two to one. What do PACs expect from congresspersons receiving their funds? Votes on important pieces of legislation. For instance, in 1982, the Used Car Dealers Association used its influence to stop the Federal Trade Commission from enacting regulations requiring that used car buyers be informed at the time of purchase of any vehicle defects known by the dealer. And in August 1982, PAC money influenced the votes of representatives on a nuclear reactor project. One hundred percent of those who received at least $3,000 in PAC contributions voted for the reactor, while only 29 percent of those who received no such contributions voted for the project.[76]

In a system where candidates are dependent on money for their success in winning office, PACs have become the closest thing to legal vote buying ever witnessed in U.S. politics. Many feel that PACs represent a clear and present danger to U.S. democracy, for an obvious reason: The poor, minorities, youth, unorganized labor, and other economically disadvantaged groups are not represented in Washington by powerful lobbies. As a result, legislation affecting the interests of the powerless has little chance of success in Congress, especially when it conflicts with the interests of the rich and powerful. In the end, democracy is weakened. Senator Edward Kennedy pointed out this problem in the late 1970s:

> Representative government on Capitol Hill is in the worst shape I have seen it in my . . . years in the Senate. The heart of the problem is that the Senate and the House are awash in a sea of special-interest campaign contributions and special-interest lobbying.[77]

The Candidate-Selection Process

Closely related to the discussion of PACs is the process by which political candidates are nominated. Being wealthy or having access to wealth are essential for victory because of the enormous cost of running a successful campaign. It costs up to $3 million to elect a senator and as much as $600,000 to elect a representative. This means, then, that the candidates tend to represent a limited constituency--the wealthy. "Recruitment of elective elites remains closely associated, especially for the most important offices in the larger states, with the candidates' wealth or access to large campaign contributions."[78]

The two-party system also works to limit candidates to a rather narrow range. Each party is financed by the special interests--especially business.

> When all of these direct and indirect gifts (donations provided directly to candidates or through numerous political-action committees of specific corporations and general business organizations) are combined, the power elite can be seen to provide the great bulk of the financial support to both parties at

the national level, far outspending the unions and middle-status liberals within the Democrats, and the mélange of physicians, dentists, engineers, real-estate operators, and other white-collar conservatives within the right wing of the Republican party.[79]

Since affluent individuals and large corporations dominate each party, they influence the candidate-selection process by giving financial aid to those sympathetic with their views and by withholding their support from those who differ. The parties, then, are constrained to choose candidates with views congruent with the elite monied interests.

THE BENEFITS THAT ELITES SEEK FROM THE STATE

From what we have said about lobbying, election financing, and candidate selection, it is obvious that corporate elites devote considerable resources to political activities, and for good reasons. The state not only regulates the capitalist economy, but also (federal, state, and local government) now accounts for 32.2 percent of the gross national product. Two-thirds of these goods and services stem from spending by the federal government alone.[80] Thus, elites seek favorable legislation (or prevention of unfavorable legislation), as well as tax breaks, subsidies, and lucrative government contracts. Such contracts include everything from multi-billion-dollar weapons systems to office furniture and paint. These contracts are not only influenced by the decisions of congressional members but are often the charge of various bureaucrats with the federal government. For example, the Government Services Administration (GSA) is in charge of securing virtually all office supplies for the entire federal government. Thus, favors from lobbyists are also from time to time dispensed to bureaucrats, as well as elected members of Congress. These favors are illegal when they include kickbacks (payments by contractors that usually involve a certain percentage of the contract in which a firm is interested). But other favors may simply include the promise of a job with the company upon completion of government services. While not illegal, these types of deals are unethical.

In addition, a host of independent regulatory agencies (e.g., Federal Communications Commission, Interstate Commerce Commission, Federal Trade Commission) have some impact on virtually every large and small business in the United States. The personnel in these agencies are not infrequently the target of various lobbying and other efforts (e.g., the promise of a job in the industry they regulate). Often, certain staff members of these agencies come from the industries they oversee, and in some cases, the industries involved requested the initial regulation.

Finally, we cannot leave this discussion without a brief mention of the influence that elites possess over the enactment or lack of enactment of legislation that defines *what is* and *is not against the law* in the first place. Examples of such influence are legion.

Item: In 1977, the House passed a bill to create a Federal Consumer Protective Agency by a vote of 293 to 94; it was defeated in the

Senate by a filibuster.   The bill was opposed by the National Association of Manufacturers, the National Association of Feed Chains, and some 300 other companies and trade associations.[81]

Item: The automobile industry got the Justice Department to sign a consent decree that blocked any attempt by public or private means to sue them for damages occurring from air pollution.

Item: Many of the nation's antitrust laws appear, on the surface, to be actions that regulate business. However, many of these laws were actually requested by big business. Such laws, as will we see in Chapter 2, exclude new competitors from the marketplace and have been used to reduce the influence of labor unions. Such laws have also functioned to increase public confidence in the quality of food and drugs by having such products certified safe by government inspection. For example, the 1906 Meat Inspection Act received a lot of support because of the muckracking activities of Upton Sinclair, who exposed the bad conditions in the meat-processing industry. However, this also delighted the large meat-packers; it helped them export successfully by meeting the high safety standards required by European countries. Nonetheless, the action crippled smaller companies. Americans were left with poor quality meat and low wages.[82] Such laws often help create uncompetitive (monopolistic) situations and are usually welcome (even favored) by big businesses. Moreover, such laws are rarely enforced and the penalties for breaking them tend to be miniscule.

Numerous additional examples could be cited, showing how, time and time again, corporate officials and politicians have, without penalty, violated laws or prevented acts from being made public that involved the theft of great amounts of money or the taking of many lives.

Here we have another of the great problems in dealing with elite deviance: All laws are not administered equally. Those laws that are administered most seriously tend to be those related to the deviance of the powerless nonelites. This process works in very subtle ways but nevertheless ensures a bias in favor of the more affluent.

One way in which this bias operates is illustrated by examining the priority given investigation and prosecution of corporate crimes within the federal government. Despite some advances noted in recent years, corporate crime remains a low priority.

Item: In 1977 and 1978, the Department of Justice spent only 5.1 percent of its resources on white-collar crime and public corruption.

Item: For fiscal year 1979, the Department of Justice's Criminal Fraud Section, which is responsible for federal prosecutions of illegal payments made overseas by U.S. corporations, all government-program fraud cases, and all oil fraud cases, possessed a total budget of only $2.4 million and a staff of only fifty attorneys.

Item: As of 1979, the Law Enforcement Assistance Administration had devoted less than 3 percent of its discretionary research grants to programs related to elite crime. As of 1980, the federal government still possessed no centralized statistical capability to index the extent of elite and other white-collar crimes. Yet for

years, the FBI, via its Uniform Crime Reports, has monitored so-
called street crimes involving both violence and crimes against
property (e.g., burglary).[83]

Quite clearly, white-collar crime does not draw the attention of
government and law enforcement officials. And for this reason, it does
not draw the resources. In fact, the Reagan administration has cut back
the funding designated for white-collar prosecutions by the Justice
Department, and the FBI has lost 15 percent of its economic crime
investigators due to budget cuts.[84]

The Criminal Justice section of the American Bar Association
issued this conclusion:

> For the most part within the Federal agencies with direct
> responsibility in the economic crime offenses area, available
> resources are unequal to the task of combatting economic crime.
> The ABA . . . also found that in cases where "seemingly
> adequate resources exist, these resources are poorly deployed,
> underutilized, or frustrated by jurisdictional considerations."[85]

Thus, the bias of the federal law enforcement effort, as well as state and
local efforts (see Chapter 2), remains slanted toward the crimes of nonelites.

THE CLASSIFICATION OF ELITE DEVIANCE

The bias of the law enforcement effort in areas other than elite
deviance has had dramatic consequences for the scholarly study of such
acts. Federal-granting agencies and elite foundations have, historically,
provided little funding for the study of elites. The first empirical study of
elite deviance was not published until 1940 (Sutherland's *White Collar
Crime*), and there has been what Clinard and Yeager describe as "little
follow-up research, with only minimal study being carried out on illegal
corporate behavior."[86]

With such minimal study devoted to the subject, such terms as
white-collar crime have become quite ambiguous. The head of the FBI
recently defined white-collar crime as "crimes that are committed by
non-physical means to avoid payment or loss of money or to obtain
business or personal advantage where success depends upon guile or
concealment."[87] Moreover, he applied the term to crimes committed by
persons from every level of society, including both elites and nonelites.

The Justice Department's current definition of *white-collar crime*
is so ambiguous that it is difficult for criminological researchers to
determine the targets of FBI investigations in this area. This definition of
white-collar criminality includes just about everything that is both illegal
and nonviolent, involving "traditional notions of deceit, deception, concealment, manipulation, breach of trust, subterfuge, or illegal circumvention."[88]

This definition is so nonspecific that it could include everything from welfare cheating by the poor to antitrust violations by upper class business men. . . . [W]hat is clear is that the Justice Department has drastically altered and expanded the usual definition of white-collar crime as it has previously been understood by both academic social science and law enforcement.[89]

The view of elite deviance discussed here differs considerably from these definitions. First, our concern is only with persons of the highest socioeconomic status. That is, we have defined the elites of U.S. society as comprised of corporate and government officials. We have done this because of the enormous wealth and power that resides in the nation's political economy--the relationship between the economic and political institution. We have, therefore, not included in our discussion labor unions or organized criminal syndicates, except in so far as there are relationships between these organizations and corporate and governmental entities that are deviant (as when the CIA hired Mafia members to assassinate Castro).

Second, we also hasten to include unethical/immoral acts in the category of elite deviance. This is not a view that is shared by all students of the subject. One criminologist described a similar classification as "definitional quicksand."[90] In a way, this is true. What is criminal is often easily understood by studying only those acts that are codified in criminal statutes. This would make our task relatively easy. But such an approach overlooks many complexities. For example, in most instances, "only a short step separates unethical tactics from violations of law. Many practices that were formerly considered unethical have now been made illegal and (are) punished by government."[91] Such acts include air and water pollution, bribes made overseas by multinational corporations, the disregard of safety and health standards, and false advertising. Thus, what is considered unethical at one point in time often becomes illegal later.

We concede that the definition of what is unethical is, like deviance itself, often in the eye of the beholder and thus subject to intense debate. Nevertheless, as one observer states:

> It is all too human to bracket law breaking with immorality, to assume that a (person) who offends against the law is ipso facto less moral than one whose activities remain within the legally permitted. Yet a few moments' honest reflection will convince us that the mere fact of transgressing the legal code or not tells us very little about our spiritual condition.[92]

Our position is that it is unavoidable and, indeed, desirable that students of deviance concern themselves with our spiritual condition. As Galliher and McCartney, two criminologists, have pointed out:

> If sociology makes no moral judgement independent of criminal statutes, it becomes sterile and inhumane--the work of moral eunuchs or legal technicians. . . . If moral judgements above and beyond criminal law were not made, the laws of Nazi Germany would be indistinguishable from the laws of many other

nations. Yet the Nuremberg trials after World War II advanced the position that numerous officials of the Nazi government, *although admittedly acting in accordance with German laws*, were behaving in such a grossly immoral fashion as to be criminally responsible. . . . In the Nuremberg trials, *representatives of the Allied governments--France, England, the Soviet Union, and the United States--explicitly and publically supported the idea of a moral order and moral judgements independent of written law*. . . . The claim was that . . . the defendants had committed atrocities against humanity. . . . The example of Nuremberg shows that moral judgements by students of crime can be made independently of particular cultural definitions of crime.[93]

Thus, the inclusion of unethical acts in the study of elite deviance represents not merely a residual category but the cutting edge of a neglected and important field of inquiry.

Third, one view of white-collar crime differentiates acts of personal enrichment from acts that are committed on behalf of one's employer.[94] This often becomes a difficult distinction to maintain when studying the deviance of elites because some elites own the organizations in which (and on behalf of whom) they commit such acts. This distinction is probably easier to maintain when discussing political corruption than it is when discussing economic deviance. However, many politicians receive illegal payments or campaign contributions for the purpose of winning elections, not necessarily for the purpose of hiding such monies in secret bank accounts or making other personally enriching expenditures.

Also, some acts of employees, committed on behalf of employers, are indirectly personally enriching. Often such acts are committed for the purpose of ensuring job security or for obtaining a promotion within the organization. This is not to say that employees never embezzle funds for personal use or that politicians do not take graft for the purpose of adding to their personal bank accounts. Our point is simply that the distinction between acts that are personally enriching and acts committed on behalf of maintaining and/or increasing the profitability or power of an organization in which one is owner or employer is difficult to maintain when examining various acts of elite deviance.

Therefore, our view of elite deviance includes three types of acts: (1) economic domination; (2) government and governmental control; and (3) denial of basic human rights.[95]

Acts of Economic Domination

These acts include crimes and unethical deeds that are usually committed by single corporations or by corporations in league with other organizations (e.g., the CIA). Typically, such crimes include violations of antitrust laws, which prohibit the formation of monopolies, price fixing, and false advertising. These crimes also involve defrauding consumers, pollution of the environment, and bribing politicians, both at home and overseas. Acts of economic domination also include crimes committed by business, such as not correcting unsafe working conditions and the deliberate manufacture of unsafe goods and hazardous medicines and foods.   And, as mentioned, there are instances where corporations illegally enter into business ventures with organized criminal syndicates.

It is important to note that some acts of economic deviance that are illegal in the United States are legal abroad.   For example, in one instance, an organic mercury fungicide, which was banned by law for sale in the United States, was used in Iraq to coat by-products of 8,000 tons of wheat and barley.   This resulted in 400 deaths and 5,000 hospitalizations among Iraqi customers.[96]   This dumping of unsafe products is a $1.2 billion business.   It is perceived as being unethical by journalists, government officials, and certain businesspeople.   Nonetheless, it is not illegal.

Crimes of Government and Governmental Control

We have discussed the unethical and generally unfair advantage gained by corporations in their efforts to influence government policies. In this section, we consider tax loopholes and other forms of "corporate welfare," including subsidies and certain special favors granted in doing business with the government.

This category includes a host of acts involving the usurpation of power. Involved here are the Watergate crimes, crimes of electioneering, and other acts involving violations of civil liberties, graft, and corruption designed to perpetuate a given administration and to enrich its members further.   Also included are those crimes committed by the government against persons and groups who are supposed threats to national security, such as crimes of warfare and political assassination.[97]

Related to offenses against those viewed as threats to national security are violations of individual civil rights, including illegal surveillance by law enforcement agencies, infiltration of law-abiding political groups by government agents, and denials of due process of law.

Many unethical acts are also committed by governmental organizations and officials. Some examples include classifying certain types of information as secret simply to cover up embarrassing incidents, making campaign promises that candidates know they cannot or will not keep, defining a situation as a genuine crisis where no real crisis conditions exist, letting out government contracts without competitive bidding, and allowing cost overruns on such contracts.

Elite Deviance as Denial of Basic Human Rights

Related to both deviance by corporations and deviance by governments are actions that contribute to various types of social injuries. Included here are threats to the dignity and quality of life for specific groups and humanity as a whole. Such practices as racism and sexism, either political or economic, fall into this category. In addition is the threat to the human race posed by the nuclear arms race.   While such notions of humanity are not always part of a nation's laws, they do enter into any value judgments made concerning the worth and dignity of individuals.

A body of international agreement and law contains some basic notions concerning human rights. Most nations of the world, including undemocratic nations, now agree that such rights should include the provision of basic material needs, as well as freedom from torture, arbitrary arrest and detention, assassination, and kidnapping.

Thus, the criminal and unethical acts of corporations and government, plus violations of basic human rights, that are part of certain bodies of international agreements subscribed to by the United States constitute the subject matter of elite deviance.

THE CONDITIONS LEADING TO ELITE DEVIANCE

In the remainder of our inquiry into the various types of elite deviance, several assumptions will be made regarding the causes, costs, and consequences of such actions.

First, organizations are often characterized by what has been termed "the shield of elitist invisibility."[98] This refers to actions, as well as heads of political organizations and governmental agencies, being frequently shrouded in secrecy. Corporate management and government officials are often shielded from the press, government investigators, and boards of directors (in the case of corporations) by virtue of the power they possess over information. For example, the illegal payments made by the Gulf Oil Company during the 1970s were kept secret from the board of directors by Gulf's chief executive officer over eighteen months after the scandal made headlines.

Such deceptions are possible in huge organizations. Corporations are often international organizations, characterized by "complex and varied sets of structural relationships between the boards of directors, executives, managers, and other employees on the one hand, and between parent corporations, corporate divisions, and subsidiaries on the other."[99] These complex relationships often make it impossible for outsiders and many insiders to determine who is responsible for what. Such structural complexities make it relatively easy to perform a host of acts corporate managers wish to be kept secret.

Next, the benefits involved in such deviance far outweigh the risks of apprehension and penalty. For example, a Senate Judiciary Subcommittee on Antitrust and Monopoly estimated that the dollar amount of corporate crime ranges from between $174 and $231 billion per year.[100] This is more than all other types of crime plus the cost of running the entire criminal justice system combined. No source can give exact estimates concerning the costs of political corruption and various kickbacks, but the New York Times estimated that business bribery and kickbacks, at least a portion of which goes to politicians, may run as high as $15 billion per year.[101] Thus, the monetary rewards of corporate and politicial crime are vitually without parallel.

Coupled with these rewards are minimal risks. From 1890 to 1970, only three businesspeople were sent to jail for violations of the Sherman Antitrust Act (see Chapter 2 for details), and from 1946 to 1953, the average fine levied in such cases was $2,600 (with $5,000 being the maximum possible).[102]

One can see that there is very little incentive not to violate some laws. And as criminologist Donald Cressey has stated, "Some businessmen have so little respect for the law that they would prefer an antitrust indictment to being caught wearing argyle socks. . . . They do so because they do not believe in these laws. This is another way of saying that they consider such laws . . . illegitimate."[103]

The prime goal of business is to make a profit, and, according to the business ideology, government regulation is often viewed as meddling (see Chapter 2). In summary, organizational structure, complexity, and primary goals (e.g., autonomy and profit) all help to shield top-level officials from the scrutiny of the press and the law. In addition, the lenient penalties established for much elite deviance are ineffectual deterrents.

THE CONSEQUENCES OF ELITE DEVIANCE

The consequences of elite deviance to U.S. society are thought to be monumental by most experts. Consider the following:

1. It is estimated that five times as many persons each year die from illnesses and injuries contracted on the job (100,000 to 200,000 persons) than are murdered by all street criminals.[104] (See Chapters 3 and 4 for details.)

2. We have observed that public confidence in our economic and political elites has drastically declined as revelations of elite deviance have taken place. In addition, many criminologists believe that deviance by elites provides either motivation or rationalization for nonelites to commit profit-oriented crimes.[105]

3. The power of elites to help shape criminal law and its enforcement raises serious questions regarding the racial and class biases of the criminal justice system's traditional equating of the crime problem in the United States with street crime.[106]

4. The monetary costs of elite deviance are thought to contribute substantially to inflation. As mentioned, estimates range from $174 to $231 billion in the prices added to goods and services. (See also Chapter 8.)

5. It will be demonstrated that elite deviance has been an important cause of the persistence and growth of organized crime in the United States. This assistance has been provided by both economic and political elites (see Chapter 2).

Also, one sociologist has argued that there exists a symbiotic (mutually interdependent) relationship between deviance by elites and deviance by nonelites. This is because elite deviance greatly affects the distribution of power in society. Much elite deviance is aimed at maintaining or increasing the proportion of wealth and power that rests in elite hands. Given the inequitable distribution of such resources, the most powerless and economically deprived members of society suffer from social conditions "that tend to provoke powerless individuals into criminality."[107]   Likewise, it is possible that elites, who view themselves as respectable members of society, view the deviance of the powerless as the genuinely dangerous type of crime faced by society.   Such elite attitudes result in elites viewing themselves as morally superior to nonelites and the crimes that they themselves commit as not really criminal. Thus, elites may be even more likely to violate legal and ethical standards because of the deviance of nonelites, which is, in part, caused by the inequitable distribution of resources, the existence of which are, in turn, related to elite power.

Finally, the consequences listed above regarding elite deviance constitute a mere beginning in this regard. The relationship between the acts of the powerful and those of the powerless—especially deviant acts—are not well investigated by scholars. Moreover, the behavior of elites, in so far as it effects an alienation and loss of confidence among nonelites, undoubtedly has additional negative consequences about which we have much to learn.

What is clear is that elite deviance possesses numerous important social, economic, and political consequences for all of society.   Only a few of the most dramatic of these consequences will be examined in this volume.

CONCLUSION

This chapter has introduced the topic of *elite deviance*. Because of the Vietnam conflict, Watergate, and numerous recent incidents involving corporate and governmental wrongdoings, elite deviance has become a major public concern.   Closer examination reveals that the deviant acts of economic and political elites are not random events. They are related to the very structure of wealth and power in the United States and to the processes that maintain such structures.

Moreover, aside from being illegal or unethical (at least according to the norms maintained by persons outside the organization committing the deviant act), elite deviance has several basic characteristics:

1. It occurs because it furthers the goals of economic and political organizations—namely, the maintenance or increase of profit and/or power.

2. It's committed with the support of the elites, who head such organizations.   Such support may be open and active or covert and implied.

3. It may be committed either by elites and/or employees acting on their behalf.[108]

Finally, such deviance is important because it possesses many negative consequences for society, including high prices, dangerous products, and the increased motivation to commit deviance on the part of nonelites.   Despite all of the public attention recently devoted to elite deviance, it remains a poorly understood, and hence unresolved, social problem in our society.   Since corporations and government now touch nearly every aspect of our daily lives, it behooves all of us to learn as much as possible about the dimensions and possible solutions to this type of deviant behavior.

NOTES

1. *San Francisco Examiner,* 7 December 1983. p. A-6.
2. *San Francisco Chronicle,* 23 November 1983, p. A-6.
3. G. Gallup, Jr., *The Gallup Report,* July 1983 (Wilmington, DL: Scholarly Resources, Inc.), 4.
4. G. Gallup, Jr., *The Gallup Report,* October 1983 (Wilmington, DL: Scholarly Resources, Inc.), 4.
5. See, for example, Sissela Bok, "People Feel They Are Being Lied to More by Politicians," *U.S. News and World Report,* 31 March 1980, 37; and Gallup, *The Gallup Report,* October 1983, 4.
6. See Sam Adams, "Vietnam Cover-Up Playing War with Numbers," in *Focus: Unexplored Deviance,* ed. C. Swanson, 93-105 (Guilford, CN: Dushkin, 1978) (article originally appeared in *Harper's,* May 1975); and A. Rogow, *The Dying of the Light* (New York: Putnam, 1975), 261-71.
7. See Michael Parenti, *Democracy for the Few,* 3rd ed. (New York: St. Martin's Press, 1980), 154-55.
8. See Alan Wolfe, *The Seamy Side of Democracy,* 2nd ed. (New York: Longman, 1978), vii.
9. Mark Green, *Who Runs Congress?* 4th ed. (New York: Dell, 1984), 234.
10. Arthur S. Miller, "Declining Faith in Government Institutions," *Society* 17 (January/February 1980), 3.
11. See "Opinion Roundup," *Public Opinion* 5 (October/November 1979), 31.
12. See M. Clinard and P. Yeager, "Corporate Crime: Issues in Research," *Criminology* 2 (August 1978), 260.
13. S. Balken et al., *Crime and Deviance in America: A Critical Approach* (Belmont, CA: Wadsworth, 1980), 170.
14. J. Roebuck and S. C. Weeber, *Political Crime in the United States: Analyzing Crime by and against Government* (New York: Praeger, 1978), 86.
15. Clinard and Yeager, 260.
16. "End of the Great Engine Flap: Settlement of Suit against GM for Use of Chevrolet Engines in Other Cars," *Time,* 2 January 1978, 66.
17. See J. Conyers, Jr., "Corporate and White-Collar Crime: A View by the Chairman of the House Subcommittee on Crime," *American Criminal Law Review* 17 (March 1980), 290; and W. E. Blundell, "Equity Funding: I Did It for the Jollies," in *Crime at the Top: Deviance in Business and the Professions,* ed. J. Johnson and J. Douglas, 153-85 (Philadelphia: Lippincott, 1978), 182.

18. Irwin Ross, "How Lawless are Big Companies," in *Florida 2000: Creative Crime Control*, ed. L. A. Wollan, 39-46 (Tampa: Florida Endowment for the Humanities, 1983), 39 (originally appeared in *Fortune*, 1 December 1980).

19. Mark Green, *Winning Back America* (New York: Bantam, 1982), 229, 231.

20. Ralph Nader and Ronald Brownstein, "Beyond the Love Canal," *The Progressive* 44 (May 1980), 28, 30.

21. Green, *Winning Back America*, 229.

22. "Toxicity," *The People* 95:111 (31 August 1985), 4.

23. *New York Times*, 19 April 1983, p. A-6; *New York Times*, 6 July 1983, pp. A-1, B-10; and Currie and Skolnick, 391.

24. G. Geis, "Upper World Crime," in *Current Perspectives on Criminal Behavior: Original Essays in Criminology*, ed. A. Blumberg, 114-37 (New York: Knopf, 1974), 116.

25. See R. Kramer, "Corporate Criminality: The Development of an Idea," in *Corporations as Criminals*, ed. E. Hochstedler, 13-38 (Beverly Hills: Sage, 1984), 18; and C. Little, *Understanding Deviance and Control* (Itaca, IL: Peacock, 1983), 214.

26. See Alex Thio, *Deviant Behavior* (Boston: Houghton Mifflin, 1978), 353.

27. See M. Mintz and J. Cohen, *Power, Inc.* (New York: Viking, 1976), xix.

28. J. Gould and W. Kolb, *A Dictionary of the Social Sciences* (New York: Free Press, 1964), 234.

29. Suzanne Keller, "Elites," in *International Encyclopedia of the Social Sciences*, vol. 5, ed. D. Sills (New York: Free Press/Macmillan, 1968), 26.

30. T. Dye and H. Zeigler, *The Irony of Democracy*, 3rd ed. (North Scituate, MA: Duxbury, 1975), 4. For an excellent summary of the evidence supporting the existence of an elite, see Harold Kerbo and Richard Della Fave, "The Empirical Side of the Power Elite Debate," *The Sociological Quarterly* 20 (Winter 1979), 5-220.

31. Dye and Zeigler, 14, 19, 235.

32. Currie and Skolnick, 25.

33. Thomas Dye, *Who's Running America?* 3rd ed. (Englewood Cliffs, NJ: Prentice-Hall, 1983), 38.

34. Thomas Dye, *Who's Running America?* 2nd ed. (Englewood Cliffs, NJ: Prentice-Hall, 1979), 234-35.

35. Ben Bagdikian, *Media Monopoly* (Boston: Beacon Press, 1983), 3.

36. Maurice Zeitlin, "Who Owns America? The Same Old Gang," *The Progressive* 42 (June 1978), 14-19.

37. Zeitlin, 14-19.

38. Zeitlin, 14-19.

39. See G. David Garson, *Power and Politics in the United States* (Lexington, MA: D. C. Heath, 1977), 181.

40. These figures are taken from Peter Evens and Steve Schneider, "The Political Economy of the Corporation," in *Critical Issues in Sociology*, ed. Scott McNall (Chicago: Scott, Foresman, 1980), 221.

41. Evens and Schneider, 222.

42. The Patman Committee, 1968, "Investments and Interlocks Between Major Banks and Major Corporations," in *American Society, Inc.,* ed. I. Zeitlin, 70-76 (Chicago: Markham, 1970), 74, 75.

43. Dye (3rd ed.), 50.

44. Evens and Schneider, 222. See also Subcommittee on Government Affairs (U.S. Senate), *Voting Rights in Major Corporations* (Washington, D.C.: Government Printing Office, 1978).

45. Garson, 181, 182, 185.

46. G. William Domhoff, *Who Rules America Now?* (Englewood Cliffs, NJ: Prentice-Hall, 1983), 77. Such power also stems from the fact that the U.S. upper class contributes heavily to political parties, campaigns, and political action committees (PACs) (see discussion that follows). Moreover, its media ownership aids it in gaining an "impact on the consciousness of all (social) classes in the nation." From D. Gilbert and J. Kahl, *The American Class Structure* (Homewood, IL: Dorsey Press, 1982), 348-49.

47. G. William Domhoff, *Who Rules America?* (Englewood Cliffs, NJ: Prentice-Hall, 1967), 87-96.

48. T. R. Dye and J. W. Pickering, "Governmental and Corporate Elites: Convergence and Differentiation," *Journal of Politics* 36 (November 1974), 905.

49. P. Freitag, "The Cabinet and Big Business: A Study of Interlocks," *Social Problems* 23 (December 1975), 137-52. See also R. J. Barnet, *The Political Economy of Death* (New York: Atheneum, 1969), 88-89.

50. R. Weissberg, *Understanding American Government* (New York: Holt, Rinehart, and Winston, 1980), 310.

51. This point and the discussion that follows are based on R. A. Garner, *Social Change* (Chicago: Rand McNally, 1977), 252-54. For a right-wing conspiratorial view, see Gary Allen, *None Dare Call It Conspiracy* (Rossmoor, CA: Concord Press, 1971).

52. Garner, 253.

53. For a summary of such differences, see Dye (2nd ed.), 190-95.

54. See William Chambliss, ed., *Criminal Law in Action* (Santa Barbara, CA: Hamilton, 1975), 230.

55. Garner, 253.

56. Cited in Garson, 183. A more detailed discussion of such monopolization and its effects is found in Chapter 3 of this volume.

57. Michael Parenti, *Power and the Powerless* (New York: St. Martin's Press, 1978), 22.

58. Dye (3rd ed.), 60.

59. Dye (2nd ed.), 126.

60. Dye (2nd ed.), 29.

61. See T. H. White, *The Making of the President 1972* (New York: Atheneum, 1973), Chapter 8; Domhoff, *Who Rules America?* 79-83.

62. Parenti, *Democracy for the Few,* 168.

63. Herbert J. Gans, *Deciding What's News* (New York: Pantheon, 1979), 12.

64. Gans, 14.

65. G. M. Tabor, "Capitalism: Is It Working?" *Time*, 21 April 1980, 55.

66. Dye (2nd ed.), 115-16.

67. Michael T. Klare, *War Without End* (New York: Knopf, 1972), 77.

68. G. William Domhoff, *The Powers That Be: Processes of Ruling Class Domination in America* (New York: Vintage, 1978), 118.

69. Parenti, *Democracy for the Few*, 226.

70. Mark Green and Jack Newfield, "Who Owns Congress?" *The Village Voice*, 21 April 1980, p. 16.

71. Michael J. McManus, "The Tyranny of Special Interests," *Rocky Mountain News*, 9 September 1979, 69.

72. See Warren Weaver, Jr., "What is a Campaign Contributor Buying?" *New York Times*, 13 March 1977, p. E-2.

73. "Shake-Up at Gulf--The Ripples Spread," *U.S. News and World Report*, 26 January 1976, 70.

74. A. Etzioni, *Capital Corruption* (New York: Harcourt, Brace, and Jovanovich, 1984), 3.

75. W. C. Cooper, "Take Back Your Dirty PAC Money," *The Nation*, 7 May 1983, 565; Green, *Who Runs Congress?* 30-31.

76. Green, *Who Runs Congress?* 35.

77. Cited in "TRB from Washington," *The New Republic*, 11 November 1978, 2. See also "Hidden Army of Washington Lobbyists," *U.S. News and World Report*, 25 July 1977, 31.

78. Walter D. Burnham, "Party System and the Political Process," in *The American Party System*, 2nd ed., ed. William N. Chambers and Walter D. Burnham, 257-307 (New York: Oxford University Press, 1975), 277.

79. Domhoff, *The Powers That Be*, 148.

80. Tabor, 54.

81. Morton C. Paulson, "What Is Business Afraid Of?" *The National Observer*, 5 October 1974, 14.

82. Frank Pearce, *Crimes of the Powerful* (London: Pluto Press, 1976), 87.

83. Conyers, 291, 299. See also Chapter 2 of this volume.

84. M. Green and J. F. Berry, "Capitalist Punishment: Some Proposals," *The Nation*, 13 June 1985, 732.

85. ABA Section on Criminal Justice, Committee on Economic Offenses, March 1977, 6-7, cited in Conyers, 290.

86. Clinard and Yeager, 256.

87. William Webster, "Examination of FBI Theory and Methodology," in Conyers, 276.

88. Attorney General of the United States, *National Priorities for the Investigation and Prosecution of White-Collar Crime* (Washington, D.C.: Government Printing Office, 1980), ii.

89. David R. Simon and Stanley L. Swart, "The FBI Focuses on White-Collar Crime: Promises and Pitfalls," *Crime and Delinquency* 30 (January 1984), 109. Another good discussion of this issue can be found in R. Akers, *Deviant Behavior: A Social Learning Approach*, 3rd ed. (Belmont, CA: Wadsworth, 1985), 231.

90. See Geis, 117.

91. Clinard and Yeager, 264.

92. John B. Mays, *Crime and the Social Structure* (London: Faber

and Faber, 1967), 39.

93. J. F. Galliher and J. L. McCartney, *Criminology: Power, Crime, and Criminal Law* (Homewood, IL: Dorsey Press, 1977), 10.

94. See H. Edelhertz et al., *The Investigation of White-Collar Crime* (Washington, D.C.: U.S. Government Printing Office, 1977), 7.

95. For an extended discussion of this typology, see Richard Quinney, *Class, State and Crime* (New York: McKay/Longman, 1977), 50–52.

96. See Mark Dowie, "The Corporate Crime of the Century," *Mother Jones* 9 (November 1979), 24.

97. Quinney, 51.

98. W. C. Scott and David K. Hart, *Organizational America* (Boston: Houghton Mifflin, 1979), 40.

99. Clinard and Yeager, 265.

100. Ovid Demaris, *Dirty Business* (New York: Harper's Magazine Press, 1974), 12.

101. See "Companies' Payoffs in U.S. Come Under New Scrutiny," *New York Times*, 16 March 1976, p. A-1.

102. See Ralph Nader and Mark Green, "Crime in the Suites," *The New Republic*, 29 April 1972, 19. The maximum fine was raised to $50,000 in 1955; however, this is still a pittance compared with the multimillion-dollar profits of most large corporations.

103. Donald Cressey, "White Collar Subversives," *Center Magazine* 6 (November/December 1978), 44.

104. See "Job Hazards," *Dollars and Sense* 56 (April 1980), 9.

105. See, for example, Geis, 114.

106. Conyers, 293.

107. Thio, 85, 89.

108. For further discussion of these issues, see N. David Ermann and Richard J. Lundman, eds., *Organization Deviance* (New York: Oxford University Press, 1978), 7–9.

CHAPTER 2

Elite Deviance and The Higher Immorality

THE NATURE OF THE HIGHER IMMORALITY

The U.S. business community has, in recent years, become concerned with its television image. For example, in 1981, United Technologies took out a full-page ad in a leading journal of social criticism, offering an explanation for the negative portrayals of corporate executives on television. According to United Technologies, in past years, minorities were typically the villains in television programs. But this changed with the civil rights movement of the 1960s, when minorities won a more favorable image in virtually all types of media. This change created a bad-guy void, and screenwriters have chosen business executives to fill it. United Technologies commissioned its own study and found that, in over 75 percent of the programs in which they appeared, businesspeople were presented as either J. R. Ewing-type scoundrels or incompetent bunglers. Where, puzzled UT, did televisionwriters ever get the notion that larceny and incompetence characterize the U.S. business community?[1]

Where, indeed! We believe that these prime-time images of corporate executives and other elites (e.g., politicians, such as Boss Hog) featured in the media come straight out of news stories and other factual accounts of real life in the United States. A few examples from the recent past will illustrate this point.

Item: On January 16, 1981, Harris Katleman, chairman of the board of 20th Century Fox, was asked to resign after submitting questionable expense-account vouchers. Likewise, David Begelman, then president of Columbia Pictures, forged names of acquaintances on $61,000 worth of checks. When actor Cliff Robertson reported that Begelman had forged his name on a $10,000 check, Robertson was blacklisted from film roles for about four years. The court later dismissed all charges against Begelman. Moreover, Alan Hirschfield, Columbia's chief executive officer, was fired by the board of directors for insisting that Begelman be prosecuted. All of this was done because the board was afraid of scandal and felt a personal fondness for Begelman.[2]

Item: From 1979 to 1982, "124 corporations and 147 individuals pleaded or were found guilty of bid rigging on highway projects in fourteen states."[3]   This case was the largest criminal antitrust investigation in Justice Department history.   As a result, more than 100 corporate officials have gone to jail for an average of four months, unusually harsh sentences for white-collar crime cases.

Item: In late 1983, President Reagan signed an order approving the use of lie detector tests for civil servants accused of leaking information to the press; the test could be administered whether or not it was established that any leak had actually taken place. (A Deputy Attorney General testified, however, that the president signed no such order.)   President Reagan also ordered all White House officials to sign lifetime agreements to submit all future writings for government clearance.[4]

Item: In 1981, President Reagan created a Foreign Intelligence Advisory Board, calling it a group of "trustworthy and distinguished citizens outside the government."[5]   The board was given the task of assessing the performance of intelligence and counterintelligence agencies.   Reagan appointed his millionaire-friend Alfred Bloomingdale to this highly sensitive post.   Bloomingdale was the only board member without academic or government service credentials in the area of intelligence.

Bloomingdale had wanted to be named a U.S. Ambassador, but his personal reputation was so suspect that the president settled for appointing him to a post that did not require Senate confirmation.   Reagan had good reason: Bloomingdale not only kept a mistress, Vicki Morgan, who he supported to the tune of $18,000 a month; he was "also a notorious sadist who derived sexual pleasure by inflicting physical pain on Morgan and numerous prostitutes."[6]   Ms. Morgan was later murdered before she could complete a book detailing her relationship with Bloomingdale and, reportedly, other members of the Reagan White House.

Item: In 1983, Donald J. O'Hara, city manager of Niagara Falls, New York, received $8,500 from Neuco Industries, the parent company of a corporation contracted to perform part of the cleanup project at the Love Canal toxic chemical site.   This contract for the cleanup was the only one not awarded on a competitive basis. As a result, Neuco added 20 percent for overhead and profit on most expenses.   New York state investigators claimed that the state was overcharged $4-$5 million.   O'Hara, the bribed city manager, subsequently was hired by a subsidiary of the same company for a $40,000-a-year post in Florida.[7]

Item: Judging from his books, columns, and TV show, the only federal agency that William F. Buckley really approves of is the CIA. He certainly doesn't like the federal agencies that monitor the ethical conduct of businesspeople.   In 1977, we found out why Buckley doesn't like the SEC: SEC staff investigators recommended to the full commission that Buckley be prosecuted for insider fraud and false reporting.

Buckley is a millionaire businessman.   His family has extensive holdings in oil and broadcasting.   Buckley has long favored more tax loopholes for the oil industry and less regulation of broadcasting.

The *Wall Street Journal* revealed that Buckley had used one of his companies--Starr Broadcasting--to help bail him out of a bad investment in a chain of Texas drive-in theaters. As the *Journal* reported: "Mr. Buckley defends the transaction as an arms-length sale, even in the face of new evidence of self-dealing." Buckley was recently forced to resign as chairman of the board of Starr by the other directors, in the hope that the corporation itself won't be named in any SEC legal action.

In 1978, Mr. Buckley signed a consent decree with the Securities and Exchange Commission. Charged with violating the federal securities laws, Mr. Buckley and two other defendants in the case agreed to make a restitution payment of $1.8 million. Mr. Buckley also agreed to an order preventing him from being an officer or a director of a publicly owned company for a period of five years.

The great benefit to humankind from this episode is not the potential civil-fraud case against Buckley: In the *Wall Street Journal* story, Buckley--who postures with the certainty of a Nobel Prize economist--admitted: "I am no good with figures. I don't understand them. . . ."[8]

Sociologist C. Wright Mills once remarked that "as news of higher immoralities breaks (people) often say, 'Well another one got caught today,' thereby implying that the cases disclosed are symptoms of a much more widespread condition."[9] Mills used the term *higher immorality* to describe a *moral insensibility*[10] among the most wealthy and powerful members of the United States' corporate, political, and military elite (which he termed *the power elite*). For Mills, the higher immorality translated into a variety of unethical, corrupt, and sometimes illegal practices, which were viewed as a systematic, institutionalized feature of contemporary U.S. society.

In business and in government, Mills felt, many transactions are accomplished via interpersonal manipulation. One type of such manipulation by the successful is using a false front: pretending to be interested in what other have to say, attempting to make others feel important, and radiating charm and self-confidence (despite one's own insecurities). Obviously, if social relations are based on insincere feelings, such activities would be characterized by a good deal of alienation on the part of the participants.

In addition, Mills felt that some business and political arrangements included the favors of prostitutes. The sexual favors of these high-priced call girls are often paid for with executive expense-account allotments[11] (which will be discussed later). Aside from interpersonal manipulation and the peddling of high-priced vice, the higher immorality also includes: (1) unethical practices relating to executive salaries and expense accounts; (2) unfair executive and corporate tax advantages; (3) the deliberate creation of political and/or economic crises by the power elite; (4) the manipulation of public opinion; and (5) the violation of antitrust and other laws relating to political corruption.

Since Mills described these various types of deviance in the 1950s, the nation has witnessed scandal after scandal involving these various forms of the higher immorality. Thus, an up-to-date analysis of the nature and significance of the higher immorality is in order. This chapter is concerned with executive salaries and expense accounts, laws relating to the incomes of corporate executives and corporations, the creation of phony crises by the power elite, and violations of antitrust laws. We will also consider one form of the higher immorality only hinted at in Mills' provocative analysis--the relationships between the wealthy and powerful and members of organized crime.

The Higher Immorality and Corporate Compensation: Salaries, Taxes, and Perks

Since the higher immorality involves the pursuit of money, the mechanisms by which money is obtained and retained are very important. As Mills put it:

> Higher income taxes have resulted in a whole series of collusion between the big firm and higher employee. There are many ingenious ways to cheat the spirit of the tax laws, and the standards of consumption of many high-priced men are determined more by complicated expense accounts than by simple take-home pay.[12]

The accuracy of Mills' description can be gauged by a study of all the various rewards granted top corporate executives. Table 2-1 lists the annual salaries, bonuses, and long-term income (stock options) paid to a number of top executives in 1983.

Corporate executive compensation, without expense accounts and other perks, dwarfs the annual salaries of the highest-paid politician in the United States ($200,000) and the highest-paid military officers ($45,000). The data make clear that one of the most widely used and effective devices for the amassing of corporate wealth is the corporate stock option. A stock option is "a right given a corporate executive to buy his company's stock at sometime in the future, at a specified price the date the option is granted."[13] For example, suppose an executive is given an option to buy 100,000 shares of his or her company's stock on January 15, 1981, and on that day the price of such stock is $75 per share. The executive may have contracted to buy the stock at $50 per share back in 1979. The executive may still purchase the stock at $50 per share. The profit on the stock amounts to $25 per share on 100,000, or $250,000. The executive does not pay income tax on this windfall but does pay capital-gains tax. Such taxes, however, are only 40 percent, considerably less than the income tax one would pay on such an amount.

If the numbers in this example sound outrageous, consider again the data in Table 2-1. These statistics indicate that, on the average, stock options were worth between $1 and $4 million in long-term benefits in 1983. But even these figures do not tell the entire story. Consider William Marquard, American Standard's chairman. The table shows that he received $671,000 from the amount of stock options he exercised in 1983. Yet *Business Week* claims that, had he exercised *all* of his stock options, Marquard could have realized an additional $3 million in compensation![14] A number of the executives on this list could have gained additional millions by the exercise of all stock options. Thus, such annual compensation totals are often misleading.

Consider also the case of Harold Geneen, ITT's chairman. Geneen retired from the corporation in January 1980. But during that year, ITT paid Geneen $450,000 as a consultant. And beginning in 1981, when his pension plan began, Geneen receives yearly payments of $250,000 in consulting fees, $130,000 from various company retirement plans, and an additional $112,000 from yet another employment contract.[15] And this is in a country where millions of workers are not covered by any pension plan at all!

Nonetheless, let us continue with our examination of stock options. Some corporations have plans that allow them to withdraw high-price stock options and publish new ones to reflect lower market prices. Some corporations even provide low-cost or no-interest loans so stock options may be purchased. Sometimes no repayment of the loan's principal (actual amount of the loan) is required until the executive "dies, retires, quits, or goes bankrupt."[16] And if the stock price falls further, executives are commonly permitted to turn their shares back to the company at the time the loan is cancelled. Hence, executives are not subject to the risks on the market that plague the bulk of the nation's stockholders.

Another innovative plan, called *stock appreciation rights* (SAR), further confirms Mills' claim regarding executive avoidance of taxation. Instead of paying money for stock shares, executives merely collect from the company money or stock shares equal to any increase in the stock's value. Doing this allows executives to escape paying capital-gains taxes and any money for the stock option. By 1977, 80 percent of the top 200 industrial corporations had opted for the SAR alternative.

Other advances in tax avoidance have occurred in recent years. One plan, adopted by 29 percent of companies with sales of over $3 million, allows executives to choose options that make stock payments on either a spread-out or lump-sum basis, resulting in more tax savings. Such plans are usually so complex that company stockholders are unable to understand them, especially when the details are hidden in the fine-print sections of stockholder reports. Such practices involve deceiving stock-holders and prevent any stockholder revolts.

Another stock-option plan permits executives to purchase stock at its book-value price. Rather than buying stock at market prices, executives buy it at a price per share equal to the company's assets minus its liabilities. This price rarely declines and usually increases greatly, regardless of stock market swings. Later, executives are permitted to sell the stock to the company at its new book value.

The perks (perquisites) of corporate life are not limited to salaries, bonuses, and stock options. Indeed, the corporate-compensation landscape now represents a form of corporate socialism for top executives. Among the tax-exempt perks enjoyed by corporate managers are

> financial counseling, tax and legal assistance, company automo-
> biles and chauffeur services (for business and sometimes for
> personal use), company-provided planes, boats, and apartments
> (for business and sometimes for personal use), company paid or
> subsidized travel, recreation facilities, club memberships, liberal
> expense accounts, personal use of business credit cards . . . com-
> plete medical coverage, including . . . home, health care, dental,
> and   psychiatric   care--all   without   outlays   by   the
> executive . . . college expenses for children, "social-service sab-

Table 2-1
Twenty-Five Highest Paid U.S. Corporate Executives, 1983 (earnings in thousands of dollars)

Executive	Company	Salary	Bonus	Salary plus bonus	Long-term income	Total compensation
1 Frederick W. Smith, chmn	Federal Express	—	—	$414	$51,130	$51,544
2 Charles P. Lazarus, chmn	Toys 'R' Us	$315	$1,098	1,413	42,360	43,773
3 W. John Devine, exec v-p	Toys 'R' Us	130	256	386	15,045	15,431
4 Norman Ricken, pres	Toys 'R' Us	150	320	470	7,458	7,928
5 Seymore Ziv, exec v-p	Toys 'R' Us	100	160	260	7,458	7,718
6 Robert P. Jensen, chmn, pres	GK Technologies; Penn Central	537	225	762	3,000	3,762
7 Hicks B. Waldron, pres	R.J. Reynolds Industries	303	284	587	2,995	3,582
8 William A. Marquard, chmn, pres	American Standard	—	—	671	2,687	3,358
9 George L. Shinn, chmn	First Boston	—	—	2,000	1,090	3,090
10 Stuart D. Watson, chmn Heublein	R.J. Reynolds Industries	244	137	381	2,633	3,014
11 Richard K. Eamer, pres	National Medical Enterprises	415	260	675	2,047	2,722
12 Harrington Drake, chmn	Dun & Bradstreet	—	—	750	1,701	2,451
13 Richard L. Gelb, chmn	Bristol-Myers	580	386	966	1,405	2,371

14	Peter T. Buchanan, pres	First Boston	—	—	1,900	445	2,345
15	Robert Anderson, chmn	Rockwell International	515	462	977	1,341	2,318
16	Hubert Faure, exec v-p	United Technologies	320	244	564	1,640	2,204
17	James J. Gavin Jr., senior v-p	Borg-Warner	210	234	444	1,714	2,158
18	David Mahoney, chmn	Norton Simon	638	250	888	1,145	2,033
19	Ray C. Adam, chmn (retired)	NL Industries	392	213	605	1,362	1,967
20	Robert A. Charple, pres	Cabot	—	—	517	1,434	1,951
21	Alva O. Way, former pres	American Express	—	—	627	1,293	1,920
22	Robert O. Anderson, chmn	Atlantic Richfield	575	222	797	1,112	1,909
23	William P. Tavoulareas, pres	Mobil	—	—	1,172	656	1,828
24	Jerry E. Dempsey, pres	Borg Warner	260	221	481	1,340	1,821
25	J. Robert Fluor, chmn	Fluor	—	—	1,073	733	1,806

* Reflects change in control contract provisions.
Source: *Business Week*, 21 March 1984, 188. Reprinted with permission.

baticals," and the best and most complete form of disability, accident, and life insurance.[17]

Among the most controversial of such perks is the expense account. This tax-avoidance device allows individual businesspeople to deduct up to 70 percent of the cost of entertaining business associates from income taxes. If the account is a company account, all of it may be deducted from corporate income tax as a cost of doing business. The practice has produced some lavish deductions, fascinating justifications, and scandalous tax results. Under this practice, some corporations give gifts to customers at Christmas. Such gifts have included $1 billion in whiskey and over $2 billion in automobiles and jewels, all tax deductible.

Gifts are but one aspect of the expense account. Theater and sports tickets, nightclub outings, country-club memberships, yacht maintenance, corporate hunting lodges, and other vacation retreats are paid for (in effect) by the U.S. taxpayer. In one Internal Revenue Service case, a dairy owner and his wife were allowed (by the presiding judge) to deduct $16,443 for a six-month African safari The safari was claimed as an "ordinary and necessary" business expense because movies of the trip were used as advertising for the dairy. Large corporations typically provide upper-level sales personnel with expense accounts of $700 to $900 per week. One executive of a small eastern corporation was provided an expense account that paid his apartment rental, meals, drinks, dues at a country club, entertainment expenses, and an occasional trip overseas (for purposes of studying business methods that would make his firm more competitive). While the man's actual salary was $35,000, the expense account made his salary and benefits equivalent to a $98,000 position. His $8,300 income tax bill would have been $62,600 had his expense account been taxable.[18]

The symbol of the expense account is the three-martini lunch. Many expensive restaurants claim that they would go out of business without the expense-account lunch. The question has been posed why business lunches are any more or less a legitimate expense than the lunches of construction workers, janitors, professors, doctors, or any other professionals. Moreover, it could easily be argued that food, housing, clothes, and entertainment are a necessary expense for any working person. Most people could not show up at their jobs without proper attire, so why should not all working people be allowed to deduct such items from taxes?

Certainly, the three-martini lunch and other expense-account perks are not deviant or immoral in the same sense that murder, bribery, and other crimes are immoral. In part, such perks are mere indicators of the types of advantages the business elite has been able to secure for itself, advantages that many feel are, at the least, unfair and prone to unethical abuses.

However, other advantages secured by the elite--especially those relating to tax laws and private foundations--are important because they have, in some instances, facilitated both political and economic crimes. Such advantages deserve a closer look.

The State of Welfare for the Well-Off:
Tax Breaks and Subsidies

Under the U.S. system of government has grown what is known as a dual-welfare system. Programs for the poor are termed "relief," "welfare," "assistance," or "charity."[19] Programs for the rich, however, are called "tax expenditures," "subsidies," "price supports," "parity," and the like.

The dual-welfare system is an integral part of the higher immorality, allowing the rich to become richer at the expense of the middle class and the poor. The mechanism by which the rich are allowed to retain their wealth is the tax loophole. Rich individuals and corporations were provided tax loopholes (now called "tax expenditures" by government) that amounted to $330 billion in 1984.[20] In fact, from 1981 to 1983, corporate tax loopholes, including the expense account, allowed fifteen major corporations to pay no federal corporate income taxes whatsoever. These firms and their earnings are listed in Table 2-2. About twenty years ago, one-third of the taxes collected by the federal government came from corporations. Today, tax breaks granted to corporations have reduced that amount to a mere 8 percent.

Congress has provided many special tax breaks for U.S. corporations. Some of the most important are discussed in the following sections.

Investment tax credit. From 1962 to 1969, the investment tax credit saved U.S. corporations $13.5 billion in taxes. It was repealed in 1969 but reinstituted in 1971 as the job-development credit. This credit allows a company to reduce its tax bill by 7 percent of the amount invested in new equipment that is expected to last seven years or more. This means a piece of equipment priced at $100,000 saves a corporation $7,000 in taxes and ends up costing (in reality) only $93,000. This break was granted corporations on the theory that buying new equipment will create additional jobs. This theory has yet to be proven. In fact, from 1969 to 1971, the sales of corporations benefiting most from the investment tax credit rose 12.5 percent, but employment in such companies actually decreased by 5.2 percent, or 500,000 jobs.[21]

New features were added to the investment tax credit under the Reagan administration. Businesses were allowed to deduct a percentage of the price of most new investments: 6 percent for assets that could be depreciated over three years; 10 percent for all other categories. Newly eligible items included petroleum-storage facilities and leased railroad cars.[22]

The asset-depletion range. Over one-half of the benefit from asset depletion goes to the largest 103 U.S. manufacturing corporations. This tax law makes an allowance for wear and tear on equipment by allowing a depreciation deduction. In reality, there is no way of knowing how long a piece of equipment will last; it merely depends on how quickly

Table 2-2
Firms Paying No Corporate Income Tax, 1981-1983

Firm	1983 Net Earnings (in thousands of dollars)
American Financial Corporation	167,002
Boeing Company	355,000*
Centrex Corporation	39,572
Champion International Corporation	82,160
Columbia Gas System	173,735
Dow Chemical Company	334,000*
General Dynamics	286,600
General Electric	2,024,000*
Greyhound Corporation	105,499
Grumman Corporation	110,746
Lockheed Corporation	262,800
Rio Grande Industries	32,562
Singer Company	31,600
Transamerica Corporation	198,424
U.S. Home	27,640

* In addition, a refund of over $100 million was made to this company over the three-year period.
   Source: Adapted from *Denver Post*, 6 October 1984, pp. 2-B, 1-A; *Fortune*, 30 April 1984, 274-300; *Fortune*, 11 June 1984, 172-94.

a given company decides to replace it.   Before the asset-depletion allowance, most equipment had to be depreciated over a ten-year period for tax purposes.   Now, however, a company is allowed to depreciate equipment over an eight-year period, 20 percent faster than before.   Of course, such equipment lasts eight years, ten years, or even longer.   The odd thing about the asset-depletion range is that it comes at a time when 25 percent of the nation's plant capacity is already underused.   Hence, the need for new equipment is suspect.

In 1981, the Reagan-sponsored tax bill contained several unique depreciation items.   The depreciation lifetimes of some items were reduced from thirty-six years to three years (e.g., cars, trucks, research equipment, and younger race horses).   Most buildings were allowed to depreciate over ten years, compared to sixty years under the old law. Most new schedules were much shorter than those of previous administrations, allowing tax-free depreciation allowances to be built up long before property and equipment actually wear out.

Moreover, the Reagan legislation actually allowed companies to buy and sell tax breaks by pretending to lease equipment from each other. Economist Frank Ackerman offers this analogy: A poor family, who pays no income tax, lets a rich family legally adopt their children for tax purposes.   The children actually remain with their family of origin, but the adoption provides the rich family with a tax exemption.   The rich family saves $500 in taxes, and the poor family is given a portion of this savings.   If individual families did this, it would be fraud.   Only corporations can do it legally.[23]

Indeed, in 1982, Ford Motor Company sold its tax benefits to IBM, which amounted to a net gain of $100-$200 million for IBM. Through similar arrangements, General Electric received a $100-million refund, Chrysler made $26 million, and a bankrupt railroad made $50 million in two years. And American Oil (AMOCO), with a pretax income of $3.5 billion, was able to reduce its taxes by $159 million.[24] Eighty percent of these new tax benefits go to the nation's largest 1,700 corporations.[25] This means that, by 1990, the federal income tax on corporations will be nearly nonexistent.

This and other features of the Reagan plan will have reduced government revenues by $750 billion between 1981 and 1984 and by $1 trillion between 1984 and 1988. Meanwhile, government deficits zoomed from $40 billion in 1980 to $210 billion in 1982. Indeed, by 1984, corporate tax breaks cost the federal treasury $150 billion. By 1986, such breaks will cost $250 billion a year.

Perhaps worst of all is the realization that there is no proof that large corporations are actually spending money on new plants and equipment, which is the stated goal of the new tax breaks. Moreover, by 1978, before the breaks, large corporations had already accummulated some $80 billion in uninvested capital. For example, U.S. Steel was badly in need of modernizing its plants. Instead of doing so, it shut down many of them. Then, in 1982, U.S. Steel bought Marathon Oil for $6 billion.[26]

Taxes and multinational corporations. Many multinational corporations take advantage of foreign tax credits, which allow a company to pay taxes on profits made overseas, where taxes are usually less, and to pay no taxes on such profits in the United States. This has made some nations--including Liechtenstein, Panama, and Liberia--tax havens for large corporations. The practice of setting up dummy corporations overseas to which items are sold only on paper (for purposes of tax avoidance) is also common. Phillip Stern has described one such practice:

> To understand, visualize a scene on a windswept shore of Nova Scotia. A seemingly ordinary industrial process is under way. The good ship *Gypsum Prince* is tied up to a special jetty, awaiting her cargo: gypsum rock, the stuff of which wallboard, plaster and other building materials are made. A conveyor belt reaches across the jetty and over the ship as the rock, mined by a Canadian company named Canadian Gypsum, reaches the end of the belt . . . and tumbles into the hold of the ship. Simple. . . .
>
> But all is not as simple as it appears. For, at the instant each piece of rock reaches the end of the conveyor belt, a sale takes place: ownership of the rock passes from the mining company, Canadian Gypsum, to Export.
>
> But Export . . . has only the briefest use for the rock, for, the instant it hits the hold of the *Gypsum Prince*, Export sells the rock . . . --at a profit of 50 cents to a ton--to U.S. Gypsum, Inc. (U.S.G.), the major American gypsum company.
>
> And that is the sum and substance of what Export does (or did) for its million-dollar-a-year profit: it held paper ownership of a couple of million tons of gypsum rock during the fleeting instants of its fall from conveyor belt to ship hold.

Why this legal sleight of hand? It *sounds* like an exceedingly poor business . . . until you learn that Export is wholly owned by U.S. Gypsum, so that USG is, in effect, paying the million dollars to itself. . . . Export qualifies, under U.S. tax law, as a "Western Hemisphere trade corporation" (known, in the tax trade, as a WHTC) whose profits are taxed at a substantially lower rate than those of its parent, USG. Approximate tax savings during 1957 and 1958: $300,000. No wonder USG didn't mind paying the million-dollar profit to an empty corporate shell for doing nothing.

But that was not the limit of the tax-saving possibilities inherent in the situation at the Nova Scotia jetty. . . . Export was not USG's only "corporate child." The Canadian mining company was also a "child." And so was the good ship *Gypsum Prince*--or, to be more precise, the Panamanian corporation (Panama Gypsum, Inc.) that owned the *Gypsum Prince*.

Why a Panamanian corporation?   Because . . . Panama imposes no taxes whatever on the profits of corporations. . . . It was all a financially incestuous arrangement: over a four-year period, USG paid its *wholly owned* shipping company (Panama) $17,684,823 to carry gypsum from its *wholly owned* mines in Nova Scotia to its *wholly owned* processing in the United States. Now just suppose that USG chose to pay Panama something "extra" (above the lowest competitive shipping rate) for doing that--as the U.S. government alleged in a court action against USG. The government contended that the overcharge amounted to between 25 and 60 percent--but if the "extra" amounted to just 10 percent, the effect would be to reduce by nearly $2 million the profits of USG (taxable at the American 48 percent rate) and to increase by $2 million the profits of USG's corporate offspring, Panama, *which are not taxed at all*. Approximate tax saving during 1957 and 1958: about half a million dollars.[27]

Despite the tax advantages granted to corporations, individuals who own controlling interests in corporations also tend to do all they can to ensure that their fortunes are passed on to their kin. In order to escape inheritance and other taxes, a boon to such individuals has been the tax-exempt foundation.

Foundations: Charity and the Higher Immorality

The purpose of foundations is supposedly to facilitate charitable contributions. In 1976, U.S. foundation assets totalled $35.1 billion.[28] Setting up a tax-exempt foundation exempts all assets therein from income and capital-gains taxes, as well as most inheritance taxes. On the surface, this seems morally upright because such funds are, after all, given to worthy causes. Underneath, however, the reality is somewhat different.

Item: In the late 1960s, millionaire Spenser Collins established the St. Genevieve Foundation. His foundation, it seems, spent $100,000 on two twin sisters. One sister was housed in a duplex, paid for by

Mr. Collins' foundation, and the other was given a five-bedroom house, for which she was paid $36,000 to act as caretaker. Mr. Collins' favors, however, were not appreciated by the government, which, subsequently, tried and found him guilty of tax evasion. While Mr. Collins' case represents a violation of foundation law, it also demonstrates the economic crime that is invited by such arrangements.[29]

Item: The late Nelson Rockefeller, while governor of New York, set up a Government Affairs Foundation. Between 1961 and 1964, the governor gave $310,469 to the Foundation, but it paid out exactly zero dollars in charitable causes. Instead, Frank Moore was paid $120,000 in salary and $40,000 in expenses to act largely as Rockefeller's political liaison in various state matters. Essentially, Rockefeller had gained a full-time political liaison at tax-deductible costs.

Item: From 1961 to 1964, the Standard Oil Foundation of Chicago made charitable grants of $5,459,967, but $2,059,736 was donated to the American Oil Foundation of Indiana, which is owned by Standard Oil!

Foundations excel at investing money and escaping taxation. A government study of 1,300 foundations found that 180 of them owned 10 percent or more of a corporation's stock (often enough to gain controlling interest in a company).[30] Far from being strictly charitable, foundations play a major role in the corporate decisions that affect the private sector of the economy, as well as politics.

Moreover, there have been incidents of government interference in the awarding of private foundation grants. This has especially been the case with the Central Intelligence Agency (CIA). In 1966, the CIA disbursed $400,000 through the J. M. Kaplan Fund to a research institute. The institute, in turn, financed research centers in Latin American countries, which also drew support from the Agency for International Development (a U.S. foreign-aid agency), Brandeis and Harvard Universities, and the Ford Foundation. The CIA also sponsored the travel of various social scientists to communist countries. The Kaplan Fund had also been financed by foundations, although it was not even listed with the Internal Revenue Service. This suggests that the foundation was fraudulently created by the CIA. Seven other foundations were discovered to have been CIA-created conduits, but the purposes or amounts of money given have never been made public. Why the CIA went into the charity business, which is a clear violation of its charter, has also gone unexplained.[31]

Foundation money has been used for a number of causes that have nothing whatever to do with charity, and, as such, represents one more form of the higher immorality. The Ford Foundation, for example, has lent large sums of money to private corporations, in effect, competing with private banks. Howard Hughes created the Hughes Medical Institute to ensure the liabilities of a number of Hughes' own companies. Other foundations have made loans to businesspeople for the purpose of closing business deals. Foundation grants have also: (1) bankrolled political candidates; (2) financed experiments with school decentralization in black slums; (3) supported militant political organizations, both on the left and the right; (4) financed the foreign travels of staff of U.S. senators; and

(5) financed the activities of moderate (middle-class) civil rights organizations, which have largely failed to understand or alleviate the problems of poor ghetto blacks (who rarely receive such money without strings).[32] In short, foundations have been used for purposes that have nothing whatever to do with charity.

Given all of the special tax privileges granted to corporations and superrich individuals, as well as the abuse to which such privileges are subject, there is little wonder that a 1977 Harris poll found that over two-thirds of the public believed that tax laws are written for the benefit of the wealthy, not the average person.[33]

Welfare for the Rich: Subsidies

In addition to all the tax loopholes created for the rich and the corporations, many more billions of dollars in benefits are paid by the government. These benefits are called *subsidies*, and they are made in the form of payments, low-interest loans, and/or in-kind benefits (whereby services of various kinds are provided by the government). Such generosity is extended to many different industries. However, it tends to benefit most of the largest and wealthiest interests.

In agriculture, for example, the lion's share of such payments go to the largest individual and corporate farmers "to limit the production of crops by buying up crop surpluses . . . keeping prices (to consumers) and profits high while subsidizing the expansion of giant corporate farms at the expense of family farms."[34] Among others receiving subsidies are oil companies, a bowling alley in Dallas, an Ohio radio station, and the Queen of England (for not producing crops on the Royal Family's Mississippi plantation).[35]

In 1973, 63 percent of the agricultural subsidies went to the wealthiest 19 percent of farmers, while the bottom half of the farm population received only 9 percent of such subsidies. And some of the farm interests that receive such payments include present and former members of the Senate Agricultural Committee, which sets policy on agricultural subsidies.[36]

By 1982, farm subsidies had become the nation's largest welfare program, totalling $28 billion, $3 billion more than farm income. Twenty-five percent of such subsidies went to just 4.6 percent of U.S. farmers, who produce 80 percent of all farm income, averaging over $100,000 per year.

Moreover, there is evidence that such subsidies have been illegally administered. The Payment-In Kind (PIK) program pays farmers for crops stored at government expense in return for leaving acreage fallow (unplanted). In 1982, President Reagan dropped the congressionally mandated ceiling on how much direct government payment farmers could receive. Government Accounting Office lawyers declared the amount of subsidies paid to farmers to be $18.8 billion, instead of the $2.9 billion estimated by Reagan budget chief Stockman.[37]

The effect of such subsidies on farm prices is to raise the floor (bottom) price on farm products, making U.S. food exports uncompetitive. As a result, farm exports declined $5 billion from 1982 to 1983. Farm subsidies thus keep food prices from falling and transfer money from consumer to producer at home.[38]

Among the most suspect of direct subsidies were those given International Telephone and Telegraph (ITT) and General Motors (GM) for damages inflicted on their plants in Germany during World War II. GM collected $33 million for damages to its truck plant, which produced trucks used by the Nazis throughout the war. ITT owned plants that produced bombers for the Nazi Air Force, which were used (among other things) to destroy Allied shipping. Ironically, ITT produced direction finders for the Allies that were designed to protect Allied convoys from enemy attack! ITT received $27 million for damages inflicted by Allied planes on its German plants.[39] Thus, inadvertently, both GM and ITT aided the Nazi war effort and were, in effect, reimbursed by the U.S. government for doing so.

To say the least, "subsidies go to a bewildering array of industries, seemingly without rhyme or reason."[40] About $200 million go to private aviation interests for the building of private airports, where corporate jet aircraft, among other planes, land. Another $57 million or so go to private air freight and passenger carriers as reimbursement for business losses. About $86 million are granted to the cane and beet sugar producers to produce sugar. And $6 billion are handed to the nation's railroads, the stockholders of which are now enjoying record dividends, despite a long history of private mismanagement.

Some interesting loans are also made. Such loans have bankrolled much of the nation's hospital and private housing construction via FHA and VA mortgages. Lockheed was guaranteed a $250-million loan in the early 1970s to keep from going bankrupt. The giant firm was later involved in bribery scandals that aided in undermining U.S. foreign policy objectives. At the time the Lockheed loan was made, the "Federal Government had outstanding . . . $56 billion in direct loans . . . $167 billion in loan guarantees . . . a total of $224 billion--twice the sum of all commercial and industrial loans that commercial banks had outstanding."[41] This seemingly nonsensical subsidy parade takes place in part to keep inefficiently managed corporations afloat at the taxpayers' expense.

In 1980, the U.S. government lent Sabena Air Ways of Belgium $31 million at 8 percent interest so it would buy two American-made DC10 jets instead of two European aircraft. The loan, in effect, helped support McDonnell-Douglas, who produce the DC10.[42]

Businesses whose sole customer is the government commonly receive subsidies. Large defense contractors are often granted free use of government laboratories, equipment, electricity, and so on. One study estimated the amount of government-owned facilities in the hands of various defense contractors at $13 billion.[43] This in an industry with profit margins among the highest in the private sector of the economy! The consequences of extending such benefits to defense contractors are explored in Chapter 5.

In sum, the various subsidies and tax breaks "have been totalling $117 to $125 billion a year." In 1983, $409 billion was extended in guaranteed loans and subsidies.[44] The continuation of such advantages is dependent on large corporations and wealthy individuals being able to m nipulate public opinion in their favor. Such manipulation is a very important aspect of the higher immorality.

THE HIGHER IMMORALITY
AND THE CREATION OF CRISIS

One aspect of the higher immorality identified by Mills concerns the concept of *crisis*.

> Crisis is a bankrupted term because so many men in high places have evoked it to cover up their extraordinary policies and deeds. As a matter of fact, it is precisely the absence of genuine crisis that has beset our morality.   For such crises involve situations in which men at large are presented with genuine alternatives, the moral meanings of which are clearly open to public debate. Our higher immorality and general weakening of older values have not involved such crises. . . .[45]

Perhaps nothing in our recent experience so confirms Mills' words as the energy crisis of the 1970s.

The oil industry is the giant of the capitalist system. Oil accounts for one-fifth of all profits in the manufacturing sector of the economy, making oil the richest industry in the world.[46]   By the early 1970s, however, several situations at home and around the world threatened to reduce oil profits. Let's review these conditions.

At home, the oil-depletion allowance (allowing oil companies to deduct a certain percentage of their income) had been reduced (in 1969) from 27.5 to 23.5 percent.   The oil companies thus expanded their overseas operations in order to take advantage of the foreign tax credit, which, between 1971 and 1974, reduced their U.S. tax bills by 75 percent.[47]   Also at home, from 1960 to 1972, small, independent oil companies had increased their share of the domestic gasoline market from 10 percent to 25 percent.   The number of new oil wells in the United States had steadily declined between 1956 and 1972. Indeed, total drilling had declined from 208 million to 86 million feet per year; 20,000 flowing wells had been capped in California alone.   This reduced U.S. oil production by five billion barrels a year. Only one new major oil refinery had been built in the United States between 1968 and 1972.[48]

Overseas, the large oil companies, which from 1948 until the late 1960s had controlled 42 percent of the oil reserves in the Mideast, began having problems. By 1970, Arab nations began demanding a larger share of control over the production of their own oil.

> In that year the new revolutionary government of Kaddafi in Libya withheld production in order, successfully, to force a price increase on Occidental, an independent whose operations relied on Libyan oil. Because of the better terms offered Arab states by the independents, the Arab "take" had been edging up. But Occidental's capitulation threatened to open the gate to soaring profits for OPEC in the 1970s.
>
> In February, 1971, the Teheran Conference was called to deal with the rapidly shifting situation.   Here the large oil companies tried to press for a united front vis-à-vis OPEC. They sought to avoid the sort of disunity marked by Occidental's caving in to Libyan demands. The oil companies were undercut, however,

not only by the independents but also by the U.S. State Department itself. The department, seeking better Arab-American relations, let it be known that the United States was not committed to a single-agreement approach. Failing to reach accord, the oil companies agreed to concessions to the Arab governments.[49]

The excuse to increase profits and ensure their increase for the future came in October 1973. During the Arab-Israeli War, the Arab-dominated OPEC nations announced an embargo on oil exports to the West. They also announced a dramatic increase in the price of crude oil from $2.50 to about $11 per barrel. The oil companies then announced a dramatic shortage of imported oil and stated that the demand for domestic oil could do nothing but increase. Thereupon, the oil companies announced increased prices for domestic crude oil equal to the increases in OPEC oil. The price of oil soon quadrupled.

This was only the beginning of the fabricated crisis. The truth seems to be that there was no embargo (withholding of oil) by OPEC. Imports for the last three months of 1973 were 32 percent above those for the last three months of 1972![50] The withholding of gasoline by the oil companies from the U.S. customer had quite an impact.

Item: From 1973 to 1974, oil company profits increased 80 percent. The oil companies claimed the profits were needed for new exploration of oil. However, the oil companies invested in such things as real estate, entertainment, and a department store chain, as well as coal and uranium. Indeed, by 1975, the oil companies owned 50 percent of the United States' nuclear fuel, 54 percent of the coal reserves, and 45 percent of the uranium reserves.[51]

Item: Oil withheld from independent dealers drove many of them out of business. By May 1973, 1,200 independent gasoline stations had closed, and by the end of the year, 10,000 independent stations had ceased operations.[52]

Item: The oil companies also used the artificial crisis to exact concessions from the government. The large companies had contributed a lusty $7 million to the Nixon campaign of 1972. Not surprisingly, they had little problem finding sympathy for their wishes.

Item: A deal was closed with the Soviet Union and Communist China involving the purchase of $45.6 billion of natural gas. This involved sale by the oil companies of $10 billion of pipeline, supertankers, and liquefaction equipment. The Soviet gas was to be sold at prices up to three times higher than domestic natural gas.

Item: Congress granted permission to build the Alaskan pipeline. The pipeline was not to extend across Canada, where it would be integrated into pipelines in the Midwest, but 798 miles across Alaska. The result was, in the late 1970s, a glut of crude oil on the West Coast, some of which was exported to Japan, while shortages of unleaded gasoline developed throughout the United States, sending gasoline prices soaring. The pipeline was constructed by the oil companies themselves, in partnership with the state of Alaska, at a cost overrun that was estimated at 800 percent. Moreover, the oil companies were also granted a profit on the crude oil that flows through the pipeline, on the transporting of the oil, on its refinery, and on the final sale of the refined product.

Item: In 1973, President Nixon removed all quotas and tariffs on imported (expensive) oil and substituted scaled license fees of twenty-one cents a barrel for five years. New oil refineries, however, were allowed to use 75 percent of the imported oil free of such fees. Exxon thereupon announced plans to expand its domestic refining capacity by 30 percent.

Item: By 1977, the annual acreage of federal lands leased for oil exploration on the U.S. Continental Shelf had tripled.

Item: President Nixon proposed that the oil companies be granted additional tax reliefs amounting to 12 percent of the cost of producing new wells and a 7 percent increase added to the 90 percent "dry hole" write off, thus allowing investors to deduct ninety-seven cents of every dollar lost from wells that failed to produce oil.

Item: In December 1973, Nixon classified all oil produced over the amount produced in 1972 as "new crude" and, hence, free from any price controls. "Old crude" was allowed to rise $1 a barrel to provide a further incentive to the oil companies to raise production.

The final irony in the energy crisis of 1973 was that, in September and October, oil storage tanks in the United States were so full that many tankers were diverted to Europe, where their contents were sold at higher prices. In Holland and Israel, which were also embargoed by the Arabs, there were no lines at gas stations. But in those countries, there were no government price controls that the oil companies had to fight to remove.[53]

The 1973-1974 oil crisis contained elements of the lack of public debate that Mills claimed were characteristic of crisis creation. In June 1973, a report issued by the Federal Trade Commission stated that the oil shortage "was the result of anticompetitive practices fostered by government regulations and manipulated by major oil companies to protect their profits."[54] The report accused the oil companies of using tax breaks to make huge profits in drilling for oil, while running their refining, distributing, and marketing operations so cheaply that independent producers were undersold and outcompeted. Moreover, the FTC claimed that the large oil producers had ensured adequate gasoline supplies for their own gasoline stations, while refusing to sell gasoline to independent stations. The FTC concluded that the large oil companies obtained profits that were "substantially in excess of those they would have obtained in a competitively structured market."[55]

In response to the FTC report, Treasury Department Secretary William Simon took to the airwaves to quote a study prepared by his department's Office of Energy advisor, which characterized the FTC report as incorrect. Later, in 1974, Simon, in effect, censured information that had previously been available through the Commerce Department concerning the amounts of imported oil on grounds of national security.

In February 1979 came signs that a new energy crisis was being fabricated. A revolution in Iran, whose production accounted for 5 percent of U.S. imports, cut off oil supplies from that nation. Oil companies and pro-oil politicians immediately began threatening rationing and $1-a-gallon gasoline within a year.[56] The government and large oil companies used the crisis atmosphere to propose various plans that would benefit the oil industry in the deregulation of oil prices, the repeal of the law forbidding the export of Alaskan oil (making for more Alaskan crude and a return to full oil production in California), the exchange of Alaskan oil for Mexican petroleum, the easing of environmental regulations on coal burning, and the slowdown of the phaseout of polluting lead additives in gasoline.[57]   All this occurred when the world--and especially the United States--had a surplus of oil. The real losers in all this, of course, are the suspicious, but nevertheless, manipulated and ripped-off U.S. consumers, voters, and taxpayers.[58]

THE HIGHER IMMORALITY
AND ANTITRUST LAWS

Mills believed that much corporate crime results because it is often good business to break the laws. As he said, businesses "obey these laws, when they do, not because they feel that it is morally right, but because they are afraid of being caught." Therefore, such laws "exist without the support of firm moral convention. It it merely illegal to cheat them, but it is often considered smart to get away with it."[59]

There are several reasons why businesses sometimes consider it smart to break the laws that regulate their activity. First, many of the laws are ambiguous and contain exemptions and exclusions, leaving a great deal of room for interpretation by the courts. Second, many laws regulating business activity are hardly strict in their penalties. Indeed, many violations of business laws are settled in civil rather than criminal courts. Imprisonment under such laws is a rarity, and the fines imposed for breaking them many times amout to no more than a slap on the wrist. Finally, the enforcement of such laws is often quite lax because government devotes comparatively few resources to catching corporate offenders. This lack of enforcement can be explained by examining the Sherman Act (1890), the Federal Trade Commission Act (1914), and the Robinson-Patman Act (1936).

The Sherman Act prohibits "unreasonable restraints upon and monopolization of trade."[60] The Act also outlaws arrangements that result in price fixing or limiting access to trade or commerce (e.g., dividing market). However, the Act is loaded with exclusions and ambiguities. Thus, the Sherman Act only applies to monopolies in trade (commerce), not to monopolies in manufacturing. Moreover, under a series of cases in 1911 involving American Tobacco and Standard Oil, it was ruled that the Act applied only to *unreasonable* trade combinations and did not exclude consolidation per se. The definition of a *reasonable* combination, of course, is a matter of judicial opinion. Under the Sherman Act's price-fixing definitions, businesses that are already regulated by the federal government (such as the Civil Aeuronautics Board's regulation of the nation's airlines) are excluded from the law. This exclusion also applies to interstate water carriers, railroads, and trucks. Other loopholes are present in the act, as well. While the Act specifies that it is illegal to fix the price of a product by agreement, this practice is legal in states that authorize it under so-called fair laws.[61]

In 1914, the Federal Trade Commission Act was passed, making it unlawful to restrict competition and to engage in unfair and deceptive trade practices. However, the power of the FTC is limited. It only has the power to issue cease-and-desist orders, which it can do only upon securing the permission of a federal court. The FTC can recommend prosecution of criminal cases, but it is the Justice Department that is specifically charged with this task.

In 1936, the Robinson-Patman Act made it illegal to discriminate between various buyers of products by charging different prices to different buyers. But the act has several limitations. First, it applies only to products, not to services, which are supposedly covered by other laws. In addition, the law specifically exempts U.S. companies that have joined together for purposes of export. The antitrust laws also exempt such items as bank mergers, agricultural cooperatives, and insurance companies, which are unregulated by state laws.[62]

Lack of Antitrust Enforcement

Enforcement of the nation's antitrust laws historically has been quite lax. The Justice Department's Antitrust Division is charged with both the criminal and civil prosecution of these laws. The FBI has no expertise at all in antitrust violations. Thus, it is the Antitrust Division that has been lax in prosecuting antitrust violations.

> In 1968 . . . the division filed 16 criminal cases involving price fixing; in 1970, with a larger staff and budget, the division brought only 4 cases; by 1975, under public pressure, prosecutions rose to 29 cases. The division has fared no better in the area of monopolies; in 1968 it brought no prosecutions; in 1975 it brought 5. This is hardly an impressive record for a unit with a budget of over $20 million. . . . The FTC (Federal Trade Commission) employs 200 attorneys in its antitrust section. . . . The record of both these agencies in the area of antitrust enforcement has been extremely poor.[63]

Enforcement records for the 1960s and 1970s are consistent with the remaining history of antitrust regulation.

> From 1890 to 1959 there were a total of 1,499 antitrust cases begun by the Antitrust Division; only 729 of them were criminal actions. A total of 486 of the 729 cases were pursued to the imposition of sentence. . . . In recent years there has been a decline in the proportion of all antitrust cases which are criminal actions as opposed to civil actions: 59 percent of all cases were criminal actions in 1940-49; 48 percent were criminal cases in 1950-59; 31 percent were criminal cases in 1960-69; and only 9 percent were criminal cases in 1970.[64]

THE PENALTIES FOR CORPORATE CRIME:
THE DOUBLE STANDARD

Corporate officials convicted of price fixing and other corporate crimes invariably receive light sentences (see Chapter 3). McCormick's data demonstrate that the heaviest jail sentence imposed in a price-fixing case from 1890 (the year the Sherman Antitrust Act was passed) until 1969 was sixty days. Actually, it was not until the 1961 Electrical Conspiracy Case (discussed at length in Chapter 3) that any business-persons "were actually imprisoned purely for price-fixing and monopo-lization. No individuals were sent to jail until twenty years after the passage of the act."[65] In fact, in almost three-fourths of the cases (73.1 percent), convictions were gained, not by the government proving any wrongdoing, but by pleas of nolo contendere, under which defendants merely refuse to acknowledge guilt instead of admitting guilt, accepting whatever sentence is imposed and thereby avoiding being labeled criminal by the court. Finally, only 45 percent of the cases under the Sherman Act have been criminal in nature; the majority were tried as civil matters, which involved no jail terms. Of those cases in which jail terms were imposed and actually served, only 2 percent were tried under the Sherman Act, and almost all of these came under the Sherman Act's statutes concerning labor unions. (Unions assisting nonunion labor gain control over a labor market is a violation of section 6 of the Sherman Act.)[66]

The laxness with which antitrust laws are enforced is in part attributable to the meager resources devoted to such enforcement. Within the Justice Department, outside Washington, local federal prose-cutors--U.S. attorneys--are charged with enforcement of federal laws. In its ninety-four local offices, there are less than 2,000 attorneys for the entire nation, only 200 of whom prosecute fraud cases. At the state level, only thirty of our fifty state prosecutors had consumer fraud units. While some white-collar prosecutions can cost over a million dollars, only forty state prosecutors had budgets that exceeded a million dollars, while three had budgets in excess of $500,000. All state prosecutors combined employ less than 7,000 attorneys. (The federal government alone employs over 10,000 lawyers.) On the local level, a study of forty-one local prosecuto-rial offices in 1975 demonstrated that more than 100,000 complaints and inquiries were supposed to be handled adequately by 149 attorneys, 147 investigators, eighty-nine paralegals, and sixty-nine volunteers.[67] Obvi-ously, U.S. society has thus far failed to provide adequate enforcement of corporate criminal violations.

THE HIGHER IMMORALITY AND CORPORATE CRIME

If Mills' view of corporate crime is correct, one would expect two effects: (1) widespread violations of antitrust laws, and (2) the presence of attitudes condoning such violations. Ample evidence exists to support both propositions.

First, several studies have documented the fact that corporate illegalities are quite widespread.

Item: One study documents that, between 1945 and 1965, the Federal
           Trade Commission issued almost 4,000 cease-and-desist orders for
           legal violations by businesses for false advertising, false endorse-
           ments, removing or concealing law-required markings, false in-
           voices, mislabeling, deceptive pricing, obtaining information by
           subterfuge, and a number of legally defined acts.[68]

Item: Edwin Sutherland, who coined the term *white-collar crime,* stud-
           ied the illegalities of seventy large corporations from 1890 to
           1945. He found that there had been 980 decisions against these
           corporations. Every corporation had at least one decision against
           it, and the average number of decisions was fourteen.[69]   One
           hundred fifty-nine of the 980 decisions were made by the criminal
           courts, whereas forty-five were made by courts that were either
           under civil or equity jurisdiction, and 361 were settled by govern-
           ment commission.   Of the seventy corporations studied by
           Sutherland, thirty were either illegitimate in origin or became
           involved in illegal activities.   Eight others, he found, were
           probably illegal in origin or in beginning policies. The finding of
           original illegitimacy was made with respect to twenty-one corpo-
           rations in formal court decisions by other historical evidence in
           other cases. What Sutherland's study implies is that 60 percent of
           the corporations, or forty-two in number, with an average of four
           convictions each, are habitual criminals under the law.[70]

Item: A recent study of the largest 582 publicly owned corporations
           indicated that more than 60 percent of such firms had had at least
           one legal action initiated against them during 1975 and 1976. The
           300 parent manufacturing firms in the study had an average of 4.8
           actions initiated against them by federal agencies.   Yet, fewer
           than 10 percent of the violations resulted in any criminal penal-
           ties. Moreover, in less than 1 percent of the federal enforcement
           actions was a corporate officer sent to jail for failing to carry out
           corporate legal responsibilities.[71] When a jail term was imposed,
           "sentences almost never exceeded six months."[72]

Second, corporate executives seem well aware that many businesspeople engage in either criminal or unethical action. A 1961 survey in
the *Harvard Business Review* of some 1,700 businesspersons revealed that
four out of seven believed that individuals "would violate a code of ethics
whenever they thought they could avoid detection." One-half of those
sampled believed that the U.S. businessperson "tends to ignore the great
ethical laws as they apply immediately to his work. He is preoccupied
chiefly with gain (profit)." And 80 percent of those sampled thought that
there were accepted business practices in their industries that they
regarded as unethical.[73]   A 1970 survey of the nation's 1,000 largest
manufacturing corporations is even more shocking: Forty-seven percent
of the largest 500 companies and 70 percent of the next 500 believed that
price fixing is a common occurrence in their industries.[74]

Corporate executives and small businesspersons engage in unethi-
cal/illegal behaviors for several other reasons, too. One important factor
is the capitalist economic system and its dependence on continued profits
and economic growth.   When antitrust and other business laws are
enforced with such laxness and the penalties involved are so minimal,

violations of such laws become quite rational from a profit standpoint. Quite simply, it is much more profitable to violate such laws than to obey them.

Second, most corporate executives who are caught breaking the law often believe that what they have done does not violate the law in any serious sense. Typically, though found guilty, they believe that they have not harmed anyone.[75]

Third, corporate criminal behavior--like any other type of behavior--is learned. In the case of corporate executives, it is the corporate environment, not the street gang or the college education, that teaches and sometimes demands the learning of such behavior. Thus, a 1973 study by the American Management Association concluded that corporate executives and businesspeople must often sacrifice personal morals and ethics in order to remain in business. "About 70 percent . . . admit they have been expected, frequently or on occasion, to compromise personal principles in order to conform either to organizational standards or to standards established by their corporate superiors."[76]

In one famous case, the convicted executives made it clear that their motives in fixing prices were to increase the profits for the company and further their own careers.

> We did feel that this was the only way to reach part of our goals as managers. . . . We couldn't accomplish a greater percent of net profit without getting together with competitors. Part of the pressure was the desire to get ahead and the desire to have the goodwill of the man above you. He had only to get the approval of the man above *him* to replace you, and if you wouldn't cooperate he could find lots of faults to use to get you out.[77]

Finally, corporate crime, as well as other types of white-collar illegalities, are made worse by the ignorance and unwitting cooperation of the public. This is not to suggest that the public is necessarily stupid or gullible. Rather, it is to confirm the fact that, until very recently, consumer education and violations of law by corporations were anything but part of the public's general knowledge or specific education in the United States. The nature of profitable crime is such that it is invisible. As Thio has stated:

> It may be difficult for the victims to know that they are victimized, even if they want to find out the true nature of their victimization. Grocery shoppers, for example, are hard put to detect unlawful substances as residues of hormones, antibiotics, pesticides, and nitrates in the meat they buy.[78]

Even when corporate criminals are caught and convicted, the news media, itself made up of corporations, has not gone out of its way to report such incidents. Although many criminologists believe that public shame is a key aspect of criminal penalties,[79] the media has failed to do its part:

> Even when prosecutions have resulted in conviction, most of the news media--including *Time* and *Newsweek*, the networks,

and *The New York Times*—have failed repeatedly to recognize the
importance of adequate reporting and have ignored the cases or
have treated them trivially.[80]

The mass media, until recently, has very much underreported corporate
criminality. Such reportage may be partially responsible for convincing
corporate criminals that the illegal acts they commit are not real crimes.
This, coupled with the large majority of antitrust violations that are tried
as civil matters, means little stigma and little public shame are associated with such crimes. Whether this will change in the face of growing
public resentment of big business is yet an open question. At the moment,
it is safe to conclude that antitrust and other corporate violations are the
most profitable form of crime and carry little risk of detection and
genuine punishment.

ORGANIZED CRIME AND THE BUSINESS ELITE

As a formal matter, *organized crime* is defined as "business
enterprises organized for the purpose of making economic gain through
illegal activities."[81] We are reminded that organized crime, to be defined
as such, must display certain features:

> We have defined organized crime as an integral part of
> the American social system that brings together (1) a public that
> demands certain goods and services that are defined as illegal,
> (2) an organization of individuals who produce or supply those
> goods and services, and (3) corrupt public officials who protect
> such individuals for their own profit or gain.[82]

However, for most people, organized crime has taken its meaning
over the past twenty years from the television series, books, movies,
magazine articles, and congressional hearings (televised no less) on the
Mafia or Cosa Nostra.

The image of organized crime, as presented in the mass media, is
that of a secret international organization of Italian and Sicilian gangsters, who, via corrupton and violence, are quite successful in exerting
their will in every task they undertake. But the media image of organized
crime is probably very misleading, especially when the relationships
among legitimate businesspeople, politicians, and syndicate criminals are
examined.

That is, an element of the higher immorality in the activities of
organized crimes is largely unexplored. The higher immorality applies to
organized crime in so far as legitimate corporate and political elites
utilize the services of the Mafia (or Cosa Nostra) for unethical or illegal
purposes. This takes place when organized crime: (1) assists economic
and political elites in repressing threats to the established order; (2) assists businesses in profit-making ventures; and/or (3) assists federal officials with the carrying out of U.S. foreign-policy objectives.

Organized Crime and Repression

Organized crime has long assisted certain business and political elites in preventing and/or suppressing the powerless in society. Throughout the 1920s, businesspeople entered into union contract negotiations with gangster-dominated unions in order to ensure themselves against upsets of any kind (e.g., union unrest). Often businesspeople would join each other by creating trade associations, and the newly formed associations would negotiate with the gangster-dominated unions. Such organizations kept competition from other businesses not belonging to such associations at a minimum. The costs of such protection were usually passed on to consumers. These activities stabilized markets in small, competitive industries, such as trucking, garments, baking, and cleaning and dyeing. When prohibition ended, gangsters moved into the movie industry via these same tactics.[83]

Mafia figures have been recruited by businesses and politicians to quell labor unrest in a variety of settings.

Item: In the 1940s, Detroit automobile companies used gangsters to suppress efforts to unionize the auto industry. Gangsters like D'Anna and Adonnis were given a monopoly over the haulaway business at the Ford Motor Company in return for gaining control of the autoworker unions in the city. And even after the AFL succeeded in unionizing the auto industry, Ford still hired mobsters to act as strike breakers. In 1945 and 1946, there were 41,750 strikes in the United States, more than in the previous ten years combined, so the need for strike breakers was clear. Use of gangsters for this purpose was curtailed in the 1950s as unions supported governmental policies related to the Cold War and militant unionism, often associated with communism, declined.[84]

Item: During the late 1930s and early 1940s, the International Longshoreman's Union was infiltrated by organized criminals in New York Harbor. The docks of New York Harbor are made up of very narrow piers and gridiron street layouts, and congestion is a continual problem. Such congested conditions make it easy to disrupt traffic on the docks. These peculiar physical conditions were part of the reason why gangsters were hired to infiltrate the local International Longshoreman's Association. Because of the congestion, drivers did not bring their own loaders to the docks. Rather, loaders were hired at the pier. Loaders could be hired only through loading bosses, who were ILA union members. Such bosses charged high prices for using the labor they controlled, and a syndicate organization, Varick Enterprises, Inc., dominated this trade by charging all truckers a per-ton tax, whether they used the loaders or not. While standardized rates were eventually worked out, the Varick organization, along with the ILA and the local Tammany Hall political machine, kept control of the loading and other rackets along the docks.

Item: In the late 1930s, the West Coast ILA was a so-called clean union headed by a labor radical named Harry Bridges. Bridges had taken his union out of the ranks of the American Federation of Labor to the CIO organization, an act of militant independence. Fearing such independence, as well as the strong socialist sentiment among some New York dock workers, mobster Albert Anastasia murdered Peter Panto, a radical longshoreman leader, who worked on the Brooklyn docks. Militant left-wing union activity continued throughout the 1940s until 1951, when over a million trade unionists from twelve unions (one fifth of its membership) were expelled from the CIO in response to the Report of the Investigation of Communism in New York City Distributive Trades.

Other brutal attacks on union dissidents by mobsters occurred throughout the 1940s. This fear concerning socialism within the U.S. labor movement is responsible for the persistence of organized crime's involvement in labor racketeering and violence, at the behest of certain corporate elites. Of course,

> [b]oth employers and unions have hired gangsters to help them in industrial disputes. It has been employers who have benefited the most. One of the underlying factors was a desire to keep real wages down, and the constant use of terror to destroy rank and file organizations was condoned because of the general American fear of radicalism in the docks--so crucial to the working of the system.[85]

But labor unions are not the only entities that have been repressed by syndicate criminals. For example, some sociologists feel that organized crime has significantly contributed to the control of U.S. ghettos. Michael Tabor has argued that a conspiracy exists in the U.S. ghetto between organized crime and the police, who are corrupted by organized criminals. Tabor's analysis centers on the role of organized crime in the distribution of heroin in ghetto areas. His contention is that the selling of heroin and the creation of a small army of heroin addicts within the ghetto keeps persons who might otherwise challenge the existing social order strung out on dope and in a state of perpetual escapism from inhumane ghetto conditions.[86]

Moreover, Stephen Spitzer has argued that organized crime helps control problem populations in a number of ways. First, organized crime creates a parallel opportunity structure, a means of employment in illegal activities for persons who might otherwise be unemployed and possibly politically discontent.   The goods and services provided by organized crime to the underclasses in society do deflect their energies from the sources of their oppression.[87] In this view, organized crime, insofar as it gains a monopoly over illegal goods and services, actually aids and maintains the public order because monopoly brings with it security that one will make profits and, as a result, lessens the need for violence.

There is some evidence that the theses of both Spitzer and Tabor are correct. We know that heroin addiction is highly concentrated in the ghetto areas of the United States and that certain illegitimate gambling activities (such as numbers running) not only give poor people a source of hope that they will become wealthy, but also provide a source of employment. The *New York Times* has estimated, for example, that the numbers racket employs thousands of people in Harlem alone.[88]

Organized Crime and Profits

Aside from aiding with the control of so-called problem populations, organized crime has increased the profits for certain legitimate businesses. The most obvious source of profit provided by organized crime is as an important customer of corporations. For example, it was estimated that, by 1940, bookies were the fifth largest customer of American Telephone and Telegraph.[89] Moreover, the members of organized crime are themselves consumers of many goods and services. Given the multibillion-dollar estimates of organized criminal enterprise (i.e., $50 to $80 billion), the amount of money spent by syndicate members as both capitalists and consumers serves as a rather significant market. As Quinney has stated:

> Organized crime and legitimate businesses may mutually assist one another, as in regulating prices or commodities or enforcing labor contracts. Interdependence between the underworld of crime and the upperworld of business ensures that both systems will be maintained. Mutual assistance accompanied by the profit motive provides assured immunity.
>
> Organized crime has grown into a huge business in the United States and is an integral part of the political economy. Enormous amounts of illegitimate money are passed annually into socially acceptable endeavors. An elaborate corporate and financial structure is now tied to organized crime.[90]

The reach of the underworld business is extensive, in terms of both economic and social impact.

Item: In 1979, the Senate Subcommittee on Investigations estimated that the $150 billion yearly gross revenues of organized crime included $63 billion from narcotics, $22 billion from gambling, and an additional $8 billion from such illegal activities as prostitution, cigarette smuggling, and arson. Revenues from loansharking in the same year were estimated at $20 billion. Net profits from all activities were estimated at $50 billion dollars, a 33.3 percent on investments, all tax free. In comparison, the net profit of the United States' largest industry oil, was $23 billion in 1979.[91]

Item: Organized crime has moved into the theft of securities, stocks, bonds, and government notes, generating at least $1.2 billion dollars a year. Some experts believe that the total may be as high as $20 billion dollars a year. It is believed that such securities are stolen from either brokerage houses, banks, the U.S. mail, or individuals. Once they have been acquired, organized crime can convert the securities into cash in a number of ways: (1) by reselling them to securities brokers; (2) by placing them in banks for loan collaterals; (3) by putting them in portfolios of certain companies that are anxious to present a healthier financial picture than actually exists; (4) by transporting them to foreign countries and reselling them to banks or individuals; or (6) by simply placing them in banks where they can be used in trust or escrow accounts.

Item: With such a huge cash flow, organized crime has rapidly expanded
its investments in many types of businesses. For example:

> The Bonanno family—Joseph and his two sons—
> have tens of millions invested in dozens of businesses
> spread coast to coast: a laundry in New York City, a
> dairy farm upstate, a hotel in New Jersey, cheese compa-
> nies in Wisconsin and Canada, real estate in Tucson, a
> Phoenix supper club and until recently, according to
> federal prosecutors, U.S. Mattress, Kachina Enterprises
> and Olympic Construction. This list goes on.[92]

Item: The energy crisis has provided organized crime with unique
opportunities to enter the energy field. Some of their activities
include

> coal-equipment theft, tax-shelter schemes, schemes for
> short-weighting customers or beating the environmental
> control laws. The intrusion has grown so acute that a
> group of coal states has created Leviticus, a seven-state
> strike force for investigating organized crime in the coal
> industry. In the New York City area 200,000 gallons of
> gasoline are disappearing every week; in Texas the police
> just shut down a ring that had been siphoning a million
> dollars a month in petroleum products from oil barges in
> the Houston ship channel.[93]

Organized crime reportedly controls at least six toxic waste-
disposal companies in greater New York and Pennsylvania and is
able to dispose of such waste at half the price charged by
legitimate waste-disposal companies.[94]

Item: South Florida is now a reputed center for Mafia drug trafficking,
as well as many legitimate investments. In 1980, the amount of
money netted from the Florida cocaine and marijuana trade and
then reinvested in legitimate state businesses was estimated at $8
billion. An estimated $7 billion has now been invested in real
estate, including perhaps one-half of the hotels on Miami Beach's
ocean front and $45 million in office buildings and shopping
centers in Palm Beach and Broward counties (owned by the
infamous Lansky organization). Organized crime is also reputed
to be invested heavily in Florida's garment, trucking, produce,
citrus, cold-storage, and warehousing industries. Moreover, banks
in the Miami area launder vast amounts of cash resulting from the
lucrative drug trade. In turn, some of those involved in the South
Florida drug trade are tied to anti-Castro paramilitary operations.[95]

Item: The Mafia (and especially the Bonanno family) is reported to have
taken over a good deal of the pizza and mozzarella cheese
businesses in the United States. Organized crime allegedly owns
several major cheese businesses, including Grande Cheese in
Wisconsin; Saputo in Montreal, Canada; Maggio in Philadelphia;
and Marinos in California. And it is suspected that organized
crime owns firms that supply mozzarella for Kraft. Mafia pizza

Item: parlors operate in both downtown and suburban shopping centers in New Jersey, Pennsylvania, Texas, and Colorado.[96]

Item: Government, itself--with its billions of dollars and ten million employees--has become a target of syndicate fraud. The General Services Administration has amply illustrated the corruption that riddles government. Federal investigators have uncovered numerous secret bank accounts belonging to GSA employees that were used by government contractors--some of them with possible syndicate ties--to deposit millions of dollars in payoff money to GSA officials.[97]

Item: The Mafia's tremendous profits have also been invested on Wall Street, especially in the over-the-counter market and in companies with fewer than $1 million in assets and less than 500 stockholders. Such investments are estimated at $200 to $300 million annually.[98]

There is also evidence that a number of large corporations (e.g., Pan American Airways and the Howard Hughes Corporation) have entered into partnership with organized crime in a number of gambling casinos and resort ventures in both Las Vegas and the Caribbean.[99] Apparently certain members of the corporate elite are not above obtaining capital for purposes of expanding markets. It is not known how much capital has come from criminal syndicates for ventures of this type, but, as mentioned in Chapter 1, obtaining such capital is now against the law under the RICO statute.

Organized Crime and the Political Elite

Revelations by the Senate Intelligence Committee in 1975 disclosed the hiring of organized crime members by the CIA in the 1960s for the expressed purpose of assassinating Premier Castro of Cuba.[100] Thus, organized crime (at certain times, at least) has functioned as an instrument of U.S. foreign policy. Such escapades allegedly began during World War II when the underworld figures in control of the New York docks were contacted by Navy intelligence officials in order to ensure that German submarines or foreign agents did not infiltrate the area. It was thought that waterfront pimps and prostitutes could act as a sort of counterintelligence corps. The man whose aid was sought for this purpose was Lucky Luciano; he was reportedly quite successful in preventing sabotage on any other outbreaks of trouble on the New York docks during the war. Following his arrest and conviction for compulsory prostitution in 1936, Luciano was granted parole and given exile for life in 1954 in exchange of the aid he provided during the war.

Mafiosi assistance was also enlisted in other war-related efforts. Some locals were used by the Allies during the invasion of Sicily in 1943. Vito Genovese, a New York gangster, who had earlier escaped to Italy to flee a murder charge, became an "unofficial advisor to the American military government."[101] After the war, local Mafiosi were installed as mayors in many locations in Sicily because they were antisocialist. And in France in 1950, the CIA recruited a Corsican gangster, Ferri-Pisani, to recruit an elite terror squad for use on the Marseilles docks.   Socialist dock workers had refused to move shipments of U.S. arms bound for use in Vietnam in support of the French military effort there.   Corsican gangsters had also been used to assault the picket lines of communist unions in France and to harass union officials.   The concession granted these international criminals in exchange for such aid was the privilege of using Marseilles as the center for Corsican heroin traffic.   In Pearce's words, "The CIA had helped build the French Connection."[102]

In Cuba, it is known that dictator Batista allowed Mafia financier Meyer Lansky to set up gambling casinos in Havana in 1933.   Following Castro's closing of the casinos in the early 1960s, organized crime figures were recruited by the CIA to aid in assassinating Castro.   Finally, in Vietnam in the 1960s and early 1970s, organized crime figures cooperated with the CIA in setting up Asia's Golden Triangle, Southeast Asia's center for heroin distribution.   This triangle stretches for some 150,000 square miles across northeast Burma, northern Thailand, and northern Laos.   The CIA's involvement included transporting opium using their own airline, Air America.[103]

Finally, organized crime has long served as a source of campaign funds for political elites on virtually every level of U.S. politics, local, state, and national.[104]   At the national level, opposing organized crime factions appear to be linked to opposing political parties.   For example, following the presidential election in 1968, the Nixon administration undertook a campaign against organized crime.   This campaign was, in fact, directed at those elements of organized crime most closed allied with Nixon's Democratic opponents, especially Meyer Lansky.   Under pressure from investigations by the FBI and IRS, Lansky sold his Las Vegas casino interests to Howard Hughes and his Miami-based bank interest to Nixon confidant Bebe Rebozo.   In the meantime, teamster union leaders made an arrangement with the Nixon White House that resulted in clemency for jailed teamster chief Jimmy Hoffa in return for a campaign contribution.   Also, President Nixon was promised the availability of teamster pension funds should hush money be needed to silence the Watergate burglars.

The final attack on the Lansky faction of organized crime resulted as part of the Nixon administration's war on drugs.   The Republicans tried to close off Lansky's heroin sources by pressuring the Turkish government to enforce laws against growing opium.   Between 1969 and 1973, the amount of opium brought from Turkey into the United States fell by 50 percent.   Efforts against Lansky's Latin American opium suppliers were also instituted.

By the early 1970s, Southeast Asia's Golden Triangle had become a major new heroin source for the U.S. organized crime syndicate of Santo Trafficante, Jr., a Lansky rival in heroin trade.   Trafficante had ties to both the Nixon White House and the Laotian Chiu Chow syndicate, a major opium source in Southeast Asia and the owner of the Laotian Pepsi Cola Company, whose U.S. counterpart had longtime ties to the Nixon organization.[105]

These illustrations have led some criminologists to conclude that organized crime has served and continues to serve the domestic and foreign political goals of the U.S. political and economic elites.

CONCLUSION:
CONSEQUENCES OF THE HIGHER IMMORALITY

This chapter has discussed a series of acts that involve the exercise of elite power. C. Wright Mills coined the term *higher immorality* to denote what he felt was systematic corruption among the U.S. economic and political elite. The features of the higher immorality discussed are unique in that most of the acts are not against the law. Indeed, certain types of executive compensation--including expense accounts and stock options, corporate income taxes, and government subsidies to businesses and wealthy individuals--represent special favors that elites have secured for themselves via the passage of special legislation and are, therefore, perfectly legal.

But, as mentioned in Chapter 1, what is legal is not necessarily moral or just. Consider the tax situation for a moment. In 1972, Stern estimated that, of the $77.3 billion in tax favors granted by the federal government, only $92 million in loopholes went to the nation's six million poorest families, while twenty-four times that amount went to 3,000 families with incomes over $1 million.[106] Another study by economist Joseph Peckham concluded that people who earned less than $2,000 per year paid 44 percent of their incomes in state, federal, and local taxes. People earning $2,000 to $15,000 paid about 27 percent of their incomes in these various taxes, and those who earned over $15,000 paid about 38 percent of their incomes for taxes.

Thus, the highest tax rates were paid by the lowest income group, and the second-highest rates were paid by the highest group. This violates the spirit of our tax laws, which are supposedly based on the ability to pay.[107] These examples indicate that individuals of power and wealth are able to influence the law for their personal benefit.[108]

The consequences of tax loopholes are serious. First, such privilege creates cynicism among the majority of taxpayers, who are very much aware that the nation's tax laws favor the rich and powerful. Second, special loopholes for the wealthy create larger government deficits and increase inflation by billions of dollars per year. Third, government subsidies, which go largely to big businesses, violate the basic principles of free enterprise. Why, for example, should Lockheed and Chrysler be allowed loan guarantees to ensure that they will remain in business, while only about one in ten of the new businesses beginning in this country survives more than five years on average?[109]

We also discussed how political and economic elites attempted to convince the public of the reality of the energy crisis of the 1970s. Yet when one looks at the facts, as well as who profited from this so-called crisis, such reality become suspect. The energy crisis clearly resulted in huge increases in oil company profits, elimination of competition from independent oil dealers, and fuel bill increases in the billions for consumers serviced by multinational oil companies. Even the government's own studies indicated that the energy crisis of 1973-1974 was due to the oil companies' anticompetitive practices, not to a genuine shortage of crude oil. Such manipulation by elites, involving the creation of favorable media images of their activities and the suppression of important facts, is not illegal, unless lied about under oath. Yet how many people consider such activities moral, ethical, or just?

Finally, we have described the long history of goods and services provided political and economic elites by members of organized criminal syndicates. Members of Mafia families have suppressed labor unions, lower-classs ghetto dwellers, and anticapitalist political movements; provided capital for certain business ventures; and on numerous occasions, aided political elites in the execution of U.S. foreign and military policy. In return for such services and capital, certain elites have allowed the activities of organized criminal syndicates to grow and prosper. This, in turn, has contributed to the flourishing of trade in many cities, as well as the corruption of politicians on all levels by organized U.S. crime members (see Chapter 6). The use of capital from ilegal businesses is now against the law. And the CIA suffered no little embarrassment when it was revealed that Mafia members had been recruited to assassinate Fidel Castro. Thus, the use of organized criminal syndicates to further the goals of economic and political elites contributes to criminal activity at all levels of U.S. society, and, occasionally, results in scandal for elites. This further contributes to the decline of public confidence in elite rule.

While many of the activities that constitute the higher immorality are not illegal, they are widely regarded as unethical and often possess serious consequences for nonelites. Obviously, our discussion tends to confirm Mills' thesis that the higher immorality is an institutionalized feature of elite power in the United States.

NOTES

1. United Technologies, "Crooks and Clowns on TV," *New York Review of Books*, 5 November 1981.

2. Mary Murphy, "Bending the Rules in Hollywood," *TV Guide*, 16 January 1982, 5. A fascinating account of the Begelman case is David McClintick's *Indecent Exposure* (New York: Dell, 1982).

3. "Highway Robbery," *Newsweek*, 2 August 1982, 17.

4. W. Safire, "Paranoia in the White House," *San Francisco Chronicle*, 1 November 1983, p. 39.

5. Lloyd Shearer, "A President and His Appointees," *Parade*, 8 July 1984, 12.

6. Shearer, 12.

7. *Oakland Tribune*, 19 December 1983, p. A-4.

8. *The Village Voice*, 11 December 1978, pp. 11, 16, 28. Reprinted by permission of The Village Voice. Copyright © News Group Publications, Inc., 1978.

9. C. Wright Mills, "A Diagnosis of Our Moral Uneasiness," in *Power, Politics, and People*, ed. I. H. Horowitz, 330-39 (New York: Ballantine, 1963), 331.

10. Barry Kreisberg, *Crime and Privilege* (Englewood Cliffs, NJ: Prentice-Hall, 1975), 4. For a brief historical view of the higher immorality and corporate crime, see also S. Balkan et al., *Crime and Deviance in America* (Belmont, CA: Wadsworth, 1980), 182-84.

11. C. Wright Mills, "Plain Talk on Fancy Sex," in *Power, Politics, and People*, ed. I. H. Horowitz, 324-29 (New York: Ballantine, 1963). For

remarks by some expense-account girls themselves, see Elizabeth I. Ray, *The Washington Fringe Benefit* (New York: Dell, 1976). The service Ms. Ray performed while on the payroll of Congressman Wayne Hayes touched off a scandal in Washington that resulted in Hayes leaving Congress. Ms. Ray's story closely parallels Mills' description of the goals and means of the expense-account girl.   An anonymous article, "The Corporation Prostitute," in *Sociology: Concepts and Characteristics,* 4th ed., by Judson Landis, 354-59 (Belmont, CA: Wadsworth, 1980), claims that some corporations hire prostitutes on a permanent basis for help in closing a variety of deals, including bidding on factory sites, mergers with other companies political lobbying, undercutting competitors, gathering stockholders' proxy votes, and securing oil leases (p. 355).

12. Mills, "A Diagnosis of Our Moral Uneasiness," 334.

13. P. Blumberg, "Another Day, Another $3,000: Executive Rip-Off in Corporate America," *Dissent* 2 (Spring 1978), 159.

14. "Annual Survey of Executive Compensation," *Business Week,* 12 May 1980, 57.

15. "Annual Survey of Executive Compensation," 57; Blumberg, 162.

16. See also "It Ain't Hay, but Is It Clover?" *Forbes,* 9 June 1980, 116-48.

17. "It Ain't Hay, but Is It Clover?" 164.

18. F. Lundberg, *The Rich and the Super-Rich* (New York: Bantam, 1968), 433-35.

19. D. Tussing, "The Dual Welfare System," *Society* 2 (January/February 1974), 50-58.

20. *USA Today,* 2 July 1985, p. 5-B.   See also H. Rodgers, "Welfare Policies for the Rich," *Dissent* 2 (Spring 1978), 141; and Gary Hart, "The Economy is Decaying; the Free Lunch Is Over," *New York Times,* 21 April 1975.

21. Philip Stern, *The Rape of the Taxpayer* (New York: Random House, 1973), 214, 232.

22. Frank Ackerman, *Reaganomics: Rhetoric vs. Reality* (Boston: South End Press, 1982), 50-54.

23. Ackerman, 53.

24. Ronnie Dugger, *On Reagan* (New York: McGraw-Hill, 1983), 108.

25. F. F. Piven and R. Cloward, *The New Class War* (New York: Pantheon, 1982), 35.

26. Ackerman, 54.

27. Stern, 259-60. Copyright © 1973 by Philip Stern. Reprinted by permission of Random House, Inc.

28. Ovid Demaris, *Dirty Business* (New York: Harper's Magazine Press, 1974), 257.

29. Lundberg, 284.

30. Lundberg, 292.

31. Examples cited in Demaris, 303-4.

32. Cited in Demaris, 317-18.

33. See M. Clinard and R. F. Meier, *The Sociology of Deviant Behavior,* 5th ed. (New York: Holt, Rinehart, and Winston, 1979), 568.

34. Michael Parenti, *Democracy for the Few,* 2nd ed. (New York: St. Martin's Press, 1977), 76.

35. Parenti, 76.

36. See Robert Sherrill, *Why They Call It Politics*, 2nd ed. (New York: Harcourt, Brace, Jovanovich, 1974), 126-27; and H. R. Rodgers, Jr., *Crisis In Democracy* (Reading, MA: Addison-Wesley, 1978), 126.

37. *Oakland Tribune*, 13 December 1983, p. 38.

38. E. Currie and J. Skolnick, *America's Problems: Social Issues and Public Policy* (Boston: Little, Brown, 1984), 138-39.

39. Cited in Parenti, 77.

40. Ira Katznelson and Mark Kesselman, *The Politics of Power* (New York: Harcourt, Brace, Jovanovich, 1975), 142.

41. Sidney Lens, "Socialism for the Rich," *The Progressive* 91 (September 1975), 14.

42. Currie and Skolnick, 139.

43. Cited in Donald McDonald, "Militarism in America," in *The Triple Revolution Emerging*, by Robert Perrucci and Mark Pilisuk, 31-54 (Boston: Little, Brown, 1971), 42 (originally appeared in *The Center Magazine* 3:1, January 1970).

44. Rodgers, *Crisis in Democracy*, 127; and U.S. Department of Commerce, *Statistical Abstract of the United States, 1984* (Washington, D.C.: U.S. Government Printing Office, 1984), 324.

45. Mills, "A Diagnosis of Our Moral Uneasiness," 338.

46. David Mermelstein, "The 'Energy Crisis,'" in *The Economic Crisis Reader*, ed. D. Mermelstein (New York: Random House, 1975), 268.

47. Cited in Demaris, 228.   The oil-depletion allowance was repealed in 1975.

48. Dave Pugh and Mitch Zimmerman, "The 'Energy Crisis' and the Real Crisis Behind It," in *The Economic Crisis Reader*, ed. D. Mermelstein, 274-380 (New York: Random House, 1975), 275-76.

49. See G. David Garson, *Power and Politics in the United States* (Lexington, MA: D. C. Heath, 1977), 251-52.   See also Robert Scheer, *America after Nixon: The Age of the Multinationals* (New York: McGraw-Hill, 1974), 143.

50. Michael Tanzer, "The International Oil Crisis: A Tightrope Between Depression and War," in *The Economic Crisis Reader*, ed. D. Mermelstein, 291-305 (New York: Random House, 1975), 293-94 (originally appeared in *Social Policy* 5 [November-December 1974]).

51. K. Dolbeare and M. Edelman, *American Politics*, 3rd ed. (Lexington, MA: D. C. Heath, 1977), 51.

52. Pugh and Zimmerman, 257.

53. Demaris, 229.   The above examples of oil company profit sources due to the crisis are based on Demaris' discussion, 229-49.

54. S. F. Singer, "The Oil Crisis That Isn't," *New Republic*, 24 February 1979, 13.

55. Cited in Demaris, 228-29.

56. Demaris, 229.

57. See Alexander Cockburn and James Ridgeway, "The Worst Domino," *The Village Voice*, 19 February 1979, pp. 1, 7-8.

58. See Singer, 14-15.

59. Mills, "A Diagnosis of Our Moral Uneasiness," 335-36.

60. J. G. Vancise, *The Federal Antitrust Laws*, 3rd rev. ed. (Washington, D.C.: American Enterprise Institute, 1979), 7.

61. August Bequai, *White Collar Crime: A 20th Century Crisis* (Lexington, MA: D. C. Heath, 1978), 96.

62. Bequai, 100-101.

63. Bequai, 102.

64. John E. Conklin, *"Illegal But Not Criminal"*: *Business Crime in America* (Englewood Cliffs, NJ: Prentice-Hall, 1977), 104-5.

65. A. E. McCormick, "Rule Enforcement and Moral Indignation: Some Observations on Antitrust Convictions Upon the Societal Reaction Process," *Social Problems* 25 (October 1977), 34.

66. McCormick, 34.

67. Bequai, 148-50.

68. Lundberg, 137.

69. Quoted in Lundberg, 137.

70. E. Sutherland, "Crime of Corporations," in *White-Collar Crime*, rev. ed., by G. Geis and R. F. Meier, 71-84 (New York: Free Press), 73.

71. M. B. Clinard, *Illegal Corporate Behavior* (Washington, D.C.: Law Enforcement Assistance Administration, 1979), 108.

72. National Council on Crime and Delinquency, *Criminal Justice News Letter* 7 (26 March 1979), 2.

73. Cited in A. Rogow, *The Dying of the Light* (New York: Putnam, 1975), 89.

74. M. Green et al., *The Closed Enterprise System* (New York: Grossman, 1972), 149, 150, 472.

75. M. Clinard and R. Quinney, *Criminal Behavior Systems: A Typology*, 2nd ed. (New York: Holt, Rinehart, and Winston, 1973), 211.

76. Cited in Rogow, 89.

77. R. Smith, "The Incredible Electrical Conspiracy," in *The Sociology of Crime and Delinquency*, ed. M. Wolfgang et al., 357-72 (New York: Wiley, 1970), 363.

78. A. Thio, *Deviant Behavior* (Boston: Houghton Mifflin, 1978), 352.

79. G. Geis, "Upper World Crime," in *Current Perspectives on Criminal Behavior*, ed. A. S. Blumberg, 114-37 (New York: Knopf, 1974), 132-33.

80. Geis, 116.

81. F. A. J. Ianni and F. Ianni, eds., *The Crime Society: Organized Crime and Corruption in America* (New York: New American Library, 1976), xvi.

82. Clinard and Quinney, 225.

83. See Mary McIntosh, "The Growth of Racketeering," *Economy and Society* 2 (1973), 63-64.

84. The items in this section are from Frank Pearce, *Crimes of the Powerful* (London: Pluto Press, 1976), 140.

85. McIntosh, 64.

86. See M. Tabor, "The Plague: Capitalism and Dope Genocide," in *The Triple Revolution Emerging*, ed. R. Perrucci and M. Pilisuk, 241-49 (Boston: Little, Brown, 1971).

87. Stephen Spitzer, "Toward a Marxian Theory of Deviance," *Social Problems* 22 (February 1975), 649.

88. For details, see *New York Times*, 30 January 1975, p. 1; *New York Times*, 21 March 1975, p. 41; *New York Times*, 7 August 1975, p. 38; and *New York Times*, 4 Novermber 1975, p. 38.

89. R. King, "Gambling and Crime," in *An Economic Analysis of Crime*, ed. L. J. Kaplan and D. Kessler, 36-45 (Springfield, IL: Charles C. Thomas, 1936), 40.

90. R. Quinney, *Criminology: Analysis and Critique of Crime in America* (Boston: Little, Brown, 1975), 145.

91. The following examples are from J. Cook, "The Invisible Enterprise," *Forbes*, 29 September 1980, 60, 62, 66.

92. Cook, 70.

93. Cook, 70.

94. Cook, 70.

95. See Penny Lernoux, "The Miami Connection," *The Nation*, 18 February 1984, 186-98.

96. Cook, 70.

97. C. McCaghy, *Deviant Behavior: Crime, Conflict, and Interest Groups* (New York: MacMillan, 1976), 242.

98. McCaghy, 242. See also H. Stuart Mills, *Demystifying Social Deviance* (New York: McGraw-Hill, 1979), 84.

99. See E. Reid, *The Grim Reapers* (New York: Bantam Books, 1969), 138-39; and H. Kohn, "The Nixon-Hughes Lansky Connection," *Rolling Stone*, 20 May 1976, 41-50, 77-78.

100. See Dolbeare and Edelman, 85-89, for Senate Intelligence Committee Report excerpts on this and other CIA assassination plots.

101. Pearce, 149.

102. Pearce, 150.

103. Pearce, 151.

104. For a detailed account of organized crime as a source of political campaign contributions, see William Chambliss, *On the Take: From Petty Crooks to Presidents* (Bloomington: Indiana University Press, 1978), 150-68.

105. For details, see Chambliss; and Alan Block and William Chambliss, *Organizing Crime* (New York: Elsevier, 1981), 34-37.

106. See Phillip Stern, "Uncle Sam's Welfare Program for the Rich," *New York Times Magazine*, 16 April 1972, 26.

107. See this and other studies cited in Richard Parker, *The Myth of the Middle Class* (New York: Liveright, 1972).

108. J. Victor Baldridge, *Sociology: A Critical Approach to Power, Conflict, and Change*, 2nd ed. (New York: Wiley, 1980), 489.

109. See Michael Maccoby and K. A. Terzi, "Character and Work in America," in *Exploring Contradictions: Political Economy in the Corporate State*, ed. Philip Brenner et al., 116-61 (New York: McKay/Longman, 1974), 128.

CHAPTER 3

Corporate Deviance: Monopoly, Manipulation, and Fraud

Sociologist Stanton Wheeler, in his presidential address to the 1975 annual meeting of the Society for the Study of Social Problems, chided his colleagues for their neglect of one particular area of criminality—"the patterns of illegal activity that lie at the core of large-scale corporate, industrial society."[1]   The magnitude of this omission was revealed in 1978 by the first comprehensive investigation of corporate crime. Sociologist Marshall Clinard and his associates gathered data on the illegal actions of the 582 largest publicly owned corporations in the United States.   Among their findings were that, during a twenty-four month period: (1) 60 percent of these corporations had a legal action instituted against them by a federal agency for criminal activity; (2) of those corporations having had at least one violation, the average number of violations was 4.2—with one corporation being formally accused by the government on sixty-two occasions; and (3) almost one-half of all the violations occurred in the oil refining, automobile, and drug industries (a rate 300 percent greater than their size in the sample indicated).[2]

The neglected subject of *corporate deviance* is the focus of this chapter, as well as the next. Specifically, this chapter is devoted to five areas of corporate deviance: the problems generated by (1) monopoly; (2) price fixing; (3) price gouging; (4) deceptive advertising; and (5) fraud.

THE COSTS OF MONOPOLIES

As noted in Chapter 1, the United States has moved from competitive capitalism to a stage of monopoly capitalism. Karl Marx, well over one hundred years ago, correctly predicted this current stage.[3] Free enterprise, he argued, will result in some firms becoming bigger and bigger as they eliminate their opposition or absorb smaller competing firms. The ultimate result of this process is the existence of a monopoly in each of the various sectors of the economy. Monopolies, of course, are antithetical to the free-enterprise system because they determine the price and the quality of the products, interfering with the balance of supply and demand. This, as we will see, increases the benefits for the few at the expense of the many.

For the most part, U.S. society upholds Marx's prediction. Although there are a few corporations that are virtual monopolies (e.g., IBM), most sectors of the U.S. economy are dominated by shared monopolies. Instead of a single corporation controlling an industry, the situation is one in which a small number of large firms dominate an industry.

> When four or fewer firms supply 50% or more of a particular market, a shared monopoly results, one which performs much as a monopoly or cartel would. Most economists agree that above this level of concentration—a four-firm ratio of 50%—the economic costs of shared monopoly are most manifest.[4]

Currently, the following industries are dominated by shared monopolies: motor vehicles (where the four largest firms control 93 percent); light bulbs (90 percent); breakfast cereals (89 percent); turbines and generators (86 percent); primary aluminum (76 percent); chocolate and cocoa (73 percent); photo equipment (72 percent); brewing (64 percent); guided missiles and spacecraft (64 percent); and roasted coffee (61 percent).[5]

The existence of shared monopolies indicates the extent of concentration of U.S. business. The evidence is clear that the assets of the United States' businesses are highly concentrated in the hands of a few giants. The 200 largest, for instance, have increased their share of U.S. industry from 45 percent in 1945 to 61 percent in 1982. In 1960, the 450 largest firms controlled about 50 percent of the nation's manufacturing assets, earning 59 percent of the profits. Today, these companies have around 70 percent control, and 72 percent of all profits.[6]

The concentration of wealth among the major corporations is enormous. In 1981, the largest 500 companies had a total of $3.51 trillion in assets, with each of these companies earning more than $1.7 billion. Even among these largest of companies, the wealth is disproportionately concentrated: Of all assets held by the top 500 U.S. companies, 25 percent are controlled by the largest twelve companies, and 50 percent are controlled by the largest fifty.[7]

Two processes account for the superconcentration of assets among a few corporations: (1) growth through competition, where the fittest survive; and (2) growth through mergers. Of the two, the latter is the more significant.

In 1978, the value of conglomerate mergers was approximately $5 billion. In 1980, just two years later, the amount had increased to an astonishing $44.3 billion. In 1981, the total approached $70 billion.

The Reagan administration has encouraged such mergers by relaxing antitrust law enforcement on the grounds that efficient firms should not be hobbled. Paradoxically, President Reagan has opposed big government because it is wasteful. Nonetheless, he claims that the bigger businesses get, the more efficient they become. During President Reagan's first term (1980-1984), some very large mergers occurred. For example, Texaco bought Getty Oil for $10.1 billion, DuPont bought Conoco for $7.4 billion, and U.S. Steel bought Marathon Oil for $6.5 billion.[8]

Why do these biggest of businesses feel the urge to merge? The goal of bigness appears to be control. As Eugene Rostow has put it, "The history of corporations is the best evidence of the motivation for their growth. In instance after instance (it) appears to have been quest for monolopy power, not the technological advances of scale."[9]

The ever greater concentration of power and resources in a few corporations has important negative consequences for U.S. society, exacerbating many social problems.[10] Foremost is the overpricing that occurs when four or fewer firms control a particular market. A study by the Federal Trade Commission has estimated that, if industries with the four largest firms were reduced in control from 50 to 40 percent of sales, prices would fall by at least 25 percent. When industries are so concentrated that four or fewer firms account for 70 percent of sales, they are found to have profits 50 percent higher than the lesser concentrated industries.[11]

The existence of monopolies is costly to consumers in other ways, since they ultimately bear the costs of advertising and product changes. The irony is that consumers, even though squeezed by monopolies, are forced to finance the continuation of monopolies.

Overpricing leads to lost output because of fewer sales and excess capacity. Lost output is detrimental for three reasons. First, it reduces potential economic activity. Second, lower output substantially reduces tax revenues that, if not reduced because of lower output, could either reduce the tax burden for all or be spent to alleviate social problems. Third, another negative consequence of overcharging by monopolies is inequitable transfer cost. Excessive prices bring excessive profits. These profits then redistribute income from purchasers to the stockholders of the corporations, and 47 percent of stocks are owned by the wealthiest 0.5 percent of the population.[12] The result is that a relative handful of stockholders (the already wealthy) reap the dividends. Thus, overcharging redistributes wealth, but in the direction of greater inequalities. As Newfield and Greenfield concluded:

> It is this tiny minority of shareholding Americans that gather in the super-profits generated by the power of big business to stifle competition and manipulate prices without fear of challenge. When we recognize that officers of these superbusinesses often collect more money from their stockholdings and stock-option privileges than from their salaries, we can see where much of our money goes: not to the community at large, not to wage earners, not into more efficient products, but into the bank accounts, trust funds, and holdings of the richest 1.6 percent of Americans.[13]

Put another way--and one that is stronger and even more compelling--two Stanford economists have argued that, if there were no monopolies: (1) 2.4 percent of U.S. families would control not 40 percent of the total wealth, but only 16.6 to 27.5 percent, and (2) 93.3 percent of U.S. families would be better off, and only the wealthier 6.7 percent would be worse off. According to these estimates, without monopoly, our current maldistribution of wealth would be as much as 50 percent less.[14]

Heavily concentrated industries are also sources of inflation. When consumer demand falls, for example, the prices of products in concentrated industries tend to rise. This occurs in such different industries as automobile manufacturing and professional sports. As evidence:

> Economist John Blair studied 16 pairs of products, one from a concentrated industry [i.e., where a shared monopoly existed], the other from a more competitive one (e.g., steel building materials vs. lumber; pig iron vs. steel scraps). During the two recessions of the 1950's, the price of every unconcentrated product fell, while the price of 13 of the 16 concentrated products actually rose.[15]

In other words, when a few corporations are large enough to control an industry, they are immune from the rules of a competitive economy. The immediate consequences for consumers is that they will pay artificially high prices.

Shared monopolies also cause inflation because they can automatically pass on increased labor costs or increased taxes to the consumer. In competitive industries, on the other hand, a corporation may be forced to reduce its profit if it wants to continue to get a share of the market. Moreover, the tendency toward parallel pricing in concentrated industries means that prices only rise. When an industry leader like General Motors or U.S. Steel announces a price increase of 7 percent, within a few days, similar increases are announced by their so-called competitors. As Ralph Nader and his associates have noted, "Each firm gladly increases its profit margin by getting the same share of a larger pie. There is no incentive to keep prices down, for then all the other firms will have to come down to that price--which means the same share of a smaller pie."[16]

It is impossible to know exactly how much monopolies contribute to inflation. Certainly, the profits generated by lack of competition rather than efficiency or product superiority are hidden contributors.

The existence of monopolies also has important political consequences. The concentration of economic power undermines the democratic process in two fundamental ways. The first is overt, as the powerful marshall their vast resources to achieve favorable laws, court decisions, and rulings by regulatory agencies. They have the lobbyists, lawyers, and politicians (as noted in Chapter 1) to work for their interests. More subtly (but real, nonetheless), the powerful get their way because of the bias of the politico-economic system. Such time-honored notions as "our economic interests abroad must be protected," or "tax incentives to business will benefit everyone," and "bigness is goodness," go unchallenged because we have been socialized to accept the current system as proper. Thus, decisions continue to be based on precedent and the idea that "what is good for General Motors is good for the country" prevails. As long as such notions guide decision making, the interests of the wealthy will be served at the expense of the nonwealthy.[17]

For defenders of a free and competitive enterprise system, the existence of monopolies and shared monopolies should be attacked as un-American because the economy has become neither free nor competitive. Green made the following observation:

> Huey Long once prophesied that fascism would come to the United States first in the form of anti-fascism. So too with

socialism--corporate socialism. Under the banner of free enterprise, up to two-thirds of American manufacturing has been
metamorphosed into a "closed enterprise system." Although
businessmen spoke the language of competitive capitalism, each
sought refuge for themselves: price-fixing, parallel pricing,
mergers, excessive advertising, quotas, subsidies, and tax favoritism.   While defenders of the American dream guarded against
socialism from the left, it arrived unannounced from the right.[18]

In summary, the negative consequences of shared monopolies are
important to our understanding of elite deviance in two ways. First,
monopolies are themselves deviant because they disproportionately redistribute wealth and advantage toward the already advantaged. And
second, the existence of monopolies aids in creating an environment in
which deviant acts are encouraged. An examination of the automobile
industry will illustrate these interrelated phenomena.

Case Study: The Automobile Industry

The automobile industry is the nation's largest. One out of six
U.S. businesses is related directly or indirectly to the automobile.
Nineteen eighty-three sales data for the top 500 corporations listed
General Motors as second (with $74.6 billion in sales) and Ford as fifth
with ($44.5 billion). The major oil companies, whose fortunes are directly
related to automobile usage, were also ranked near the top: Exxon was
first, Mobil was fourth, Texaco was sixth, Standard Oil of California was
eleventh, Gulf was twelfth, Standard Oil of Indiana was fourteenth, and
Atlantic Richfield was fifteenth. Together, these companies earned $290
billion.[19]

The pivotal position of the industry in the U.S. economy is
underscored by such considerations as the following: One out of
every seven workers in this country is said to be dependent
directly or indirectly on the automobile industry; the industry
consumes about one fifth of the nation's steel production, one out
of every fourteen tons of copper, more than two out of every five
tons of lead, more than one out of every four tons of zinc, one
pound in seven of nickel, one-half of the reclaimed rubber, almost
three fourths of the upholstery leather, and substantial proportions of total national output of glass, machine tools, general
industrial equipment, and forgings.[20]

The important point is that the automobile industry is one of the
nation's most highly concentrated. In the early 1900s, 181 companies
manufactured and sold automobiles. But few were to survive. By 1927,
there were forty-four, by 1935 there were ten, and now there are only
four domestic manufacturers.
The automobile industry has become a shared monopoly. But even
this shared monopoly is in danger of greater concentration.[21]   For
example, in 1984, GM had 60 percent of all U.S. sales for domestically
built cars. This market share will likely increase even more because of

the government's insistence that the automobile industry reduce gasoline consumption in all cars sold in the United States. In 1974, the average car sold by domestic manufacturers went fourteen miles to the gallon.   At that time, federal regulations mandated that fuel economy be boosted in stages until each manufacturer produced cars averaging 27.5 miles per gallon in 1985.   Such product adaptations require massive costs for downsizing and new technologies. The bigger the company, the less these costs hurt.   For instance, GM, with $45.7 billion in assets in 1983 (650 percent greater than Chrysler's), can afford the huge costs.   Since the 1974 edict, it has spent a yearly average of $3.2 billion to overhaul its models.   These huge expenditures have given GM a lead in the fuel-economy race and an ever greater share of the market.   Thus, a positive governmental policy, aimed at solving the problem of petroleum waste, has had the negative effect of increasing the dominance of a single corporation.

GM achieved an even greater advantage when it lobbied with the other automobile manufacturers for less stringent mileage requirements, since they were unable to meet the standards set for 1985. The government accepted the automakers' argument and rescinded.   As a result, GM and Ford together saved about $200 million that would have been levied in fines for noncompliance.[22]

The advantages of being big are illustrated buy the two largest U.S. automobile companies--GM and Ford.   In 1983, these companies had assets worth $45.7 billion and $23.9 billion (respectively) and profits of $3.7 and $1.9 billion (respectively).[23]   Such huge sums allow these companies to make big capital outlays, to provide credit to their suppliers, and to pay great sums for advertising.   Moreover, they can afford a high degree of product differentiation (i.e., a number of different models and options), which further reduces competiton.   As a result of these barriers, it has been estimated that a new company would need at least $1 billion for manufacturing and another $200 million to set up a dealership network.   The result of these high-entry barriers is that, since 1923, there has not been a successful new domestic entrant into the automobile market.[24]

But how does this market control affect the consumer?   The answer is simple--the consumer pays dearly.   Let's briefly look at some examples:

1.   Competition is limited to four companies and, in reality, to one, GM.   These companies do not compete in price and quality of the product, but they do compete in advertising.   This cost is passed on to the consumer.

2.   Yearly style changes (planned obsolescence) is the industry's strategy for continued growth in sales and profits.   This policy has at least three important negative effects: (a) it increases the waste of resources; (b) it increases the likelihood of unsafe products because of insufficient time for planning and testing; and (c) it increases the huge costs paid for by the consumer.   "The cost of dynamic obsolescence is passed on to the buyer twice: first, by tacking the cost of style changes onto the price of the car (about 25 percent of the price), and, second, in the car's unnecessarily rapid loss of value."[25]

3.   Frequent style changes make it prohibitively expensive for outsiders to make spare parts.   As a result, 90 percent of automobile parts

are available only from the original manufacturers--and at a higher cost than one would pay if prices were competitive.

4. Finally, monopoly control of the automobile industry has meant that prices tend to rise regardless of the demand. During the 1973-1974 recession, the number of cars sold fell by 20 percent, yet the prices of domestic new cars were raised 9 percent.[26] Obviously, the law of supply and demand is rescinded in monopoly industries. Monopoly conditions, rather than the market, control prices, as shown in the similar price increases among the automakers. In a typical instance, when one manufacturer announces its price increase, within weeks, the others will make similar increases. If one is out of line with the others, there is a period of adjustment toward the GM price.[27] The result is higher profits for each of the companies--an average annual return on net worth between 1946 and 1967 of 16.67 percent in the automobile industry, compared to 9.02 percent in other manufacturing corporations. "In sum, the automobile industry imposes classic oligopolistic costs on its consumers."[28]

But the costs to consumers do not end here. There is considerable evidence that the automobile manufacturers actually create a deviant market structure. Sociologist Harvey Farberman has suggested that the automakers impose on their new car dealers a pricing policy that requires high volume and low per-unit profit.[29] The dealer is at the mercy of the manufacturers. If the dealer protests the situation, then he or she might lose the dealership or receive unfavorable treatment (slow delivery or not enough of the most popular models). Thus, when the manufacturers demand high volume and a low-profit margin, the dealers are forced to look for profits elsewhere in their operations. These solutions are often deviant.

One way to increase profit is to minimize one's taxes. The so-called short sale allows both buyer and seller to escape taxes. This is a tactic whereby the customer pays part of the car's cost by check and the remainder in cash. The sales manager, in turn, records the sale as the amount paid by check. The customer pays sales tax on that amount only, and the dealer does not pay income tax on the cash received. This excess cash is buried or laundered.

When an automobile agency has an abundance of trade-ins, the best are recycled back to the agency's used car retail line, while the surplus is sold to used car wholesalers. The dispersal of cars into the wholesale market often involves the receipt of kickbacks by the used car manager, as independent wholesalers must pay graft for their supply.

Another tactic to increase profits in used car sales is to provide cosmetic changes rather than improve the mechanical condition of the car. This practice is based on the knowledge that customers are especially impressed by observables such as the paint job and the interior.

Car dealers also make unusually high profits from their repair shops. These profits are elevated by two practices--flat-rate labor costs and the parts monopoly.[30] Under the industrywide tactic of the flat rate, labor for repairs is charged according to the standard amount of time a given job is supposed to take--not the time it actually takes. The result is that the customer typically pays for shop and mechanic time that were never used.

The other scam is charging for parts at the inflated retail cost. As noted earlier, the monopoly pricing of parts is exorbitant. And still another tactic to increase profits is the unnecessary replacement of parts.[31] The totals are impressive: Nearly 40 percent of all auto repairs are wasted.

In sum, the automobile industry is permeated by a rip-off mentality. Quite clearly, monopoly has costly consequences for consumers, who are vicitmized in countless ways. (For additional discussion, see Chapter 4.[32])

PRICE FIXING

The *sine qua non* of capitalism is competition. We have seen, though, that the tendency toward concentration makes a mockery of the claim that the U.S. version of capitalism is competitive. The existence of shared monopolies allows the few corporations that control an industry to eliminate price wars by parallel pricing and product homogeneity. The former depicts the practice where tacit collusion by supposed competitors achieves a common price, while the latter means that prices are going to be roughly equal because the competitors produce goods with similar specifications. Both practices are common and have the consequence of equal prices, regardless of whether the leading companies in an industry conspire to do so or not.

Prices are also manipulated to maximize profits through collusive activities of the companies supposedly in competition with each other. This practice is called *price fixing*. It refers to the explicit agreement among competitors to keep prices artificially high to maximize profits.

Price fixing is illegal and complaints are monitored and brought to court by the Antitrust Division of the Justice Department. The illegality of price fixing, however, has not deterred competing companies from conspiring to make abnormal profits through this practice, which costs consumers about $60 billion a year.[33] One review of cases from 1963 to 1972 in which price fixing was proven revealed that the practice occurred among companies producing and marketing the following: steel wheels, pipe, bed springs, metal shelving, steel castings, self-locking nuts, liquified petroleum gas delivery, refuse collection, linoleum installation, swimsuits, structural steel, carbon steel, baking flour, fertilizer, railroads, welding electrodes, acoustical ceiling materials, hydraulic hose, beer, gasoline, asphalt, book matches, concrete pipe, drill bushings, linen, school construction, plumbing fixtures, dairy products, fuel oil, auto repair, brass fittings, plumbing contracting, bread, athletic equipment, maple floors, vending machines, ready-mix concrete, industrial chemicals, rendering, shoes, garage doors, automobile glass, and wholesale meat.[34] In addition, review these current examples.

Item: In 1982, a federal investigation found 158 companies guilty of bid rigging in highway construction in fifteen states.[35]

Item: In 1984, the state of New York estimated that a monopoly to fix concrete prices resulted in overcharges at public and private

Item:
construction projects of between $40 million and $450 million a year.[36]

Item: In 1984, the federal government alleged that the major U.S. oil companies had rigged prices and contrived shortages during the 1973 Arab oil embargo.[37]

Examining a number of price-fixing cases, several researchers have tried to determine if a pattern is associated with price fixing. They concluded that "conspiracy among competitors may arise in any number of situations but it is most likely to occur and endure when numbers are small [few companies involved], concentration is high [when four or fewer firms control fifty percent or more of the market], and the product is homogeneous."[38]

We should not forget, however, that collusive arrangements to keep prices or fees artificially high are not limited to industrial sales. Price fixing in one form or another often occurs in real estate fees, doctors' fees, lawyers' fees, and tax accountants' fees, to name a few.

Although the government continues to prosecute price-fixing cases, the problem continues. Apparently, the potential for increased profits is too tempting. Moreover, when individuals have been found guilty, the punishment has been more symbolic than real. Thus, the incentives remain. Once again, profit is the primary source of motivation —and the customer be damned.

The extra profits garnered through price-fixing arrangements have an obvious impact on customers, who pay extraordinary prices for goods and services. But it also has some negative indirect effects. Two of these subtle consequences are especially noteworthy. First, larger than necessary expenditures fuel inflation. And second, extra profits exacerbate the gap between the haves and the have-nots.

For an illustration of price fixing, let's examine the most blatant incident in modern U.S. history.

Case Study: The Electrical Conspiracy

From the mid-1940s through the 1950s, virtually all electrical manufacturing firms were actively involved in collusive activities to keep prices high.[39] Twenty-nine companies--but principally General Electric and Westinghouse--eventually were found guilty of conspiring to fix prices, rig bids, and divide markets on electrical equipment valued at $1.75 billion annually. The amount of profit generated from price fixing in the electrical industry was considerable.

The result of these machinations was grossly inflated prices. Generator prices rose 50 percent from 1951 to 1959, while wholesale prices on all commodities rose only 5 percent. The Senate Small Business Committee later asserted that Westinghouse had bilked the Navy by a 500 percent overcharge on certain gear assemblies, and GE had charged 446 percent too much on another contract.[40]

An example of how the prices were fixed occurred in so-called competitive bidding for new business. Public agencies (e.g., utilities, school districts, and the government) required companies to make sealed bids for the cost of their products. The conspiring companies used this seemingly competitive practice to ensure high prices by rotating business on a fixed-percentage basis. Namely, each company was allowed the proportion of the sales equal to the proportion of the market they had controlled prior to the conspiracy. For sealed bids on circuit breakers, for example, the four participating companies divided the sales so that GE received 45 percent; Westinghouse, 35 percent; Allis-Chalmers, 10 percent; and Federal Pacific, 10 percent.

Every ten days to two weeks, working-level meetings were called in order to decide whose turn was next. Turns were determined by the ledger list, a table of who had received what in recent weeks. After that, the only thing left to decide was the price that the company picked to win would submit as the lowest bid.[41]

Four grand juries investigated price-fixing allegations in the electrical industry and handed down twenty indictments involving forty-five individuals and twenty-nine corporations. At the sentencing hearing in 1961, Judge Ganey levied fines totalling $1,787,000 on the corporations and $137,000 on different individuals. The highest corporate fines were against General Electric ($437,500) and Westinghouse ($372,500). Seven individuals were given jail sentences of thirty days (later reduced to twenty-five for good behavior), and twenty others received suspended sentences. In addition, the individuals were assessed fines ranging from $1,000 to $12,500. The corporations also faced settlements to injured parties. By 1964, for example, some 90 percent of the 1,800 claims against GE had been settled for a total of $160 million.

Several significant conclusions can be drawn from this electrical conspiracy case. First, and most obvious, this antitrust conspiracy illustrates the willful and blatant violation of the law by some of the leading corporations in the United States. Second, the highest officials in the guilty corporations escaped without fines and jail sentences. Those found guilty were vice-presidents, division managers, and sales managers--not presidents and chief executive officers. Moreover, the sentences levied were mild, considering the huge amounts of money involved. The government even ruled that the companies' payments of fines and settlements could be considered a business expense and therefore tax deductible.[42]

This type of crime is underplayed by the media. For example, on the day that the defendants pleaded guilty or *nolo contendere* (no contest), only four of the largest twenty-two newspapers made the story front-page news, and four well-known papers--the *Boston Globe, New York Daily News, Christian Science Monitor*, and the *Kansas City Times*--completely omitted the story. Five days later, when the sentencing occurred, 45 percent of the twenty newspapers with one-fifth of all the newspaper circulation in the United States did not consider the story front-page news.[43]

The parties convicted did not consider their acts immoral. Two quotes illustrate this point. First, the president of Allen-Bradley, Fred L. Loock, said, "It is the only way a business can be run. It is free enterprise."[44] Second, a GE official said, "Sure, collusion was illegal, but it wasn't unethical."[45]

The punishment for those judged guilty was incredibly light, given the magnitude of the case--a maximum of $12,500 and thirty days in jail. But more important is the discrepancy found when the sentences for these types of crimes are compared to those given to individuals guilty of street crimes. Some extreme examples are provided by Nader and Green:

> A year after seven electrical manufacturers were sent to jail for 30 days apiece, a man in Asbury Park, New Jersey, stole a $2.98 pair of sunglasses and a $1 box of soap and was sent to jail for four months. A George Jackson was sent to prison for ten years to life for stealing $70 from a gas station, his third minor offense; and in Dallas one Joseph Sills received a 1000-year sentence for stealing $73.10. Many states send young students who are marijuana first offenders to jail for five to ten years' sentence. But the *total* amount of time spent in jail by all businessmen who have ever violated antitrust laws is a little under two years.[46]

In all probability, antitrust cases like the electrical conspiracy represent only a small portion of the actual amount of price fixing in U.S. industry.[47] The potential profits are too tempting for many business executives, and the chances of getting caught are slim. The likelihood of escaping conviction, if caught, is great because of two factors: (1) the deals are made in secret and masked by apparently legal activity (e.g., sealed bids); and (2) the government's antitrust budget is very small.

PRICE GOUGING

Because private corporations are entirely profit oriented, they take whatever advantage they can to sell their products or services at the highest possible prices. Shared monopolies, as we have seen, use their control of the market to increase prices an average of 25 percent. Price fixing, of course, is another tactic to maximize profits. In this section, we will discuss yet another manifestation of profit-maximizing behavior-- *price gouging:* taking extraordinary advantage of consumers because of the bias of the law, monopoly of the market, manipulation of the market, or because of contrived or real shortages.

Whatever the means used, price gouging is a form of deviancy. Let's examine the procedures used in three areas: (1) selling to the disadvantaged; (2) taking advantage of events; and (3) extraordinary profits through convenient laws and manipulation.

Taking Advantage of the Disadvantaged

Low-income consumers are the victims of price gouging from a variety of merchants, banks and finance companies, landlords, and the like. The poor pay more due to several factors, including higher rates of street crimes in their neighborhoods, which raise the cost of doing business, and the economic marginality of the poor, making their credit especially risky. But even when these rationales are accounted for, the poor are the victims of unusually high prices, which, of course, tend to perpetuate their poverty. Many food chains find that it costs 2 or 3 percent more to operate in poor neighborhoods, yet low-income consumers pay between 5 and 10 percent more for their groceries than those living in middle-income areas. Perhaps the best example of price gouging by ghetto stores is that they tend to raise prices on the first and the fifteenth of each month because these are the days when welfare checks are received. Similarly, there is evidence that grocers in the Mississippi Delta raised prices when food stamps were introduced.[48]

Banks and other financial organizations also take advantage of the poor. Because they are not affluent and therefore have inadequate collateral or credit standing, the poor must pay higher interest rates or may be forced to deal with loan sharks because they are denied resources through the legitimate financial outlets.

The greater risk of loaning to the poor is used to justify extremely high prices in poor neighborhoods. In the jewelry business, for example, the normal markup is 100 percent, but for jewelry sold in poor neighborhoods, the markup often is 300 percent or higher. A ring selling wholesale for $50 will sell for as much as $300 in the poverty market. In order to protect themselves from possible default, credit jewelers in such a situation will try to get the maximum down payment--say $60. If so, the dealer has already made a $10-profit and the future payments are even more profit.[49]

The merchants in poor areas engage in such price gouging for several reasons: (1) the stores are essentially monopolies (no competition present); (2) the stores can argue legitimately that their costs are higher than in middle-class areas (although their prices, as we have seen, tend to exceed their increased risks by a wide margin); (3) the poor are unorganized and have no access to the powerful in society; (4) the poor are often unaware of the available avenues to complain of abusive practices; and (5) the poor tend to be apathetic because of the hopelessness of trying to change the practices of powerful banks, supermarket chains, finance companies, and other seemingly monolithic organizations. Cross has summarized the economic plight of the poor:

> Caught in a vicious cycle of poverty, the poor and the stores which serve them are trapped by the worst aspects of the free enterprise system. And it is likely that the poor are also at the receiving end of a greater amount of deliberate fraud and price discrimination than the suburban middle class.[50]

Taking Advantage of Unusual Events

The sharp entrepreneur is always looking for special events that might lead to spectacular profits. For example, when California passed Proposition 13 in 1978, local property taxes were dramatically reduced by $7 billion. This event was used by some people to increase profits substantially. For example, landlords did not reduce rents accordingly but tended to pocket the difference. And California-based corporations made an instant additional profit of $2 billion, yet did not lower prices on their products.

In the mid-1970s, a worldwide shortage caused the price of sugar to increase rapidly for U.S. consumers. This caused a concomitant rise in a number of products using sugar. The cost of candy bars increased while their size dwindled (the price tripled while the size shrunk to one-third its former size). The cost of soda also increased markedly during this period. Canned soda from vending machines went from fifteen to twenty-five cents a can. Interestingly (and revealing of the tendency of corporations to gouge whenever possible), the cost of diet soda (which, of course, contained no sugar) went up in price to twenty-five cents, as well. When the sugar shortage subsided, the cost of soda stayed at the shortage-created level and continued to increase. Also, all major soda companies had the same pricing strategy—a form of parallel pricing or price fixing.

But the best example of using a crisis to one's economic advantage—and the one that has had the greatest impact on the U.S. consumer—is the price gouging by the oil companies following the oil boycott of the OPEC countries in 1973-1974 and the shortages caused by the upheavals in Iran in 1979 (which were discussed in detail in Chapter 2).

Extraordinary Profits through Deception

Although there are many examples of price gouging because of deception, we will focus on this phenomenon in one industry—the pharmaceutical industry.

The sale of prescription and nonprescription drugs is a large industry, representing 10 percent of all medical costs in the United States (approximately $16.5 billion in 1979). About half of all prescription drugs come in two forms—under a brand name or under the generic name. Although a drug is identical chemically, if marketed under a brand name, it is very much more expensive and, therefore, profitable. Consider these examples:[51]

Item: The tranquilizer Librium, made by Hoffman-LaRoche, sells wholesale for $9.06 per 100 10-mg. tablets, while its generic substitute lists for $1.10.

Item: Hydroduiral, a drug for blood pressure made by Merck, costs $6.09 per 100 50-mg. tablets under its trade name but sells for forty-five cents under its generic equivalent.

Item: Abbott wholesales 100 tablets of crythromyacin for $15.50 while its generic counterpart wholesales for $6.20.

Item: In 1984, 20 tablets of Lomotil, an antidiarrhea pill made by G. D. Searle, cost $8.79; the same amount of this drug sold under its generic name, diphenoxylate, cost only $3.29.

Obviously, customers would save enormous sums if every prescription was filled with an available generic, yet only about 10 percent are filled with the less expensive alternative.[52] The question is, why? The answer is that drug manufacturers have done all in their power to get doctors and the public to buy the branded and more expensive drugs. Let's elaborate.

The situation in drug sales is very different from the typical purchaser-seller relationship. The choice of prescription drugs is not made by the consumer but by the physician, whose decision is not based on price but on knowledge. Doctors prescribe drugs they know about, and most of their information is supplied by large pharmaceutical firms, who spend from $3,000 to $5,000 per doctor, per year, promoting their own brand-name drugs.

Drug manufacturers also benefit by the proliferation of drugs, which leaves physicians inundated with a virtual sea of drugs and drug names. For example, sixty-one firms offered their own version of one chemical compound, PETN. Busy physicians will opt, in most cases, for the drugs that are most familiar, and drug firms do all they can to familiarize doctors with their branded (and expensive) products.

But drug companies have done more than just advertise their products to physicians. According to Ben Gordon, a drug consultant to the U.S. Senate for twenty years, "The larger drug manufacturers have been misleading and lying to the American public, to the medical profession, and to the Congress, about the quality of their drugs, as against that of the generic drugs."[53] They have used several scare tactics, such as films in which generic drugs were compared to defective cars and warnings to pharmacists that the increased use of generic drugs would cause the druggists' insurance rates to increase.[54]

Another tactic used by drug firms has been to lobby for laws prohibiting generics to be substituted for the branded drugs prescribed by physicians. At one time, all fifty states had such a law, but in recent years many have been changed. In late 1978, some forty states and the District of Columbia allowed pharmacists to substitute generic drugs for brand-name prescription drugs. Also, in 1984, Congress finally passed a law that eliminated the costly and time-consuming delays facing companies seeking government approval to market generic drugs.

This shift in the laws and the greater consumer familiarity with generic drugs has brought about a shift in policy by the large drug firms. They are fighting generics with what they call *branded generics*, which are prescription drugs that carry a different name and are priced midway between the brand-name drugs and the products that come from the generic drug houses. Although the chemicals used are identical, the large drug firms argue that the higher price of the branded generics is justified. According to Joseph Stetler, president of the Pharmaceutical Manufacturers Association, "Those larger companies have heavy investments in quality control research, which is relatively incidental, but they have a backup capability that is of value to a consumer. So there's a justification for a price differential."[55]

Such reasoning sounds good, but in many cases, the large companies do not manufacture their highly advertised products. In 1978, "20/20," the ABC newsmagazine program, visited the Mylan Pharmaceutical Company and found one machine producing erythromycin tablets. Some of the tablets were then dyed pink, others were colored yellow, while still others were made orange. The only difference among the three sets of tablets was the color, yet the three would be priced very differently. The pink version was the generic and would sell for $6.20; the yellow pills were marketed by Smith-Kline and would sell for $9.20; and the orange ones were called Bristamycin and marketed for $14.00. Similarly, at the Phillips-Roxanne Laboratories, 60-mg cidamenphene-

todene tablets were placed in a Smith-Kline bottle to be sold wholesale
for $13.20 a hundred, but when they were put in a Phillips-Roxanne
package, they sold for $10.80.   Again, the products were precisely
identical--even manufactured at the same place.[56] The only differences
were color, packaging, price, and "man in the plant," as explained by Jack
Anderson:

> Many large drug companies actually don't manufacture
> some of their highly advertised products. Usually, officials from
> a big drug company will hire a smaller firm to manufacture a
> product for them. Then the big firm will stamp its brand name on
> the product, jack up the price and sell the drug as its own. The
> big name firm is required only to send someone to the factory to
> watch over the manufacturing process. The ruse is known as "man
> in the plant."   Thus, the industry giants are able to charge
> consumers millions of dollars more than generic firms for prod-
> ucts that are essentially the same.[57]

DECEPTIVE ADVERTISING

One tenet of capitalism is expansion. Every corporation wishes to
produce an increasing amount so that profits likewise will inflate. The
problem, of course, is that the public must be convinced to consume this
ever-larger surplus.[58] One way to create demand is through advertising.
In 1973, advertising expenditures amounted to $25 billion, and by
1982 they had increased to $66.6 billion. A strong argument could be
made that advertising expenditures are wasteful in three ways: (1) they
create a demand to consume that increases the waste of natural resources; (2) they increase the cost of products, as consumers pay all the
advertising costs; and (3) the money spent serves no useful purpose (other
than profits).
But advertising is a problem to the public in another way: It is
sometimes designed to be deceptive. In a fundamental way, all advertising is deceptive because it is designed to manipulate. Symbols are used to
make the observer concerned with his or her status, beauty, age, or to
associate sex appeal with a certain look. Advertising is deceptive because
it creates desires to consume new products. But the deception we want to
consider goes beyond this type of illusion. We are concerned with a more
willful form of deception, where the goal is to sell, even through lies.[59]
A retired advertising executive discussed the cardinal principle in
U.S. advertising:

> Don't worry whether it's true or not. Will it sell? . . . The
> American people . . . are now being had from every bewildering
> direction. All the way from trying to persuade us to put dubious
> drug products and questionable foods into our stomachs to urging
> young men to lay down their lives in Indochina, the key will-it-sell
> principle and the employed techniques are the same. *Caveat
> emptor* has never had more profound significance than today,
> whether someone is trying to sell us war, God, anti-Communism

or a new improved deodorant. Deceit is the accepted order of the hour.[60]

The tendency toward deception in advertising takes two forms, blatantly false advertising and puffery. Let's examine these in turn. Several examples will show how advertising can be outright false.

Item: In 1978, the Federal Trade Commission ruled that Anacin had falsely advertised its product by claiming that it (1) relieved nervousness, tension, stress, fatigue, and depression; (2) was stronger than aspirin; (3) brought relief within twenty-two seconds; (4) was highly recommended over aspirin by doctors; and (5) was more effective for relieving pain than any other analgesic available without prescription.[61]

Item: In 1978, the attorney general of Colorado filed suit against Montgomery Ward, alleging that Ward's had regularly advertised items such as television sets and major appliances at a sale price below the so-called regular price when in reality the regular price was substantially inflated.[62]

Item: Companies commonly use bait-and-switch advertising, although it is a clear violation of FTC rules. The *bait* involves advertising a product at an extremely low price. The *switch* is made when customers arrive to buy it; there is none available, so the salespersons pressure people to buy other more expensive articles.

Item: In 1979, the nation's largest toymaker, CPG Products, a subsidiary of General Mills, was found guilty of two deceptive acts: (1) use of a television commercial that showed a toy horse being able to stand on its own--when in fact it could not--through the use of special camera techniques and film editing; and (2) use of over-sized boxes in model airplane kits that gave a misleading impression of the size of the contents.

Item: Products are advertised at exaggerated sizes. Lumber is uniformly shorter than advertised--a twelve-inch board really is eleven and one-quarter inches wide. The quarter-pounder advertised by McDonald's is really three and seven-eighths ounces. Nine-inch pies are in truth seven and three-quarters inches in diameter, because the pie industry includes the rim of the pan in determining the stated size.[63]

Item: When Libby-Owens-Ford Glass Company wanted to demonstrate the superiority of its automobile safety glass, it smeared a competing brand with streaks of vaseline to create distortion, then photographed it at oblique camera angles to enhance the effect. The distortion-free marvels of the company's own glass were shown by taking photographs of a car with the windows rolled down.[64]

Item: An analysis of news items appearing in the *New York Times* during 1974 revealed court cases of FTC rulings concerning deceptive advertising for the following: Air France, Fram Oil Filters, Ford, GM, Chrysler, American Cynamid, Clorox, Calgon, Listerine, Lysol, A&P, Sterling Drug, Kayser Pantyhose, Hardees, Carte Blanche, California Milk Producers, Skippy Peanut Butter, Sugar Association, Viceroy Cigarettes, and Jack LaLanne Health

Spas.[65]

Item: In 1984, an FTC survey of real estate advertisements for new homes in Denver found 10 percent of them to be misleading.[66]

A more subtle form of deceptive advertising is called *puffery*. This term refers to the practice of making exaggerated claims for a product. Although advertisers routinely make such false claims, and the result is deception, the law considers such practices to be legal.[67] Some examples:

"Blatz is Milwaukee's finest beer"
"Nestlé makes the very best chocolate"
"Ford gives you better ideas"
"GM—always a step ahead"
"Zenith Chromacolor is the biggest breakthrough in color TV"
"Wheaties, Breakfast of Champions"
"You can be sure if it's Westinghouse"
"Barnum and Bailey, The greatest show on earth"
"Every kid in America loves Jello brand gelatin"
"Coke is it"
"Seagram's, America's Number One Gin"
"Winston, America's Best"

Such claims are false or unsubstantiated. Even though they are considered legal, their intent is to mislead. The goal—as is always the case with advertising—is to use whatever means will sell the product. If that includes trifling with the truth, then so be it.

FRAUD

Fraud is committed when one is induced to part with money or valuables through deceit, lies, or misrepresentation. Although the law recognizes fraud as a crime, it has traditionally assumed that a fraud directed against a private individual is not a crime because of the principle of *caveat emptor*. Preston has summarized this principle:

> The buyer must accept full responsibility for a sales transaction; the seller accepts none. He must rely upon and trust nothing but his own personal inspection of his purchase, ignoring any representations of the seller which he does not confirm for himself. Any buyer who does other than this must suffer all consequences of purchases which turn out badly.[68]

This principle of the marketplace is an open invitation for fraud. Some criminologists have contended that fraud is probably "the most prevalent crime in America."[69]

The types of frauds perpetrated on victims involve a host of schemes applied to a wide variety of economic activities, as seen in the following cases.

Item: In Indianapolis, a sting operation aimed at transmission shops found that defective gears in transmissions that should have been replaced for $50 were fixed for as much as $800. Some shops even insisted that new transmissions were needed.[70]

Item: In 1984, the House Select Committee on Aging, reporting the results of a four-year study, concluded that health fraud cheats elderly Americans of more than $10 billion a year. The report estimated that elderly people spent between $4 and $5 billion a year on bogus cancer cures, $2 billion a year on questionable arthritis cures, and at least $2 billion a year on worthless products that claimed to counteract the effects of aging.[71]

Item: A 1982 Senate committee inquiry revealed evidence of kickbacks, unnecessary implantations, and waste accounting to $64 million a year in the heart-pacemaker industry.[72]

Item: So-called boiler room operations (i.e., telephone-sales scams) steal millions from gullible customers seeking fortune in oil leases, commodities markets, and stocks. In 1983, the government accused one Fort Lauderdale company, International Gold Bullion Exchange, of taking customers for more than $140 million in a three-year period.[73] Another South Florida company, U.S. Oil and Gas Corporation, guaranteed its customers in writing that, for an $8,784 investment, they would win an oil lease worth $25,000. In nine months, 66,000 people invested, yet only sixty people got leases.[74]

Item: Land fraud has occurred most commonly in areas of special allure, such as the desert, mountains, or seashore. Land, represented in brochures, media presentations, and by salespersons as having favorable characteristics, has been sold to unsuspecting buyers, even though it was without the amenities claimed. As an example of such sales deception, a newspaper ad for Lake Mead Rancheros claimed, "The Rancheros are livable now. . . . You can own a king-sized western estate with roads and electricity, water and phones available. . . . Build now and move in." In actuality, though, power and phone lines were six miles away and the nearest water was from a coin-operated pump twelve miles away.[75] Often several elements of the legitimate business community are extensively involved in land fraud: law firms, banks, title companies, real estate firms, contractors, the media, and investors. Moreover, public officials are sometimes bought to solve such problems as zoning and road construction and to curb regulatory zeal.

Item: The American Knitting Center sold imported knitting machines to persons with the promise that they, in turn, would market the garments manufactured at high prices. Twelve hundred women purchased these machines for $550 each, while they had cost the sellers between $60 and $90 each.

Item: A dance studio signed a sixty-nine-year-old widow to eight lifetime memberships, entitling her to 3,100 hours of instruction at a cost of $34,193.[76]

Item: In a fifteen-year span, some 100,000 Americans paid over $70 million for lightbulbs sold under the Torch brand. The sales were made over the phone with the salesperson claiming to be handicapped and often tearfully pleading for a sale. The bulbs were overpriced by 300 percent and were substandard in quality. Moreover, an investigation by New Jersey revealed that some of the salespersons' doctor-certified disabilities included acne, excess weight, nervousness, hernia, hay fever, and dislocated shoulder.[77]

Item: Many fraudulent schemes are based on the classic perfected by Bostonian Charles Ponzi in the 1920s; the pyramid system whereby early investors are paid off handsomely with proceeds from sales of later participants. The result is often a rush of new investors greedy for easy profits. An example of the Ponzi scam was the Home-Stake swindle perpetrated by Robert Trippet, which consisted of selling participation rights in the drilling of sometimes-hypothetical oil wells. The beauty of this plan was that, since oil exploration was involved, it provided a tax shelter for the investors. Thus, the plan especially appealed to the wealthy. As a result, many important persons were swindled of a good deal of money, including the chairman of Citibank, the head of United States Trust, the former chair of Morgan Guarantee Trust, the former chair of General Electric, and entertainers such as Jack Benny, Candice Bergen, Faye Dunaway, Bob Dylan, and Liza Minnelli. John Kenneth Galbraith, the noted economist, in reviewing a book about the Home-Stake swindle, said that it should have been titled *How the Rich Swindled Each Other and Themselves.*[78]

Item: The Equity Funding Corporation of America began in 1960 as a legitimate insurance business with $10,000.[79] In the midsixties, it became the fastest-growing life insurance company in the United States. From 1967 to 1972, sales increased from $54 million to $1.32 billion, and insurance in force from $109 million to $6.5 billion. The stock in the company went public in 1964 at $6 a share and during the company's phenomenal growth period sold for as high as $80. In April 1973, this growth was found to be the result of fraud. The corporation filed for bankruptcy and the stock was declared of no value. At a representative price of $40 a share, shareholders lost $300 million. Since 1967, it had *never* made any money. All earnings reported during those years had been false. What appeared to be growth was the result of issuing 64,000 phony policies with a face value of $2 billion. These bogus policies were then sold to other insurance companies for cash. In addition, Equity Funding routinely faked assets and earnings in its annual reports, sold counterfeit bonds, and forged death certificates. The result was that policy holders, stockholders, and other insurance firms lost between $2 and $3 billion. Other money was also indirectly lost because of the resulting scandal. For example, in the week that the *Wall Street Journal* published the story of the scandal, the value of all shares on the New York Stock Exchange dropped by $15 billion.

CONCLUSION

Two issues that have historically concerned Americans are street crimes and inflation. Our discussion in this chapter should provide new insight into both of these problems.

Street crimes, for example, are miniscule in their economic costs when compared to the costs of illegal activities by corporations. To cite just one example, the $2 to $3 billion lost in the Equity Funding fraud involved more money "than the total losses of *all* street crimes in the United States for one year."[80]

The primary sources of inflation, many argue, are huge governmental expenditures. Of course, these do impact the inflationary spiral, but the blame lies elsewhere, as well. Ignored by most critics are the sources of inflation found in our corporate economy. In 1982, U.S. consumers spent $1.08 trillion on retail items. Much of that money purchased nothing of value. We have seen that the existence of shared monopolies increases prices by 25 percent. We have seen that consumers pay all the costs of advertising, which amounted to $66.5 billion in 1982.[81] We have seen that consumers pay inflated prices brought about by price fixing and other collusive arrangements by so-called competitors. Finally, we have seen that consumers spend billions on products sold under false pretenses, products that do not perform as claimed, products identical to cheaper ones but unavailable or unknown, and the like.

The point is quite clear: These extra costs to consumers do not bring anything of value back to them. What could be more inflationary than that? Put another way, the corporate economy diverts scarce resources to uses that have little human benefit.

To conclude, Edwin Sutherland, the sociologist who first examined white-collar crime extensively, made several observations relevant to the understanding of such corporate deviant behavior as price fixing, misleading advertising, and fraud.[82]

1. The criminality of corporations tends to be persistent. Recidivism (repeat offenses) is the norm.

2. The level of illegal behavior is much more extensive than the prosecutions and complaints indicate.

3. Businesspeople who violate the laws designed to regulate business do not typically lose status among their associates. In other words, the business code does not coincide with the legal code. Thus, even when they violate the law, they do not perceive of themselves as being criminals.

NOTES

1. Stanton Wheeler, "Trends and Problems in the Sociological Study of Crime," *Social Problems* 23 (June 1976), 525. This criticism has been made by others, as well. See especially Alexander Liazos, "The Poverty of the Sociology of Deviance: Nuts, Sluts, and Preverts," *Social*

Problems 20 (Summer 1972), 103–20.

2. Marshall B. Clinard, *Illegal Corporate Behavior* (Washington, D.C.: U.S. Department of Justice, Law Enforcement Assistance Administration, 1979).   See also Marshall B. Clinard and Peter C. Yeager, "Corporate Crime: Issues in Research," *Criminology* 16 (August 1978), 255–72.

3. Karl Marx, *Capital: A Critique of Political Economy* (New York: International Publishers, 1967). Originally published in 1866.

4. Mark J. Green, Beverly C. Moore, Jr., and Bruce Wasserstein, *The Closed Enterprise System* (New York: Bantam Books, 1972), 7. Copyright © 1972 by The Center for Study of Responsive Law. Reprinted by permission of Viking Penguin Inc.

5. "Trend Toward Bigness in Business Speeds Up," *U.S. News and World Report*, 24 August 1981, 69–70. See also Daniel Zwerdling, "The Food Monopolies," *The Progressive* 39 (January 1975), 15; and Louis M. Kohlmeier, "Snap, Crackle and Divestiture," *New York Times*, 25 April 1976, Section 3, pp. 1, 9.

6. From a statement by the chairperson of the Federal Trade Commission, quoted in TRB, "Bartered Brides," *New Republic*, 17 March 1979, 3.

7. "The Forbes 500s," *Forbes*, 10 May 1981, 222–38.

8. Clemons P. Work, "The Tide of Mergers Picks Up Speed," *U.S. News and World Report*, 19 December 1983, 72; and Clemons P. Work, "Washington Wrestles to Set a Policy on Business Mergers," *U.S. News and World Report*, 26 March 1984, 77.

9. Quoted in Green, Moore, and Wasserstein, 13–14.

10. This section on the consequences of shared monopolies is taken primarily from Green, Moore, and Wasserstein, 14–26; and Jack Newfield and Jeff Greenfield, *A Populist Manifesto* (New York: Warner Paperback Library, 1972), 48–56.

11. Green, Moore, and Wasserstein, 14.

12. Richard B. DuBoff, "Wealth Distribution Study Causes Tinge of Discomfort," *In These Times*, 5–11 December 1984, 17.

13. Newfield and Greenfield, 51.

14. William Conner and Robert Smiley, quoted in Ralph Nader, Mark Green, and Joel Seligman, *Taming the Giant Corporation* (New York: W. W. Norton, 1976), 216.

15. Green, Moore, and Wasserstein, 15. See also "The Monopoly Inflation Game," *Dollars and Sense*, no. 23, January 1977, 12–13.

16. Nader, Green, and Seligman, 213.

17. For comparison, see Michael Parenti, *Power and the Powerless* (New York: St. Martin's Press, 1978).

18. Mark J. Green, "The High Cost of Monopoly," *The Progressive* 36 (March 1972), 4.

19. "The Forbes Sales 500," *Forbes*, 30 April 1984, 170–94.

20. Robert F. Lanzillotti, "The Automobile Industry," in *The Structure of American Industry*, 4th ed., ed. Walter Adams (New York: Macmillan, 1971), 256.

21. "GM's Juggernaut," *Business Week*, 26 March 1979, 62–77; and Tom Nicholson and James C. Jones, "GM: Survival of the Fittest," *Newsweek*, 25 June 1984, 52–53.

22. Reginald Stuart, "U.S. Alters Mileage Rules, Aiding Ford and GM," *New York Times*, 27 June 1985, pp. A-1, A-18.

23. "The Forbes Assets and Earnings 500," *Forbes*, 30 April 1984, 170-94.

24. Green, Moore, and Wasserstein, 244.

25. David Hapgood, *The Screwing of the Average Man: How the Rich Get Richer and You Get Poorer* (New York: Bantam, 1975), 152.

26. "The Monopoly Inflation Game," 12.

27. Lanzillotti, 282.

28. Green, Moore, and Wasserstein, 246.

29. The following is taken primarily from Harvey A. Farberman, "A Criminogenic Market Structure: The Automobile Industry," *The Sociological Quarterly* 16 (Autumn 1975), 438-57. See also W. N. Leonard and N. G. Weber, "Automakers and Dealers: A Study of Criminogenic Market Forces," *Law and Society* 4 (February 1970), 407-24.

30. For comparison, see Hapgood, 164-67.

31. For comparison, see Gerald F. Seib, "Dallas Ordinance against Car Repair Frauds," in *Crime at the Top: Deviance in Business and the Professions*, ed. John M. Johnson and Jack D. Douglas (Philadelphia: J. B. Lippincott, 1978), 319-22.

32. For a description of these techniques, see Roger Rapoport, "How I Made $193.85 Selling Cars," in *The Marketplace: Consumerism in America*, ed. by the editors of *Ramparts* with Frank Browning (San Francisco: Canfield, 1972), 39-47.

33. Orr Kelly and Ted Gest, "Reagan Revolution Takes Firm Hold at Justice," *U.S. News and World Report*, 26 April 1982, 25.

34. George A. Hay and Daniel Kelley, "An Empirical Survey of Price Fixing Conspiracies," *The Journal of Law and Economics* 17 (April 1974), 13-38.

35. *USA Today*, 26 April 1983, p. A-3.

36. Selwyn Raab, "Monopoly is Seen in Concrete Sales," *New York Times*, 14 June 1984, p. A-1. For a similar case involving an alleged national conspiracy to fix cement prices, see Chris Wells, "Cement Case: Inside Look at Business," *Los Angeles Times*, 5 August 1984, part V, p. 1.

37. *Wall Street Journal*, 17 December 1984, p. 1.

38. Hay and Kelley, 26-27.

39. The following account is taken primarily from three sources: Gilbert Geis, "White Collar Crime: The Heavy Electrical Equipment Cases of 1961," in *Corporate and Governmental Deviance*, ed. M. David Erman and Richard J. Lundman (New York: Oxford University Press, 1978), 59-79; Richard Austin Smith, "The Incredible Electrical Conspiracy," *Fortune*, Part I--April 1961, 132-37, 170-80; Part II--May 1961, 161-64, 210-24; and Green, Moore, and Wasserstein, 154-57.

40. Green, Moore, and Wasserstein, 155.

41. Smith, Part I, 137.

42. For comparison, see *Wall Street Journal*, 27 July 1964, p. 22. For the account of more recent cases of corporations and their executives receiving little if any punishment for their crimes, see Robert Stuart Nathan, "Coddled Criminals," *Harper's*, January 1980, 30-35; and "Crime in the Suites: On the Rise," *Newsweek*, 3 December 1979, 114-21.

43. Green, Moore, and Wasserstein, 152; and *New Republic*, 20 February 1961, 7.

44. Quoted in Smith, Part I, 133.

45. Smith, Part I, 135.

46. Ralph Nader and Mark Green, "Crime in the Suites," *New*

Republic, 29 April 1972, 20-21.

47. For a late-1970s example of a price-fixing violation in the forest-products industry, see Jean A. Briggs, "For Whom Does the Bell Toll?" *Forbes,* 25 June 1979, 33-36.

48. For comparison, see Jennifer Cross, *The Supermarket Trap,* rev. ed. (Bloomington: Indiana University Press, 1976), 119, 124; and Eric Schnapper, "Consumer Legislation and the Poor," in *Consumerism,* 2nd ed., ed. David A. Aaker and George S. Day (New York: The Free Press, 1974), 87.

49. Paul Jacobs, "Keeping the Poor Poor," in *Crisis in American Institutions,* 4th ed., ed. Jerome H. Skolnick and Elliott Currie (Boston: Little, Brown, 1979), 96.

50. Cross, 122.

51. The first three items are taken from three sources: "The Drugmakers Rx for Living with Generics," *Business Week,* 6 November 1978, 205; "20/20," ABC Newsmagazine, 30 November 1978. The last item is from "Prescription for Cheap Drugs," *Time,* 17 September 1984, 64-65.

52. "Generics Pose No Threat to Big Drug Firms," *Chemical and Engineering News,* 11 November 1974, 71.

53. "20/20."

54. "20/20," 19-20.

55. "20/20," 21.

56. "20/20," 21-23.

57. Jack Anderson, "Secret Documents that Unveil the Drug Industry's Deception," *Rocky Mountain News,* 28 September 1978, 65.

58. Harold Freeman, "On Consuming the Surplus," *The Progressive* 41 (February 1977), 20-21.

59. For an elaboration of the role of television in the manipulation of people, see Rose K. Goldsen, *The Show and Tell Machine: How Television Works and Works You Over* (New York: The Dial Press, 1975).

60. John Philip Cohane, "The American Predicament: Truth No Longer Counts," in *Criminology: Crime and Criminality,* 2nd ed., by Martin R. Haskell and Lewis Yablonsky (Chicago: Rand McNally, 1978), 172 (originally appeared in *Los Angeles Times,* 1 October 1972).

61. Associated Press release, 17 September 1978.

62. Associated Press release, 15 December 1978.

63. Ivan L. Preston, *The Great American Blow-Up: Puffery in Advertising and Selling* (Madison: University of Wisconsin Press, 1975), 220, 229-31.

64. Preston, 235.

65. Hugh D. Barlow, *Introduction to Criminology* (Boston: Little, Brown, 1978), 252-53.

66. Burt Hubbard, "U.S. Survey Finds 10% of Ads for City Real Estate Misleading," *Rocky Mountain News,* 17 February 1984, p. 78.

67. Preston, 18-20.

68. Preston, 32-33.

69. Edwin H. Sutherland and Donald R. Cressey, *Criminology,* 9th ed. (Philadelphia: Lippincott, 1974), 42.

70. Michael Doan, "Travelors' Advisory: Auto Ripoffs Ahead," *U.S. News and World Report,* 8 June 1984, 48.

71. Robert Pear, "Health Frauds Cost Elderly $10 Billion Annually," *Denver Post,* 1 June 1984, p. 22-A. See also Marilyn Zeitlin,

"High Pitch, High Volume: Millions Fall Prey to Hearing-Aid Hustlers," *The Progressive* 47 (May 1983), 38-39.

72. Jane Hulse, "Pacemaker Sales Abuse Revealed," *Rocky Mountain News*, 17 October 1982, pp. 8, 13.

73. Marlys Harris, "America's Capital of Fraud," *Money*, November 1983, 225-35. See also Susan P. Shapiro, *Wayward Capitalists* (New Haven, CN: Yale University Press, 1984).

74. Charles P. Alexander, "Reach Out and Bilk Someone," *Time*, 24 October 1983, 75.

75. Quoted in Robert P. Snow, "The Golden Fleece: Arizona Land Fraud," in *Crime at the Top: Deviance in Business and the Professions*, ed. John M. Johnson and Jack D. Douglas (Philadelphia: J. B. Lippincott, 1978), 138.

76. Reported in Haskell and Yablonsky, 111-12.

77. Robert J. Flaherty and Tedd A. Cohen, "Rascality Springs Eternal," *Forbes*, 20 April 1979, 87-88.

78. John Kenneth Galbraith, "Crime and No Punishment," *Esquire*, December 1977, 102-6. See also David McClintick, "The Biggest Ponzi Scheme: A Reporter's Journal," in *Swindled*, ed. Donald Moffett, 90-126 (New York: Dow-Jones Books, 1976).

79. This example is based on Raymond L. Dirks and Leonard Gross, *The Great Wall Street Scandal* (New York: McGraw-Hill, 1974); and William E. Blundell, "Equity Funding: I Did It for the Jollies," in *Swindled*, ed. Donald Moffett, 42-89 (New York: Dow-Jones Books, 1976).

80. Johnson and Douglas, 151.

81. Bureau of the Census, *Statistical Abstract of the United States, 1984* (Washington, D.C.: U.S. Government Printing Office, 1983), xxvi, 567.

82. The following is taken from Edwin H. Sutherland, *White-Collar Crime* (New York: Holt, Rinehart, and Winston, 1961), 217-33.

CHAPTER 4

Corporate Deviance: Human Jeopardy

The topic of this chapter is the corporate disregard for the welfare of people, involving the abuse of consumers, workers, and society itself. Our thesis is that the profit-maximizing behaviors practiced by corporations under monopoly capitalism are hazardous to our individual and collective health, and therefore constitute another manifestation of elite deviance.

The first part of this chapter examines three manifestations of corporate deviance that jeopardize individual health—dangerous products, food pollution, and hazardous working conditions. The second part focuses on the problems society faces from various corporate activities—the waste of natural resources and ecological contamination.

INDIVIDUAL JEOPARDY

Unsafe Products

Commonly, the concern over violence in society is directed toward murder, rape, child abuse, and riots. We do not include in the context of violence the harm inflicted on people by unsafe products. The National Commission on Product Safety has revealed that twenty million Americans are injured in the home as a result of incidents connected with consumer products. "Of the total, 110,000 are permanently disabled and 30,000 are killed. A significant number could have been spared if more attention had been paid to hazard reduction."[1] The Commission also made two additional points:

> Manufacturers have it in their power to design, build, and market products in ways that will reduce if not eliminate most unreasonable and unnecessary hazards. Manufacturers are best able to take the longest strides to safety in the least time. . . . [However] competitive forces may require management to subor-

dinate safety factors to cost considerations, styling, and other marketing imperatives.[2]

Considerable evidence points to unsafe products from clothing to toys to tires, but nowhere has the poor corporate safety record been more visible than in the automobile industry. The indictment against this industry involves two basic charges: (1) faulty design and (2) working against governmental and consumer efforts to add safety devices as basic equipment.

Production of dangerously defective vehicles. In 1929, the president of DuPont tried to induce the president of General Motors to use safety glass in Chevrolets, as Ford was already doing. The president of GM felt that this addition was too costly and would therefore hinder sales. In his reply to DuPont, he said:

> I would very much rather spend the same amount of money in improving our car in other ways because I think, from the standpoint of selfish business, it would be a very much better investment. You can say, perhaps, that I am selfish, but business is selfish. We are not a charitable institution—we are trying to make a profit for our stockholders.[3]

This example shows how the profit motive superseded the possibility of preventing deaths and serious injuries. Nor is this an isolated instance in the auto industry. We will review two representative cases, one involving GM and the other, Ford.

Ralph Nader attacked GM's Corvair in *Unsafe at Any Speed* (1972), showing how that car had many dangerous defects, including a heater that gave off carbon monoxide and an instability that increased its likelihood of overturning.[4] GM's response to this indictment was to attack Nader's credibility and hide evidence supporting Nader's allegations.[5]

Throughout much of the 1970s, the fastest-selling domestic subcompact was Ford's Pinto. From the very beginning, however, the Pinto was flawed by a fuel system that ruptured easily in a rear-end collision.[6] Preproduction crash tests established this problem, but since the assembly-line machinery was already tooled, Ford decided to manufacture the car as it was—despite the fact that Ford could produce a much safer gas tank. This decision was made partly because the Pinto was on a tight production schedule; Ford was trying to enter the lucrative subcompact market dominated by Volkswagen as quickly as possible. The time span from the conception of the Pinto to production was targeted at twenty-five months, when the normal time for a new car was forty-three months. Also involved in the decision to go with the original gas tank were styling considerations and the effort to maximize trunk space.

The profits-over-human considerations is clearly evident in Ford's reluctance to change the design of the Pinto as fatalities and injuries occurred because of the faulty gas tank. Although the company calculated that only $11 would make each car safe, it decided that this was too costly. Ford reasoned that 180 burn deaths and 180 serious burn injuries and 2,100 burned vehicles would cost $49.5 million (each death was figured at $200,000). But a recall of all Pintos and the $11 repair would amount to $137 million (see Table 4-1). In addition to the decision to leave the Pinto alone, Ford lobbied in Washington to convince government regulatory agencies and Congress that

> [a]uto accidents are caused not by *cars*, but by (1) people and (2) highway conditions. This philosophy is rather like blaming a robbery on the victim. Well, what did you expect? You were carrying money, weren't you? It is an extraordinary experience to hear automotive "safety engineers" talk for hours without ever mentioning cars. They will advocate spending billions educating youngsters, punishing drunks, and redesigning street signs. Listening to them, you can momentarily begin to think that it is easier to control 100 million drivers than a handful of manufacturers. They show movies about guardrail design and advocate the clear-cutting of trees 100 feet back from every highway in the nation. If a car is unsafe, they argue, it is because its owner doesn't properly drive it. Or, perhaps, maintain it.[7]

Meanwhile, fiery crashes involving Pintos occurred with some regularity. Liability suits against Ford increased, with judgments routinely found against Ford. In 1978, a jury in California awarded $127.8 million—including $125 million in punitive damages—to a teenager badly burned when his 1972 Pinto burst into flames after being hit in the rear by a car traveling thirty-five miles per hour. At that time, up to fifty Pinto-related civil suits were pending in various courts.[8]

In that same year, ten years after the government had begun investigating the Pinto problem, the Department of Transportation finally announced that its tests showed conclusively that the Pinto was unsafe and ordered a recall of all 1971 to 1976 Pintos. One critic of Ford's outright defiance of human considerations made this telling observation: "One wonders how long Ford Motor Company would continue to market lethal cars were Henry Ford II and Lee Iacocca [the top Ford officials] serving twenty-year terms in Leavenworth for consumer homicide."[9]

In a similar but less celebrated case, General Motors executives were repeatedly warned by test drivers and internal company documents of serious braking problems in 1980 X-body automobiles before production. The Justice Department charged that GM failed to act on the braking problem and later withheld information from federal officials regarding these cars (the 1980 Chevrolet Citation, Pontiac Phoenix, Oldsmobile Omega, and Buick Skylark). By August 1983, the government had received more than 1,700 complaints about brakes locking in the X-body cars, including accidents involving fifteen deaths when the cars went into dangerous spins.[10]

Resistance to consumer and governmental pressures to provide safety devices. The automobile industry has traditionally resisted new safety devices because the added cost might hurt sales.[11] Following tests conducted by the government and the insurance industry in the late 1950s, the government ruled that lap belts must be installed in all new cars built after January 1, 1965. The auto industry resisted (as it has since resisted other requirements such as lap-and-shoulder belts, ignition interlocks, and buzzers), despite clear evidence that these devices would be effective in saving lives: "Between 1968 and 1977, the stock of cars on the road grew

Table 4-1
$11 vs. a Burn Death: Benefits and Costs Relating to Fuel Leakage Associated with the Static Rollover Test Portion of FMVSS 208

Benefits

Savings: 180 burn deaths, 180 serious burn injuries, 2,100 burned vehicles
Unit Cost: $200,000 per death, $67,000 per injury, $700 per vehicle
Total Benefit: 180 x ($200,000) + 180 x ($67,000) + 2,100 x ($700) = $49.5 million

Costs

Sales: 11 million cars, 1.5 million light trucks
Unit Cost: $11 per car, $11 per truck
Total Cost: 11,000,000 x ($11) + 1,500,000 x ($11) = $137 million

Source: Ford Motor Company internal memorandum, "Fatalities Associated with Crash-Induced Fuel Leakage and Fires," cited in Mark Dowie, "Pinto Madness," *Mother Jones* 2 (September/October 1977), 24. © *Mother Jones.* Used with permission.

from 83 million to 112 million, an increase of 35 percent. Over the same period, traffic fatalities declined 6 percent."[12]
    Since lap belts are effective only when used, and relatively few are used, the government reasoned that safety could be improved significantly if a passive restraint such as the air bag was included as standard equipment. A study by Allstate Insurance concluded that air bags would reduce occupant crash deaths by 65 percent. Had all cars been so equipped in 1975, 9,500 fewer persons would have died in car crashes in that year instead of the 27,200 who did. Additionally, 104,000 serious injuries could be prevented each year.[13] The increased safety argument led the National Highway Traffic Safety Administration to recommend that air bags be required on all cars manufactured after April 1973. The argument that air bags save lives was not as compelling to the automobile industry, however. The expense of tooling up for such a life-saving system was considered too high. They countered with strategies such as advertising in the major newspapers and high-level lobbying in Washington. As a result, the date requiring air bags was moved back two years to August 1975. Because of further pressure from the automobile industry, the Department of Transportation continued to move the date back. By 1985, the issue was yet unresolved. The Reagan administration has decided to study the consequences of installing air bags before making any definitive decision.

Dangerous Nutrition

    The food industry is obviously big business, earning $150 billion in sales in 1982. In this section, we will examine how the food industry, in its search for more profits, often disregards the health of consumers, which constitutes deviance. We will explore four areas in which human considerations are often secondary to profit: (1) the sale of adulterated products; (2) the extensive use of chemical additives; (3) the increased use of sugar and fats; and (4) the sale of products known to be harmful.

Adulterated products. We will use the meat industry as our illustration of blatant disregard for the health of consumers. Upton Sinclair's exposé of the Chicago stockyards and meat-packing houses around 1900 showed how spoiled meat was sold, how dangerous ingredients were used in sausage (such as rats and dung), and how rats overran piles of meat stored under leaking roofs.[14] President Theodore Roosevelt commissioned an investigation of Chicago meat packers and, as a result, the Meat Inspection Act of 1906 required that meat sold in interstate commerce had to be inspected according to federal standards. However, meat processed and sold within a state was not subject to the law, omitting as late as 1967 nearly 15 percent of the meat slaughtered and 25 percent of all the meat processed in the United States. As a result:

> Surveys of packing houses in Delaware, Virginia, and North Carolina found the following tidbits in the meat: animal hair, sawdust, flies, abscessed pork livers, and snuff spit out by the meat workers. To add even further flavoring, packing houses whose meat did not cross state lines could use 4-D meat (dead, dying, diseased, and disabled) and chemical additives that would not pass federal inspection. Such plants were not all minor operations; some were run by the giants--Armour, Swift, and Wilson.[15]

In 1967, the Wholesome Meat Act was passed, specifying that state inspection standards must at least match federal standards. This was accomplished in 1971, but there have been continuing violations. One problem is "Number 2" meat--meat returned by a retailer to a packer as unsatisfactory and then resold as Number 2 meat to another customer if it meets standards of wholesomeness. As an example of how this can be abused, consider the following occurrence in a Los Angeles Hormel plant:

> When the original customers returned the meat to Hormel, they used the following terms to describe it: "moldy liverloaf, sour party hams, leaking bologna, discolored bacon, off-condition hams, and slick and slimy spareribs." Hormel renewed these products with cosmetic measures (reconditioning, trimming, and washing). Spareribs returned for sliminess, discoloration, and stickiness were rejuvenated through curing and smoking, renamed Windsor Loins, and sold in ghetto stores for more than fresh pork chops.[16]

This Hormel abuse occurred because the U.S. Department of Agriculture inspector, who was paid $6,000 annually by Hormel for overtime, looked the other way.[17]

Meat packers are also deceptive about what is included in their products. The labels on the package are not always complete. Consider, for instance, the ingredients of the hot dog:

The hot dog . . . by law can contain 69 percent water, salt, spices, corn syrup and cereal, and 15 percent chicken; that still leaves a little room for goat meat, pigs' ears, eyes, stomachs, snouts, udders, bladders and esophagus--all legally okay. There is no more all-American way to take a break at the old ball game than to have water and pigs' snouts on bun, but you might prefer to go heavier on the mustard from now on.[18]

Upton Sinclair's lurid description of the 1900s-era Chicago slaughterhouses fits some situations even today.   In 1984, Nebraska Beef Processors and its Colorado subsidiary, Cattle King Packing company--the largest supplier of ground meat to school lunch programs and also a major supplier of meat to the Defense Department, supermarkets, and fast-food chains--was found guilty of: (1) regularly bringing dead animals into its slaughterhouses and mixing rotten meat into its hamburgers; (2) labeling old meat with phony dates; and (3) deceiving U.S. Department of Agriculture inspectors by matching diseased carcasses with the healthy heads from larger cows.[19]

The Nebraska Beef-Cattle King scandal is not an isolated case. Two additional examples make this point. In 1979, a New Jersey firm was convicted of making pork sausage with an unauthorized chemical that masks discoloration of spoiled meat.   And in 1982, a California company used walkie-talkies to avoid inspectors while doctoring rotten sausage.[20]

Extensive use of additives in food. The profits from the food industry come mainly from processing farm goods through fortifying, enriching, and reformulation to produce goods that look appealing, have the right taste and aroma, and will not spoil.   More than 1,500 food additives have approved use as flavors, colors, thickeners, preservatives, and other agents for controlling the properties of food. Let's briefly look at some of these additives.[21]

Sodium nitrates and nitrates are chemicals added to keep meat products appearing blood red. Nitrates are also used to preserve smoked fish.

A variety of preservatives are used to prevent the spoilage of bread, cereals, margarine, fish, confections, jellies, and soft drinks.   The most commonly used are BHT, BHA, sodium benzoate, and benzoic acid.

About 95 percent of the color in the food we eat is the result of synthetic colors added. Red dye No. 2 was prohibited by the government when it was found to cause cancer in mice, although it is still allowed in maraschino cherries because it is assumed that no one will eat more than one or two at a time.

Flour, that all-purpose staple, is bleached and conditioned by a number of potent poisons--hydrogen acetone, benzyl peroxide, chlorine dioxide, nitrogen oxide, and nitrosyl chloride.   Also added to flour are such strengtheners as potassium bromate and ammonium presulfate.

An indirect additive that affects the health of consumers is one that is fed to animals. Diethylstilbestrol (DES), an artificial female sex hormone, fattens about 75 percent of the beef cattle in the United States. This hormone is added because it causes dramatic weight gain on less feed. It has been outlawed for use with poultry, although hens are fed arsenic because it makes them lay more eggs.

Sugar substitutes are another type of food additive that has questionable health consequences. Cyclamates was banned in 1970 after tests linked it to various types of cancer. And saccharin, another additive, has been shown to be dangerous but has not been banned; Congress has only decreed that food containing saccharin must carry warning labels. The latest sugar substitute, aspartame (or Nutrasweet), is also believed by some scientists to pose a health danger to some 50 million regular users. However, no ban or warning has been issued for products containing Nutrasweet.

There is a great deal of controversy among scientists about the results of these additives in our diet. "Altogether, laboratory tests have produced evidence that some 1,400 substances--drugs, food additives, pesticides, industrial chemicals, cosmetics--might cause cancer. But there are only a few chemicals which all the experts see as linked to human cancer."[22] Typically, government scientists disagree with the scientists hired by industry.[23] Several considerations, though, should make us cautious about what we eat.

First, many of the additives are poisons. The quantities in food are minute, but just what is the tolerance level? Is any poison, in any amount, appropriate in a food? Is there the possibility of a residue buildup in vital organs?

Second, what happens to laboratory animals fed relatively large quantities of these additives? They are poisoned; they do get cancer; and they do suffer from other maladies induced by the additives.

Finally, what happens with the interaction of these additives on humans? Scientists may be able to test the effects of a few chemicals, but what about the hundreds of thousands of possible combinations? In a slice of bread, for example, there can be as many as ninety-three possible different additives. The danger is that it takes years--maybe twenty or thirty--of a particular diet for an individual to develop cancer. Since most of the additives are of recent origin, we do not know what they may eventually cause. We do know that the average American has increased his/her yearly intake of food additives from three pounds in 1965 to about five pounds in 1977.[24] And the cancer rate continues to rise.

Why, then, do companies insist on adding these potentially harmful chemicals to our food? One possibility is that consumers demand more variety and convenience. But more important, the food industry has found that the processing of synthetic foods is very profitable. As one food marketer has remarked, "The profit margin on food additives is fantastically good, much better than the profit margins on basic, traditional foods."[25] Hightower has shown how this works:

> It gets down to this: Processing and packaging of food are becoming more important pricing factors than the food itself.
>
> Why would food corporations rather sell highly processed and packaged food than the much simpler matter of selling basics? Because processing and packaging spell profits.
>
> First, the more you do to a product, the more chances there are to build in profit margins--Heinz can sell tomatoes for a profit, or it can bottle the tomatoes for a bigger profit, or it can process the tomatoes into ketchup for still more profit, or it can add spices to the ketchup and sell it as barbeque sauce for a fat

profit, or it can add flavors and meat tenderizer to the barbeque sauce for the fattest profit of all.

Second, processing and packaging allows artificial differentiation of one company's product from that of another—in other words, selling on the basis of brand names. Potatoes can be sold in bulk, or they can be put in a sack and labeled Sun Giant, which will bring a higher price and more profit.

Third, processing and packaging allow the use of additives to keep the same item on the shelf much longer and they allow for shipment over long distances, thus expanding the geographic reach of a corporation.

Fourth, processing and packaging separate consumers from the price of raw food, allowing oligopolistic middlemen to hold up the consumer price of their products even when the farm price falls. When the spinach crop is so abundant that spinach prices tumble at the farm level, the supermarket price of Stouffer's frozen spinach souffle does not go down.[26]

What's more, American corporations, in their quest for profits, have knowingly marketed defective medical devices, lethal drugs, known carcinogens, toxic pesticides, and other harmful products overseas when they have been banned for sale in the United States. A more detailed discussion of such practices is found in Chapter 5.

Increased use of unhealthy substances in foods and efforts to convince the young to use such products. This section discusses the types of food provided by the food industry and the advertising efforts to push certain questionable items. In particular, we will address how the food industry has increased the consumption of sugar and fats.

In the previous section, we noted the problem with chemical additives. However, we did not discuss the foremost food additive—sugar. The introduction of processed foods has increased the annual amount of refined sugar consumed by the average individual from 76.4 pounds in 1909-1913 to 94.1 pounds in 1978 (even though the average household purchase of sugar itself declined in that period).[27] One of the biggest sources of sugar intake is the ingestion of soft drinks. For example, the number of gallons, per capita, consumed per year increased from 16.8 in 1962 to 39.6 in 1982.

The use of sugars presents three health dangers. First, dental disease such as cavities and gum problems are clearly exacerbated by sugar. Another problem is that refined sugar, although an energy source, offers little nutritional value. Not only does it deprive the body of essential nutrients found in complex carbohydrates, but it actually increases the body's need for certain vitamins. Finally, there appears to be a relationship between the increasingly larger proportion of refined sugar calories in the diet and the higher incidence of diabetes. In 1977, these problems, plus the problem of weight control, led the Senate Select Committee on Nutrition and Human Needs to recommend that Americans reduce their consumption of processed sugars by 45 percent to the level consumed by Americans in the early 1900s.[28]

Another trend in the U.S. diet is the increased consumption of fats. From 1900 to 1973, the average daily amount of fat consumed per person rose from 125 grams to 156 grams (the equivalent of about twenty-four pounds more per year). One source of this fat for modern Americans is the potato chip. Potato chips are 40 percent fat compared to 0.1 percent fat in baked potatoes.[29] The food processors push us to eat potato chips rather than fresh potatoes because the profit is 1,100 percent more.[30] In 1977, the Senate Select Committee on Nutrition recommended that Americans reduce their consumption of fats by 40 percent because fat consumption leads to problems of obesity, cancer (breast and colon), and heart disease.[31]

The increased consumption of additives, sugar, and fats in food by children is a special health concern. But children are an important market, and food producers have spent multimillions of dollars in advertising aimed at children. Obviously, these corporations believe that their advertising influences the interests, needs, and demands of children. This belief is backed by research findings that show that children are susceptible to this influence. One study of youngsters in grades one to five found that 75 percent had asked their mothers to purchase the cereals they had seen on television. In another study, 80 percent of the mothers of children aged two to six expressed the conviction that television ads did cause their children to ask for certain products.[32]

The nutritional problem emanating from the television advertising blitz aimed at children is that the most advertised food products are sugar-coated cereals, candies, and other sweet snack foods. One study, for example, found that 96 percent of all food advertising on Saturday and Sunday children's TV programs was for sweets.[33] This report by the Federal Trade Commission shows that these advertisements are effective, for several reasons:

> (a) children's requests for specific, brand-name cereals and snack foods are frequently, if not usually, honored by their parents; (b) very high proportions of children are able to name specific (heavily advertised) brands as their favorites; (c) when asked to list acceptable snacks, high proportions of children mention cookies, candy, cake, and ice cream, including specific (heavily advertised) products; (d) U.S. consumption of snack desserts has increased markedly since 1962, and significant proportions of the purchases are made by children.[34]

The television directed at children is effective because the advertisers have done their research. Social science techniques have been used by motivation researchers in laboratory situations to determine how children of various ages react to different visual and auditory stimuli. Children are watched through two-way mirrors, their behavior is photographed, and their autonomic responses (e.g., eye-pupil dilation) are recorded to see what sustains their interest, their subconscious involvement, and the degree of pleasure they experience.[35] Thus, advertisers have found that, if one can associate fun with a product, power, or fascinating animated character, then children will want that product.

The staff of the Federal Trade Commission has argued that all television commercials aimed at children are inherently unfair and deceptive. The young, they contend, are unable to be rational consumers. Therefore, in 1978, the Commission proposed that: (1) there be a ban on all ads for children under age eight; (2) a ban on all ads for highly sugared foods for those under eleven be enforced; and (3) there be a requirement for nutritional counter-ads to be paid for by industry. This stance has been met with derision from the advertising and corporate industries. In hearings conducted by the Commission, the advertisers and manufacturers argued against the evils of government regulation. The attorney for Mattel, a major manufacturer of children's toys, testified, "Our position, simply stated, is that the proposed ban is unconstitutional, economically injurious and unnecessary."[36] A spokesman for the National Association of Broadcasters also argued that self-regulation by the industry has worked: "Industry self-regulation has in fact been successful, and now provides the mechanisms for effective regulation of advertising to children."[37] Also at the hearings, the counsel for the Kellogg Company said that "in an American democratic capitalistic society we must all learn, top to bottom, to care for ourselves. And the last thing we need in the next twenty years is a national nanny."[38]

These arguments have been countered by others. A child psychologist agreed with the FTC ban, saying, "I'm angry. In fact, I'm mad as hell. I'm furious that the most powerful communications system and the most powerfully and persuasive educational device that has ever existed in human history is being used systematically to mislead and lie to children." Friedlander added that children under the age of six, seven, or eight "are absolutely unable to understand and defend themselves against the ulterior motives of our business system."[39]

Syndicated columnist Ellen Goodman has said:

> Personally, I can't imagine why we should allow advertisers into our homes when they behave like decadent tooth fairies offering our gullible children candy bars and Frankenberrys in return for their molars. But the thing that continues to evade my understanding is how business people have the nerve to bellow against government when they won't address their own faults and hazards. They are the ones, after all, making us choose between nutrition and regulation.[40]

Bill Moyers, after confessing a bias for the necessity of advertising in general, ended his television program with these words:

> It's astonishing to me that advertising to young children is even a matter of debate; that high-powered people with enormous skills and resources should have unbridled access to the minds of young children is no less absurd because those who profit from it consider it a sacrosanct right. If the government wanted to shower 20,000 propaganda messages a year on our children [the average number of advertisements seen annually by a child in the U.S.], we would take to the barricades and throw the scoundrels out. Yet the words of an advertising executive are treated as constitutional write when he tells the FTC: "Children, like everyone else, must learn the marketplace. Even if a child is deceived by an ad at age four, what harm is done? Even if a child perceives children in advertisements as friends and not actors, selling them something, where's the harm? . . ."

In the end, this debate is between two views of human nature. One treats young children as feeling, wondering, and wondrous beings to be handled with care because they're fragile;

the other treats them as members of a vast collective to be hustled. We shall know a great deal about our society when we know, in this battle, which view prevails.[41]

Manufacturing, advertising, and selling known harmful products. Although a number of industries have been guilty of these practices, we will consider only the tobacco industry. In 1979, fifteen years after the first Surgeon General's warning that smoking is linked to lung cancer and other ills, the Secretary of Health, Education, and Welfare issued the new Surgeon General's report on the health hazards of smoking cigarettes. The report summarized 30,000 previously published scientific studies and provided strong evidence that: (1) smoking is a leading cause of lung cancer and a major factor in heart disease, bronchitis, and emphysema; (2) the babies of mothers who smoked while pregnant were born lighter and displayed slower rates of physical and mental growth than babies born to nonsmokers; (3) two-pack-a-day smokers have a 100 percent greater risk of dying in any given year than nonsmokers; (4) smoking is especially hazardous to workers in certain occupations (asbestos, rubber, textile, uranium, and chemical industries); and (5) smoking kills 346,000 Americans and costs taxpayers $18 billion annually.[42]

No medical group or scientific group in the world has disputed the conclusion that smoking is very injurious to health, yet the tobacco industry continues to push its products (buttressed, we might add, by government subsidies). In 1982, the tobacco industry spent $800 million promoting its products,[43] much of it aimed at portraying smoking as a youthful and attractive habit. In this regard, the Federal Trade Commission has characterized cigarette advertising as follows:

> Cigarette ads associate smoking with good health, youthful vigor, social and professional success and other attractive ideas ... that are both worthy of emulation and distant from concerns relating to health. ... Thus the cigarette is portrayed as an integral part of youth, happiness, attractiveness, personal success, and an active, vigorous life style.[44]

In addition to regular advertising, the tobacco industry has countered the antismoking campaign in several ways, each of which indicates disregard for the health of consumers. First, the industry has refused to accept the evidence against smoking. They argue that the links between smoking and various diseases are merely inferences from statistics. As Bill Dwyer of the Tobacco Institute has said, "Statistics are like a bikini bathing suit: what they reveal is interesting; what they conceal is vital."[45] Representatives of the industry argue in the media and in speeches before civic groups that there is no conclusive cause-and-effect relationship between smoking and ill health. Smoking, they insist, is a matter of individual choice and not a decision to be made by government.

A second tactic used by the tobacco industry has been to shore up its power in Washington through extensive lobbying efforts and contributions to the political campaigns of key decision makers.

A more subtle strategy is the giving or withholding of advertising monies to publications depending on their editorial treatment of the tobacco issue. Accepting cigarette advertising is very lucrative. In an average year, *TV Guide* sells $20 million in cigarette advertising; *Time*,

$15 million; and *Playboy*, $12 million. A 1978 survey by the *Columbia Journalism Review* found that, in the previous seven years, not a single comprehensive article on the dangers of smoking appeared in any major national magazine accepting cigarette advertising.[46]

Another strategy used by tobacco companies to maintain or increase profits despite the obvious health dangers of their products has been to push the smokeless alternatives—chewing tobacco and snuff. The potential market for these products has been barely tapped:

> [T]he young college (or high school) athlete who would never smoke cigarettes, the white-collar office worker who is not permitted to light up on the job, the overweight ex-smoker who still craves nicotine but has been told by her doctor to give up cigarettes, the nervous air traveler stuck in the nonsmoking section of a plane. To reach that market, smokeless tobacco manufacturers have concentrated on making their product more attractive to use, primarily through developing mild-tasting, flavored and discreetly disposable varieties such as Skoal Bandits.[47]

The catch: chewing tobacco presents real health dangers.

> There's only one cloud on the smokeless horizon. The folks who are more concerned with preventing diseases of the mouth and gums than with making profits for tobacco companies are increasingly, if belatedly, starting to warn smokeless users that such products may be even more harmful than cigarettes. The 1982 Surgeon General's Report states unequivocally that "certain tobacco products, such as snuff, have the highest level of such carcinogens (i.e., nitrosamines) in any consumer product taken into the body." Several studies have shown an increased connection between the use of chewing tobacco and snuff and cancers of the mouth, pharynx, and esophagus. The most widely quoted of these is a North Carolina case-control study of white women with oral and pharyngeal cancer, reported in the *New England Journal of Medicine* in 1981. The investigators concluded that "the exceptionally high mortality from this cancer . . . is primarily related to chronic use of snuff." The data showed a 400 percent increase in mouth cancer and a fifty fold increase in cancer of the cheek and gums in users of the product as compared with nonusers.[48]

Finally, tobacco companies look to expand their market overseas, particularly in the developing countries. These countries do not harass tobacco companies by forcing them to warn users of the potential dangers. They also present a growing market. Philip Morris, for example, sells more than 175 brands in 160 countries, and its foreign sales have been growing rapidly.[49] The foreign market also provides companies with a market for the high-tar brands that are losing sales in the United States. The problem with all this, of course, is that the tobacco firms are promoting the use of a known health hazard for their own profit.

Dangerous Working Conditions

In a capitalist economy, workers represent a cost to profit-seeking corporations. The lower management can keep labor costs, the greater will be their profits. Historically, this has meant that workers labored for low wages, inferior or nonexistent fringe benefits such as health care, and in unhealthy environments. The labor movement early in this century gathered momentum because of the abuse experienced by workers.

After a long and sometimes violent struggle, unions were successful in raising wages, adding fringe benefits, and making conditions safer. But owners were slow to change and worker safety was (and continues to be) one of the most difficult issues. Many owners of mills, mines, and factories continue to consider the safety of their workers a low-priority item, presumably because of the high cost.

The mining industry provides an excellent example of this neglect. Even as late as the 1970s, coal-mining firms have refused to comply with state and federal safety regulations. ABC News found, for instance, that the mining companies, when fined for violating safety regulations, not only refused to make the mines safer but also declined to pay the fines. In 1974, there were some 91,000 unpaid fines worth some $20 million.[50] In 1981, an explosion in a Colorado mine killed fifteen workers. Since 1978, that mine had received 1,133 citations and fifty-seven orders for immediate correction of known dangers from federal inspectors, but the owners did nothing.[51] Work in the mining industry is hazardous enough, even when owners diligently comply with safety regulations. So when they do not, as is often the case, the workers are doubly jeopardized. Recent data show that the hazards for miners are increasing. "Death rates in coal mining rose to 0.07 per 200,000 employee hours in the first quarter of 1984 from 0.04 in 1983."[52]

Despite the owners' reluctance to make industry safer, there have been some improvements. The probabilities of cave-ins, fires, and other plant disasters are much less now than in the days before unionization. This does not mean, however, that occupational dangers have been significantly reduced. The dangers today are invisible contaminants such as nuclear radiation, chemical compounds, dust, and asbestos fibers in the air. The dangers from these contaminants are increasing because the production of synthetic chemicals has increased so dramatically, from 1.3 billion pounds in 1940, to 96.7 billion pounds in 1960, and to 306.6 billion pounds in 1977.[53] The magnitude of this problem is underscored by the fact that more than 20 million Americans work with one or more of the chemicals known to be neurotoxic, that is, to do damage to the human nervous system.

The extent of job-induced illnesses is impossible to ascertain exactly, primarily because some diseases require many years of exposure to produce effects in the skin, lungs, blood chemistry, nervous system, or various organs. The government estimates that about 100,000 Americans die and 390,000 are disabled annually because of occupational diseases. They also estimate that at least 20 percent of all cancer cases are linked to the workplace. And as many as 20 million Americans are exposed to chemicals at work that can make them sterile or cause miscarriages and birth defects.[54]   Table 4-2 summarizes the dangers that millions of persons face as a result of their occupations.

Consider the following examples of the specific risks of continued exposure in certain industries.

Item: Workers in the dyestuffs industry (working with aromatic hydrocarbons) have about thirty times the risk of the general population of dying from bladder cancer.[55]

Item: The wives of men who work with vinyl chloride are twice as likely as other women to have miscarriages or stillbirths.[56]

Item: In 1978, Occidental Chemical Company workers handling a pesticide DBCP were found to be sterile as a result of the exposure, substantiating a 1961 study by Dow Chemical that indicated that DBCP caused sterility in rats.[57]

Item: A 1976 government study determined that, if 129,000 workers were exposed to the current legal level of cotton-dust exposure, over a period of time, 23,497 would likely become byssinotics (victims of "brown lung").[58]

Item: Starting with 632 asbestos workers in 1943, one researcher determined each of their fates after twenty years of employment. By 1973, 444 were dead, a rate 50 percent greater than for the average white male. The rate for lung cancer was 700 percent greater than expected, and the rate for all types of cancers was four times as great.[59]

The case of Karen Silkwood is a well-known illustration of industry's disregard for the safety of its employees. Karen Silkwood, a plutonium-plant worker, charged that the Kerr-McGee plant in which she worked was unsafe and that she was contaminated by plutonium radiation exposure. After her death in a somewhat questionable car accident, Karen's family sued Kerr-McGee. During the trial, Kerr-McGee employees testified that they were provided little or no training on the health hazards involved in handling plutonium. They were never told that radiation exposure could induce cancer. Attorneys for Kerr-McGee argued in court, however, that there had been no documented case of plutonium cancer in humans. This was countered by the testimony of Dr. John Gofman, one of the first physicists to isolate plutonium, who said that Ms. Silkwood had an instant "guarantee of cancer based on her exposure."[60]

Industry has historically ignored data or stalled through court actions rather than make their plants safer. Two examples forcefully make this point.

In 1970, an Italian toxicologist reported that long-term intermittent exposure of rats to vinyl chloride in air resulted in the production of several types of cancer.[61]   This was the first test on the possible carcinogenicity in the plastics industry. In 1972, these earlier findings were confirmed by a major study supported by British, Belgian, and French firms. Cancer was found at the lowest level tested, fifty parts per million. (At that time the permissible exposure level for U.S. workers was 500 ppm.) Representatives of U.S. industry were given the full details of these studies in January 1973 but entered into an agreement with the

Table 4-2
Ten Suspected Hazards in the Workplace

Potential Dangers	Diseases that May Result	Workers Exposed
Arsenic	Lung cancer, lymphoma	Smelter, chemical, oil-refinery workers; insecticide makers and sprayers--estimated 660,000 exposed
Asbestos	White-lung disease (asbestosis); cancer of lungs and lining of lungs; cancer of other organs	Miners; millers; textile, insulation, and shipyard workers--estimated 1.6 million exposed
Benzene	Leukemia; aplastic anemia	Petrochemical and oil-refinery workers; dye users; distillers; painters; shoemakers--estimated 600,000 exposed
Bischloromethylether (BCME)	Lung cancer	Industrial chemical workers
Coal dust	Black-lung disease	Coal miners--estimated 208,000 exposed
Coke-oven emissions	Cancer of lungs, kidneys	Coke-oven workers--estimated 30,000 exposed
Cotton dust	Brown-lung disease (byssinosis); chronic bronchitis; emphysema	Textile workers--estimated 600,000 exposed
Lead	Kidney disease; anemia; central-nervous-system damage; sterility; birth defects	Metal grinders; lead-smelter workers; lead storage-battery workers--estimated 835,000 exposed
Radiation	Cancer of thyroid, lungs, and bone; leukemia; reproductive effects (spontaneous abortion, genetic damage)	Medical technicians; uranium miners; nuclear-power and atomic workers
Vinyl chloride	Cancer of liver, brain	Plastic-industry workers--estimated 10,000 directly exposed

Source: Occupational Safety and Health Administration; Nuclear Regulatory Commission; U.S. Depts. of Energy, Interior, plus other sources. Reprinted from U.S. News and World Report, 5 February 1979, 42. Copyright 1979 U.S. News & World Report, Inc.

European consortium not to disclose the information without prior consent. The U.S. organization involved in this agreement, the Manufacturing Chemists Association, failed to disclose the dangers of vinyl chloride despite a request from a government agency for all available data on the toxic effects of vinyl chloride. The data were finally revealed to the government fifteen months later when three workers exposed to vinyl chloride at a B. F. Goodrich plant died of angiosarcoma of the liver.   According to a special committee report of the American Association for the Advancement of Science, the Manufacturing Chemists Association had deliberately deceived the government, and "because of the suppression of these data, tens of thousands of workers were exposed without warning, for perhaps some two years, to toxic concentrations of vinyl chloride."[62]

Unlike vinyl chloride, the health dangers of asbestos have long been known.   The link with asbestosis, a crippling lung disease, was established in 1900 and the relationship between asbestos and lung cancer was first noted in 1935.   Studies of asbestos insulation workers in subsequent years have revealed a death rate from lung cancer seven times normal and a death rate from all causes three times that of the general population.[63]

Despite these facts, asbestos workers have been consistently uninformed about the serious health hazards associated with working in that industry.   In a Johns-Manville plant, for example, company doctors diagnosed lung disease in workers yet never told them that their lung problems were related to asbestos.

Plants have also been lax about meeting government standards for exposure. The maximum exposure level set by the government was twelve fibers per cubic meter for plants that had government contracts.   An inspection of an asbestos plant in Tyler, Texas, revealed, for instance, that 117 of 138 samples in the plant exceeded the limit.   The government fined the owner of the plant, Pittsburgh Corning, a total of $210 for these violations.

When the hazards of working with asbestos became more generally known, the industry reacted by sponsoring research to disprove the dangers of asbestos.   One such industry study was faulty on at least two counts.   First, it used researchers who had long been consultants to industry and therefore might be suspect for their lack of objectivity. Second, the study examined workers who had worked a relatively short time. Since lung cancer has a latent period of twenty years or so, the use of short-term workers in the study had the effect of whitewashing the real situation.[64]

The lack of concern for the safety of workers in the plastics and asbestos industries is typical of other industries, as well. Safety regulations for cotton dust have been opposed by the textile industry. As usual, industry argued that it would cost billions to clean up the mills, jobs would be lost, and prices to consumers would rise dramatically.   Similarly, copper refiners have resisted rigorous safety regulations. For example, a study of mortality among Tacoma smelter workers found the death rate from lung cancer to be between three and four times as high as normal and ten times as high for workers exposed to the highest toxic concentrations. Moreover, a study found that children within a half mile of the smelter had absorbed as much arsenic as the workers themselves.[65] Despite these findings, the owner of the smelter in Tacoma, ASARCO, led an industrywide campaign against the government's new standards. Again, the company offered the familiar argument that the costs of compliance would be $100 million, adding fifteen cents to the now seventy-two cents needed to produce a pound of copper.

This raises the critical question: At what point are profits more important than human lives? Speaking of the cotton industry, which is representative of other major industries, one observer has argued:

> In a society in which profits did not take precedence over people ... the finer points of byssinosis [brown lung disease] would have been considered tangential long ago and the road to its prevention would now be clear: Better air filtration systems would have been installed and other capital expenditures made. But in the United States, where society is tuned to a different chord, the present delay over preventive measures, like the oblivion which preceded it, is rooted not in science and technology but in economics and politics--in the callous traditions of the cotton industry and in government's compromising ways.[66]

Finally, we should ask: What is a crime? Is it not when a victim is hurt (physically, emotionally, or financially) by the willful act of another? When 100,000 Americans die annually from occupationally related diseases, is there the possibility of crime?

Officially, these deaths and the human suffering induced by willful neglect for worker safety are not considered crimes. (See Chapter 1 for the discussion of criminal versus noncriminal deviance.)   One observer, Joel Swartz, has argued that these deaths should be considered as criminal--as murders.

> By any legitimate criteria corporate executives who willfully make a decision to expose workers to a dangerous substance which eventually causes the death of some of the workers, should be considered murderers. Yet no executive has ever served even a day in jail for such a practice, and most probably are well rewarded for having saved the company money. The regulatory apparatus that is complicit with such practices should of course be considered an accomplice.[67]

But the guilt does not stop with corporate executives, as Swartz goes on to argue:

> In the long run it is not the outright deception, dishonesty and cunning of corporate executives, doctors and bureaucrats which is responsible for the problem. Rather, the general functioning of the system is at the heart of the problem. ... The tremendous toll in occupational illnesses results from the oppression of one class by another. The people who own corporations try to exact as much wealth as they can from the workers. Improvements in working conditions to eliminate health hazards would eat into the profits that could be exacted. ... In particular the asbestos industry would rather spend millions of dollars trying to prove that asbestos is safe, than spend the money necessary to eliminate exposures. In oil refineries many of the exposures to chemicals result from inadequate maintenance of plant equipment. Maintenance costs come to 15 percent of total refinery costs, but these costs are considered controllable. In other words, skipping on maintenance is a good way to cut costs. Only the worker suffers. Another reason that the system causes occupa-

tional illnesses is the pressure it applies for expansion, especially in certain industries such as chemicals and plastics. The chemical industry, especially, is able to reap high profits by rapidly introducing new chemicals. ... Thus demands that chemicals be adequately tested before use, and the possibilities that new chemicals found to be dangerous might be banned, constitute a tremendous threat to the industry.... The ultimate reason for the problem is the drive of corporations to extract as much profit as possible from the workers. But to continue to function this system requires constant efforts by people from corporate executives to scientists to bureaucrats. These efforts result in a staggering toll in death and disease which should qualify the perpetrators as criminals by any reasonable human standards. But the system, functioning the way it is, rewards certain criminals very handsomely. The ultimate success in the battle to improve health and safety conditions will require getting rid of these criminals, and the system which enables them to operate.[68]

COLLECTIVE JEOPARDY

In the first part of this chapter, we focused on the hazards that individuals face at work or from the products they purchase. In this section, we broaden our scope somewhat. Here the victims of corporate deviance are not individuals per se but the collectivities of people who comprise individual communities, U.S. society, and even the world. Our discussion will center on two broad areas of this collective jeopardy--the waste of natural resources and ecological damages.[69]

The Waste of Resources

Since the earth's creation billions of years ago, the ecosystem has worked interdependently, relatively undisturbed by the impact of human beings. But recent developments have begun to disturb the delicate balance of nature. Explosive population growth, modern technology, and high rates of consumption have combined to pollute the environment and deplete resources. We will focus on the waste of resources.

A most pressing concern for humanity is the accelerated rate of the consumption of nonrenewable resources. Obviously metals and fuels (except for wood and sun) are finite. And the greater the number of people, the greater these resources will be consumed. If technology is added to the equation, the result is a further increase in the ratio of resource depletion.

Mineral resources have remained relatively untouched until the last 100 years or so.

Total mineral production during the last thirty years was greater than that from the beginning of the Bronze Age until World War II. The Unites States Bureau of Mines estimates that world consumption of aluminum will be twice today's level in nine years, that use of iron will double in a decade and a half, and that demand for zinc will double in 17 years.[70]

The problem is exacerbated further because these resources are not evenly distributed. The indigenous reserves of minerals and fuel of those countries that industrialized first are being exhausted. And these are the very nations in which the demand is greatest. Western Europe must now import nearly all of the copper, phosphate, tin, nickel, manganese ore, and chrome ore it uses. In 1950, the United States depended on foreign sources for 50 percent or more of four of the thirteen basic minerals; by the year 2000, it is expected to rely on imports for at least 50 percent of twelve of these thirteen minerals.

Except for coal, the major deposits of raw materials are found in the poor and developing nations of the world, yet because of high technology, most of these resources are consumed by only about one-fourth of the world's population. Because these resources are rapidly diminishing (except for coal), severe shortages and dislocations will occur. The well-endowed countries (e.g., the OPEC cartel) will raise prices and be able to trade their surpluses for other needed resources. The high-technology countries, and therefore those with the greatest appetite for natural resources, will in the short run not be hurt because they will be able to purchase the necessary resources. In the long term, however, the technological societies will suffer for at least three reasons. First, as the resources are exhausted (and not replaced by adequate synthetics or renewable fuels such as the sun, wind, and tides), these societies will be forced to reduce their productivity, resulting in economic dislocations and dissatisfactions. Second, discontentment will also be found in the resource-rich nations. Although they benefit monetarily, they doubtless will eventually feel exploited as their resources are dissipated. Quite certainly, these countries will insist on even higher prices for their resources as they near depletion, which will increase the probability of hostile acts by wealthy nations against resource-rich nations.

A third source of international unrest brought about by the disproportionate use of limited resources by the wealthy nations will be from the have-not nations. The gap between the haves and the have-nots will continue to widen as the rich get the benefit of more resources and whatever gains are accomplished by the have-nots are cancelled by the rapid population growth. The result from such a situation is the heightened likelihood of hostile outbreaks between the rich and poor nations as the latter become more and more desperate in their need for resources.

The United States is the world's largest per-capita consumer of the world's resources. One example makes the point: The United States, with only 5 percent of the world's population, consumes 30 percent of the world's energy resources. The enormous U.S. consumption of energy and raw materials is a huge drain on U.S. and world storehouses.

Why do we consume so much? Although there are many reasons, we will focus on the major one--the American economic system, a system based on profits, the quest for which is never satiated. Companies must grow. More sales mean more profits. Sales are increased through advertising, product differentiation, new products, and creative packaging. Advertising creates previously nonexistent demand for products. The introduction of new products makes the old ones obsolete. Product differentiation (many models with different features) is redundant and wasteful, but it increases sales. The automobile industry is an excellent illustration of both product differentiation and planned obsolescence. Minor styling changes for each model year, with massive accompanying advertising campaigns, have the effect of making all older cars obsolete, at least in the minds of consumers.

Writing in 1960, Vance Packard warned of the waste demanded by our economic system.[71] Progress through growth in profits is maximized by consumers who purchase products because they feel the need to replace old ones when they are used up or outmoded. This supposed need is promoted by manufacturers who produce goods that do not last long or who alter styles so that consumers actually discard useable items. These two marketing strategies--creating obsolescence through poor quality and through desirability--produce growing profits. But both strategies are fundamentally based on waste, which is a societal problem that cannot continue indefinitely.

One type of obsolescence is positive--the introduction of a new product that outperforms its predecessor. However, even this type can be orchestrated to increase waste and profit. The technology may exist for a major breakthrough, but the manufacturer or industry may choose to bring out a series of modifications that eventually lead to the state of the art. The rationale for this procedure is to saturate the potential market with the stepped-up technology and then move to the next stage of develop- ment, and so on until the major breakthrough is attained. In this way, the consumer purchases a number of products rather than immediately purchasing the ultimate. The history of high-fidelity sound equipment provides a good illustration of this marketing principle.[72]

The waste of our throw-away age is easy to see. Beverages are packaged in convenient disposable cans. Meat can be purchased in disposable aluminum frying pans, to be thrown away after one use. TV dinners are warmed and eaten in the same containers. We can purchase disposable cigarette lighters and plastic razors with built-in blades. What's more, we junk seven million cars annually, as well as ten million tons of iron and steel.[73] These are but a small sample of the products that are quickly used and destroyed.

As another example of resource waste, let's look at the cost to society of the packaging policies of a single company. Bruce Hannon, an engineer at the University of Illinois, did an environmental impact study of McDonald's, the hamburger chain, when that company was less than half its present size. Hannon found that "McDonald's packaging consti- tuted a phenomenal drain on natural resources. It took the sustained yield of 315 square miles of forest to keep McDonald's supplied with paper packaging for one year."[74]

To maximize profits, one must minimize costs. Among other things, this search for profits results in abusing the environment. Con- sider the role of the profit motive in raping the land, which is the ultimate waste of resources.

It is cheaper to extract minerals from the earth by strip mining than to remove them carefully and restore the land to its original state. Because the costs of restoration are subtracted from profits, mining companies have vigorously resisted governmental efforts to curb the environmental abuses of strip mining. The following is a description of the waste that occurs in the strip-mining process.

In the flat country of western Kentucky, where thousands of acres had already been devastated by strip mining, the coal seams lie only thirty to sixty feet beneath the surface. The overburden is scraped off and the coal is scooped out. Inevitably such topsoil as the land affords is buried under the towering heaps of subsoil. When the strippers move on, once-level meadows and cornfields have been converted to jumbled heaps of hardpan, barren clay from deep in the earth. This hellish landscape is slow to support vegetation and years elapse before the yellow waste turns green again. In the meantime, immense quantities of dirt have crept into the sluggish streams, have choked them, and brackish ponds have formed to breed millions of mosquitos.

The evil effects of open-cut mining are fantastically magnified when practiced in the mountains. Masses of shattered stone, shale, slate, and dirt are cast pellmell down the hillside. The first to go are the thin layer of fertile topsoil and such trees as still find sustenance in it. The uprooted trees are down the slopes by the first cut. Then follows the sterile subsoil, shattered stone, and slate. As the cut extends deeper into the hillside, the process is repeated again and again. Sometimes the "highwall," the perpendicular bank resulting from the cut, rises ninety feet; but a height of forty to sixty feet is more often found. In a single mile, hundreds of tons are displaced.

Each mountain is laced with coal seams. Sometimes a single ridge contains three to five veins varying in thickness from two-and-a-half to fourteen feet. Since each seam can be stripped, a sloping surface can be converted to a steplike one.

After the coal has been carried away, vast quantities of the shattered mineral are left uncovered. Many seams contain substantial quantities of sulfur, which when wet produces toxic sulphuric acid. This poison bleeds into the creeks, killing minute vegetation and destroying fish, frogs, and other stream dwellers.[75]

This devastation of the land and its inhabitants is perpetrated by the owners of coal companies for two reasons. Foremost, this type of operation is very profitable. For example, in 1962, a small crew with an auger and a fleet of trucks made a profit of $15 a minute working a four-to-six-foot-seam.[76] Second, until recently, laws have allowed companies complete authority over the land they controlled. The historical bias of the courts toward the coal companies is seen in some of their decisions.

Item: The courts ruled that the rights to mine included the authority to cut down surface trees without compensating the owners of the land.

Item: The courts ruled that the companies had the right to divert and pollute all water in or on the lands over which they had mineral rights.

Item: The courts ruled that the companies could build roads wherever they desired.

Item: When a gob dam (created by dumping refuse from mining into streams) broke during a 1945 storm, causing a flood and tremendous damage in Pike County, Kentucky, the court ruled that the Russell Fork Coal Company was innocent of wrongdoing and negligence because the rain was an act of God.[77]

Summarizing the situation, Caudill stated, "The companies, which had bought their coal rights at prices ranging from fifty cents to a few dollars an acre, were, in effect, left free to do as they saw fit, restrained only by the shallow consciences of their officials."[78]

Pollution of the Environment

The assault on the environment is the result of an ever-larger population, higher rates of consumption, and an increasing reliance on technology. These are worldwide trends. "Not only are more societies acquiring more efficient tools wherewith to exploit the earth; nearly everywhere, there are increasing numbers to do the exploiting, and befoul the air, water, and land in the process."[79] As an example, let's look at one major consequence of the increased use of technology—heat pollution.

Thermal pollution takes two basic forms: waste heat from the generation of electric power that (1) raises the temperature of the water (affecting fish and plant life in waters), and (2) increases heat in the atmosphere. Obviously, a rapidly expanding population increases the demands for more electricity and more industrial output, thereby adding to the creation of heat. Moreover, the addition of seventy or eighty million people each year (the current world rate) adds heat to the atmosphere just by the metabolism of these bodies.

The consequences of heat pollution are enormous. We know, for example, that the climate of cities differs from the surrounding countryside due to the dissipation of heat from the human activities there. Cities are warmer, cloudier, rainier, and foggier. As urban areas spread, they present great forces for climatic change.

According to one recent estimate, the Boston-Washington megalopolis in the year 2000 will contain fifty-six million people on 11,500 square miles, the dissipation of heat will be equal to 50 percent of the solar energy incident on that surface area in the winter, and 15 percent of the corresponding figure in the summer. If the present global rate of increase in energy consumption— approximately five percent per annum—should persist for another century and a half, man's dissipation then would be equal to ten percent of the solar energy absorbed over the entire surface of the globe, or one-third of the solar energy absorbed over land. Simple calculations suggest a corresponding mean global temperature increase of about 13 degrees Fahrenheit.[80]

If this scenario occurred, the thirteen-degree rise in world temperature would melt the ice at the poles, flooding much of the land surface and causing unbelievable climatological and ecological disruptions.

Another source of heat is the greenhouse effect, which is caused by the existence of more carbon dioxide than nature's mechanisms can recycle. Modern technology, through its reliance on the burning of fossil fuels, is the source of great quantities of carbon dioxide. Just like the glass roof of a greenhouse, the molecules of carbon dioxide allow sunlight to reach the earth's surface but block the escape of heat radiating off the ground. According to the theory, the earth's heat level will rise five degrees Fahrenheit over the next thirty to one hundred years because of this greenhouse effect. Obviously, the earth's climate will be changed unless the world's usage of fossil fuels (oil, oil shale, tar sands, and coal) is reduced dramatically in the near future.[81]

There is a countervailing force, however, that is believed to have a cooling effect. It, too, comes from pollution: airborne dust, which is increased in every daily activity from suburban driving to farming the soil.

Periods of global cooling have been recorded over the past two centuries after major volcanic eruptions spewed tons of dust particles into the air. Meteorologist Helmut Landsberg estimates that, along with world population, the amount of dust in the atmosphere has doubled since the 1930s, despite the absence of major volcanic eruptions. Some scientists fear that increased amounts of atmospheric dust may act as insulation, reflecting the sun's rays away from the earth and lowering temperatures.[82]

So, technology creates in its wake two forces, one which screens the sun out and the other which traps the heat in. Although both effects are negative for human life as we know it, the exact impact of these forces is not fully understood. Clearly, climate will be affected, but we are unsure of its exact nature. What is known is that when modern technology tampers with the climate, it produces negative consequences.

Heat pollution, however, is only one form of pollution. In the short term, anyway, it is the least hazardous. Pollution comes in many forms and we are all guilty. Each of us pollutes as we use fossil fuel transportation, burn wood in our fireplaces, use aerosol sprays, kill weeds with pesticides, and throw away junk. Indirectly, we pollute when we use electricity, heat our homes with natural gas, and use the thousands of products created by industry.

But what influences our consumer choices? Do we have a choice to travel by mass transit? Do we have a choice to buy products transported by truck or rail (railroads are much less polluting because they are more efficient)? Do we have a choice to use soap instead of detergents? The role of the corporations in limiting our consumer choices is an especially instructive way to understand how a laissez-faire economic system works to the ultimate detriment of people and society.

In a capitalist system, private businesses make decisions based on making profit. This places the environment in jeopardy. Best and Connolly have shown how corporate decision makers choose alternatives that have negative impacts on the ecology.[83] They describe the logic of capitalism in the following:

Under such circumstances [capitalism] it is quite irrational for any individual producer or consumer to accept the
higher costs involved in curtailing various assaults on the environment. Thus a company that purified the water used in
production before disposing it into streams would add to its own
costs, fail to benefit from the purified water flowing downstream,
and weaken its competitive market position with respect to those
companies unwilling to institute purified procedures. Since it is
reasonable to assume that other companies in a market system
will not voluntarily weaken their position in this way, it is
irrational for any single company to choose to do so. . . . Thus a
range of practices which are desirable from the vantage point of
the public are irrational from the vantage point of any particular
consumer or producer. And a range of policies which are rational
from the vantage point of individual consumers and producers are
destructive of the collective interest in preserving nonrenewable
productive resources and in maintaining the environment's capacity to assimilate wastes.[84]

Why, for example, does the United States depend on an irrational
transportation system? If mass transit for commuting replaced the
automobile in our urban centers, 50 percent of the fuel now consumed by
cars would be saved. Best and Connolly argue that the automobile
industry has intervened to suppress a viable mass transit alternative.
Three facts buttress their argument. First, in the middle twenties,
General Motors, sometimes with Standard Oil and Firestone, purchased
control of electric trolley and transit systems in forty-four urban areas.
After purchase, the electric-rail systems were dismantled and replaced by
diesel-powered bus systems, supplied by General Motors. When the
systems were subsequently sold, part of the contract stated that no new
equipment could be purchased that used a fuel other than gas. GM
favored the diesel bus because its life was 28 percent shorter than its
electric counterpart, resulting in more profit for the company. Standard
Oil and Firestone obviously benefited from such an arrangement.[85] The
result is well known: We are dependent on gasoline for transportation and
our cities are smothered in toxic emissions of carbon monoxide, lead, and
other deadly chemical combinations from internal-combustion engines.
Other examples come from the substitution of synthetic for
organic materials. Industry decided to displace soap with synthetic
detergents because the profit margin increased from 30 percent of sales
to 52 percent.[86] The decision was not made by consumers but by
management. These decisions and others (e.g., the change from wool and
cotton to synthetic fibers; plastics substituted for leather, rubber, and
wood; and synthetic fertilizers replacing organic fertilizers) have often
been incompatible with good ecology because the new chemicals are
sometimes toxic and/or nonbiodegradable.
Remember, citizens as voters and consumers were not involved in
these decisions to shift from organic to synthetic products. Rather the
decisions were made for them--and, it turns out, against their long-term
interests--by companies searching for more lucrative profits. Barry
Commoner has claimed that these new technologies have invariably been
more polluting but were introduced nontheless because they yielded higher
profits than the older, less-polluting displaced technologies. Moreover,

the costs to the consumers are borne in the increased health hazards and in the cost for cleaning up the environment.

> Environmental pollution is connected to the economics of the private enterprise system in two ways. First, pollution tends to become intensified by the displacement of older productive techniques by new ecologically faulty, but more profitable technologies. Thus, in these cases, pollution is an unintended concomitant of the natural drive of the economic system to introduce new technologies that increase productivity. Second, the costs of environmental degradation are chiefly borne not by the producer, but by society as a whole, in the form of "externalities." A business enterprise that pollutes the environment is therefore being subsidized by society; to this extent, the enterprise, though free, is not wholly private.[87]

Pollution, as we have seen, is a direct consequence of an economic system in which the profit motive supersedes the concern for the environment. This is clearly seen when corporations are unwilling to comply with government regulations and to pay damages for ecological disasters such as oil spills.

Although the government appears passive in its relationship with the business community, there is a strong bias in its action or inaction toward this group. This bias is readily seen in the government's relatively cozy relationship with the largest polluters, the corporations.[88] Ralph Nader, the consumers' advocate, has provided several illustrations of how the benefits accrue to the wealthy few, causing this upside-down effect.

Item: Who defines violence? The answer, according to Nader, is that those who define violence are those who perpetuate most of it. While the government focuses its attention on the violence that occurs from street crimes, it tends to ignore the violence that emerges from the chemical assault on the environment. Much more is lost in money and health through pollution than crimes of street violence, yet only the latter is defined officially as violence.

Item: Before the recent liberalization of marijuana laws in the 1970s, when an individual in some states could get a jail sentence exceeding ten years for smoking pot, industrialists knowingly smogging a city could be fined just a few hundred dollars for each day they continued.

Item: If you throw a banana peel out of your car window in Yosemite, you will be fined $25, yet the oil companies responsible for the 1969 oil spill in Santa Barbara paid nothing.

Item: Why is it a crime for an individual to relieve himself in Puget Sound when a corporation can do it twenty-four hours a day?

Item: Suppose you own a fifteen-room house and rent out rooms to six tenants. You employ several people, such as a cook, gardener, and janitor, and to keep costs down you throw all your garbage and trash out into the street. The city officials do not permit this wanton disregard for the welfare of the city and its citizens. You argue, however, that you must keep your costs down in order to contribute to the employment of some of the city's inhabitants. If forced to pay for garbage collection or recycling of waste materials, your profit would be reduced and you would have to close down, throwing your few employees out of work. Faced with your threat, the city says that you must desist. The problem is that your operation is not big enough. If you employed thousands of employees, then the city would very likely allow you to continue your pollution of the environment for fear of what the possibility of thousands added to the unemployment rate would do to the city, a clear case of industrial extortion.[89]

Item: In 1976, Allied Chemical Corporation pleaded no contest to 940 counts of violating federal water pollution laws by the discharge of the pesticide ingredient Kepone and other chemicals into the James River of Virginia. The corporation was fined $13.2 million. Allied gave $8 million to finance an independent environmental foundation in Virginia to show its good faith. As a result, a federal judge reduced the fine to $5 million. (Allied had asked to have the fine reduced to $1.4 million because it was "contrite and sincere.") Because Allied was allowed to have the fine reduced by the amount it voluntarily gave the foundation, it was allowed an $8-million tax write-off because it had made a contribution that would not have been possible had the money been paid as a fine.[90]

These examples illustrate that the present laws are minimal in their effect. Moreover, the efforts of the administrative agencies operating under the regulatory laws have been superficial at best. Typically, governmental intervention has had the effect of being but a symbolic slap on the wrist, and the pollution of the environment has continued virtually unabated. The government, apparently, will not or cannot push the largest and most powerful corporations to do anything that is unprofitable.

These corporations are not only the largest polluters but they have a vested interest in the status quo. General Motors and Ford, for example, resist the attempts by Congress to make cars less polluting because the necessary devices add to the cost of automobiles, which might curb sales. The government has been successful in achieving gradual change, but the power of the automobile industry has also been successful in making the government go much slower than the proenvironment lobbies would like.

The government, thus, has enacted laws to curb pollution, but they are very mild indeed. Turner has listed the defects in these conservation laws:

1. The laws are often phrased in ambiguous language, making prosecution difficult.

2. The laws typically mandate weak civil penalties and hardly every carry criminal penalties.

3. The vast majority of the laws do not attack the sources of pollutants, but rather require treatment of pollutants after they have been created.

4. Many state antipollution laws are enacted with "grandfather clauses" which allow established companies to continue

their harmful activities.[91]

The mildness of the pollution laws and their enforcement indicate the power of the powerful to continue their disregard for people and nature in their search for profits.   The government could take a much firmer stance if it chose to do so.   Suppose, for example, that the situation were reversed:

> Can you possibly reverse this situation and imagine the poor polluting the streams used by the rich, and then not only getting away with it and avoiding arrest, but also being paid by the rich through the government to clean up their own pollution?[92]

In such a case, how would the poor be treated?   The answer is obvious. The powerful would punish them severely and immediately curb their illegal behaviors.   The implication is that whoever has the power can use it to his or her own benefit, disregarding the masses and nature.

CONCLUSION

In this chapter, we have shown conclusively the fundamental flaw of capitalism.   Corporations are formed to seek and maximize profits.   All too often, the result is a blatant disregard for human and humane considerations.

It is too simplistic to say that corporations are solely responsible for these dangers to individuals and society.   In many cases, consumers insist on convenience rather than safety.   They would rather smoke or drink diet cola with saccharin than have the government demand that they quit.   Moreover, consumers typically would rather take an unknown risk than pay higher prices for products, which would pay for the cost of cleaning up the pollution.   So, too, workers would rather work in an unsafe plant than be unemployed.   But for the most part, these attitudes are shaped by corporate advertising and corporate extortion (threatened higher prices and unemployment if changes are enforced).   Also, corporations are guilty of efforts to persuade us that the dangers are nonexistent or minimal when the scientific evidence is irrefutable.   They also do everything possible to block efforts by the government and consumer groups to thwart their corporate policies.   For example, despite studies that estimate 75 to 90 percent of all cancers are environmentally related, corporations have refused to alter their behavior.   Instead, they counterattack in two characteristic ways:

> Monsanto Chemical Co. . . . has embarked on a costly advertising campaign to persuade us that chemical products are essential to our way of life.   More than 100 industrial corporations have banded together to form the American Industrial Health Council, a lobby that is spending more than $1 million a year to combat the stricter carcinogen controls proposed by the Occupational Safety and Health Administration (OSHA).[93]

The probusiness approach argues that risks are inherent in living. But the consumer is the ultimate arbiter. He or she may choose. If he or she doesn't buy dangerous or wasteful products, then industry will provide alternative products to suit the wishes of the consumer.[94] Likewise, the worker in an asbestos plant or a cotton mill can change jobs if he or she feels the current one is unsafe.

Companies continue to argue that what goes on in the market-place is not within the domain of government. We argue, to the contrary, that the government must provide a watchdog function. We also argue that individuals do not have the simple options that the corporations suggest. We buy the products that are available. Our attitudes are shaped by advertising. Employees cannot shift from one job to another in the hopes of finding safer conditions, when most of the plants in the industry for which they are trained have similar problems and when the unemployment rate is high.

The dangers pointed to in this chapter direct attention to the fundamental irrationality of our economic system. Whenever profits supersede the health of workers and consumers, when corporate decisions encourage enormous waste and pollution, then the economic system is wrong and will ultimately fail.

NOTES

1. National Commission on Product Safety, "Perspectives on Product Safety," in *Consumerism: Search for the Consumer Interest,* ed. David A. Aaker and George S. Day (New York: The Free Press, 1974), 321-22. See also Amitai Etzioni, "Mindless Capitalism, an Unyielding Elite," *Human Behavior* 4 (November 1975), 11-12; and Ralph Nader, ed., *The Consumer and Corporate Accountability* (New York: Harcourt Brace Jovanovich, 1973), 51.

2. National Commission on Product Safety, 325, 322.

3. Quoted in Morton Mintz and Jerry S. Cohen, "Crime in the Suites," in *The Consumer and Corporate Accountability,* ed. Ralph Nader (New York: Harcourt Brace Jovanovich, 1973), 79.

4. Ralph Nader, *Unsafe at Any Speed: The Designed-In Dangers of the American Automobile* (New York: Bantam, 1972).

5. Morton Mintz, "Confessions of a GM Engineer," in *The Consumer and Corporate Accountability,* ed. Ralph Nader, 301-9 (New York: Harcourt Brace Jovanovich, 1973). For a similar situation among tire manufacturers, see "Forewarnings of Fatal Flaws," *Time,* 25 June 1979, 58-61.

6. The following is taken from Mark Dowie, "Pinto Madness," in *Crisis in American Institutions,* 4th ed., Jerome Skolnick and Elliott Currie (Boston: Little, Brown), 23-40 (originally appeared in *Mother Jones* 2 [September/October 1977], 24-25).

7. Dowie, 30, © *Mother Jones,* used with permission. This is the argument made in Walter Guzzardi, Jr., "The Mindless Pursuit of Safety," *Fortune,* April 1979, 54-64.

8. Associated Press release, 14 September 1978.

9. Dowie, 39.

10. H. Joseph Hebert, "Files Show GM Knew X-Car Brakes Locked," *Denver Post*, 21 October 1983, pp. 1-A, 12-A.

11. The following is taken from Fred R. Harris, "The Politics of Corporate Power," in *Corporate Power in America*, ed. Ralph Nader and Mark J. Green (New York: Grossman, 1973), 27-29; and "Detroit Fights Airbags," *Dollars and Sense*, July/August 1978, 6-7.

12. "Detroit Fights Airbags," 6.

13. "Detroit Fights Airbags," 7.

14. Upton Sinclair, *The Jungle* (First published in 1905. Reprint, New York: New American Library, 1960).

15. Charles H. McCaghy, *Deviant Behavior: Crime, Conflict, and Interest Groups* (New York: Macmillan, 1976), 215.

16. Harrison Wellford, *Sowing and Wind: A Report from Ralph Nader's Center for Study of Responsive Law on Food Safety and the Chemical Harvest* (New York: Grossman, 1972), 69.

17. McCaghy, 216.

18. Robert Sherrill, cited in McCaghy, 216 (originally appeared in *New York Times Book Review*, 4 March 1973, p. 3). See also Gene Marine and Judith Van Allen, *Food Pollution: The Violation of Our Inner Ecology* (New York: Holt, Rinehart, and Winston, 1972), Chapter 2; and Jennifer Cross, *The Supermarket Trap: The Consumer and the Food Industry*, rev. ed. (Bloomington: Indiana University Press, 1976), Chapter 9.

19. Neal Karlen, "A 'Mystery Meat' Scandal," *Newsweek*, 24 September 1984, 29; and Mark Thomas, "Ex-Cattle King Worker Acknowledges Fraud," *Denver Post*, 31 January 1984, pp. 1, 11.

20. Norm Brewer, "Bad School Meat Spurs Crackdown in Inspecting," *USA Today*, 21 December 1983, p. 8-A.

21. The following discussion of additives is taken primarily from Daniel Zwerdling, "Food Pollution," in *The Capitalist System*, 2nd ed., ed. Richard C. Edwards, Michael Reich, and Thomas E. Weisskopf, 19-24 (Englewood Cliffs, NJ: Prentice-Hall, 1978). See also Jacqueline Verrett and Jean Carper, *Eating May Be Hazardous to Your Health* (Garden City, NY: Doubleday Anchor Books, 1975).

22. Julie Miller, "Testing for Seeds of Destruction," *The Progressive* 39 (December 1975), 37-40. See also Richard F. Spark, "Legislating against Cancer," *The New Republic*, 3 June 1978, 16-19.

23. It is even possible that financial ties to huge food corporations may shade the so-called expert testimony of nutritionsists, as argued by Benjamin Rosenthal, Michael Jacobson, and Marcy Bohm, "Professors on the Take," *The Progressive* 40 (November 1976), 42-47.

24. 1965 data are from Marine and Van Allen, 38; 1977 data are from Hugh Drummond, "Add Poison for Flavor and Freshness," Mother Jones 2 (April 1977), 13.

25. Quoted in Zwerdling, 20.

26. Jim Hightower, *Eat Your Heart Out: Food Profiteering in America* (New York: Vintage, 1975), 58-59. Copyright © 1975 by Jim Hightower. Reprinted by permission of Crown Publishers, Inc.

27. U.S. Senate, Select Committee on Nutrition and Human Needs, *Dietary Goals for the United States*, 2nd ed. (Washington, D.C.: U.S. Government Printing Office, 1977), 30; and U.S. Bureau of the Census, *Statistical Abstract of the U.S.: 1979* (Washington, D.C.: U.S. Government Printing Office, 1979), 127.

28. U.S. Senate, Select Committee on Nutrition and Human Needs, 33.

29. U.S. Senate, Select Committee on Nutrition and Human Needs, 35, 19.

30. Hightower, 631.

31. U.S. Senate, Select Committee on Nutrition and Human Needs, 35-48.

32. Marilyn Elias, "How to Win Friends and Influence Kids on Television (and Incidently Sell a Few Toys and Munchies at the Same Time)," *Human Behavior* 4 (April 1974), 20. For an extensive review of research, see National Science Foundation, *The Effects of Television* (Washington, D.C.: U.S. Government Printing Office, 1976).

33. Federal Trade Commission, *Staff Report on Television Advertising to Children* (Washington, D.C.: U.S. Government Printing Office, 1978), 57.

34. Summarized in U.S. Commission on Civil Rights, *Window Dressing on the Set: An Update* (Washington, D.C.: U.S. Government Printing Office, 1979), 49.

35. Elias, 16-23.

36. Michael Weinstock, quoted in *Broadcasting* 96 (22 January 1979), 25.

37. John Summers, quoted in *Broadcasting* 96 (26 March 1979), 84.

38. Frederick Furth, quoted in "Keep Out of the Reach of Children: Bill Moyers' Journal," 30 April 1979 (p. 3 of transcript).

39. Bernard Friedlander, quoted in *Broadcasting* 96 (2 April 1979), 64.

40. Ellen Goodman, "Why Allow Decadent Tooth Fairies to Invade Our Homes?" *Rocky Mountain News*, 5 December 1978, p. 61. For an opposite opinion, see Christopher De Muth, "Hands Off Children's TV," *Rocky Mountain News*, 15 April 1979, p. 55

41. "Bill Moyers' Journal," 11.

42. See "Slow Motion Suicide," *Newsweek*, 22 January 1979, 83-84; United Press International release, 12 January 1979; and Associated Press release, 12 January 1979.

43. U.S. Census Bureau, *Statistical Abstract of the United States 1984* (Washington, D.C.: Government Printing Office, 1983), 568-69.

44. Cited in Ruth Darmstadler, "Snuff and Chaw: The Tobacco Industry Plugs Nicotine by Osmosis," *Business and Society Review* 47 (Fall 1983), 24. Copyright © 1983, Warren Gorham & Lamont, 210 South Street, Boston, MA 02111. All rights reserved.

45. Gwenda Blair, "Why Dick Can't Stop Smoking: The Politics Behind our National Addiction," *Mother Jones* 4 (January 1979), 36.

46. Blair, 40, 42.

47. Darmstadler, 24.

48. Darmstadler, 24-25.

49. Eric Eckholm "Four Trillion Cigarettes," *The Progressive* 42 (July 1978), 26. For a discussion of the U.S. tobacco invasion in the Middle East, see "Tobacco Inroads," *Newsweek*, 2 October 1978, 106. See also Albert Huebner, "Exporting Cancer," *Rocky Mountain News*, 1 July 1979, p. 60.

50. ABC News Special, "West Virginia: Life, Liberty, and the Pursuit of Coal," 1976.

51. G. M. Seigel, "Safety Citations at Dutch Creek Called Average," *Rocky Mountain News,* 22 April 1981, p. 24.

52. Mine Safety and Health Administration data, cited in "Behind Gains In On-the-Job Health, Safety," *U.S. News and World Report,* 11 June 1984, 39.

53. "Is Your Job Dangerous to Your Health," *U.S. News and World Report,* 5 February 1979, 39.

54. Betty Holcomb, "Occupational Health: The Fetus Factor," *Ms.,* May 1983, 40-42.

55. Philip Cole and Marlene B. Goldman, "Occupation," in *Persons at High Risk of Cancer,* ed. Joseph F. Fraumeni, Jr., (New York: Academic Press, 1975), 171.

56. Dorothy McGhee, "Workplace Hazards: No Women Need Apply," *The Progressive* 41 (October 1977), 25.

57. Daniel Ben-Horin, "The Sterility Scandal," *Mother Jones* 4 (May 1979), 51-63.

58. Jeanne Schinto, "The Breathless Cotton Workers," *The Progressive* 41 (August 1977), 29.

59. Reported in Samuel S. Epstein, *The Politics of Cancer* (San Francisco: Sierra Club Books, 1978), 84-86. See also Lea Zeldin, "The Asbestos Menace," *The Progressive* 42 (October 1978), 12.

60. Reported in "Silkwood Vindicated," *Newsweek,* 28 May 1979, 40, 102-6.

61. Epstein, 100-12.

62. J. T. Edsall, "Report of the AAAS Committee on Scientific Freedom and Responsibility," *Science* 188 (1975), 687-93 (reported in Epstein, 103-4).

63. See Richard Doll, *British Journal of Industrial Medicine* 12 (1955), 81.

64. The following account is taken primarily from Joel Swartz, "Silent Killers at Work," *Crime and Social Justice* 10 (Spring/Summer 1975), 15-20.

65. Roger M. Williams, "Arsenic and Old Factories," *Saturday Review,* 20 January 1979, 26.

66. Schinto, 28. For a description of how the government has waffled in this area, see "Brown Lung Compromise," *The Progressive* 42 (August 1978), 13.

67. Swartz, 18. Reprinted by permission of *Crime and Social Justice,* P.O. Box 4373, Berkeley, CA, 94704.

68. Swartz, 19-20. Reprinted by permission of *Crime and Social Justice,* P.O. Box 4373, Berkeley, CA, 94704.

69. Portions of this section are taken from D. Stanley Eitzen, *Social Problems* (Boston: Allyn and Bacon, 1980), Chapters 3 and 11.

70. Lester R. Brown, Patricia L. McGrath, and Bruce Stokes, *Twenty-Two Dimensions of the Population Problem,* Worldwatch Paper 5 (Washington, D.C.: Worldwatch Institute, 1976), 58.

71. Vance Packard, *The Waste Makers* (New York: David McKay, 1960).

72. Packard, 55-56.

73. Paul R. Ehrlich and Anne H. Ehrlich, *Population/Resources/Environment: Issues in Human Ecology,* 2nd ed. (San Francisco: W. H. Freeman, 1972), 159.

74. Cited in Max Boas and Steve Chain, *Big Mac: The Unauthorized Story of McDonald's* (New York: New American Library, 1976), 74.

75. From Harry M. Caudill, *Night Comes to the Cumberlands* (Boston: Little, Brown, an Atlantic Monthly Press Book, 1963), 311-12; used with permission. See also Harry M. Caudill, *Theirs Be the Power: The Moguls of Eastern Kentucky* (Urbana: University of Illinois Press, 1983); and John Egerton, "Appalachia's Absentee Landlords," *The Progressive* 45 (June 1981), 42-45.

76. Caudill, *Night Comes to the Cumberlands*, 314.

77. Caudill, *Night Comes to the Cumberlands*, 306-24.

78. Caudill, *Night Comes to the Cumberlands*, 307.

79. Harold Sprout and Margaret Sprout, *The Context of Environmental Politics* (Lexington: The University Press of Kentucky, 1978), 17.

80. Paul R. Ehrlich and John P. Holdren, "The Heat Barrier," *Saturday Review*, 3 April 1971, 61. See also Lamont C. Cole, "Thermal Pollution," *Bioscience* 19 (November 1979), 989-92.

81. "Is Energy Use Overheating the World?" *U.S. News and World Report*, 25 July 1977. See also Stephen H. Schneider and Lynne E. Mesirow, *The Genesis Strategy: Climate and Global Survival* (New York: Delta, 1976); and Brown, McGrath, and Stokes, 35-37.

82. Brown, McGrath, and Stokes, 35-36.

83. The following is taken primarily from Michael H. Best and William E. Connolly, "Nature and Its Largest Parasite," in *The Capitalist System*, 2nd ed., ed. Richard C. Edwards, Michael Reich, and Thomas E. Weisskopf, 418-25 (Englewood Cliffs, NJ: Prentice-Hall, 1978), excerpted from their book *The Politicized Economy* (Lexington, MA: D. C. Heath, 1976).

84. Best and Connolly, 419.

85. Best and Connolly, 420-21.

86. Barry Commoner, "The Economic Meaning of Ecology," in *Crisis in American Institutions*, 4th ed., Jerome H. Skolnick and Elliott Currie (Boston: Little, Brown), 285, excerpted from *The Closing Circle* (New York: Alfred A. Knopf, 1971).

87. Commoner, 291.

88. See Barry Weisbert, "The Politics of Ecology," *Liberation*, January 1970, 20-25.

89. The above examples are taken from two speeches by Ralph Nader at Colorado State University, May 1970 and November 1977.

90. Associated Press release, 2 February 1977.

91. Jonathan H. Turner, *Social Problems in America* (New York: Harper and Row, 1977), 419-20.

92. James M. Henslin and Larry T. Reynolds, *Social Problems in American Society*, 2nd ed. (Boston: Holbrook, 1976), 220-21. See also Michael Parenti, *Power and the Powerless* (New York: St. Martin's Press, 1978), 19-20.

93. "The Politics of Cancer," *The Progressive* 43 (May 1979), 9.

94. See Guzzardi, 54-64; and "Diseased Regulation," *Forbes*, 19 February 1979, 34.

CHAPTER 5

National Defense, Multinational Corporations, and Human Rights

In this chapter, we will focus on the international dimensions of deviance by economic and political elites. Namely, we will examine three types of acts: (1) unethical or illegal practices relating to U.S. defense policy; (2) the conduct of multinational corporations abroad; (3) violations of human rights by nations supported by the United States.

Item: In December 1983, Republican Senator William Roth summoned the press to his congressional office to show them a Christmas tree that he had decorated with ornaments representing purchases made by the Defense Department. Among the items on the tree were a nine-cent screw for which the Pentagon paid $37, a $17 hammer for $435, a thirteen-cent nut for $2,043, a $3 washer for $387, and a two-and-one-half-cent antenna for $7,417.[1]

Item: In December 1984, a Union Carbide plant located in Central India sprang a leak and spread a cloud of deadly methyl isocyanate gas over some of the poorest slums of Bhopal. More than 2,500 people were killed and as many as 100,000 were seriously injured in what has been declared the worst industrial accident in history. When Warren Anderson, a Union Carbide board chairman, flew to Bhopal to discuss relief aid with local authorities, he was promptly arrested and required to post bail of 25,000 rupees ($2,100). Mr. Anderson was charged with "corporate and criminal liability." A number of important legal and ethical questions have been raised by the tragedy at Union Carbide's Bhopal plant. San Francisco-based attorney Melvin Belli filed a suit in U.S. District Court in Charleston, West Virginia, on behalf of the victims, asking for $5 billion in compensatory damages and $10 billion in punitive damages. There are also questions regarding Union Carbide's possible bankruptcy.

The exact cause of the Bhopal accident has not been established. Meanwhile, Union Carbide has shut down its methyl isocyanate plant in Tennessee in response to public pressure.

Item: According to Union Carbide's own inspectors, the Bhopal plant did
not meet U.S. safety standards, and it had not been inspected by
the firm's headquarters auditors since 1982, two and one-half
years before the accident.   Such troubling issues concerning
safety standards at Third World facilities of multinational corporations clearly need to be resolved.

Item: The Bhopal plant did not possess the type of computer system
found in more sophisticated plants, such as Union Carbide's West
Virginia facility, which is capable of monitoring plant functions
and quickly alerting staff to the presence of leaks.   Instead,
workers have claimed that the management relied on them to
sense escaping gas.   Namely, safety depended on the watering
eyes of plant workers to detect leaks of methyl isocyanate.   This
human detection system clearly violated specific orders issued by
the parent company in their technical operations manual.   Bhopal
plant workers have also reported that training levels and requirements for education and work experience were sharply reduced
and that the staff at the plant had been reduced from twelve to
six employees in 1983, with no corresponding increase in the use
of automated equipment.[2]

THE MILITARY-INDUSTRIAL COMPLEX

Beginning with the divisive and tragic Vietnam War (1964-1975), a
host of incidents has heightened public concern regarding the United
States' defense and foreign policies.   A few specific examples illustrate
this point:

1. Numerous government investigations, from the 1950s to now,
have revealed many unethical, wasteful, and sometimes illegal practices
involving Pentagon officials and defense contractors.

For example, in 1976, Senator William Proxmire (Dem., Wisc.)
identified fifty-nine defense officials and high-ranking military personnel
who had been entertained by defense contractors at various hunting
lodges.   It was revealed that the costs of such entertainment—several
hundred-thousand dollars—had been added to the costs of defense contracts.   One contractor, Northrop, agreed to pay back $2.3 million in fees
that were added to the contracts for entertainment and illegal campaign
contributions.

2. Certain practices of multinational corporations in their overseas business dealings have also come under scrutiny.

By 1979, over 350 major corporations had admitted making illegal
or improper payments to foreign governments totaling some $750 mil-
lion.[3] The Nader organization compiled a list of some of the largest firms
involved (Table 5-1).   The table reveals that some companies began
making payments shortly after the end of World War II.   Moreover, some
of these same companies were involved in making illegal campaign contributions in the United States, as well.

Table 5-1
Corporations Admitting Illegal or Improper Payments

Company	Date	Amount	Nature of Payments	Source
Alcoa	1972-74	$4,000,000	foreign payments from secret fund	CiB, p. 147
American Home Products	1971-75	$6,462,000	foreign political contributions	SEC
Boeing Co.	1970-75	$70,000,000	foreign commissions	CiB, p. 141
Carrier Corp.	1972-75	$2,614,000	foreign commissions	SEC
Chrysler	1971-76	$2,438,000	secret funds abroad foreign payments	6/77 8K
Cities Service	1971-75	$1,049,400	foreign payments	CEP
Dresser Industries	1971-75	$24,000	payments to foreign officials	SEC
Exxon	1963-75	$56,771,000	foreign political contributions	SEC
FMC	1973-75	$200,000	foreign payments to secure sales	CiB, p. 141
Ford Motor Co.	1973-74	$60,000	payments to foreign political parties	CiB, p. 144
General Tire & Rubber	1950s-75	$1,349,000	foreign and domestic political payments	SEC
B. F. Goodrich Co.	1971-75	$124,000	foreign commissions	SEC
Goodyear Tire & Rubber	1970-75	$846,000	payments to foreign officials	SEC
Gulf Oil Corp.	1960-73	$6,900,000	foreign political contributions	CiB, p. 158
Ingersoll-Rand	1971-75	$797,000	payments acknowledged but not described	CEP
Koppers Co.	1971-75	$1,500,000	foreign payments	CEP
Kraftco Corp.	1969-75 1972-76	$699,500 $550	foreign payments domestic campaign contributions	SEC
3M Co.	1963-72	$545,799	secret fund for domestic political campaign contribs.	SEC
	1975	$52,000	foreign payments	SEC
Reynolds Metals Co.	since 1970	N.A.	undisclosed amounts to foreign political parties	CiB, p. 147
R. J. Reynolds Ind.	1968-73	$190,000	payments to presidential and congressional candidates, disguised by diverting royalties	CiB, p. 148
	since 1968	$5,500,000	payments to foreign officials and governments, disguised on books as commissions	CiB, p. 148
	1971-75	$19,000,000	foreign rebates to shippers by SeaLand, a subsidiary	CiB, p. 148

Table 5-1 (continued)

Company	Date	Amount	Nature of Payments	Source
Rockwell Int'l	1971–75	$676,300	foreign payments to secure sales	SEC
Standard Oil Co. of Ind.	1970–75	$1,359,400	foreign payments	SEC
Tenneco Inc.	N.A.	$865,480	foreign payments	SEC
AMAX Inc.	1972–76	$64,877	foreign payments	CEP
Armco Steel Corp.	1971–75	$18,060,000	foreign payments	CEP
Atlantic Richfield	1969–76	$262,000	foreign payments	CEP
Boise Cascade	1971–76	$340,100	foreign payments	CEP
Champion International	1971–75	$537,000	foreign payments	CEP
Clark Equipment	1971–76	$95,000	foreign payments	CEP
Coca-Cola	N.A.	$300,000	foreign payments	CEP
Dart Industries	1971–76	$126,000	foreign payments	CEP
Dow Chemical	N.A.	$2,500	foreign payments	CEP
Firestone Tire & Rubber	1970–76	$97,000	foreign payments	CEP
GAF Industries	N.A.	N.A.		CEP.
General Electric	1972–75	$550,000	foreign payments	CEP
General Foods	1971–76	$162,751	foreign payments	CEP
H. J. Heinz	1971–76	N.A.	foreign payments	CEP
Hercules, Inc.	1971–75	$597,000	foreign payments	CEP
Marcor Inc. (Mobil)	1971–76	$635,517	foreign payments	CEP
Mobil Oil	1970–73	$2,000,000	foreign contributions to Italian political parties	N.A.
Monsanto	1971–76	$533,300	foreign payments	CEP
J.C. Penney	1971–75	$373,000	foreign payments	CEP
Ralston Purina	1970–76	$154,000	foreign payments	CEP
Scott Paper	1971–76	$229,000	foreign payments	CEP
Shell Oil	1969–73	$6,600,000	Royal Dutch Shell and British Petroleum to Italian political parties	N.A.
Stauffer Chemical	1975–76	$7,500	foreign payments	CEP
Weyerhaeuser	1971–76	$1,180,000	foreign payments	CEP
White Motor	1971–75	$1,016,000	foreign payments	CEP
Xerox Corporation	1973–75	$100,000	foreign payments	CEP
United Aircraft	1971–76	$2,040,000	sales fees to foreign government employees or officials	SEC
Westinghouse Electric	N.A.	$323,000	foreign payments	SEC

Table 5-1 (continued)

---

* Key: SEC—Report of the Securities and Exchange to the U.S. Senate Committee on Banking Housing and Urban Affairs, May 1976; CiB--*Corruption in Business* (New York: Facts on File, 1977); CEP--*The Invisible Hand: Questionable Corporate Payments Overseas* (New York: Council on Economic Priorities, 1976); 8K or 10K-Forms filed with SEC on dates indicated.

Source: Jack Newfield, "Crime in the Suites: Will Congress Go Easy on Corporate Crooks?" *The Village Voice,* 20 October 1979, 12. Reprinted by permission of *The Village Voice.* Copyright © News Group Publications, Inc., 1979.

In the 1970s, the Interfaith Center on Corporate Responsibility (ICCR) organized an international boycott against the Nestlé Company. The ICCR claimed that Nestlé's sale of baby formula to inhabitants of various poor nations throughout the world was causing the death of some 10,000 babies per year because the formula was being mixed with impure water. Moreover, the people buying the formula were so poor that they could not afford continued purchase of the product, resulting in cases where the formula was so diluted that babies' health was endangered. One tropical health expert, Dr. Derrick Jelliffee, estimates that the sale of such formula by Nestlé and other companies (e.g., Bristol Myers and American Home Products) contributes to some "ten million cases of severe infantile starvation and diarrhea a year" in poor nations.[4]

3. Finally, President Carter placed foreign policy emphasis on U.S. nonsupport of regimes that violate basic human rights. But by late 1979, with the capture of the American embassy in Tehran, columnist Jack Anderson claimed that little had been done to improve the situation. Indeed,

> The Iranian crisis is only the latest, and most dramatic, evidence of the enmity the United States has aroused by its support of repressive dictators in the name of anti-communism. . . . In South America and Africa, we continued to prop up the regimes of generals who beat their countrymen with one hand and rob them with the other. . . . In Argentina and Chile, we continue to back repressive military regimes to protect U.S. business interests.[5]

Certainly, we could cite numerous examples of such deviant acts of international proportion. Our thesis is that these acts are caused by the structure of the international political and economic system. More specifically, the unequal relationships between the United States and its allies in Western Europe and Japan, and between the United States and the Third World nations of Asia, Africa, and Latin America, have created an environment in which certain types of illegal and objectionable practices tend to flourish. Such practices are often justified or over-looked by the U.S. press because of an ideology that stresses anti-communism, free enterprise, and the need for a strong national defense. Nevertheless, for reasons made clear below, such practices and their causes deserve careful examination. Our analysis begins with an inquiry into the nature of the U.S. military establishment.

The Defense Establishment and Its Origins

In 1945, the United States emerged victorious from World War II, its economy and military forces intact. There was, at that time, a crucial need to help rebuild the war-torn economies of Western Europe. In addition, the communist revolution in China (1949) pointed out the neces- sity of preventing newly independent Third World nations from entering the communist orbit. Thus, from 1945 to 1975, $170 billion in loans and grants were made by the United States to friendly nations all over the world.[6] In return for such aid, recipients agreed to adopt the dollar as the standard currency of exchange and to give U.S. firms certain advanta- geous trade and investment opportunities.

Those nations agreeing to accept U.S. aid were to be protected by a worldwide U.S. military network. By 1969, the United States had "1,517,000 uniformed personnel in 119 countries . . . in 429 major and 2,972 minor military bases"[7] (aside from the substantial commitment in Vietnam at that time). Since World War II, U.S. troops and naval forces have been involved in 215 so-called shows of force and have intervened militarily in Korea, Lebanon, the Dominican Republic, Vietnam, and, most recently, Grenada and Nicaragua (through employment of mercenary contras).[8] Militarily, the United States has provided what the Douglas Aircraft Company, in a report for the Army Research Office, called the "Pax Americana" (the American peace).[9]

These strategies have resulted in an unprecedented situation: Between 1945 and 1977, the United States spent an astounding $1,500 billion on defense.[10] Moreover, an additional $1 trillion has been spent on defense since Reagan took office in 1980. These expenditures, together with the nearly worldwide deployment of U.S. military forces, have created a huge permanent military establishment.

In fact, on January 13, 1961, outgoing President Eisenhower warned of the consequences of the military-industrial complex in his farewell address:

> In the councils of government, we must guard against the acquisition of unwarranted influence, whether sought or unsought, by the military-industrial complex. . . .
>
> We must never let the weight of this combination en- danger our liberties or democratic processes. We should take nothing for granted. Only an alert and knowledgeable citizenry can compel the proper meshing of the huge industrial and military machinery of defense with our peaceful methods and goals, so that security and liberty can prosper together.[11]

Despite Eisenhower's warning, the military-industrial complex has con- tinued to increase in both size and influence. Moreover, the nature of the complex is poorly understood by the public. It is not a malevolent

conspiracy, as some believe, but an interrelated "community of interests".[12] It is really a "MITLAMP (military-industrial-technological-
labor-academic-managerial-political) complex":

1. The military sector consists of some two and one-half million
active-duty military personnel; their current pay and allowances comprise
about 30 percent of the defense budget. In addition, in 1982, military
retirees and veterans received payment of approximately $14,900,000,000.
Finally, in 1983, over $24 billion was budgeted for the Veterans Adminis-
tration, which wields considerable political pressure.[13]
2. The industrial segment consists of over one hundred defense
contractors whose economic base consists of the weapons portion of the
defense budget. In 1973, some 3,233 retired officers worked for such
companies. And between 1979 and 1983, 1,455 additional officers above
the rank of colonel accepted positions with defense contractors (along
with 335 civilian Pentagon employees with equivalent rank and thirty-one
NASA employees).[14]
3. The labor component of the complex consists of part of the
Pentagon workforce, 5 percent of whom are directly involved and 16
percent of whom are indirectly involved in military matters.
4. The academic division of the MITLAMP complex consists of
university departments involved in Pentagon-funded research on various
U.S. campuses. In 1984, twelve universities received over $10 million
each in grants from the Defense Department. Two universities—John
Hopkins and MIT—received over $260 million each.[15]
5. The managerial component consists of the 7.8 percent of U.S.
managers that are directly involved in administering the intellectual,
scientific, technological, and manpower requirements essential to
MITLAMP goals. Another 9 percent of the managerial workforce is
indirectly employed in such administration.
6. Finally, the political component of the MITLAMP complex
consists of congresspersons whose districts contain military facilities
and/or employers receiving defense contracts. Such members often sit on
those congressional committees (such as the Senate and House Armed
Services committees) that oversee the Pentagon budget.

At the apex of the military-industrial complex stand the so-called
National Security Managers—a group of politicians, civil servants, and
businesspersons—who tend to rotate among various posts in the Pentagon,
Department of State, Atomic Energy Commission, the FBI, the CIA, the
agencies that administer foreign aid and certain national and international
police training programs, the White House, and big business. Such people
(as was mentioned in Chapter 1) sit on the boards of trustees of the
universities who receive the bulk of defense-related research funds, and
compose the directors of leading foundations who fund the think tanks and
elite associations that regularly make policy recommendations to the
executive branch of the federal government. This set of relationships is
diagrammed in Figure 5-1.
Not surprisingly, the corporations that receive the most financial
benefit from defense contracting are the same multinational corporations
whose overseas holdings are protected by the military-counterinsurgency
umbrella provided by the United States' worldwide military establishment.

Figure 5-1
Elites and the Military–Industrial Complex*

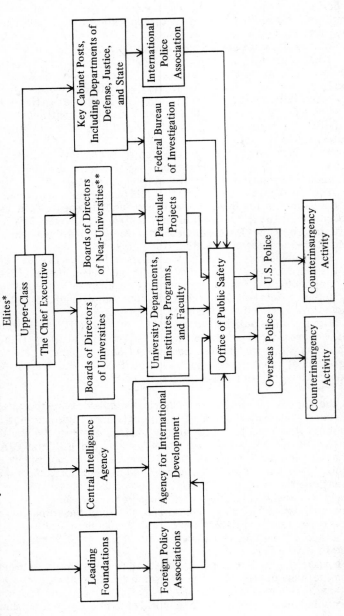

*Includes defense contractors.   **"Think-Tanks" (e.g., Rand Corp).

Source: John C. Leggett, *Taking State Power* (New York: Harper and Row, 1973), 377.   (Original title: Figure 4, "Schematization, Amplified in the Text, of the Support of and Concern for the Office of Public Safety on the Part of the Upper Classes.)   Copyright © 1973 by John C. Leggett.   Reprinted by permission of Harper & Row, Publishers, Inc.

As the Chasins have pointed out, "At least 205 firms ranking in the top 500 manufacturing corporations" are "significantly involved in military production."[16] Moreover, "the top 100 corporations monopolize three-fourths of the contracts."[17] With the defense budget hovering near the $250-billion mark in 1985 and with "half the Defense budget spent on prime military contracts for the development, production, or deployment of weapons," the opportunity for profits is great.[18] These opportunities are enhanced greatly by the practice of awarding more than half of defense contracts with no competitive bidding.

In fact, the government's own investigations have revealed surprising patterns of unethical practices. In 1965, the Comptroller General described the following aspects of the military-contract system to a House committee:

> 1. Excessive prices in relation to available pricing information.
> 2. Acceptance and payment by the government for defective equipment.
> 3. Charges to the government for costs applicable to contactors' commercial work.
> 4. Contractors' use of government-owned facilities for commercial work for extended periods without payment of rent to the government.
> 5. Duplicate billings to the government.
> 6. Unreasonable or excessive costs.
> 7. Excessive progress payments held by contracts without payment of interest thereon.[19]

Among these items are $13 billion in government-owned land, buildings, and equipment, which in some cases greatly reduces the need for any capital investments by a contractor.

One of the most notorious defense-contract practices is known as "buying in." Using this device, contractors set very low bids on the costs of weapons systems, but, should the costs rise (and they inevitably do), the government agrees to pay for such increases under a contract-change notice. Here changes are made by either the Pentagon or the contractors. And in a complex weapons system, the number of such notices runs, at times, into thousands of dollars.[20] The practice has resulted in two negative consequences: (1) the so-called cost overrun, where the original price of an item easily multiplies; and (2) the Defense Department's receipt of weapons of very questionable quality (in some cases, no weapons at all are received). Some examples:

Item: Richard Stubbing, a defense analyst with the Bureau of the Budget, studied thirteen aircraft and missile programs contracted for since 1955 at a cost of more than $40 billion. He found that 60 percent of the electronic components in these systems failed to perform acceptably.

Item: In 1968, the Pentagon stated that, in the previous fifteen years, $8.8 billion had been socked into sixty-seven military contracts that were cancelled, either because the Defense Department (DOD) decided it could not use them or because the projects failed to meet military requirements.[21]

Item: By 1982, various congressional studies and the General Accounting Office (GAO) estimated that fraud and waste in the Defense Department cost at least $15 billion per year, including $6.9 million in misuse of military aircraft and $2.6 billion for 256 consultant contracts, 80 percent of which were awarded on a noncompetitive basis.

Item: In 1983, the Air Force disposed of $700 million in spare parts, many of which were still in good condition. The Army sold an $8,000 machine, still unopened in its original packaging, for $65. Other items, also in their original cartons, were sold back to the Pentagon by salvage dealers.[22]

Item: Many of the weapons systems completed are of inferior quality. In 1980, a Defense Department memo showed that the F-15 fighter plane was combat-ready only 56 percent of the time; the F-111D fighter plane performed only 34 percent of the time and required ninety-eight maintenance hours per flight. The M-1 Abrams tank broke down every forty-three miles and got 1,400 feet per gallon in "mileage." In fact, the tank is so awkward that it must be accompanied by a fuel truck and bulldozer so that its position can be fortified.[23]

Item: J. P. Grace, head of a commission appointed by President Reagan to improve management and reduce costs within the federal government, estimates that fourteen weapons systems begun in 1983-1984 will end up costing 2.3 times as much as the amount of funds likely to be available for their production. According to Grace, as much a $100 billion in defense spending could be saved over a three-year period by adopting such practices as competitive bidding.[24]

Item: On October 4, 1982, the Navy committed itself to purchase sixty-three F-18 fighter aircraft, plus an additional 1,300 F-18s over the next decade, at an estimated cost of $22.5 million apiece. On the same day that the Navy signed the contract for the planes, test pilots completing a five-month evaluation of the F-18 reported that it was unsuitable for Navy use because it could not fly far enough with a full load of fuel and equipment to reach a combat target and then return to base. Despite this report, the Navy stood by its commitment and ordered the planes.

Item: A GAO report issued in April 1982 concluded that, over the past decade, the cost of 182 major defense projects had increased from $233 to $424 billion. Some individual price increases were estimated at over 1,000 percent. In all, there was a 91 percent chance of a cost overrun totalling at least 53 percent, not counting any increases for inflation.[25]

Defense contractors also practice "pyramiding profits": Prime contractors purchase components for systems from subcontractors, who in turn purchase other components from other subcontractors. Each company involved bills the company to whom it sells costs plus profits, which is perfectly legal; but taken to an extreme, this system breeds gigantic amounts of profit taking.

One example of pyramiding occurred in the 1950s when Western Electric was given the contract for the Nike missile, and, subsequently, the launcher for the missile. Western Electric subcontracted the launcher project to Douglas Aircraft, who subcontracted the project to a subsidiary of U.S. Steel. The U.S. Steel affiliate's bill for the transaction, including its profit, was $13.5 million. The Douglas company manufactured the covers that fit over the missile and earned over $1.2 million on the transaction--a return of over 36,000 percent on its original investment. Western Electric based its bill to the government on Douglas' reported costs and profit, $14.7 million. Western Electric's total investment was $14,293, charged for inspecting equipment on various army bases. Its profit on the transaction amounted to almost $1 million, a return on investment of over 6,000 percent. The pyramiding arrangement can, then, allow the prime contractor and each subcontractor to add on tremendous profits at each level of the pyramid.

The costs to the government in some defense contracts have reached unbelievable proportions at times. Several years ago the Boeing aircraft corporation delivered eighty-two beds to the Air Force at a cost of $1,080 per bed. Standard Air Force beds were usually purchased for around $38 each.[26]

Undoubtedly, the most famous of all cost overruns is that of the C-5A transport aircraft. The C-5A case demonstrates the excess costs, as well as shoddy quality of goods, sometimes delivered to the Department of Defense. One hundred fifteen of the Lockheed crafts were contracted for at a cost of $3.2 billion. And this cost increased by a whopping 67 percent, to $5.2 billion.

The safety and performance record of the C-5A has been a disaster. The plane has been involved in a number of tragic incidents. In 1971, following the initial delivery of fifteen C-5As to the government, it was found that the

> C-5 suffers major technical breakdown once an hour of flight time. The unenviable pilot of the giant jet should anticipate, according to the General Accounting Office, that his landing gear alone will fail once every four hours. One of the planes already accepted by the Air Force and picked at random by the GAO auditors for inspection had 47 major and 149 minor deficiencies. Fourteen of the defects, the GAO reported to Congress, "impair the aircraft's capability to perform all or a portion of six missions" assigned to it.[27]

In May 1973, the last of eighty-one C-5As was delivered to the Air Force, thirteen months behind schedule. Following the delivery, several additional incidents occurred:

1. In 1973, the Air Force was to supply Israel with emergency material following an Arab invasion, but it was discovered that some thirty-six C-5As could not be used because they needed repairs. Ten more transports were grounded for lack of parts. Mechanical malfunctions in other C-5As caused twenty-nine flights to be terminated and forty others to be delayed.

2. In 1975, a C-5A leaving Saigon crashed, killing more than one hundred Vietnamese orphans bound for the United States.[28]

3. Throughout the 1970s, problems with the C-5A continued to escalate. In one six-month period, 3,327 defects were found in the plane's landing gear, and an additional $1.3 billion was needed to strengthen the

craft. Thus, airplanes proven to be faulty, costing $28 million each in 1965, ended up costing $65 million by 1970, and, finally, $85 million in 1979.[29]

The C5-A's history also reveals the miseries bestowed on those who blow the whistle on such abuses. In the early 1970s, Earnest Fitzgerald, a Pentagon efficiency analyst, exposed the initial cost overrun of the C-5A. Once he made the news public, Fitzgerald was transferred to Thailand, where he was placed in charge of overseeing the building of a bowling alley. Subsequently, as part of a cost-reduction move, his position was abolished and he was fired. It took a congressional investigation to get Fitzgerald rehired by the Defense Department. However, during the period that Fitzgerald exposed the plane's cost, the Air Force Office of Special Investigation (OSI) undertook to open his personal mail and tried to uncover information that they could use to discredit him. An OSI report characterized Fitzgerald as "pinchpenny," as evidenced by the fact that he drove an old car, a Rambler.[30]

Fitzgerald was also involved in another instructive incident concerning the Mark II electronic and electrical system of the F-111 fighter. The contract for the system was given to the Autonetics Division of North American Aviation with an initial bid of $750,000 per unit; but with the usual overrun, the cost skyrocketed to $4.1 million per unit. In an attempt to hold down costs, Fitzgerald met with the project's director, Major General Zoeckler. After Fitzgerald complained of the program's rising costs, the general replied, "Inefficiency is national policy," necessary for the attainment of such social goals as employment and aid to businesses.[31]

Whether inefficiency is national policy throughout the economy is an open question. That waste and inefficiency often take place in defense contracting is a fact that has dismayed even some members of the defense establishment. Nevertheless, the presence of waste, fraud, and corruption on such a massive scale has prompted some to speculate about the importance of defense spending to the U.S. economy. Michael Parenti insists that "military appropriations are the single most important source of investment and profit for corporate America."[32]

Robert Sherrill also argues this economic issue. Eleven hundred major American corporations employ 700,000 workers in the production, design, testing, and evaluation of weapons systems. To reduce the military budget significantly would, therefore, cause a depression in many areas of the nation. Even the supposedly cost-conscious Reagan administration has allowed defense contractors in economically depressed areas to bid as much as 5 percent more than contractors from other areas and still be awarded weapons contracts.[33]

Conservative businessman J. P. Grace estimates that about two-thirds of all congressional districts contain or are near military installations. However, only 312 of these 4,000 defense installations are necessary and significant to U.S. defense. Most installations represent storage and support facilities and employ fewer than 150 people. Yet Congress requested $6 billion more than did the Defense Department for the fiscal-year 1985 defense budget.[34] Why? Because such money will funnel into congressional districts, creating a few jobs and giving congressional members reelection themes.

In addition to buying-in and cost-plus contracting, several other wasteful and inefficient practices are commonplace in the defense industry:

      1. "Goldplating" is the tendency to build into new systems needless levels of technological sophistication. The purchase of exotic features is encouraged by competition between the military services and among the corporations, and is relatively uncontrolled because of military self-regulation in the definition of tactical needs.

      2. "Managers without power" cannot effectively supervise contracts. Weapons programs tend to be overseen by middle-ranking military officers who must carry every decision to superiors and who are prevented from developing expertise by frequent job rotation.

      3. "Concurrency" is the practice of beginning weapons production before development is complete, to speed deployment and cut lead time. Problems discovered later must be corrected on already produced units, driving up costs.[35]

Defense contracting seems to invite incidents of fraud. For example, in the early 1970s, the B. F. Goodrich Company was granted a contract to develop the brake assemblies on the Air Force's A7D fighter aircraft. When the models developed by Goodrich consistently failed to pass their own laboratory tests, Goodrich engineers began falsifying test data and changing testing methods so that the brakes would meet Air Force specifications. Upon being tested on the actual aircraft, the brakes malfunctioned, causing a number of near crashes. Because of the nature of the doctored test data, Goodrich employee Kermit Vandivier (who later appeared as the government's witness) resigned. In his letter of resignation, Vandivier described a falsified report that was sent to the Air Force:

> As you are aware, this report contained numerous deliberate and willful misrepresentations which, according to legal counsel, constitute fraud and expose . . . myself and others to charges of conspiracy to defraud. . . .[36]

In the end, no charges of fraud were brought against either Goodrich or any of its officials. Goodrich merely announced that it would replace its original brake system with a new and better one.

Other examples of illegal or unethical practices with the Defense Department have included outright bribery. Between 1971 and 1974, Northrop had hired a number of special consultants, including military and congressional officials. One such consultant was General John Blandford, a former aide to Senator Mendel Rivers, head of the House Armed Services Committee, which oversees the Pentagon's budget in the House of Representatives. (Blandford had also offered his services to Lockheed and Fairchild Industries.) One Northrop project in which Blandford and Rivers were involved was the development of the Northrop F-5. This plane was never purchased by the Pentagon. Instead, it was developed by the government and donated to the United States' Asian allies.

In all, these consultants were paid $5.5 million. In addition, Northrop paid Blandford $40,000-$60,000 through another consultant, Frank DeFrancis, for protection in dealing with the company's competitors.[37] DeFrancis was paid a total of $500,000. Auditors investigating Northrop ruled that payments to DeFrancis were improperly billed to the government by Northrop. Finally, Northrop paid the former head of the Air National Guard, General Wilson, $115,000 in expenses, which auditors documented went for entertainment in Northrop's hunting lodge, lobbying, and illegal political contributions.

The incidents of corruption, graft, and inefficiency that make defense contracting so profitable continued into the late 1970s. A 1978 study by the General Accounting Office reported that fifty-five major weapons systems accounted for an increase totaling an amazing $86 billion.[38] In late 1978, columnist Jack Anderson reported staggering amounts of waste and theft in procurement within the Defense Department itself. The Defense Personnel Support Center, which handles contracts for clothing, food, and medical supplies, became the focus of an investigation by the FBI, the General Accounting Office, the DOD's inspector general, and the Senate Permanent Subcommittee on Investigations. Accounting procedures at the Center were reported to be so inept that it may be impossible to determine how much inventory has been stolen or is missing.

> The Philadelphia center scandal was touched off by an innocent error by a mail clerk at the facility. Seeing a check for $250,000 to be mailed to P. Morris Co., the clerk sent it off to a legitimate defense supplier, the Philip Morris tobacco company. Philip Morris returned it with a letter explaining that the firm had already been paid once for the order.
>
> Closer examination of the check showed that it was supposed to have been sent to P. Morris Co., a dummy corporation with an answering-service address in Philadelphia. Someone at the support center had been making out duplicate checks which were to be sent to phony contractors and cashed by participants in the scam.
>
> Investigators tracked down some $1.6 million in fake payments which were ready to be mailed out. But the FBI was unable to pinpoint the culprits. Because of the lax accounting procedures, there were hundreds of possible suspects who could have engineered the ripoff.[39]

Since some $1.2 billion in orders could not be validated due to the nature of the center's accounting system, thirty professional accountants were sent from Washington to look into the matter. Such waste and theft is, however, only a small portion of the costs of defense to American society.

The Consequences of Defense Policies

By the mid-1970s, many economists and social analysts had escalated their criticisms of the social costs of defense. First, there was the Vietnam War, with its $150-billion price tag and loss of 55,000 American lives. The social costs of Vietnam are something from which American society has yet to recover. By 1968, three and one-half years into the war's escalation, these costs were already prohibitive. Terrence McCarthy calculated that, by 1968, the war had:

> reduced the purchasing power of the consumer's dollar by almost 9 percent;
> distorted the economy by adding only 1.6 million production workers to manufacturing payrolls compared with 2.3 million to government payrolls;
> caused a loss in housing construction of at least 750,000 dwelling units;
> raised interest rates to the highest levels in a century; . . .
> raised the interest-bearing federal debt by $23 billion; . . .
> generated the greatest threat of inflation since the Civil War. . . .[40]

According to a 1977 study by the Center for Defense Information, "military spending is one of the least effective ways to create jobs."[41] In fact, the net impact of military spending in 1977-1978 was the loss of slightly over one million jobs in the United States, mainly in the frostbelt areas of the nation, which were hardest hit by the recession. The same study also indicated that $1 billion spent in state and local government would create seventy-two thousand new jobs, compared with twenty-seven thousand jobs in the civilian sector of the economy, but only eighteen thousand defense-sector positions, and thirty-seven thousand military-sector jobs.[42]

Although unethical and illegal defense contracting practices have been supported by American beliefs in free enterprise and the need for a strong national defense, ironically, neither has been provided by the system.

Another criticism stems from the growing realization that defense spending is a major cause of inflation, robbing consumers of purchasing power.

> Virtually all economists agree . . . that military spending tends to be inflationary. This is because it puts money into the hands of workers without expanding the supply of goods they can buy--the consumer market for missiles and the like being somewhat limited--thereby driving up the prices of goods like autos and refrigerators and machine tools.
> [Also, arms makers on cost-plus contracts] tend to bid up the prices of resources and skilled labor. This produces a cost-push effect that feeds inflationary pressure throughout the rest of the economy.[43]

Despite these criticisms, defense spending continues to absorb over one-half of the money in the federal budget that is not a fixed cost and one-half of the federal research and development finds. By 1986, military spending will account for 83 percent of the value of everything humanmade on the ground surface in the United States. A mere 7 percent

of the defense spending from 1981-1986 could have completely rehabili-
tated U.S. Steel Corporation's outdated plants and equipment, and the
cost of a single F-18 aircraft could modernize the machine-tool stock of
the entire U.S. economy.

The continued growth of military spending has contributed to
international tension between the United States and the Soviet Union, who
are locked in an international arms race.   More arms make it less likely
that either country would survive a full-scale war and thus create more
insecurities.   The only alternative is to enter into treaties that limit the
production of weapons, which would, of course, diminish the profits that
accrue from military spending.   In the meantime, by mid-1983, the United
States had produced 30,000 deliverable nuclear warheads, twelve thousand
of which could be used against the Soviet Union.[44]   In addition, former
senator J. W. Fullbright notes that the Reagan administration plans to
spend another $222 billion between 1983 and 1989 for continued develop-
ment of nuclear weapons, which will add seventeen thousand nuclear
weapons to the U.S. arsenal by 1993.[45]

Another frightening aspect of nuclear arms is the Reagan administration's public announcements concerning nuclear war itself.   Reports
indicate that Reagan administration officials consider a nuclear war to be
"winnable."   The loss of up to 150 million lives would be "acceptable" in
such a confrontation.

In direct opposition, nearly two-thirds of the U.S. population
favors a verifiable nuclear weapons freeze as an alternative to a
continued arms race.[46]   This contrast in attitudes illustrates a significant
characteristic of elite deviance:

> In this society anybody who contemplates murdering a
> single individual is considered either mentally unstable or a
> potential criminal.   But people within this (the Reagan) adminis-
> tration are making statements about nuclear war that contem-
> plates the death of hundreds of millions of human beings.   The
> same moral and legal restraints should be applied to these people
> as to ordinary citizens who contemplate the death of only one
> human being.[47]

The United States already possesses enough nuclear weaponary to
destroy the 218 Soviet cities with a population of 100,000 or more over
230 times.   Should a nuclear war erupt, it is estimated that both the
Unites States and the Soviet Union would lose 95 to 120 million citizens,
and three-fourths of their respective economies would be destroyed.[48]

Despite these catastrophic potentials, the military-industrial
complex continues to spend millions of dollars each year to convince itself
and the American public of the dangers of Soviet aggression and of the
United States' inferior position in the arms race.   General David Shoup,
former Commandant of the Marine Corps and head of the Joint Chiefs of
Staff, has noted that all service associations (i.e., the Association of the
U.S. Army, the Navy League, and the Air Force Association) publish
journals that reflect the "party line" within the various services.   Defense
industries support these journals with expensive ads that also lend
credence to the anti-Soviet viewpoint.   Thus develops an atmosphere
among active-duty and retired personnel that allows them to believe their
own propaganda, contributing to the creation of what General Shoup has

termed a militaristic culture, where force of arms is viewed as an acceptable solution to international problems.[49]

The defense department also possesses an immense propaganda apparatus. Its various public-relations divisions employ over 6,000 people who lobby before Congress, make their own movies, aid Hollywood moviemakers in making films, sponsor conferences for both defense contractors and civic organizations, and provide speakers to educate civic organizations concerning the nature of the communist threat.[50] To date, there has been no effective organization capable of either countering the militaristic view of the world situation or of informing the American people of the international dimensions of deviant behavior, which are masked by the complex's appeals to patriotism and anticommunism.

Moreover, some critics believe that the prevalence of an exaggerated Cold War ideology (i.e., fear of the Soviet military threat) sometimes results in the manipulation of public opinion in order to win increased defense funds. H. R. Rodgers argued this point in the early 1970s:

> If all else fails, the Pentagon can always use its secret weapon to get its way—the big scare. Despite the fact that the United States already has the nuclear capacity to drop the equivalent of six tons of TNT on every person on earth, the scare campaign always centers on some alleged deficiency in our military capacity. During recent years we have had the bomber gap scare, which led to a considerable increase in defense spending. Only after the funds were committed was it discovered that at the time of the supposed bomber shortage, the United States had 680 bombers and the Soviet Union had between 150 and 200. . . . Recently we have had the missile gap: once again, after the funds were spent, it came to light that the Pentagon had exaggerated Russian missile strength by 30 times.[51]

And in the late 1970s, we faced a naval gap. The U.S. Navy claimed in 1978 that, over the last fifteen years, the Soviet Union had launched 205 major combatants compared to 165 for the United States. Yet subsequent investigations revealed that most of the Soviet's major warships were small patrol boats and escort vessels, and that, regarding major surface warships, the United States had actually outbuilt the Soviet Union 122 units to fifty-seven.

In 1976, one national news magazine reported that the Soviet Navy possessed 3,300 ships, while the United States had only 478. However, even U.S. admiral Stansfield Turner (later director of the CIA) had to admit that the figures included every "seventy-five foot tugboat and barge, and comparing heaven knows what."[52]

Another factor in the overestimation of Soviet military strength is that largely unreliable data are used. For example, the CIA determines how much the Soviets spend on equipment and labor by estimating how much such items would cost in the United States. This is hardly a valid comparison, considering the small labor costs in the Soviet Union. Moreover, the CIA assumes that Soviet draftees receive the same pay as U.S. soldiers. According to this logic, each time U.S. service members receive a pay raise, so do the Soviets. Thus, for every $1-million U.S. pay increase, the CIA estimates a $2-million increase in the Soviet military budget! This estimation is also unrealistic because military pay in the Soviet Union is much lower than that in the United States. A Soviet recruit earns about $8 a month, whereas a U.S. recruit earns about $500. Moreover, U.S. estimates of its own military strength rarely compare spending by NATO nations with those of the Warsaw Pact, which are lower, on average.

Finally, estimates of national military strength are, by nature, quantitative. They say little concerning the quality of weapons. In general, U.S. weapons are thought to be more lightweight, more accurate, and more efficient than their Soviet counterparts. This is especially true of missiles, combat aircraft, and radar sensors.[53]

This is not to say that the Soviet Union represents no threat to U.S. interests. However, there is a genuine need for an honest, objective appraisal of the Soviet threat. As yet, the Pentagon has not provided such an appraisal for the American public.

This lack of accountability may ultimately work against the Pentagon as it faces a genuine crisis in preparedness due to its policy of throwing money into costly and sophisticated weapons systems. Recent reports indicate critical needs for such basic items as spare parts, ammunition, and adequately trained personnel. The problem, again, is a question of priorities:

> There are far too many extremely costly programs in the military budget today. We cannot simultaneously: acquire a vast new arsenal of nuclear weapons; expand costly forces for defending countries in Europe and Asia; add to substantial forces for rapid intervention everywhere in the world; enlarge a very expensive navy for development on all the world's oceans; develop new weapons which are always better than Soviet weapons; and keep existing forces at a high level of readiness and training.[54]

Thus, perhaps the most significant consequence of the practices described above is that they limit U.S. ability to muster a truly adequate defense capability.

DEVIANCE AND MULTINATIONAL CORPORATIONS

The Structure of the International Economy

Deviant behavior by multinational corporations stems in large part from the structure of the economic relationships between multinational corporations and foreign countries (especially Third World). What began as a need to rebuild war-torn economies and stimulate trade had, by the 1970s, become an important aspect of the U.S. economy. Thus, during the 1960s, American multinational firms invested $47 billion overseas, largely in Western Europe and Canada, creating some 3.3 million new jobs in foreign nations. By 1976, U.S.-owned firms were selling more goods overseas ($212 billion) than U.S.-based firms were exporting (only $76.6 billion).[55]   Thus, American-owned foreign companies now sell three dollars' worth of goods overseas for each dollar's worth of goods exported overseas from the United States.

In Asia, Africa, and Latin America (the Third World), U.S. military and foreign aid has created a safe environment for investment by U.S. multinational corporations.   Between 1946 and 1976, the United States gave $69,197 billion in military aid to the nations of Asia, Africa, and Latin America. During this period, U.S. business investments in these areas jumped from $5.7 billion in 1950 to $28.5 billion in 1974.[56] The importance of these investments to industrialized nations is great: They account for two-thirds of the net income received from all foreign investments.[57]

With so much profit and investment potential at stake, both in Western Europe and the Third World, it is not surprising that a good deal of bribery money has been spent to secure contracts and other favors relating to a positive business climate. But the need for profits and economic growth are only part of the reason for the expansion of U.S. business overseas.

A second reason for the profitability of overseas business activity relates to labor costs. The companies listed in Table 5-2 are firms whose employees are unionized. Even though only about 20 percent of the labor force is unionized, union members receive higher wages than nonunionized workers.   Large corporations in the United States thus face high labor costs, and are, therefore, motivated to find less expensive labor. Table 5-2 reveals that wages in the Third World are very low, usually two to three dollars per hour less than comparable wages in the United States. Thus, in Haiti, women are paid $2.70 a day for making thirty to forty baseballs, which the Rawlings Company sells for $3.50 to $4.00 each in the United States.[58]

This search for cheap labor has several negative consequences for U.S. society.   Specifically, as U.S. business moves abroad, at home, "unemployment mounts; the importation of foreign goods increases which results in a flow of dollars abroad; and as our balance of payments deficit increases, the value of the dollar declines relative to other currencies, which increases inflation and causes other economic problems."[59] While none of this is criminal or unethical, it does illustrate that the goals of multinational corporations center around the pursuit of profits and investments.   What may be beneficial to the nation as a whole is not necessarily of major concern.

Another of the needs of U.S. economic life concerns a dependence on foreign countries, especially poor (Third World) nations, for strategic raw materials. "One half of the sixty-two strategic materials listed by the Department of Defense require 80% to 100% importation, and five-sixths require at least 40%. Three fourths of these materials are taken from underdeveloped areas."[60] One such key ingredient is bauxite, which is used to make aluminum (for airplanes) and other materials.

According to Zeitlin, 80 to 90 percent of the bauxite supply comes from foreign sources.[61]   Probably most important is that the United States is self-sufficient only in a few industrial resources, such as sulphur, magnesium, and coal, and is depleting its supply of these and other resources so rapidly that dependence on foreign sources will probably continue to increase in the future.

Our position is that the nature of the U.S. economy--with its needs for investment outlets, cheap labor, and access to scarce raw materials--has created an environment in which certain types of deviance tend to occur.   In recent years, such deviance by multinational corporations has centered around illegal payments to foreign governments and the exporting of hazardous goods.

Table 5-2
Differential Hourly Wage Rates in Selected Industries:
Underdeveloped Nations vs. the United States

Industry	Average Hourly Rate (in dollars)	
	Underdeveloped Nations	United States
Consumer electronic products		
Hong Kong	0.27	3.13
Mexico	0.53	2.31
Taiwan	0.14	2.56
Office-machine parts		
Hong Kong	0.30	2.92
Taiwan	0.38	3.67
Mexico	0.48	2.97
Semiconductors		
Korea	0.33	3.32
Singapore	0.29	3.36
Jamaica	0.30	2.23
Wearing apparel		
Mexico	0.53	2.29
British Honduras	0.28	2.11
Costa Rica	0.34	2.28
Honduras	0.45	2.27
Trinidad	0.40	2.49

* Hourly wage rates for a given country and the United States are for comparable task and skill levels.
Source: Richard L. Barnet and Richard E. Muller, *Global Reach* (New York: Simon and Schuster, 1974), 127. Copyright © 1974 by Richard L. Barnet and Richard E. Muller. Reprinted by permission of Simon and Schuster, Inc.

Multinationals and Bribery

According to Sorensen, a *bribe* may be defined as:

> a payment voluntarily offered for the purpose of inducing a public official to do or omit something of his (her) lawful duty, or to exercise his (her) official discretion in favor of the payor's request for a contract, concession of privilege on some basis other than the merits.[62]

By the 1970s, even the most ardent supporters of America's multinational corporations have admitted that "companies can't condone the practice (of bribery). Responsible executives are right to insist that it shouldn't happen. Many companies have rules prohibiting it. . . . But nearly four years of increasingly sensational disclosures add up to a lot of monkey business."[63]   The disclosures of bribery of foreign governments and of American officials reveal a disturbing pattern of corporate secrecy, unaccountability to stockholders, and, in some cases, the undermining of U.S. national security and foreign policy. Corporations insist that bribes are an established custom in many foreign countries and are a necessary part of doing business, but the effect and nature of many of the bribes seem to cast some doubt on this claim. A member of the Securities and Exchange Commission has called the practice of international bribery something of a "national crisis," and an examination of the situation on a case-by-case basis leaves little doubt about the accuracy of the charge.[64]

Lockheed: bribes at the taxpayers' expense? From 1969 to 1975, the Lockheed Corporation spent $202 million, paying agents to deliver the money and bribe government officials in Indonesia, the Philippines, Saudia Arabia, Japan, France, Germany, Turkey, Italy, and the Netherlands. Laundered funds in secret Swiss bank accounts, top-secret memos, slush funds, the toppling of governments, and suicides by some of the figures involved characterized the intrigue. Lockheed had been given a $250 million loan guarantee by the U.S. government in 1971 in an effort to stave off bankruptcy. However, it became clear that Lockheed's connections with the U.S. government ran much deeper than being able to secure loans.

Item: In October 1975, a set of papers were made public revealing that Lockheed was aided by the CIA in making bribes to the Indonesian government. When President Sukarno of Indonesia was deposed in a coup, Lockheed asked the American Embassy in Jakarta to have its CIA staff inquire about the relationship of Izaac Dassad, Lockheed's agent, and the new government. The inquiries revealed that Dassad had a good relationship with the new regime. Subsequently, Lockheed arranged for its agent to deliver bribes to Indonesian Air Force officials involving the status of $300,000 in spare airplane parts and $40 million in plane sales in 1973-1974. The bribes were treated as commissions that amounted to 3 percent of the price of the planes and 5 to 10 percent of the other contracts, totalling over $1.2 million dollars. In addition, Lockheed's chairman later revealed that many of the bribes were claimed on the company's income tax return as direct business deductions.

Item: During the early 1970s, in Saudia Arabia, Lockheed retained the services of Adnan N. Khashoggi, president of Triad, the Arab world's first multinational conglomerate. Lockheed paid Mr. Kashoggi a staggering $106 million over a five-year period in supposed commissions and bribes. Some of this money went directly under the table to Saudi officials and other funds were deposited in secret bank accounts of the officials in Lichtenstein and Switzerland. Through a complicated arrangement with Kashoggi's companies and Lockheed's subsidiaries in Switzerland, Lockheed arranged for taxes on the deals to be paid in Switzerland, where the tax rate is much lower than in the United States. And the dummy corporation set up in Switzerland by Lockheed rerouted some of the profits to the United States, where no profits were claimed because amounts equalling the rerouted profits were deducted as costs for marketing services (provided, of course, by Kashoggi's firm). Thus, the money moved from the Saudi government, to Lockheed in Switzerland, to Lockheed in California, to Khashoggi in Switzerland. The losers on the deal were taxpayers in both Switzerland and in the United States.[65]

Item: In 1975, a hearing by the Senate Subcommittee on Multinational Corporations revealed that Lockheed had, in some cases, paid bribes for contracts where no competition for its products existed. Lockheed virtually admitted that bribery is profitable because bribes are not only deducted from taxes, but are tacked onto contracts in the form of costs. Moreover, paying bribes where no competition exists means that foreign governments are encouraged to spend money on products like arms, when such money might go for other necessary commodities, like food.

Item: In 1976, it was revealed that Lockheed had paid commissions of about $7 million to its Japanese agent, Yoshio Kodama, a known right-wing political extremist and convicted war criminal. Kodama was hired in order to convince a Japanese airline to contract for some 130 Lockheed Tri-Star jets. Kodama had also been instrumental in helping Lockheed obtain a contract from the Japanese government in 1958 for its F-104 fighters. Lockheed also convinced the Japanese to cancel an existing contract with Grumman, another American firm. In this deal, about $5.6 million in bribes was paid. Talks in 1972 among Japanese Prime Minister Tanaka, President Nixon, and Secretary of State Kissinger resulted in the Japanese agreeing to purchase $320 million in U.S. civilian aircraft. Shortly after this meeting, the Japanese airline announced a cancellation of a contract with McDonnell-Douglas in favor of a Tri-Star purchase. It is not known if President Nixon and Secretary of State Kissinger played a role in this transaction. Later that year, Prime Minister Tanaka and twenty Japanese industries and political officials were sent to jail for their actions relating to the Tri-Star deal.[66]

Item: In addition to the Japanese crisis, in 1976, it was revealed that Lockheed had paid some $8 million in commissions and bribes to agents in Turkey, France, Italy, Germany, and Japan, as well as an additional $1.1 million to a highly placed Netherlands official. Moreover, Lockheed paid $12 million to the West German Christian Social Union, a right-wing political group, to influence a Tri-Star deal there. Files on the transaction mysteriously disappeared from the Defense Ministry, according to a former West German defense minister.   In sum, the influence of Lockheed on the international scene has not been beneficial either to American taxpayers or to American foreign policy.

Lockheed has invaded the treasury of a dozen nations . . . destabilized the governments of three allies, undermined NATO . . . boosted inflation, and prompted a series of newspaper sensations that appeared to have resulted in suicides as far apart as Tokyo and L.A. (including the suicide of one of its former executives).[67]

By 1976, bribery scandals among U.S. multinational corporations had become almost commonplace.   United Brands, Northrop Aviation, Phillips Petroleum, Exxon, Gulf Oil, and Mobil Oil had all been implicated in major episodes of bribery abroad.   Exxon, whose slogan relates to building a strong America, was exposed as secretly donating campaign funds to the Italian Communist Party. The president of United Brands, Eli Black, leaped forty-four floors to his death in 1975 over revelations that his company had paid the president of the Honduras and other Honduran officials $1.25 million in order to have the tax rate on bananas exported from the Honduras lowered by seventy cents per box.[68]

In the late 1970s, the Bechtel corporation hired Yoon Sick Cho, a Korean American, at $90,000 a year, to bid on Korean nuclear power contracts.   Reportedly, Cho spent at least $60,000 on gifts for Korean officials in an effort to influence the government.   In addition, it is possible that Secretary of State George Schultz and Secretary of Defense Casper Weinberger, both Bechtel executives at the time, knew about the illegal payments and either approved or condoned them.[69]

In almost all these cases, no one was convicted of a crime.   Most of the executives held responsible for these policies were either promoted and given sizable raises or retired with generous pensions and valuable blocks of stock

The Foreign Corrupt Practices Act was finally passed in early 1978, making international bribery illegal and punishable by up to $1 million in fines and five years in jail. Finally, in June 1979, Lockheed was convicted of eight felony counts (four of wire fraud and four of making false statements), as well as two misdemeanors in concealing its bribes to Prime Minister Tanaka of Japan in 1973-1974.   Lockheed was not convicted under the law that prohibits bribery, but was fined $647,000 for concealing such bribes.[70]   No Lockheed officials were sent to jail for their crimes.

Whether this law will deter corporations from making illegal payoffs remains to be seen. From 1977 to 1984, only thirteen cases were tried under the act, and another ninety-six cases were closed without prosecution.   Many businesses have lobbied to weaken the act's chief provisions. And under the Reagan administration, the Justice Department unit charged with the act's enforcement has been pared down.[71]

The consequences of bribery by multinationals. It has been noted that bribery by multinationals is now a crime. This is the case not merely because such payments are immoral, but because this practice has resulted in a number of very negative consequences to the corporations themselves and to America's foreign policy and economy.   Such consequences result in part because bribes made by multinational corporations are hidden from the stockholders. Such secrecy within the corporation means several things:

> 1. The prospective investor or stockholder, as well as the government, does not have an accurate financial picture of the corporation, and
> 2. These practices can be concealed only through various devious means or through improper accounting procedures, both of which endanger the credibility of corporations.[72]

Thus, at home, revelations of corporate bribery have caused distrust among both stockholders and the public at large.

Abroad, the bribery of foreign officials, especially in countries where it is viewed as unethical or illegal, has endangered U.S. relations with other governments. This was particularly the case in Japan, where the Lockheed scandal helped create the greatest post-World War II crisis in Japanese politics. Clearly the communists could not have hoped for a more successful event.

Bribes by multinationals also endanger corporate operations from an internal standpoint:

> In abiding or abetting corruption of public officials, a company gradually corrupts itself. No organization can remain for long in a state of moral schizophrenia, violating legal or ethical norms abroad while seeking to maintain its institutional integrity at home. In time, the lower standards accepted as the way of life abroad will corrupt standards of corporate life at home.[73]

Finally, it has been suggested that such bribes have not only failed to accomplish the goal of increasing business abroad, but they may have actually been detrimental to such commerce. Sorensen has insisted that there

> was no gain to our country's balance of payments or economy when U.S. companies paid bribes to win a contract that would otherwise have gone to another U.S. company. On the contrary, the added cost of these improper contracts to the host country further weakened the market for other U.S. exporters. The fact that some American companies have succeeded in these countries without the payment of bribes is an indication that U.S. exports will not suffer all that severely from an end to such payments. Those governments desirous of obtaining U.S. technology and

quality will unquestionably learn to buy our goods without any special inducement.[74]

Thus, bribery by multinationals appears to carry with it a number of ironic and negative consequences for U.S. society as a whole.   The same may be said about another deviant practice of some multinational firms, the exportation of hazardous products.

The Practice of Corporate Dumping

By the late 1970s, a practice known as *corporate dumping* had aroused a good deal of concern among certain public-interest groups and governments agencies.   The practice involves exporting goods that have either been banned or not approved for sale in the United States.

Most often, the greatest market for such unsafe products is among the poor of the Third World. Hazardous products are often legal in such countries.   And because many of the poor in these nations are illiterate, they are often unaware of the hazards involved with the use of such products.

Examples of the products involved in corporate dumping are growing at a rapid pace.

An undisclosed number of farmers and over 1,000 water buffalos died suddenly in Egypt after being exposed to leptophos, a chemical pesticide which was never registered for domestic use by the Environmental Protection Agency (EPA), but was exported to at least 30 countries.

After the Dalkon Shield intrauterine device killed at least 17 women in the United States, the manufacturer withdrew it from the domestic market.   It was sold overseas after the American recall and is still in common use in some countries.

No one knows how many children may develop cancer since several million children's garments treated with a carcinogenic fire retardant called Tris were shipped overseas after being forced off the domestic market by the Consumer Product Safety Commission (CPSC).

Lomotil, an effective anti-diarrhea medicine sold only by prescription in the U.S. because it is fatal in amounts just slightly over the recommended doses, was sold over the counter in Sudan, in packages proclaiming it was "used by astronauts during Gemini and Apollo space flights" and recommended for use by children as young as 12 months.

Winstrol, a synthetic male hormone, which was found to stunt the growth of American children, is freely available in Brazil, where it is recommended as an appetite stimulant for children.

Depo-Provera, an injectable contraceptive banned for such use in the United States because it caused malignant tumors in beagles and monkeys, is sold by the Upjohn Co. in 70 other countries, where it is widely used in U.S.-sponsored population control programs.

450,000 baby pacifiers of the type that has caused choking

deaths have been exported by at least five manufacturers since a ban was proposed by the CPSC. 120,000 teething rings that did not meet recently established CPSC standards were declared for export and are on sale right now in Australia.[75]

In some cases, corporate dumping has been aided by government policy. In one instance, the population office of the Agency for International Development (AID) purchased hundreds of shoe-boxed-sized cartons of unsterilized Dalkon Shields for distribution in the Third World. The birth-control device--which causes uterine infections, blood poisoning, spontaneous abortion in pregnant women, and perforation of the uterus--was sold to AID at 48 percent discount because of its unsterile condition.[76] The device was distributed in forty-two nations, largely in the Third World. Moreover, insufficient information concerning the use and hazards of the shield accompanied the shipment.

Some companies dump workplace hazards, as well as hazardous products, in poor nations. One example is the case of asbestos, a cancer-causing agent. Thanks to the Occupational Carcinogens Control Act of 1976, fines of $1,000 for violations and $5,000 for repeat violations are provided for U.S. manufacturers who expose workers to carcinogenic agents. However, no such regulations protect workers from contracting cancer from asbestos fibers. On the contrary, Mexican law merely provides a light fine ($45 to $90) for failure to warn workers that they are working around a health hazard. As a result, U.S. asbestos makers increasingly locate plants in Mexico and other Third World nations with lax workplace hazard laws (e.g., Brazil) and are now producing quantities of asbestos there.[77]

Corporate dumping is undesirable for two main reasons. First, it poses serious health hazards to the poor and uninformed consumers of the Third World, which, in the long run, contributes to the anti-Americanism of many nonaligned nations. And such anti-Americanism is not infrequently exploited by communist bloc nations. Second, many types of corporate dumping produce a boomerang effect. That is, some of the hazardous products sold abroad by U.S. companies are often used in the manufacture of goods that are exported to the United States and other developed nations.

> The "vast majority" of the nearly one billion pounds of pesticides used each year in the Third World is applied to crops that are then exported *back* to the U.S. and other rich countries. . . . This fact undercuts the industry's main argument defending pesticide dumping. "We see nothing wrong with helping the hungry world eat," is the way a Velsicol Chemical Company executive puts it. Yet, the entire dumping process by-passes the local population's need for food. The example in which DBCP manufactured by Amvac is imported into Central America by Castle & Cooke to grow fruit destined for U.S. dinner tables is a case in point.[78]

The boomerang effect of corporate dumping may represent the breeding ground of yet another major scandal regarding the practices of multinational corporations and certain U.S. government agencies in the Third World.

　　We are not suggesting that deliberate racist and genocidal policies are being practiced by certain corporations and government agencies. What we are suggesting is that corporate dumping may well have such effects on the nonwhite people of the world.　The same may be said concerning support by corporations and government for regimes that violate human rights.

HUMAN RIGHTS, MULTINATIONALS, AND U.S. FOREIGN POLICY

　　Under Presidents Ford and Carter, the United States went on record as supporting the cause of human rights around the world.　In a United Nations speech of March 17, 1977, President Carter pledged to "work with potential adversaries as well as . . . close friends to advance the cause of human rights."[79]

　　The United States is also a party to the International Bill of Rights.　Passed by the UN General Assembly in 1948, this document supports a variety of civil and economic rights and specifically pledges member nations not to subject anyone to "torture or to cruel, inhuman or degrading treatment, or punishment" or to "arbitrary arrest, detention, or exile."[80]

　　Finally, the United States is also a signatory to the famous Helsinki Agreement of 1975, which contains a detailed human rights clause, specifically stating that participating nations will "respect human rights and fundamental freedoms, including freedom of thought, conscience, religion, or belief, all without distinctions as to race, sex, language, or religion."[81]　Thus, by pronouncement and by legal agreement, the United States has firmly committed itself to the cause of human rights.

　　Unfortunately, there is a mounting body of evidence that indicates that U.S. policymakers have, on many occasions, either placed in power and/or aided in retaining power some of the world's most repressive dictatorships.　The chief characteristic of such regimes is that they are right-wing, military dictatorships, and, hence, friendly to the goals of multinational capitalism.　Chomsky and Herman have stated that, with U.S. support (ranging from foreign aid to military protection), many Third World regimes have done away with democratic practices and instituted brutally repressive measures, including arbitrary imprisonment, torture, death squads, and kidnapping.

　　In fact, a pattern has been established, showing that U.S. economic and military aid (and aid from U.S.-dominated lending agencies) has been "positively related to investment climate (for U.S. multinationals) and inversely (negatively) related to the maintenance of the democratic order and human rights."[82]　This relationship is described in Table 5-3. Moreover, the decline in aid for South Korea and Chile is somewhat misleading.　In South Korea, the decline was caused by the end of expenditures for the Vietnam War, in which South Korea participated.

Table 5-3
Relationship Between U.S. Aid, Investment Climate, and Human Rights in Ten Countries

Country	Strategic Political Dates (1)	Positive (+) or Negative (–) Effects on Democracy (2)	(–) Means an Increased Use of Torture or Death Squads (3)	(–) Means an Increase in No. of Political Prisoners (4)	Improvement in Investment Climate: Tax Laws Eased (+) (5a)	Improvement in Investment Climate: Labor Repressed (+) (5b)	Economic Aid (% Change) (6)	Military Aid (% Change) (7)	(6) + (7) (% Change) (8)	U.S. and Multi-national Credits (% Change) (9)	Total Aid (8) + (9) (% Change) (10)
Brazil	1964	–	–	–	+	+	+ 14	–40	– 7	+ 180	+ 112
Chile	1973	–	–	–	+	+	+558	– 8	+259	+1,079	+ 770
Dominican Republic	1965	–	–	NA	+	+	+ 57	+10	+ 52	+ 305	+ 133
Guatemala	1954	–	–	NA	+	NA	NA	NA	NA	NA	+5,300
Indonesia	1965	–	–	–	+	+	– 81	–79	– 81	+ 653	+ 62
Iran	1953	–	–	–	+	+	NA	NA	NA	NA	+ 900
Philippines	1972	–	–	–	+	+	+204	+67	+143	+ 171	+ 161
South Korea	1972	–	–	–	+	+	– 52	–56	– 55	+ 183	+ 9
Thailand	1973	+	+	NA	–	–	– 63	–64	– 64	+ 218	+ 5
Uruguay	1973	–	–	+	+	–	11	+ 9	– 2	+ 32	+ 21

Source: N. Chomsky and E. S. Herman, "U.S. vs. Human Rights in the Third World," *Monthly Review* 29 (July/August 1977), 30–31. Reprinted by permission.

And the decline in aid for Chile was, in fact, due to a successful right-wing coup (supported by the CIA) in 1973; high levels of aid had been given before that date.

Between 1973 and 1978, the United States continued its aid to many of the regimes cited by Chomsky and Herman, as well as to others cited by organizations like Amnesty International, the UN Commission on Human Rights, and the International Commission on Human Rights for persistent "torture, assassination, and arbitrary arrest."[83]

Moreover, the Foreign Assistance Act of 1974 provides that the president "shall substantially reduce or terminate security assistance to any government which engages in gross violations of . . . human rights."[84] Under this act, it became illegal (as of July 1, 1975) to provide aid to any law enforcement organization (e.g., police prisons) of any foreign government. However, under the International Narcotics Control Act, both training and weapons have been given to police departments in many foreign countries, including those listed in Table 5-3.

In the cases of Guatemala (1953), Iran (1953), the Dominican Republic (1965), and South Vietnam (1963), either U.S. troops and/or the CIA played an active role in actually installing such regimes, either through aid or armed forces or both.[85] Aside from bringing favorable advantages to multinationals, these regimes have done little to improve the lot of the people over whom they rule. This is especially the case in Latin America.

Item: In 1973, following a U.S.-supported coup that overthrew Chilean President Allende, a socialist, 45,000 people were arrested, tortured, killed, and/or exiled. Several university facilities were closed down, all left-of-center political parties were prohibited, and press censorship was rigidly enforced.

Item: Following a 1965 invasion by U.S. Marines, a wave of torture swept the Dominican Republic in 1970. A disappearance or murder was reported every thirty-four hours. Moreover, in 1975, it was reported that the Philip Morris Company had paid over $136,000 in bribes to various Dominican officials in return for preferential tax ruling and other favors.[86]

One of the most significant examples of such support concerns Iran. In 1953, the CIA was responsible for placing the Shah's family in power when it assisted in overthrowing leftist Prime Minister Mohammad Mossadeq in a violent coup. From 1953 until the 1979 Khomeini revolution, Congress, the U.S. military, the CIA, and private corporate interests all supported the Shah's army and secret police with various types of aid. Under the U.S. Office of Public Safety program, between 1961 and 1973, Iran received $1.7 billion. This money was used to purchase police hardware (e.g., guns, teargas grenades, computers, patrol cars, and so on) and to train 179 Iranian police officials at the International Police Academy in Washington, D.C. (and other special U.S. police schools). From 1946 to 1976, Iran received $1.6 billion under a variety of U.S. military-assistance programs. These programs involved outright grants of arms, equipment, and services; credit for the purchasing of U.S. arms; training of Iranian military personnel; and subsidies awarded under an act designed to aid threatened pro-U.S. regimes.

Between 1950 and 1976, 11,025 Iranian military officers received training under these programs.

Iran also purchased arms from private concerns. For example, the Bell Helicopter Company helped Iran develop a Sky Cavalry Brigade, operating from helicopters, which was modeled after similar U.S. units that fought in Vietnam.[87] Finally, between 1971 and 1978, the United States sold Iran $15 billion in military supplies.[88] Moreover, at the moment of the revolution, some 40,000 military advisors,[89] along with an unknown number of CIA agents, were stationed in Iran. In short, the United States had a long history of assistance to the Shah's regime.

While the Shah was in power, almost 1,500 people were arrested every month. In one day alone (June 5, 1963), the SAVAK (Iran's secret police) and the Shah's army killed 6,000 Iranian citizens. Amnesty International's report for 1975 indicated that Iranian authorities had arrested and imprisoned between 25,000 and 100,000 political prisoners.[90] The Iranian press was strictly controlled by the police under the Shah's direct orders. Minorities were not allowed to learn their native languages, and poverty was widespread. Iran was a nation in which political stability was maintained by repression--a nation on the brink of massive political turmoil.

Since 1973, Iran has been one of a number of nations cited for constant abuses of human rights by organizations such as Amnesty International, the International Commission of Jurists, and the UN Commission on Human Rights.[91] Thus, while U.S. officials and the press knew full well what was taking place in Iran, the government continued to support the Shah with various types of military aid and the press remained nearly silent on the Shah's abuses.

By mid-1980, the United States had paid a tragic price for its rather blind support of the Shah's regime: In 1979, an anti-American revolution led by Moslem holy man Ayatollah Ruhollah Khomeini, exiled from Iran by the government in 1963, overthrew the Shah's rule. U.S. support for the Shah may also have been partially responsible for the catastrophic increases in oil prices since 1973 (see Chapter 2). A number of sources, including Jack Anderson and CBS's "60 Minutes" have reported that the Shah:

1. was installed in power in the 1950s when the Rockefellers helped arrange the CIA coup that overthrew the Mossadegh;

2. demonstrated his gratitude to the Rockefellers by making heavy deposits of his personal funds in the Rockefeller-owned Chase Manhattan bank;

3. raised Iranian oil prices in 1973-1974 by 470 percent, with the approval of then Secretary of State Henry Kissinger, a Rockefeller associate. (This cost the oil-consuming nations of the West an estimated $95 billion in inflated oil prices.)[92] The price hike was requested by the Shah in part to purchase American-made arms;

4. was admitted into the United States for medical care in 1979 as a result of pressure by Chase Manhattan president David Rockefeller and Henry Kissinger.[93] As a result, in November 1979, militants overran the U.S. Embassy in Tehran, capturing sixty-one U.S. employees. An aborted effort to rescue the hostages in early May 1980 resulted in the deaths of eight U.S. servicemen. "While the hostages' release was successfully negotiated in January of 1981, in December of 1979 Chase

Manhattan filed a $366 million lawsuit against the Iranian government, largest of the over 300 suits filed against the Iranians. The suit is still pending in the Courts.[94]

Since then, the Khomeini regime has spread anti-American fever throughout the Middle East. In October 1983, a truck driven by members of a Khomeini-supported regime smashed into a Beirut, Lebanon, building housing U.S. Marines, killing 241 servicemen.[95] Such terrorism and instability has seriously weakened perception of the strength and consistency of U.S. foreign policy.

U.S. support for the Shah was quite profitable for the Chase Manhattan bank, which continues to be the repository for the Shah's sizable fortune, and the Exxon Oil Company, which is controlled through Rockefeller trust funds and private holdings.[96]   Yet these events have never been investigated by Congress. The consequences suffered in return for U.S. support for the Shah are also indicative of other consequences of supporting regimes that violate human rights.

In Central America, another trouble spot, U.S. support for authoritarian dictatorships contributes to suffering and political instability throughout the region.

Item: From 1976 to 1983, some 15,000-20,000 residents of Argentina simply disappeared. Many were tortured to death and then buried in secret locations in unmarked graves by Argentina's military dictatorship. In 1982, the U.S.-backed government declared amnesty for those responsible for the disappearances of these 20,000 suspected subversives, which primarily benefited those guilty of torture and murder. However in December 1983, Argentina elected a democratic government under Raul Alfonsin, and judicial action began against many of those military officers responsible for the crimes.[97]

Item: In El Salvador, a poor Central American nation, 2 percent of all families own 60 percent of the nation's most fertile land. And between 1961 and 1975, the number of families owning no land at all grew from 30,000 to 167,000. Between 1979 and 1983, some 40,000 civilians were killed largely by government-supported, right-wing death squads, and 20 percent of the Salvadoran population (800,000 people) became refugees. U.S. aid to El Salvador between 1979 and 1984 was $100 million, six times that provided in the previous twenty-nine years, despite the fact that the government's death squads brutally raped, tortured, and murdered four U.S. nuns in 1980.

Amnesty International has declared that the Salvadoran death squads are a gross violation of human rights. Nonetheless, aid continues, as the Reagan administration continues to argue that the situation is constantly improving. Meanwhile, investments in El Salvador by U.S.-based multinational corporations, such as Chevron, Texaco, and Kimberly-Clark, total $100 million.[98]

Item: In another poor Central American nation, Guatemala, the United States sponsored a CIA-directed coup in 1954 when it was learned that Guatemala's president, Jacobo Guzman, planned to redistribute 387,000 of the 500,000 acres of Guatemalan land owned by a

U.S.-based company, United Fruit.   Secretary of State John Foster Dulles, whose law firm had represented United Fruit in the 1930s, and CIA director Allan Dulles (John's brother and former president of United Fruit), launched a massive public relations campaign accusing Guzman's government of being Communist. The CIA coup that overthrew the Guatemalan president replaced him with a U.S.-trained army officer, Castillo Armas.   Under Armas, political parties and trade unions were abolished, and U.S. aid totalling $6 million was used to thwart guerrilla resistance in the 1960s in which 10,000 people were killed and 100,000 people were left refugees. Even the U.S. State Department criticized the operation.

Since 1954, 80,000 Guatemalan civilians, mostly peasants, have been murdered, many, women and children.   Eyewitness accounts report children being hacked to death with machetes, their heads smashed against walls, while infants were thrown into the air and bayoneted.   In 1982 alone, 80,000 peasants fled Guatemala, and Amnesty International estimates another 10,000 were killed.   Yet the Reagan administration insists criticism of Guatemala is a "bum rap."[99]

Since July 1982, the Guatemalan government has been involved in the attempted genocide of ethnic groups living on its northern border, violating a 1948 UN convention against genocide (to which Guatemala was a signatory). In August 1983, General Montt was overthrown in a barracks coup and replaced by another military leader, General Victories.   At the time of the coup, unemployment was 40 percent and business was angered over Montt's policies restricting oil investment.

Following the coup, the Reagan administration quickly approved an aid package totalling $10.25 million in military aid and $66.5 million in development aid for fiscal 1984.   Reports indicated that the new Guatemalan leader had conferred with U.S. officials two days before the cup aboard the U.S. ship *Ranger*, anchored off the Nicaraguan coast.   In late August, General Victories announced closer military ties with El Salvador, including provision for new training camps in Guatemala to instruct Salvadoran military personnel in counterinsurgency tactics.   A military alliance was quickly concluded with El Salvador and Honduras, largely against Nicaragua.

Item: Between 1929 and 1979, the U.S.-backed Samosa family ruled Nicaragua with a dictatorial hand. Ousted by a popular revolution in 1979, Samosa's former supporters are now being armed and trained by the CIA in Central America and Miami.   While the revolutionary Sandanista government has reduced illiteracy in Nicaragua from 50 to 12 percent, redistributed land, and achieved self-sufficiency in food production, its regime was forced to turn to the Soviet Union for aid when the Reagan administration cut off $30 million in funds approved under the Carter presidency.

Since 1980, the United States has engaged in a covert war against Nicaragua, training counterrevolutionaries in more than a dozen Latin American nations, giving $3.1 million in military aid to the Honduran military, and arming 4,000-10,000 men in Nicaragua itself. The United States has also illegally mined harbors in Nicaragua and refused to accept judgment against this action by the World Court. The CIA has also used the Salvadoran Air Force to fly sorties over Nicaragua.[100]

The Consequences of Support for Repressive Governments

The assessment of U.S. support for regimes that violate human rights may be made by viewing (1) the conditions of people who live under such regimes, and (2) the effect of such support on U.S. foreign policy. It must be stressed that the inhabitants of the Third World often exist under conditions that violate elementary human rights. Thus, throughout Asia, Africa, and Latin America:

An estimated 1.5 billion people are without effective medical care.

Developing countries have an average of 4,000 people per doctor; in some, the ratio goes above 50,000 per doctor.

Half the school-age children are not yet in schools.

10,000 persons per day in the Third World die from starvation, and another 1.5 billion suffer from malnutrition.

Unemployment in the Third World is now 30% in most countries.

Per capita income in most Third World nations ranges from less than $250 per year (e.g., Ethiopia, India, Kenya, and Pakistan) to less than $1,600 per year (e.g., Turkey, Mexico, and Chile).

More than 700 million adults are unable to read and write.[101]

To the extent that U.S. support for such regimes is based on arms rather than development, U.S. policy becomes a factor in exacerbating these wretched conditions. By 1983, yearly U.S. weapons sales to foreign nations had reached $23 billion. In 1983, the United States was the major supplier to at least twenty of the world's nations engaged in war at the time. Moreover, in 1982-1983, the United States signed another $24 billion in arms-export agreements.[102]

While it is true that not all Third World peoples live under repressive dictatorships, the majority of Third World governments are repressive. Such sales of weapons help maintain repressive regimes and fuel wars in the Third World. They do not foster peaceful economic development.

In the India-Pakistan War of 1965, for example, "the Sherman tanks of the Indian Army battled the Patton tanks of the Pakistani Army."[103] These weapons were sold to the two nations with the promise that they would be used defensively to resist communist aggression, yet they helped fight a war between the two noncommunist nations. Such incidents have also taken place between Israel and her Arab neighbors. Certainly, U.S. arms sales to nations in conflict are not the sole cause of such wars. But the presence of arms may contribute to the heightening of tensions. In any case, it is unfortunate that a world that spends $200 billion a year on arms cannot (or will not) spend funds for projects so desperately needed in the Third World, including:

Annual cost for ending world illiteracy in five-year pro-
gramme. Estimate by UNICEF: $1.6 billion.

Annual cost for making "real impact" on the development
crisis. Estimate by World Bank Chief Robert McNamara: $15
billion.

Annual cost for investment in land and water needed for
poor nations to meet food production targets. Estimate by U.N.
Food and Agriculture Organization: $4.5 billion.

Money needed now by poor countries to maintain essential
imports. Estimate by World Bank, Washington: $5.5 billion.

Cost for solving the crisis of cities and human settlements. Estimate by environment expert Barbara Ward: $25
billion.

Annual cost for supplying everyone in the poor world with
basic maternal health and family planning services. Estimate by
food and population expert Lester Brown: $2 billion.[104]

U.S. support for dictatorships in underdeveloped countries does
help create a favorable business climate for multinational firms. However, the economic activity of multinationals is often a hindrance to
development of such countries. Consider, for example, the effects of
repatriation (return of profits made overseas to the corporation's home
base):

From 1950 to 1970 ... U.S. firms added $1.7 billion to
their holdings in four ... countries--Chile, Peru, Bolivia, and
Venezuela--primarily to increase production of such export commodities as copper, tin, and oil. But in the same period, these
multi-nationals repatriated $44.2 billion to the United States,
leaving a net loss to those countries of $9.5 billion.[105]

This net loss often translates into massive indebtedness, with such debts
usually owed to multinational banks, governments, and other lending
institutions made up largely of members from advanced industrial countries. The results have been very favorable for multinational banks, but
devastating to Third World nations. From 1965 to 1972, overseas assets of
U.S. banks grew from $9 billion to $90 billion. By 1976, U.S. banks held
$181 billion in overseas assets, a 100 percent increase over four years.[106]

A great share of such assets were actually loans to Third World
governments. In 1972, the total indebtedness of Third World nations to
foreign lenders was $50 billion.[107] By the late 1970s, this indebtedness
reached about $200 billion, a 300 percent increase.[108] By 1982, Third
World governments owed $640 billion, an increase of nearly 1,200 percent
over just ten years.[109]

This means that certain multinational companies have an immense
stake in preserving certain Third World governments so they may collect
on their loans. Such stakes have sometimes required multinationals to
favor foreign policy measures that are bitterly opposed by the U.S. public.
The Panama Canal treaties are a case in point. Thirty-nine percent of the
national budget of Panama is spent just to pay the interest on that
nation's national debt of $1.8 billion, 77 percent of which is owed to

multinational banks.   Ronald Steel claims that it was for this, and other reasons favorable to business interests, that multinational firms lobbied hard for the passage of the canal treaties, which assured Panama an income from the canal, plus various foreign aid payments, which in turn assured Panama's creditors that repayment would continue.[110]   The passage of the treaties also meant continued military assistance to the repressive regime of General Torrijos.   This, despite polls showing a majority of Americans opposed the treaties!

Not only does support for repressive regimes inhibit economic development and foster unpopular foreign policy measures, such support often has a detrimental effect on American foreign policy, as well. That is, repressive regimes and U.S. support of them are often quite unpopular with Third World peoples. As seen in Iran, such support has touched off revolutions in nations that are anti-American and often anticapitalist, as well.   U.S. support for regimes that violate human rights sometimes has the effect of driving poor nations into the hands of the communists. This has been the case with Cuba and certain African nations, and may yet be the case with Nicaragua, the Philippines, and dozens of others. Thus, the policy designed to prevent communist influence in developing nations often has precisely the opposite effect.

CONCLUSION

In this chapter, we have examined those U.S. defense and foreign policy areas in which deviance abounds: questionable defense contracting practices, bribery, the sale of hazardous goods by multinational firms, and U.S. support for repressive Third World regimes. A closer look at these types of deviance indicates that they are quite interrelated.   That is, many of the corporations involved in defense contracting with the federal government have also been found guilty of bribery overseas (e.g., Lockheed and Northrop). And many of these same firms are enriched by U.S. arms sales to repressive regimes.   Likewise, the needs of the U.S. economic system for cheap labor, raw materials, and investment outlets have contributed immensely to the worldwide deployment of U.S. military forces and U.S. support for dictatorships, which are obstensibly anticommunist.

The results of these policies are profitable for major corporations in the short run but may be devastating to the nation and much of the world in the long term. Waste, inefficiency, and cost overruns within the Defense Department threaten to create domestic inflation and a weakened U.S. military capability.   And bribery, the sale of hazardous products, and support for repressive regimes often foster resentment toward the United States, further weakening her strength at home and abroad.   Such practices also hinder the economic development of the world's poorest and most desperate citizens. In short, nothing less than the future well-being of the United States and much of the world is now at stake, in part because of such deviance.

NOTES

1. H. Block, *Herblock Through the Looking Glass* (New York: W. W. Norton, 1984), 67.

2. *Jacksonville Times-Union*, 28 January 1985, p. A-5, and *Denver Post*, 13 December 1984, p. 12-D.

3. J. Newfield, "Crime in the Suites: Will Congress Go Easy on Corporate Crooks?" *The Village Voice*, 29 October 1979, 12.

4. C. Watson, "Campaign Wins Some Concessions," *Multinational Monitor* 1 (Winter 1978/1979), 12.

5. Jack Anderson column, *Washington Post*, 30 December 1979, p. B-7.

6. S. Lens, "Thirty Years of Escalation," *The Nation*, 27 May 1978, 624.

7. H. Magdoff, "Militarism and Imperialism," in *The Capitalist System*, ed. R. C. Edwards et al., 421-26 (Englewood Cliffs, NJ: Prentice-Hall, 1972), 425.

8. Lens, 624.

9. M. T. Klare, *War without End: American Planning for the Next Vietnams* (New York: Knopf, 1972), 25.

10. R. L. Sivard, "Arms or Alms," *National Catholic Reporter* 24 (8 April 1977), 8.

11. Dwight D. Eisenhower, "Farewell Address," in *The Military-Industrial Complex*, ed. C. W. Pursell, Jr. (New York: Harper and Row, 1972), 206-7.

12. Senator William Proxmire, *Report from Wasteland: America's Military-Industrial Complex* (New York: Praeger, 1970), 162.

13. Reprinted from A. Sanseri, "The Military-Industrial Complex in Iowa," in *War, Business, and American Society: Historical Perspectives on the Military-Industrial Complex*, ed. B. F. Cooling, 158-70 (Port Washington, NY: Kennikat Press, 1977), 158-59; and Department of Commerce, *Statistical Abstract of the United States, 1984* (Washington, D.C.: U.S. Government Printing Office, 1983), 332, 539.

14. James Fallows, *National Defense* (New York: Random House, 1981), 65.

15. "Top Non-profit Defense Contractors," *The Chronicle of Higher Education*, 10 July 1985.

16. H. Chasin and B. Chasin, *Power and Ideology* (Cambridge: Schenkman, 1974), 167.

17. M. Pilisuk and T. Hayden, "Is There a Military-Industrial Complex which Prevents Peace?" in *The Triple Revolution Emerging*, ed. R. Perrucci and M. Pilisuk, 73-93 (Boston: Little, Brown, 1971), 77.

18. A. Yarmolinsky, *The Military Establishment* (New York: Harper and Row, 1973), 67.

19. D. McDonald, "Militarism in America," in *The Triple Revolution Emerging*, ed. R. Perrucci and M. Pilisuk, 32-53 (Boston: Little, Brown, 1971), 36 (originally appeared in the *The Center Magazine* 3 [January 1970]).

20. McDonald, 42.

21. McDonald, 42.

22. Block, 69.

23. F. Ackerman, *Reaganomics: Rhetoric or Reality* (Boston: South End Press, 1982), 64-67.

24. J. P. Grace, *Burning Money: The Waste of Your Tax Dollars* (New York: Macmillan, 1984), 95, 99.

25. S. Tobias et al., *What Kind of Guns Are They Buying for Your Butter?   A People's Guide to National Defense* (New York: Morrow, 1982), 249.

26. L. P. Ellsworth, "Defense Procurement: Everyone Feeds at the Trough," in *The Monopoly Makers*, ed. M. Green (New York: Grossman, 1974), 230-32. See also comment by Congressman Aspin, cited in S. Melman, *The Permanent War Economy: American Capitalism in Decline* (New York: Simon and Schuster, 1974), 44 (originally appeared in *New York Times*, 29 August 1972).

27. See Congressional Quarterly, *The Power of the Pentagon* (Washington, D.C.: Congressional Quarterly, Inc., 1972), 88-90.

28. M. Mintz and J. Cohen, *Power Inc.* (New York: Viking Press, 1976), 276-77.

29. Jack Anderson, "C-5A Costs Up Again," *Jacksonville Times-Union*, 26 July 1979, p. A-9; and Harold Freeman, *Toward Socialism in America* (Cambridge, MA: Schenkman, 1979), 40.

30. Mintz and Cohen, 277-following.

31. A. E. Fitzgerald, *The High Priests of Waste* (New York: W. W. Norton, 1972), ix.

32. M. Parenti, "More Bucks From the Bang," *The Progressive* 44 (July 1980), 27-30.

33. R. Sherrill, *Why They Call It Politics*, 4th ed. (New York: Harcourt, Brace, Jovanovich, 1984), 114, 120.

34. Grace, 90-91.

35. Steven Rosen, ed., *Testing the Theory of the Military-Industrial Complex* (Lexington, MA: D. C. Heath, 1973), 18-19.

36. Kermit Vandivier, "Why Should My Conscience Bother Me?" in *In the Name of Profit*, ed. R. Heilbroner, 3-31 (New York: Doubleday, 1972), 28.

37. Mintz and Cohen, 150.

38. T. Coffin, "Conversion, the Answer to Inflation and Recession," *The Washington Spectator* 2 (1 February 1979), 1.

39. Jack Anderson, "Defense Department Procurement Waste, Theft Staggering," *Florida Times-Union*, 10 November 1978, p. 6-A.

40. Terence McCarthy, "What the Vietnam War Has Cost," *New University Thought* 6, no. 4 (Summer 1968).

41. *The Defense Monitor* 7 (September/October 1977,) 3.

42. M. Anderson, "The Empty Pork Barrel," in *Defense Sense*, ed. R. Dellums, 184-203 (Cambridge, MA: Ballinger, 1983), 189-96.

43. Quoted in Coffin, 1.

44. G. R. LaRoque, "Preparing to Fight a Nuclear War: The Reagan Arms Budget," in *Defense Sense*, ed. R. Dellums, 109-24 (Cambridge, MA: Ballinger, 1983), 110; F. Holzman, "Administration Misrepresentation of Soviet Military Spending," in *Defense Sense*, ed. R. Dellums, 96-107 (Cambridge, MA: Ballinger, 1983); and M. Raskin, "U.S. Foreign Policy . . . Imperialism and Military," in *Defense Sense*, ed. R. Dellums, 57-68 (Cambridge, MA: Ballinger, 1983), 57.

45.   J. W. Fulbright, "National Security and the Reagan Arms Build

up," in *Defense Sense,* ed. R. Dellums, 69-77 (Cambridge, MA: Ballinger, 1983).

46. Sherrill, 133.

47. H. Caldicott, *Missile Envy* (New York: Morrow, 1984), 38.

48. Sivard, 1.

49. D. Shoup, "The New American Militarism," in *Crisis in American Institutions,* ed. Jerome H. Skolnick and E. Currie (Boston: Little, Brown, 1973), 269.   See also W. Fulbright, *The Pentagon Propaganda Machine* (New York: Liveright, 1970).

50. See Colonel J. Donovan, *Militarism, U.S.A.* (New York: Scribner, 1970), 191-210; and Fulbright.

51. H. R. Rodgers, *Crisis in Democracy: A Policy Analysis of American Government* (Reading, MA: Addison-Wesley, 1978), 145.

52. G. Ott, "Now It's a 'Naval Gap,'" *The Progressive* 9 (September 1978), 22.

53. Center for Defense Information, "U.S. Soviet Military Facts," *The Defense Monitor* 6 (June 1984), 5, 6.

54. Center for Defense Information, *The Defense Monitor* 3 (April 1980), 1.

55. H. Magdoff, "The U.S. Dollar, Petrodollars, and U.S. Imperialism," *Monthly Review* 30 (January 1979), 12.

56. See A. Edward et al., eds. *The Capitalist System,* 2nd ed. (Englewood Cliffs, NJ: Prentice-Hall, 1978), 478.

57. A. Ebert-Miner, "How Rawlings Uses Haitian Women to Spin Profits Off U.S. Baseball Sales," *Multinational Monitor* 7 (July 1982), 11.

58. C. H. Anderson, *The Political Economy of Social Class* (Englewood Cliffs, NJ: Prentice-Hall, 1974), 278; R. Scheer, *America After Nixon* (New York: McGraw-Hill, 1974), 163-64; and D. Tiranti, "High Finance and Small People," *The New Internationalist* 69 (November 1979), 61.

59. T. Sullivan et al., *Social Problems: Divergent Perspectives* (New York: Wiley, 1980), 190.

60. C. H. Anderson, 280.

61. I. Zeitlin, *Capitalism and Imperialism* (Chicago: Markham, 1972), 103.

62. T. Sorensen, "Improper Payments Abroad: Perspectives and Proposals," *Foreign Affairs* 54 (July 1976), 722.

63. G. Breckenfeld, "Multinationals at Bay: Coping with the Nation-State," in *Readings in Social Problems: Contemporary Perspectives,* ed. P. Wickman, 170-76 (New York: Harper and Row, 1977), 174 (originally appeared in *Saturday Review,* 24 January 1976). Mr. Breckenfeld is on the board of the editors of *Fortune* magazine, a leading business periodical.

64. Mintz and Cohen, 153. The following section on multinational and corporate bribery is based heavily on their excellent discussion.

65. J. Hougan, "The Business of Buying Friends," in *Unexplored Deviance,* ed. Dushkin, 130-43 (Guilford, CN: Dushkin, 1978), 134 (originally appeared in *Harper's,* December 1976).

66. Mintz and Cohen, 153.

67. Hougan, 130.

68. Mintz and Cohen, 147.   See H. Maurer, "Bananagate," *The Progressive* 40 (July 1976), 30-34.

69. M. Dowie et al., "Bechtel: A Tale of Corruption," *Multinational Monitor* 5 (May 1984), 7.

70. "Lockheed Fined $647,000 for Secret Payoffs," *Florida Times-Union*, 2 June 1979, p. B-5.

71. Dowie, "Bechtel: A Tale of Corruption," 7-9.

72. M. Clinard, *Illegal Corporate Behavior* (Washington, D.C.: Law Enforcement Assistance Administration, 1979), 200.

73. P. Gabriel, "A Case for Honesty in World Business," *Fortune*, December 1977, 50.

74. Sorensen, 729.

75. Mark Dowie, "The Corporate Crime of the Century," *Mother Jones* 9 (November 1979), 24-25. © *Mother Jones* Magazine. Used with permission.

76. Barbara Ehrenreich et al., "The Charge: Genocide; The Accused: The U.S. Government," *Mother Jones* 9 (November 1979), 28.

77. B. Castleman, "Industries Export Hazards," *Multinational Monitor* 1 (Winter 1978/1979), 14.

78. David Weir et al., "The Boomerang Crime," *Mother Jones* 9 (November 1979), 43.

79. J. Cockcroft and F. Cockcroft, *The Nation*, 18 November 1978, 523.

80. "The International Bill of Rights," in *The New Politics of Human Rights*, by J. A. Joyce, 237-82 (New York: St. Martin's Press, 1978), 239.

81. "Excerpts from the final act of the 1975 Helsinki Conference," in *Human Rights and American Diplomacy: 1975-1977*, by J. F. Buncher, 11-17 (New York: Facts on File, 1977), 12.

82. N. Chomsky and E. S. Herman, "U.S. vs. Human Rights in the Third World," *Monthly Review* 29 (July-August 1977), 29.

83. M. Klare, *Supplying Repression: U.S. Support for Authoritarian Regimes Abroad* (Washington, D.C.: Institute for Policy Studies, 1977), 8.

84. Klare, 15-16.

85. Klare, 25-26.

86. G. MacEoin, "A Continent in Agony: Latin America on the Road to Fascism," *The Progressive* 3 (March 1979), 17.

87. For several interesting assessments, consult the following articles: Richard Falk, "Iran's Home-Grown Revolution," *The Nation*, 10 February 1979, 135-37; A. Cockburn and J. Ridgeway, "The Worst Domino," *The Village Voice*, 19 February 1979, pp. 1, 11-12; W. Laqueur, "Trouble for the Shah," *The New Republic*, 23 September 1978, 18-21; M. Kondracke, "Who Lost Iran," *The New Republic*, 18 November 1978, 9-12; and F. Halliday, "Shah's Dreams of Economic Growth Become Nightmares," *In These Times*, 26-28 December 1978, 9.

88. Klare, 20, 33, 36, 41, and 45.

89. Kondracke, 12.

90. R. Baraheni, "Terror in Iran," *New York Review of Books*, 28 October 1976, p. 21.

91. Amnesty International, *Report on Torture* (New York: Farrar, Straus, and Giroux, 1975), 227-29.

92. J. Anderson, "Kissinger Cleared Iran's Oil Gouge," *Washington Post*, 5 December 1979, pp. 13-17.

93. J. Anderson, "Rockefeller-Shah-Kissinger Connection," *Washington Post*, 26 December 1979, p. D-12; and "60 Minutes," 4 May 1980.

94. *New York Times*, 11 November 1980, p. 3.

95. Block, 269.

96. J. Anderson, "Kissinger Cast in a Questionable Light," *Washington Post*, 10 December 1979, p. C-27.

97. R. A. White, *The Morass* (New York: Harper and Row, 1984), 29-30.

98. Caldicott, 160; J. Kwitney, *Endless Enemies* (New York: Cogdon/Weed, 1984), 10-11.

99. Caldicott, 98; White, 97.

100. Caldicott, 100.

101. Sivard, 9; Scheer, 163-64; and Tiranti, 61.

102. Sherrill, 128; *The Defense Monitor* 6 (June 1984), 6-7.

103. Freeman, 46.

104. J. Roebuck and S. C. Weeber, *Political Crime in the United States* (New York: Praeger, 1978), 76.

105. *Daily World in U.N. Action Pact for World Development* (New York: United Nations Information Division, n.d.), 1.

106. S. Lens, "The Sinking Dollar and the Gathering Storm," *The Progressive* 5 (May 1978), 23.

107. "The IMF," *Multinational Monitor* 7 (July 1983), 1.

108. Lens, 23.

109. "The IMF," 1.

110. Ronald Steel, "Beneath the Panama Canal," *New York Review of Books*, 23 March 1978, p. 12.

CHAPTER 6

Political Corruption: Continuity and Change

Political corruption is an integral part of U.S. politics.[1] As we will see, Watergate was not an aberration, but just another instance in a long series of political crimes by public officials.

Political corruption is defined as "any illegal or unethical use of governmental authority for personal or political gain."[2] Corruption occurs, then, to accomplish one of two goals--material gain or power. This chapter is divided into two sections, one discussing each goal. In each case, we will illustrate political corruption at one or more of the various levels of government--community, state, and national. We should note at the outset, however, that the examples used are just a small sample of the political crimes--known and unknown--that have occurred throughout U.S history.[3]

MONEY AND POLITICS

Money and politics have always been closely intertwined. Since political campaigns are costly, candidates must either be relatively affluent or accept monies from the wealthy or special interests. We have discussed some aspects of the money/politics relationship already, but our concern in this section is with another facet--graft.

Political *graft* is the illegal act of taking advantage of one's political position to gain money or property. Graft can take several forms. First is the outright bribe, where an individual, group, or corporation offers money to a public official for a favor. Or the government official may demand money in return for a favor, which is political extortion. Second is a subtle form of bribery, where the public figure accepts exorbitant lecture fees from organizations or accepts retainers at his or her law office. A third type occurs when a public figure is offered the opportunity to buy securities at a low price; then, when the price goes up, the briber purchases the securities back, at a great profit to the bribee Finally, a fourth variant is the kickback, where contractors, engineering and architectural firms, and others pay back the official responsible for granting a lucrative government contract with a percentage of that contract.

We will discuss all these forms of graft as we examine the various fields in which they occur.

Fields of Graft

The government--city, state, and national--is involved in a number of activities, including law enforcement, the granting of contracts, the use of public funds, the hiring/firing of employees, tax assessment, and land use. Quite certainly, all of these activities are prone to corruption.

Purchasing goods and services. The federal government spends billions of dollars on an array of goods and services from U.S. business, including military hardware, space systems, research projects, musical instruments, desks, clothing, and brooms. One agency alone, the General Services Administration (GSA), buys about $5 billion in goods and services each year.[4] One estimate is that the graft in the GSA costs taxpayers roughly $66 million annually.

Repair contractors and suppliers have also been guilty of graft, billing the government for work never performed and for undelivered materials. For example, one firm was paid to paint 2.4 million square feet of space in a federal building containing only 1.9 million square feet. Also, store managers have accepted money and other gifts from firms that sell to the government; in return, the companies were allowed to charge in excess for their merchandise. What's more, GSA officials have deliberately purchased inferior goods at premium prices for their personal gain, with both the companies and the GSA officials sharing in the bounty. For example, from 1974 to 1977, several contractors pleaded guilty to charges of bribery, with one claiming that he divided $310,000 with GSA employees while doing only $60,000 in legitimate work.[5]

Bidding for contracts is a process especially susceptible to bribery, especially when the bidding is not competitive. Approximately 90 percent of all contracts for new weapons systems are exempt from competitive bidding so that the Defense Department may select the superior system rather than just the most economical one. Unfortunately, this process is especially open to graft.

What does it take to win a defense contract? The answer is not easy, for there are many possibilities, including superior design, more efficient programs, performance on schedule, and better quality control. Perhaps most important is influencing a few key personnel in the Pentagon, as noted in Chapter 5. A good deal of time and money is spent on this cause, including the hiring of former military officers by industry. Jack Anderson describes this practice:

> The giant contractors, such as Northrop Corporation and Rockwell International, court Pentagon officials assiduously. The way to many a defense contract has been greased by a mixture of booze, blondes, and barbeques. The brass hats and the industrialists shoot together in duck blinds. They ski together on the Colorado slopes. They drink together and play poker together. And invariably, the tab is picked up by some smiling corporate executive. The relationship is so cozy that many Pentagon officials, upon retirement, got to work for the companies that had come to them for contracts. ... It's a rare contractor that doesn't employ a few retired generals and admirals who are on a firstname basis with the Pentagon's big brass. ...[6]

According to Anderson, in the mid-1970s, 715 former Pentagon "bigwigs" had found employment with top defense contractors. For instance, Northrop Corporation had sixty-four ex-Pentagon officials on staff. It is not surprising, therefore, that Northrop managed to secure $620.3 million in military contracts. Similarly, Boeing Corporation, with forty-eight former Pentagon officials, contracted $1.56 billion in Pentagon business. And Rockwell International, which hired thirty-six exofficials, received $732.3 million in defense contracts.[7]

At the local level, competitive bidding is avoided in several ways. So-called emergencies are exempt. So it was that James Marcus, New York City's water commissioner under Mayor John Lindsay, gave an $840,000 contract without bidding to a firm that had agreed to pay a kickback for cleaning a reservoir in the Bronx.[8] Purchases below a specified amount are also not subject to competitive bidding. One creative way to stay below the cutoff in such a situation is to split the contract into smaller parts so that each part can be awarded without bidding.

A common exception to competitive bidding is in the purchase of professional services by engineers, architects, auditors, and others. While the rationale for this exception is logical—that is, the need for a specialist may mean that there is no competition—the negotiation process is vulnerable to graft. The most celebrated case involving this type of corruption caused Spiro Agnew to resign as vice-president of the United States. Let's briefly look at this interesting and common type of graft.[9]

During the 1960s, suburban Baltimore County was growing rapidly. This growth required the creation of new streets, sewers, and bridges, as well as numerous rezoning decisions. Great sums of money were made by those fortunate to receive favorable zoning or contracts from the county. A government investigation revealed that those favorably treated (including contractors, architectural firms, and engineering firms) often kicked back 5 percent to those responsible for the decision. This practice of kickbacks was not new. In fact, it was a time-honored Maryland custom.

Included among those regularly receiving kickbacks was Spiro Agnew. The payoffs began in 1962, when Agnew became Baltimore County executive and continued when he became governor in 1967; even as late as 1971, when Agnew was vice-president, he received a payment in the basement of the White House. Agnew received these payments for all the design jobs in the county, and later, as governor, he received a percentage of the highway contracts and other engineering work. While serving as vice-president the payments continued, amounting to $80,000 during those few years.

During the dark days of the Watergate investigation, the inquiry into Agnew's possible criminal activities became public. The evidence against him was irrefutable, and he was forced to plea bargain to reduce the penalty. Agnew resigned, plead no contest to one charge of income-tax evasion, and was given a sentence of three years of unsupervised probation and a fine of $10,000.

Public funds. The use of public monies is a ready source of corruption by those in political power. Government units at all levels have discretionary powers over money collected, waiting to be spent. The state treasurer, for instance, is custodian over many millions of dollars. Commonly, these funds are deposited in banks to obtain interest for the state. But which banks and at what interest rate? The choice is certainly not a random one. The criteria used by some officials include several factors: (1) which banks have given financial support to the candidates and/or party in power; (2) where politicians are shareholders of bank stocks; and (3) which banks will make loans at favorable rates to powerful public officials or to their business associates.

One case of the questionable use of public funds involved Matthew Quay, the state treasurer of Pennsylvania, for thirty years during the late 1800s.[10] Quay demanded political contributions from banks; if they complied, he would in return deposit state monies at no interest. This practice deprived the state of the revenue from interest (e.g., $100 million at 6 percent yields $6 million in interest). Quay was also guilty of political extortion.

Public property. Another potential area for corruption is the misuse of public property. Government officials have discretionary powers over public lands. They decide, for example, which ranchers get grazing rights, which lumber companies have rights to timber lands, and what policies will control the extraction of minerals and petroleum from lands owned by the government. Fortunes can be made or lost depending on favorable access to these lands. Of course, such a situation is susceptible to bribery and extortion.

Early in U.S. history, there were several instances of the improper use of political influence in the disposition of public lands. One example involved a large area of virgin land west of South Carolina known as the Yazoo territory (much of which is now Alabama and Mississippi), which was claimed by the federal government, Georgia, and numerous Indian tribes. In 1794, the Georgia legislature sold its land (30 million acres) to four companies for 1.5 cents per acre. "The haste of the legislature in concluding such an unprofitable sale was apparently the result of the attentions paid them by the companies which had peddled shares at very low prices to nearly all the legislators."[11]

This congressional largesse to help business for mutual gain was typical after the Civil War.

> Congressmen gave huge grants, subsidies, and loans to railroad promoters--and bought their stocks at preferred prices or accepted gifts outright. . . . In 1876 they repealed all restrictions on the sale of public federal land in the South, ordering it sold to private interests as soon as possible--and got huge shares of it as the silent partners of the timber speculators who bought it.[12]

The most infamous case involving the fraudulent use of public lands was the Teapot Dome scandal. During the administration of Warren Harding (which, along with that of Ulysess S. Grant, is considered among the most corrupt in U.S. history), a scandal broke concerning the leasing of oil lands. In 1921, Secretary of the Interior Albert Fall persuaded President Harding and the Navy Secretary to transfer naval oil reserves from the Navy to his jurisdiction in the Interior Department. When this was accomplished, Fall then transferred the oil reserves at Teapot Dome, Wyoming, and Elk Hills, California, to two private oil producers--Henry Sinclair and E. L. Doheny--for their use. The leases were signed secretly and without competitive bidding. In return, Fall collected $100,000 from Doheny for Elk Hills and $300,000 from Sinclair for Teapot Dome. When the scandal broke, the government cancelled the leases. Fall was sent to prison for a year (the first cabinet officer in U.S. history to be put in prison), but no penalties were given to the two guilty oil companies or their officers.

Tax assessment and collection. The taxation function of government is one that has enormous potential for graft. Tax assessors have great latitude because many of their decisions are subjective. They are obvious targets for bribes to reduce assessments. In the 1920s, Chicago had a particularly corrupt tax system. Individual members of the board of review could raise, lower, or eliminate assessments made by the tax assessors. Workers in Chicago's political machine "were rewarded by ridiculously low assessments, a precinct captain's house being assessed at one-fifteenth the value of a similar house next door."[13]

The situation in Cook County (where Chicago is located) has not changed much since the 1920s when it comes to taxation. In 1972, the county assessor was investigated by the state for assessing certain properties on a system subject to manipulation and preference. Upon learning of the pending investigation, the assessor, P. H. Cullerton, reassessed nine high-rise properties in Chicago, adding $34 million to the city's tax base.[14]

Officials at the federal level are also susceptible to bribes involving taxation. Internal Revenue Service personnel investigating income tax evasion can be bribed to look the other way. So, too, can customs officials. An additional example of an abusive practice involving taxes is illustrated by the 1875 Whiskey Ring scandal, which broke during the Grant administration. Over 350 distillers and government officials were indicted for defrauding the government of tax revenues. This was accomplished when distillers falsified reports on the amount produced and bribed government inspectors to verify the fraudulent reports.[15]

Regulation of commercial activities. Government officials are required by law to inspect foods (such as grain and meat) to ensure that they are not contaminated and to grade them according to quality. Again, we know of numerous instances when agents have received bribes to allow questionable items to pass inspection.

Abuses also abound in government efforts to control certain business activities, such as gambling and the sale of alcohol. Because these activities are generally restricted by law, the granting of licences is a lucrative plum for which people are willing to pay extra. They are also willing to pay for favorable legislation. In a celebrated 1960 case, Governor Otto Kerner of Illinois was bribed by certain racetrack interests for political favors. The bribe was subtle because it was in the form of stock. Kerner was offered racetrack stock for a fraction of its value. He paid $15,079 for stock, which he later sold for $159,800 (a profit of 1,050 percent). This was a disguised bribe in return for Kerner's help in securing legislation favorable to the racetrack owned by the donor of the securities.[16] Not so incidentally, the donor, Marjorie Everett, also contributed $45,000 to Kerner's 1960 campaign and another $40,000 in 1964. These monies, plus the sweet stock deal, seem related to some of Governor Kerner's decisions concerning racing:

1. Kerner directed the chair of the Harness Commission to cancel the dates awarded a competitor of Mrs. Everett and to divide them among two other tracks, one owned by Mrs. Everett. (When the chairman resisted, he was forced to resign.)

2. Kerner was instrumental in getting parimutuel taxes on a graduated basis rather than a fixed percentage, saving Mrs. Everett and her co-owners of Washington Park $3 million between 1966 and 1968.

3. Kerner signed a bill abolishing the troublesome Harness Commission, giving its duties to the Racing Board, whose membership was expanded with Kerner appointments.

Kerner was found guilty in federal court of bribery and conflict of interest in 1973.[17]

Zoning and land use. The areas of zoning, planning, and building codes are highly subject to graft, since the decisions can provide or eliminate great financial advantage.   Decisions in these areas can establish which individuals or organizations will have a monopoly.   Overnight, such decisions can make cheap land valuable or priceless land ordinary.   And the decisions can force all construction to be done by certified employees.   And so on.   Again, we can see that the government's discretionary powers, while necessary, can be abused by government officials and businesspeople. The problem, of course, is that the decisions are not always made in the public interest.

The examples of graft in zoning decisions are plentiful, but we will only present one illustrative case.[18]   From 1950 to 1970, a small borough in southern New Jersey—Lindenwold—had undergone rapid population growth, tripling in size. In this setting, a group of speculators was able to make a 2,400 percent gross profit on a tract of sixty-nine acres because of favorable zoning decisions greased by bribes. They purchased the land at public sale for $40,000. At that time, the land was relatively cheap because of strict zoning and a clause that demanded the land be developed within a specified time or revert back to the municipality. The investors then used $30,000 for payoffs to the borough tax assessor and the secretary of the county tax board, which allowed the investors to exceed the deadline without any construction. Another $90,000, given to the mayor, the tax assessor, and at least one councilman, got the land rezoned for townhouses, making it much more salable than when it was zoned for industry. The land was then sold for $1 million, which meant a gross profit of $960,000, or a net profit of $840,000 when the expenses for bribes were deducted. Once again, the political decisions, orchestrated with money, were lucrative to all parties--except the public.

The legislative process. Persons serving in legislatures, municipal councils, or on boards of county commissions are targets for bribes because their lawmaking powers are so crucial to the monied interests. There are two special problems in detecting whether bribery occurs in legislatures. First, legislators (and candidates for other offices as well) receive campaign contributions. And second, it is difficult to assess the motivations of how a person votes. Is he or she beholden to those who contributed to the candidate's political campaign, or does the individual have a sincere belief that such a vote was in the best interests of the region or nation?

We cannot answer this question with certitude, but the data seem to indicate that money makes a difference. In 1981, for example, nineteen of the twenty-two members of the House Ways and Means Committee who received contributions from the commodities industry voted for a measure giving traders a tax break. Of the thirteen members who received no money from the commodities industry, eight voted against the bill.[19]

Thus, the passage of favorable laws or the defeat of unfavorable ones may result directly from financing by special interests. So, too, may special interests receive beneficial governmental rulings and the maintenance of tax loopholes. Since these investments pay off, it is only rational for special interests to donate to the candidates of both parties to ensure that their interests are served. The result is that the wealthy have power while the less well-to-do and the poor exert no leverage on office holders.

To counter the potential and real abuses of large contributions, the presidential campaigns of 1976, 1980, and 1984 were financed from public funds. Congressional candidates, however, were allowed to accept contributions from individuals and special interest groups. Most of this money has come from special interest groups through PACs (political action committees.) These groups represent many interests, including labor unions, doctors, realtors, auto dealers, teachers, oil interests, and defense contractors. Each PAC may give up to $5,000 to any candidate in a primary and another $5,000 to any candidate in a general election. However, as *U.S. News and World Report* observed, "PACs of every ilk have a way of contributing their allowed $5,000 chunks to candidates who either have voted 'right' or had better do so shortly."[20]

In 1974, PACs provided congressional candidates with $12.4 million; in 1976, they provided $22.6 million, and in 1978, $35 million. In 1980, PACs contributed $50 million to congressional races, and in 1982, the amount jumped to $199 million, leading some cynics to comment that the United States has "the best Congress that money can buy."[21]

No one can prove that receiving a PAC contribution automatically buys a vote. But the evidence leads to such a conclusion. For example, in 1982, the National Automobile Dealers' Association opposed a law proposed by the Federal Trade Commission that would require used-car dealers to disclose known defects to potential buyers. Through various PACs, the dealers' association made campaign contributions of over $840,000 to more than 300 senators and congresspersons. Eighty-five percent of these representatives voted against the used-car rule, killing it by more than a two-to-one margin.[22]

Another example of PAC influence concerns a congressional vote on funding the Clinch River nuclear breeder reactor in 1981. Ralph Nader's Public Citizen's Congress Watch observed that the five companies involved in designing and building the reactor contributed a total of $280,000 to members of Congress. Of the eleven representatives who received more than $3,000, ten voted to build the reactor; the other was absent at the time of the vote. Of the representatives who received $1,500 to $3,000, 76 percent voted for the project. And of the representatives who did not receive any money, 71 percent voted to kill it.[23]

Another case shows how business PACs regard their political contributions as good business investments. In 1980, the top ten defensecontractors had contracts worth $23 billion to manufacture military hardware. During the 1982 political campaign, PACs representing these large defense corporations contributed more than $1.5 million to various officeholders and candidates.[24]

What effect does receiving campaign contributions and other favors have on a legislator? Will his or her actions be biased? Clearly it is difficult to affirm that a legislator acted because of money, as Amick has argued:

> When people are exercising legislative roles, they have to be given wide latitude. The law can and does forbid them to sell their votes, but it cannot force them to cast those votes in an objective way, or an intelligent way, or a well-informed way. And there is no test that can be designed that will automatically disclose whether a given vote is corrupt; the necessary freedom given to legislators to make honest decisions also makes it easier for them to get away with making dishonest ones.[25]

The relationship between receiving money and favorable decisions by legislators is not always a subtle one, however. A few examples make this point, beginning with the Credit Mobilier scandal.[26] In the late 1860s, some of the major stockholders of the Union Pacific Railroad concocted a scheme whereby they would get their company, the railroad, to contract with their construction company, Credit Mobilier. This cozy arrangement allowed the conspirators to charge Union Pacific exorbitant costs. In effect, then, the money that Union Pacific raised through the sale of stocks went to the construction company, which made enormous profits. Concerned over a possible congressional investigation, one member of the conspiracy, who was also a U.S. representative from Massachusetts, Oakes Ames, gave away or sold Credit Mobilier stocks at very low cost to selected members of Congress. In 1872, the bribes were exposed, which led to the expulsion of Ames and another congressman, James Brooks. Also implicated were the outgoing vice-president of the United States and a future president, James A. Garfield.

Another instance of an outright bribe occurred in 1910 when the American Bridge Company bribed New York legislators to defeat a bill that would have improved the procedure for constructing bridges by requiring a referendum and approval by the state engineer.[27]

More recently, we have seen the efforts of Tongsun Park to purchase favorable legislation. Park, a Korean businessman, gave thirty-one congressional members $850,000 in cash from 1968 to 1975 (in addition to throwing lavish parties and giving expensive gifts). Park testified, under immunity, that he bribed Louisiana Congressman Otto Passman, who served as chair of the Foreign Relations Committee, to get South Korea to appoint Park as its sole rice agent. The bribe was successful, as Park became that agent and made $9 million in commissions during a four-year period.[28]

Finally, from 1971 to 1983, thirty-two current or former members of the House of Representatives went to prison, faced criminal charges, or were disciplined by their colleagues.[29] The list of charges included: mail fraud, salary kickbacks from aides, accepting bribes, election-law violations, defrauding the government, making false statements to the government, tax evasion, and perjury. The largest congressional scandal in recent years was the FBI sting operation known as ABSCAM. This operation set up a fictional Arab sheik, Kambir Abdul Rahman, who offered financial inducements to legislators for their favors. Meetings between the sheik and legislators were secretly videotaped. Seven legislators (six representatives and one senator) were indicted and convicted of accepting cash or stock as bribes for their favorable influence. Most noteworthy, only one legislator, Senator Larry Presler of South Dakota, was offered the rich inducement but refused the bribe.[30]

Law enforcement. Formal law enforcement policy begins with the police, who decide if a law has been broken. They must interpret and judge: What behavior is "disorderly"? How much noise is a "public nuisance"? When does a quarrel become a "criminal assault"? When does protest become "riotous"? What constitutes "public drunkenness"?

These questions reveal that the police have great decisional latitude. Unlike other aspects of the criminal justice process, the police often deal with their clients in isolation, their decisions not subject to review by higher authorities. According to Skolnick, "Police work constitutes the most secluded part of an already secluded system and therefore offers the greatest opportunity for arbitrary behavior."[31]

The police, then, have the power to continue or terminate the criminal-processing procedure. Accordingly, the position of the police personnel exposes them to extraordinary pressures. The President's Commission on Law Enforcement and the Administration of Justice noted:

> The violations in which police are involved vary widely in character. The most common are improper political influence; acceptance of gratuities or bribes in exchange for nonenforcement of laws, particularly those relating to gambling, prostitution, and liquor offenses, which are often extensively interconnected with organized crime; the "fixing" of traffic tickets; minor thefts; and occasional burglaries. ... Government corruption in the United States has troubled historians, political reformers, and the general public since the middle of the 19th century. Metropolitan police forces--most of which developed during the late 1800's when government corruption was most prevalent--have often been deeply involved in corruption. The police are particularly susceptible to the forms of corruption that have attracted widest attention--those that involve tolerance or support of organized crime activities. But the police, as one of the largest and most strategic groups in metropolitan government, was also likely targets for political patronage, favoritism, and other kinds of influence that have pervaded local governments dominated by political machines.[32]

Police corruption is most likely with the enforcement of so-called victimless crimes. Legislatures have typically enacted laws to enforce the morality of the majority, making criminal certain offensive acts that may harm the individual who performs them but not others. Laws prohibiting gambling, sex between consenting adults, pornography, liquor, and drug usage create such victimless crimes. Over 80 percent of the police work in the United States has to do with the regulation of private morals. While many police officers are unwilling to accept bribes from murderers and thieves, they may accept them from the perpetrators of victimless crimes, for several reasons: (1) they believe these crimes are harmless and impossible to control anyway; (2) they may feel strong community pressures against enforcement of such laws; and (3) they face organized crime, with its threats and enticements, which encourages cooperation.

The following examples illustrate the level of police corruption noted by the Knapp Commission for New York City in the early 1970s.[33]

Item: In the five plainclothes divisions where investigations were concentrated, a strikingly standardized pattern of corruption was uncovered: Plainclothesmen, participating in what is known as a "pad," collected regular biweekly or monthly payments of as much as $3,500 from each of the gambling establishments in the area under their jurisdiction and divided the take in equal shares. The monthly share per man (the "nut") ranged from $300 and $400 in midtown Manhattan to $1,500 in Harlem. Those supervisors involved received a share and a half.

Item: Corruption in narcotics enforcement lacked the organization of the gambling pads, but individual payments--known as "scores"-- were commonly received and could be staggering in amount. Investigation revealed another standard pattern: Corrupt officers customarily collected scores in substantial amounts from narcotics violators, which were either kept by the individual officer or shared with a partner and, perhaps, a superior officer. Scores ranged from minor shakedowns to payments of many thousands of dollars. The largest narcotics payoff uncovered in this investigation was $80,000. According to information developed by the State Investigation Commission and gathered in recent federal investigations, the size of this score was not at all unique.

Item: Uniformed patrolmen, particularly those assigned to radio patrol cars, were involved in gambling pads smaller than those received by plainclothes units and received regular payments from construction sites, bars, grocery stores, and other business establishments. These payments were usually made on a regular basis to sector car patrolmen and on a more irregular basis to others. Individual payments to uniformed police were small, usually under $20. However, payments were often so numerous that they added substantially to an individual's income. Other less regular payments to patrolmen included those made by afterhours bars, bottle clubs, tow trucks, motorists, cab drivers, parking lots, prostitutes, and defendants trying to fix their cases in court.

The organization of power. So far, we have focused on public officials who have taken bribes or demanded them from monied interests. More important than these random and sometimes patterned actions are the organizational forms that promote a climate where corruption flourishes. We will examine briefly three of these organizational forms-- organized crime, the political machine, and the invisible government.

1. *Organized crime and corruption.* Organized crime involves business seeking profit by supplying illegal goods and services, especially drugs, prostitution, pornography, gambling, and loan sharking (see Chapter 3). The profits from organized crime are enormous. Of course, we cannot know the exact figures, but it is estimated that the gross income of organized crime is twice that of all other kinds of illegal activity. In 1979, estimated revenues from organized rackets were more than $150

billion: $22 billion from gambling, $63 billion from narcotics, $8 billion from pornography and prostitution, and the remaining from such activities as cigarette bootlegging and loan sharking.[34] The net income of organized crime is higher than that of any single legitimate industry.

Several characteristics of organized crime help perpetuate it.[35] First, organized crime supplies illegal goods and services that are in great demand. In other words, one reason for the continued existence of organized crime is that it fills a need. If victimless crimes were decriminalized, organized crime would be left with products and services that could be easily and cheaply supplied from legitimate sources, thereby possibly destroying organized crime's profits and existence.

A second characteristic of organized crime is that it depends on the corruption of police and government officials for survival and continued profitability. Bribery, campaign contributions, delivery of votes, and other favors are used to influence police personnel, government attorneys, judges, media personnel, city council members, and legislators. Each of the major crime families has at least one position in their organization entitled "corrupter."

> The person occupying this position bribes, buys, intimidates, threatens, negotiates, and sweet-talks himself into a relationship with police, public officials, and anyone else who might help "family" members maintain immunity from arrest, prosecution, and punishment. . . . More commonly, one corrupter takes care of one subdivision of government, such as the police or city hall, while another will be assigned a different subdivision, such as the state alcoholic beverage commission. A third corrupter might handle the court system by fixing a judge, a clerk of court, a prosecutor, an assistant prosecutor, a probation officer.[36]

The role of organized crime is a very important source of political corruption at all levels, not just at the level of the police. William Chambliss discusses this in the introduction to his book on corruption in Seattle, Washington:

> Money is the oil of our present-day machinery, and elected public officials are the pistons that keep the machine operating. Those who come up with the oil, whatever its source, are in a position to make the machinery run the way they want it to. Crime is an excellent producer of capitalism's oil. Those who want to affect the direction of the machine's output find that the money produced by crime is as effective in helping them get where they want to go as is the money produced in any other way. Those who produce the money from crime thus become the people most likely to control the machine. Crime is not a by-product of an otherwise effectively working political economy: It is a main product of that political economy. Crime is in fact a cornerstone on which the political and economic relations of democratic-capitalist societies are constructed.
>
> In every city of the United States, and in many other countries as well, criminal organizations sell sex and drugs, provide an opportunity to gamble, to watch pornographic films, or

to obtain a loan, an abortion, or a special favor. Their profits are a mainstay of the electoral process of America and their business is an important (if unrecorded) part of the gross national product. The business of organized crime in the United States may gross as much as one hundred billion dollars annually--or as little as forty billion--either way the profits are immense, and the proportion of the gross national product represented by money flowing from crime cannot be gainsaid. Few nations in the world have economies that compare with the economic output of criminal activities in the United States.[37]

2. *The political machine.* The political machine became the dominant pattern of government for United States cities in the last part of the nineteenth century. This type of government is formed when a clique gets elected to all the major posts in a city. Once in, the leaders use their appointing power to fill the municipal boards, thus controlling the decision-making apparatus. To stay in power, the political organization actively seeks votes. One technique to get votes is to appoint key persons from various factions in the community who deliver the votes of their followers. The other method is to gain the allegiance of voters by providing them with governmental services or public works projects that appeal to large voting blocs. The city is also organized so that each precinct and ward has a machine representative who uses patronage, bribes, favors, and other techniques to keep the voters in his or her district loyal to the machine. Political machines have been almost universally corrupt. The pattern of corruption is not limited to the city, however; usually, there are links to the state and national levels.

The corruption of U.S. cities was typical around the turn of the century.

The pervasiveness of machine politics and of the accompanying corruption in nineteenth-century America is astounding. In his *American Commonwealth* James Bryce estimated that the government of every American city with more than 200,000 inhabitants was corrupt during this last quarter-century. Many cities of 50,000 to 200,000 were corrupt, and even several cities smaller than 50,000 were riddled with corruption, although on a less grandiose scale than, say, New York or San Francisco. The findings of the municipal historian Ernest S. Griffith are also grim. He noted that from 1870 to 1900 Newark was the only large city to remain reasonably honest. The New England towns of Cambridge, Worcester, and Springfield were the only medium-sized cities he discovered that were consistently uncorrupt. Every city he examined in the middle states and all the Southern cities except Atlanta, Charleston, and possibly Richmond and Memphis were persistently or intermittently corrupt. In the West only Oakland and in the mid-West only Milwaukee seem to have avoided the corruption tendency of politics in this era.[38]

For an example of graft rampant in one political machine, let's briefly examine the situation in New York City under the nefarious Boss Tweed, where the Tweed Ring robbed the city of somewhere between $30 and $200 million from 1866 to the mid-1870s.[39]

William March Tweed and two associates gained control of Tammany Hall, New York City's Democratic party organization, in 1863. Under Tweed, the organization gained popular support in the city by providing public works and by actively courting the foreign born, about one-half of the city's population in 1870. Ward leaders helped their constituents by finding jobs, fixing minor problems with the law, and remembering families on special occasions. As a result, the ward captains could deliver votes--and power.

Tweed used this power to become wealthy as he and his associates orchestrated the city government to extract money.

The most accessible and secure source of income was from graft on municipal contracts. Before 1869, city contractors expected to pay 10 percent in graft to the machine. Under Tweed this rapidly rose to 65 percent, of which 25 percent went to Tweed, while the remaining 40 percent was distributed among lesser accomplices. The history of the New York Court House is the most familiar and notorious example of the ring's method of operation. Planned in 1868 at a cost not to exceed $250,000, the Court House under Tweed management eventually absorbed over $8 million of city revenue. Many of the contracts were lent to friends of the ring or to companies owned by the ring's members at inflated prices. The ring collected its 65 percent from the contract on top of the inflated prices. All the costs were passed along to the taxpayers.[40]

As a result of these frauds and others, Boss Tweed and his associates plundered the city. "Of every tax dollar, only fifteen cents went for legitimate uses. The rest went into the pockets of the ring, the overpaid builders, or bribe-welcoming officials."[41]

3. *The invisible government and legal graft.* Who really rules a city, a state, or the nation? The obvious answer is that elected officials do, since they make the laws and enforce them. But a strong case can be made that, at each level of government, there is a permanent alliance of special interests that is more powerful than the elected government.

We live in a nation where private profit is officially perceived as the maximum good--the engine of all progress. The permanent government . . . at the national level where giant oil companies, defense contractors, and multinational corporations have effectively defined the nation's priorities and allocated its resources through a long series of administrations that have unswervingly agreed with Calvin Coolidge's observation that "the business of America is business." In the early 1960s, John Kennedy quickly learned that a president, no matter how popular, who confronts the combined interests of corporate America is walking into a meat grinder. Faced with the choice between massive public works and social spending, or the "trickle-down" economics of business to cure the Eisenhower recession, he found it expedient, in the face of a carefully orchestrated corporate propaganda campaign, to opt for investment credits for industry and tax cuts that aided the wealthiest segment of society. In dealing with the nations balance-of-payments problems, he encountered the same wall of opposition and finally observed: "It's a ridiculous situation for us to be squeezing down essential public activities in order not to touch private investment and tourist spending—but apparently that's life."

"Life" hasn't changed much in Washington, New York, or hundreds of other cities across the land as we begin the nation's third century. *Corporate power still dominates public need.*[42] (Italics added.)

Chapter 7 will focus on this phenomenon at the national level. In this chapter, we will examine how it works at the municipal level, using New York City as the case study. Newfield and DuBrul argue forcefully that a permanent, invisible, and unelected government holds ultimate power over public policy in New York City.[43] It is a government of bankers, brokers, developers, landlords, union leaders, and lawyers. The power of this loose confederation of elites is in their control of institutions, money, property, and even the lawmaking process. It gets its way no matter who the voters elect as mayor or council members.

Whenever an assemblyman casts a vote, or when a public-works project is begun, or when a developer gets a zoning variance to build a highrise, or when federal funds come into a district, or when a decision is made to raise the interest rates that the banks charge the city—in all these situations, the real decision-makers are usually off stage, and unknown to the public.[44]

This permanent government makes enormous sums of money through what Newfield and DuBrul call *legal graft*. The money they receive is not under the table; instead, it is paid in the form of finder's fees, title insurance, city contracts, interest-free deposits of the city's funds, zoning variances, insurance premiums, bond-sale commissions, public-relations retainers, real estate leases, mortgage closings, and legal fees. For example, from 1954-1969, Robert Moses, head of the New York Port Authority, spent over $4.5 billion on public works for over fifteen years. Much of that money was spent for legal graft. For instance, three Democratic politicians shared the insurance business from the Triborough Bridge and Tunnel Authority, worth $100,000 annually in commissions. All of the insurance for the 1964 World's Fair was funneled to one insurance agency, providing it with $3 million in commissions. All of the legal fees for the Fair Corporation were given to the law firm of a former city administrator, who had helped draft the legislation exempting the Fair Corporation from the city's Code of Ethics.[45]

When Yankee Stadium was refurbished, Mayor Lindsay used urban-renewal funds, saying that it would cost but $24 million, including $2 million to rehabilitate the streets and shops around the stadium. The stadium was eventually completed at a cost of $101 million, and the $2 million for the community was never spent. As expected, some contractors did very well. One outfit—Kinney Systems—was awarded a contract without competitive bidding to build two parking garages and remodel another. They were paid $22 million, a management fee from the city, most of the parking fees collected, and a $2-million tax exemption. The city counsel who negotiated the contract in 1972 was, by 1976, working for Kinney Systems as a lawyer.[46]

Legal graft occurs in every conceivable area of city activities, resulting in money, patronage, and other perquisites. In the case of New York City, citizens pay multimillions annually for which they receive nothing. Ironically, though, New York's severe fiscal problems are typically blamed on a variety of sources other than the graft perpetuated by the invisible government.

CORRUPTION AND POWER

In this section, we will discuss the illegal and unethical means used by various people and organizations to gain, retain, or enlarge political power. We will focus on four problem areas: the powerful controlling the powerless, the administration of elections, the conduct of campaigns, and the influence of money in elections. In conclusion, we will elaborate on the various forms of political corruption manifested in the Watergate-related crimes.

The Powerful Controlling the Powerless

The hallmark of representative democracy is that all people have the fundamental right to vote for those who will administer and make the laws. Those in power have often defied this principle of democracy, however, as they have minimized, neutralized, or even negated the voting privileges of the lower classes, minorities, third parties, and the opposition.

The writers of the Constitution, who represented wealth and property, were concerned about the potential power of the masses.[47] Thus, they objected to democracy as we know it today. Their attitude was well-stated by Alexander Hamilton:

> All communities divide themselves into the few and the many. The first are the rich and the well born, the other the mass of the people. The voice of the people has been said to be the voice of God; and however generally this maxim has been quoted and believed, it is not true in fact. The people are turbulent and changing; they seldom judge or determine right. Give therefore to the first class a distinct, permanent share in the government. They will check the unsteadiness of the second and as they cannot receive any advantage by a change, they therefore will ever maintain good government.[48]

Even more blatant was the statement by Governor Morris at the Constitutional Convention:

> The time is not distant when this Country will abound with mechanics and manufacturers [industrial workers] who will receive their bread from their employers. Will such men be the

secure and faithful Guardians of liberty? ... Children do not
vote. Why? Because they want prudence, because they have no
will of their own. The ignorant and the dependent can be as little
trusted with the public interest.[49]

As a result of this type of thinking (which, by the way, was
characteristic of the complaints by intellectuals throughout history until
the last one hundred years or so[50]), the Constitution was designed to
retain the power among the propertied few, while utilizing seemingly
democratic principles. The appearance of democracy actually had the
effect of fragmenting the power of the masses.

> By separating the executive, legislative and judiciary
> functions and then providing a system of checks and balances
> among the various branches, including staggered elections, execu-
> tive veto, Senate confirmation of appointments and ratification of
> treaties, and a two-house legislature, they [the Founding Fathers]
> hoped to dilute the impact of popular sentiments. To the extent
> that it existed at all, the majoritarian principle was tightly locked
> into a system of minority vetoes, making swift and sweeping
> popular actions nearly impossible.[51]

The blatant disregard for the masses, as determined by the Constitution,
is seen in the following provisions.

Item: The senators from each state were to be elected by their
respective state legislatures. The Seventeenth Amendment,
adopted in 1913, finally provided for the direct election of
senators.

Item: The election of the president was, on the surface, to be decided
by the voters, but in reality, the president was to be selected by
an electoral college composed of political leaders. This procedure
allowed the upper classes to control the presidential vote, regardless of the popular vote. Each state had as many electors as it
had senators and representatives. Each political party would
select a slate of electors, who would vote for president if their
party's candidate carried the state. Interestingly, and indicative
of the contempt for the masses, some states allowed their
electors to vote for anyone, not necessarily the presidential
candidate of their party. (Five states still retain that right.)[52]

The 1876 election illustrates how the electoral college
can run counter to the popular will: The winner, Republican
Rutherford B. Hayes, received some 250,000 fewer votes than his
Democratic opponent, Samuel J. Tilden. Two sets of returns
arrived from three southern states, each having one set that
showed a Republican plurality and another with a Democratic one.
The issue was resolved by a special commission of Congress,
which gave all the disputed nineteen electoral votes to Hayes,
making him the winner by one electoral vote. A deal was made
whereby the southern Democrats aligned with northern Republicans because Hayes promised that: (1) all remaining federal
troops in the three states would be removed; (2) the federal
government would subsidize a southern transcontinental railroad;
and (3) a southerner would be appointed to the cabinet.[53]

Item: Supreme Court justices were to be nonelected. They were to be appointed to life tenure by the president and confirmed by the Senate.

Item: The matter of who was allowed to vote was left to the individual states, which meant, in effect, the disenfranchisement of many voters. All the states disallowed women from voting (changed in 1919 by the passage of the Nineteenth Amendment). All the states denied voting to those held in bondage (changed following the Civil War by the passage of the Fourteenth Amendment). And in various states, it was common to require that voters own certain amounts and kinds of property.

Other nondemocratic practices occurred throughout the states early in U.S. history, some continuing into the present. Most significant was the limiting of political candidates to the wealthy—candidates had to pass steep property qualifications for holding office. This meant that most voters could not qualify as candidates. "The result was that the gentry, merchants, and professionals monopolized the important offices."[54]

An important historical example of this relationship between the wealthy and political leaders is the robber barons of the late nineteenth century. These so-called captains of industry—including Jay Gould, Andrew Carnegie, Pierpont Morgan, John D. Rockefeller, and Cornelius Vanderbilt--made fabulous fortunes, often with the aid of favorable government actions but most notably through chicanery, ruthless plundering, and conspiracy. They were successful clearly because of a cozy relationship with a government, involving several tactics. For instance, at the formal level, some robber barons ruled in the highest councils of government as senators and cabinet members. Moreover, their lawyers and other employees were sometimes appointed to government office, as well. Robber barons made large contributions to the political campaigns of candidates from both parties, and they freely used bribes when necessary. Summarizing the robber-baron philosophy, Frederich Townsend Martin said:

> It matters not one iota what political party is in power, or what President holds the reins of office. We are not politicians or public thinkers; we are the rich; we own America; we got it, God knows how; but we intend to keep it if we can by throwing all the tremendous weight of our support, our influence, our money, our political connection, our purchased senators, our hungry congressmen, our public-speaking demagogues into the scale against any legislation, any political platform, any Presidential campaign, that threatens the integrity of our estates.[55]

Throughout U.S. history, it has been common practice for the majority in legislatures (at all levels) to revise political boundaries for their advantage. This tactic, known as *gerrymandering*, occurs when the party in power designs the political boundaries to negate the power of the opposition. Assume, for instance, that the Democrats control the state legislature. The boundary lines can be redrawn in order to take Republican strongholds from problematic districts, placing them in nearby strong Democratic districts. The Democratic district is strong enough to absorb the Republicans without losing their advantage, and in the former

Republican district, the Democrats have a better chance of gaining control.

Although the Fourteenth Amendment to the Constitution gave blacks the right to vote following the Civil War, the white majority in the southern states used a variety of tactics to keep them from voting. Most effective was the strategy of intimidation. Blacks who tried to assert their right to vote were often subject to beatings, destruction of property, or even lynching. The more subtle approach, however, was quite effective in eliminating the black vote in the southern states. Through legal means, laws were passed to achieve illegal discrimination. One tactic was the white primary, which excluded blacks from participating in the party primary. The Constitution prohibited the states from denying the vote on the basis of race. A political party, however, since it was a private association, could discriminate. The Democratic party throughout most of the South chose the option of limiting the primary to whites. Blacks could legally vote in the general election but only for the candidates already selected by whites. And since the Democratic party in the South was supreme, the candidate selected in the primary would be the victor in the general election. This practice was nullified by the Supreme Court in 1944.

Other legal obstacles for blacks in the South were the literacy test and the poll tax, which were eventually ruled illegal by the Supreme Court, but only after many decades of denying blacks the right to vote. Both obstacles were designed as two southern suffrage requirements to admit whites to the electorate and exclude blacks, without mentioning race. The literacy test and its related requirements were blatantly racist.[56] The object of the test was to allow all adult white males to vote, while excluding all blacks. The problem with this test was that many whites would also be excluded because they were also illiterate. In response, legislators in various southern states contributed alternatives to the literacy requirements that would allow the illiterate whites to vote. One loophole was the "grandfather clause, which, using Louisiana law as the example, exempted persons from the literacy test who were registered voters in any state on January 1, 1867, or prior thereto, the sons and grandsons of such persons, and male persons of foreign birth naturalized before January 1, 1898." Another alternative designed to allow illiterate whites to vote was the understanding clause, which allowed a person who could not read any section of the Constitution to qualify as an elector if he could understand and give a reasonable interpretation of what was read to him. This procedure gave registrars great latitude to decide who could vote. Thus, they had the ability to discriminate, which they did uniformly. A similar law in some states authorized registration of illiterates if they were of good character and could "understand the duties and obligations of citizenship under a republican form of government."

Unfortunately, efforts by whites to limit the power of blacks is not just an historical anomaly. A number of racist strategies are still employed. Howard Ball, head of the political science department at Mississippi State University, has noted a number of "voting wrongs" still used by the white power structure in Mississippi to keep whites in power even though blacks hold a numerical majority.

1. Holding at-large elections in multimember legislative districts gives whites the advantage even when outnumbered because more than

twice as many whites as blacks are registered voters.

   2. Counties have been gerrymandered to dilute black voting strength. As a result, blacks, who represent 35 percent of Mississippi's population, hold only 7 percent of the county supervisor positions.

   3. Once blacks have been successful in winning elections, elective offices have been changed to appointive ones.

   4. White subdivisions have been annexed to produce municipalities, thus diluting the black vote.

   5. Polling places have been switched literally the night before an election.[57]

Election Frauds

   Certainly more than one election has been won through illegal activities. Violence and intimidation have been used by the supporters of certain candidates to control the vote. Various forms of harassment were used especially prior to 1850, when voting was done orally. This practice allowed bystanders to know how votes were cast and thus intimidate or punish persons who voted contrary to their wishes. In this century, violence has been aimed at southern blacks to keep them from registering, thus ensuring white supremacy.

   Most election frauds involving illegal voting, false registration, and bribery have occurred in areas of one-party dominance, especially in cities controlled by a political machine. This has kept the machine in power at the local level and has delivered votes in state and federal elections to one party, thus increasing the scope of the machine's power.

   In the heyday of machine politics, the use of repeaters and personators—to "vote early and often"--was widespread, from the North Side in Kansas City to the South Side in Chicago, from the Strip in Pittsburgh to South of the Slot in San Francisco. No less important, and generally used in conjunction with these, was the practice of wholesale manipulation of registration lists. The names of aliens (sometimes as the result of illegal naturalization), minors, and nonresidents were added to the registration list, along with fictitious names and the names of reliable nonvoters. In combination, such illegal techniques could yield large numbers of fraudulent votes. In the 1869 election in New York, for example, between 25,000 and 30,000 votes were attributed to repeating, false registration, and illegal naturalization.[58]

   These tactics have been used throughout history to influence elections in the United States. For example, Harry Truman would not have been elected senator from Missouri without the help of 50,000 fraudulent votes from the Pendergast machine in Kansas City.[59] So, too, have more recent Democratic victories been predicated on the massive help from Mayor Daley's delivery of the votes in Cook County, Illinois.

   Votes have also been purchased and continue to be today, especially in poor areas, through bribes of money and liquor. The *Los Angeles Times* alleged, for example, that $5,000 was channeled through four black ministers for street money to recruit votes during the Carter campaign in the 1976 California primary.[60]

Another form of election fraud is to bypass the manipulation of the voters in favor of forgery and false accounting by election officials. Corrupt election officials can (1) complete ballots when the voter has failed to vote for a particular office, (2) declare ballots for the opposition invalid by deliberately defacing them or marking two preferences for a single office, (3) destroy ballots for the opposition, (4) add premarked ballots to the total, and (5) simply miscount.

One of the most famous instances of election fraud involved the election of Lyndon Johnson to the Senate.[61] In 1948, Johnson ran for the Democratic nomination (which meant election in Democratic Texas) against Governor Coke Stevenson. Stevenson won the primary by 71,000 votes but lacked a majority in the crowded field. A runoff was then held with the two top vote getters—Stevenson and Johnson. Stevenson again won, or so everyone thought. Days after the polls had closed, a questionable correction of the vote from Duval County gave Johnson 202 more votes than the original count, enough to give him the Democratic nomination by eighty-seven votes. The new vote was orchestrated by George B. Parr, the Democratic county boss. It was alleged that the new votes came from the graveyard and Mexico; some Chicanos testified that Parr had voted their names without their knowledge. When the defeated candidate charged fraud, the Senate voted to investigate. Senate investigators found, however, that the ballots had mysteriously been destroyed. The investigation ended and Johnson became a senator, taking a big step in his political career, which later included terms as the powerful majority leader of the Senate and finally, as president of the United States.

Unfair Campaign Conduct

Political campaigns often involve illegal or at least immoral behavior by the competitors and their supporters to achieve the advantage over their opponents. Behavior such as espionage, bribery, sabotage, crowd agitation, lying, innuendo, and the like occur quite regularly. The primary goal of these tactics is to negate the opponent's strengths, which can be done by spreading rumors about his/her character, especially regarding the candidate's sex life and association with unsavory individuals, such as communists and criminals. For example, in 1983, Bill Allain was elected governor of Mississippi, despite a very rough campaign. Allain's opponent, Leon Bramlett, accused him of having sexual relations with three black transvestites. Allain denied this involvement and was able to win the election. Afterward, the three transvestites repudiated their allegations, claiming they had been paid to lie.[62]

Another tactic has been to place hecklers in an opponent's rally, which the Mondale-Ferraro campaign accused the Reagan campaign of doing in the 1984 presidential race. Or opponents can steal campaign information, as occurred when Reagan forces secured secret information from the Carter campaign prior to the crucial television debates in the 1980 election. In other instances, billboards have been defaced, public address systems and lights for rallies have been sabotaged, and blacks have been hired to pose as workers for the opposition going door-to-door in so-called redneck precincts.

Political dynamiting, another common tactic, gives the voters misinformation about the opposition.[63] This may be accomplished by designing, printing, and distributing pamphlets and brochures that blacken the candidate's reputation, which may be distributed at the end of the campaign so the victim has no time to respond to the charges. The techniques here may be blatant, such as those used by Richard Nixon in his early campaigns for office. He defeated Jerry Voorhis for a House seat in 1946 by stating that Voorhis had been formally endorsed by a labor group (PAC) tainted with known communists. (Voorhis, in fact, was a vigorous anticommunist during his four terms in the House and was never endorsed by the PAC.) A newspaper ad placed by Nixon in that campaign proclaimed, "A vote for Nixon is a vote against the Communist-dominated PAC with its gigantic slush fund."[64] Another alleged violation in this campaign was the hiring of workers by Republican headquarters to work at a phone bank asking people at random, "Did you know Jerry Voorhis was a Communist?"

In 1950, Nixon was elected to the Senate after a race characterized by unethical attacks on his opponent, Helen Gahagan Douglas, a liberal, three-term congresswoman. According to the campaign rhetoric, Douglas was "soft on communism." Moreover, "On 353 times the actress candidate voted exactly the same as Vito Marcantino, the notorious Communist party-line Congressman from New York." She was called the "pink lady" and described, along with Marcantino, as a hero of the communist movement. A pamphlet, colored pink, was distributed to thousands of voters.

> On September 9, in San Diego, Nixon stated that "if she [Douglas] had her way, the Communist conspiracy would never have been exposed, and Alger Hiss would still be influencing the foreign policy of the United States." . . . On November 1, Nixon repeated an earlier charge . . . that Douglas "gave comfort to Soviet tyranny."[65]

The Nixon campaign was aided by favorable treatment in many of California's newspapers. A cartoon that appeared in two Hearst papers, the *San Francisco Examiner* and the *Los Angeles Examiner*, is illustrative of this political help:

> The cartoon, entitled "Rough on Rats," shows Nixon resolutely standing guard with a shotgun in front of a walled farm. His sleeves are rolled up, and in addition to the shotgun, he carries a net labeled "Communist Control." Uncle Sam is farming contentedly behind the wall, while rats (labeled variously, "Appeaser," "Professional Pacifist," "Conspirator," "Spy," "Soviet Sympathizer," and "Propagandist") run about. Hearst cartoons and editorials in those days left very little to the imagination. The editorial under this cartoon, for example, accuses Douglas of favoring "reckless government spending" and "giving away atomic bomb secrets" and of opposing military assistance programs, Selective Service, the Communist Control Act . . . and "weeding out poor security risks."[66]

The Nixon-Douglas campaign rhetoric was based on falsehood and smears. Ms. Douglas was not a communist sympathizer. She did vote on the same side as Marcantino 354 times, but so did Nixon, 112 times, the gap being primarily the difference between Republican and Democratic votes on various issues. But in this case, slander was a successful tactic, as Nixon won 56 percent of the vote.

Tactics need not be as blatant as Nixon's but can be more subtle, like Johnson's famous anti-Goldwater television advertisement in 1964: It never mentioned Goldwater or his "hawk" position; instead, it showed a child amid nature with an atomic mushroom cloud exploding in the distance.

The impact of television in campaigns has been significant in developing and manipulating opinion. In this case, the tactic is not directed at smearing an opponent but by building a particular image of the candidate of choice. Scenes showing one's war exploits or role as a devoted parent, dedicated humanitarian, lover of nature, or whatever, are displayed without reference to the candidate's positions on the issues. The intent of these brief ads (generally thirty or sixty seconds long) is strictly to manipulate the viewers to think positively of the candidate. There is a debate as to whether this technique is moral or not.

This very issue was raised in the 1984 presidential election, as the Reagan campaign employed a strong image-building technique. Reagan's strategy was to act and appear presidential, evoking confidence and determination and speaking in platitudes about American strength and patriotism. Lost in this carefully prepared rhetoric were clear-cut, definitive positions on the political issues at hand. Nonetheless, Reagan won the election by a landslide.

Another borderline technique that has emerged with the growth of the computer is the use of form letters. Millions of letters can be mailed in a political campaign that give personalized messages referring to the recipient's race, ethnicity, religion, children (by name), issues they favor or oppose (e.g., abortion, busing). Again, the effort is the manipulation of voters by making it appear as if the candidate is taking a personal interest in his or her concerns. The Nixon campaign of 1972, for example, could employ 35,000 different combinations in a single letter. This tactic, though legal, subverts the intent of democracy.

Money in Elections

Democracy is a system of government that expresses the will of the people. In theory, since all persons and groups have a right to contribute to the candidate or party of their choice, all interests and points of view will be represented. In practice, however, wealthy individuals and large organizations provide the most money and have the greatest influence on the political process, as we have discussed earlier.

Money intrudes in a variety of ways to thwart democracy, not just through the voluntary contributions to the few. One problem is that political leaders may extort money, producing two sets of victims. One set is the businesses and individuals dependent on the government for contracts, favorable laws, and sympathetic regulation. When confronted with the charge that he had authorized an illegal political contribution of company funds, the chairman of the board of a large corporation replied, "A large part of the money raised from the business community for political purposes is given in fear of what would happen if it were not given."[67] Maurice Stans, Nixon's chief fundraiser in the 1972 campaign, who gathered some $60 million, was especially adept at this form of extortion.

> Stans would approach potential donors threatening that if they did not contribute the desired sum, he would initiate unfavorable pollution action against their corporations. He would take this action, he said, through the Pollution Council he helped establish at the Commerce Department. The scope of Stans' fundraising operations while he was still Nixon's Secretary of Commerce was revealed recently by two oil company executives. They told the Senate Watergate committee that a hundred-thousand-dollar contribution was expected from all large corporations.[68]

The other set of victims of political extortion are government employees, who are forced to make campaign contributions. Although such contributions were made illegal by federal law in 1967, they continue to be required, although perhaps less frequently. The practice has most commonly occurred at state and local levels and has been connected to the patronage system. Around 1900, the rate varied from 10 percent of one's salary (in Louisiana), to a sliding scale of from 3 to 12 percent. In 1972, state employees in Indiana paid 2 percent of their salaries to the party in power.[69]

Closely related to political extortion is the sale of jobs for contributions. This used to be a common practice for postmasterships and other federal positions. Apparently, it is still possible for the most prestigious jobs.

> It is clear that the sale of embassies flourished extensively under Richard Nixon, his 1972 campaign reaping $1,324,442 merely from the eight individuals who headed embassies in Western Europe at the time. After this reelection, Nixon made ambassadors of a further eight individuals, each of whom had given no less than $25,000 to the campaign, and in aggregate $706,000. In February, 1974, Herbert Kalmback, Richard Nixon's personal attorney, pleaded guilty to a charge of promising J. Fife Symington, the ambassador to Trinidad and Tobago during 1969-71, a more prestigious European ambassadorship in return for a $100,000 contribution to be divided between Republican senatorial campaigns and the Committee to Re-elect the President.[70]

Pervasive throughout the money/politics connection is routine circumvention of the law.[71] Candidates and donors commonly exploit loopholes. They give less than the amount the law requires must be reported, but they give in multiples to a number of committees, each of which supports the same candidate. Another ruse is to give money to others, who then make donations in their name. Corporations evade restrictions on giving by laundering money through other sources or by contributing to trade associations such as the National Association of

Manufacturers, which, in turn, pass the money on to the candidates of the original donor. They may also give bonuses to their employees, which are then given as individual contributions. Unions may assess their members a fee, which is then given to the unions' candidates. As noted earlier, some of the largest corporations have given money under the table in a variety of ways to finance candidates. Indeed, a good share of talent in our largest organizations and political organizations is devoted to finding ever more creative ways to outwit the letter and the intent of the law for their political and monetary advantage.[72]

Watergate

The Watergate-related crimes, committed by government officials, represent the acts of official secrecy and deception taken to the extreme.[73] They demonstrate forcefully and fearfully just how far away from the Democratic ideal the U.S. political system had moved at the time and how close it was to approaching totalitarianism. In the words of David Wise:

> Watergate revealed that under President Nixon a kind of totalitarianism had already come to America, creeping in, not like Carl Sandburg's fog, on little cat feet, but in button-down shirts, worn by handsome young advertising and public relations men carrying neat attache cases crammed with $100 bills. Men willing to perjure themselves to stay on the team, to serve their leader. It came in the guise of "national security," a blanket term used to justify the most appalling criminal acts by men determined to preserve their own political power at any cost. It came in the form of the ladder against the bedroom window, miniature transmitters in the ceiling, wiretaps, burglaries, enemies lists, tax audits, and psychiatric profiles.
>
> It is not easy to write the world totalitarian when reporting about America, but if the word jars, or seems overstated, consider the dictionary definition: "Of or pertaining to a centralized government in which those in control grant neither recognition nor tolerance to parties of differing opinion."
>
> And that is very close to what happened, for, as we learned from the Watergate investigation, the enormous power of the government of the United States, including the police power and the secret intelligence apparatus, had been turned loose against the people of the United States, at least against those who held differing opinions, against the opposition political party, and the press.[74]

The Watergate investigation revealed a number of criminal and undemocratic actions by President Nixon and his closest advisors.[75]

Item: Burglars, financed by funds from the Committee to Reelect the President, broke into and bugged the headquarters of the Democratic party in the Watergate apartment complex. These individuals were paid hush money and promised executive clemency to

Item: protect the president and his advisors.

Item: Burglars also broke into the office of the psychiatrist of Daniel Ellsberg, the person who leaked the Pentagon Papers to the press. These papers, of course, were instrumental in showing the public how they had been systematically deceived by a series of president during the long Vietnam War.

Item: While the trial was in session, the White House offered the judge in the Ellsberg case the possibility of his being named director of the FBI.

Item: President Nixon's personal attorney solicited money for an illegally formed campaign committee and offered an ambassadorship in return for a campaign contribution. Money gathered from contributions, some illegally, was systematically laundered to conceal the donors. Much of this money was kept in cash so when payoffs occurred, the money could not be traced.

Item: President Nixon ordered secret wiretapping of his own aides, several journalists, and even his brother. Additionally, he had secret microphones planted in his offices to record clandestinely every conversation.

Item: The director of the FBI destroyed vital legal evidence at the suggestion of the president's aides.

Item: John Mitchell, Attorney General of the United States, participated in preliminary discussions about bugging the Democratic headquarters. He even suggested that one means of gaining information about the Democrats was to establish a floating bordello at the Miami convention.

Item: The president's men participated in a campaign of dirty tricks to discredit various potential Democratic nominees for president, including the publication and distribution of letters, purporting to come from Senator Muskie, claiming that Senator Jackson was a homosexual.

Item: The White House requested tax audits of administration opponents.

Item: The White House used the CIA in an effort to halt the FBI investigation of Watergate.

Item: President Nixon offered aides Robert Halderman and John Erlichman as much as $300,000 from a secret slush fund for their legal fees after they were forced to resign.

Item: The president and his advisors, using the cloak of national security, strongly resisted attempts by the special prosecutor, the courts, and Congress to get the facts in the case. Various administration officials were found guilty of perjury and withholding information.

Item: When the president, under duress, did provide transcripts of the tapes or other materials, they were edited.

Item: The president, on television and in press releases, lied to the United States public, over and over again.

This infamous list of discretions comprises a tangled web of activities that posed a significant threat to the United States' democratic political system. All the efforts were directed at subverting the political process so that the administration in power would stay in power, regardless of the means. There was a systematic effort to discredit enemies of the administration, to weaken the two-party system, and to control the flow of information to citizens.

Although the Nixon administration was guilty of these heinous acts, we should not assume that Nixon was the first U.S. president to be involved in such chicanery. Watergate was no sudden aberration. Rather, it was the end result of government practices that have been significant throughout U.S. history.

CONCLUSION

Our task in this chapter has been to focus on the dark side of politics. Hopefully, politics is not completely corrupt, as one may be tempted to conclude from our discussion.

We have looked at two types of political deviance—the use of political clout for material gain and the unfair means used to gain, maintain, or increase political power. In both cases, the deviance can be achieved by corrupt individuals or by a corrupt system. But even when accomplished by individuals, the important sociological point is that the deviance is only possible because the elite occupy positions of power. Because of the duties and powers inherent in their political positions, they are susceptible to the appeals of the monied interests who want to use them, or they are persuaded by the appeal of greater power.

Although political corruption is found in all types of societies and in all types of political and economic systems, the amount of political corruption found in the United States is astounding. Benson, after carefully studying the phenomenon, offers this conclusion:

> Today it is probably fair to say that America has as much corruption, both absolutely and proportionately, as any other modern constitutional democracy. There are no international indices of corruption, but the available data indicate that corruption here is at least as severe and extensive as in other modern democracies. American idealism does not appear to be reflected in our political ethos.[76]

Why is the United States plagued by this high rate of political corruption? The answer is complex and requires an understanding of the historical factors, character, values, and political-economic systems that characterize the United States. The rip-off mentality that pervades the economic system is found throughout the social structure, as this chapter has amply demonstrated. The goal of the individual or corporate success supersedes group concerns; therefore, any means are used to achieve the goal. The following chapter should provide further insight into this complex societal problem.

NOTES

1. The organization and many of the examples used in this chapter are from two sources: George C. S. Benson, *Political Corruption*

in America (Lexington, MA: Lexington Books, D. C. Heath and Company, 1978), Reprinted by permission of the publisher, Copyright 1978, D. C. Heath and Company; and George Amick, *The American Way of Graft* (Princeton, NJ: The Center for Analysis of Public Issues, 1976).

2. Benson, xiii.

3. In addition to Benson and Amick, the following source provides an excellent review of the magnitude of political crime in the United States: Carl J. Friedrich, *The Pathology of Politics* (New York: Harper and Row, 1972).

4. The following is taken from "Another Scandal Breaks Open in Washington," *U.S. News and World Report*, 11 September 1978, 82; and "A Sweeping Benefit of the GSA Scandal," *Business Week*, 2 October 1978, 78-86.

5. United Press International release, 24 October 1978.

6. Jack Anderson, "Weapons Makers and Pentagon Brass and Happy Family," *Rocky Mountain News*, 1 February 1976, p. 51.

7. Anderson, 51.

8. Amick, 40-41.

9. The Agnew case is taken primarily from Amick, 42-50; and J. Anthony Lukas, *Nightmare: The Underside of the Nixon Years* (New York: Viking, 1976), Chapter 12.

10. Benson, 11, 127; and Gerald J. McCullouch, "Pennsylvania: The Failure of Campaign Reform," in *Campaign Money*, ed. Herbert E. Alexander (New York: Macmillan, 1976), 226-27.

11. Benson, 69.

12. Frank Browning and John Gerassi, *The American Way of Crime* (New York: G. P. Putnam's Sons, 1980), 214.

13. Benson, 12.

14. Amick, 98-99.

15. Benson, 81-82.

16. Amick, 146-49.

17. Amick, 109-14.

18. Amick, 76-94.

19. Mark Green, "When Money Talks, Is It Democracy?" *The Nation*, 15 September 1984, 202.

20. Marvin Stone, "Political Spending: Running Wild," *U.S. News and World Report*, 23 October 1978, 112.

21. Amitai Etzioni, *Capital Corruption: The New Attack on American Democracy* (New York: Harcourt Brace Jovanovich, 1984), 6. See also Pat Ordoensky, "Incumbents, Chairmen Reap Most Donations," *USA Today*, 1 November 1984, p. 9-A; Mark Green, *Who Runs Congress?* 4th ed. (New York: Dell, 1984); and Larry J. Sabato, *PAC Power: Inside the World of Political Action Committees* (New York: W. W. Norton, 1984).

22. "The Death Lobby," *The Nation*, 11 October 1982, 196-97.

23. Cited in Otis Pike, "The Cancer of Congressmen and Campaign Funds," *Denver Post*, 31 August 1982, p. 2-B.

24. Etzioni, 104.

25. Amick, 77.

26. Amick, 146-49.

27. Benson, 13.

28. Green, *Who Runs Congress?* 255-58.

29. Green, *Who Runs Congress?* 235-39.

30. Green, *Who Runs Congress?* 258-62.

31. Jerome H. Skolnick, *Justice without Trial: Law Enforcement in Democratic Society* (New York: John Wiley, 1966), 14.

32. President's Commission on Law Enforcement and the Administration of Justice, "The Challenge of Crime in a Free Society," in *Official Deviance*, ed. Jack D. Douglas and John M. Johnson (Philadelphia: J. B. Lippincott, 1977), 254-55.

33. These three examples are taken from *The Knapp Commission Report on Police Corruption* (New York: George Braziller, 1973), 1-3.

34. James Cook, "The Invisible Enterprise," *Forbes*, 29 September 1980, 60.

35. These characteristics are taken from Charles H. McCaghy, *Deviant Behavior: Crime, Conflict, and Interest Groups* (New York: Macmillan, 1976), 233-35.

36. Donald R. Cressey, *Theft of the Nation: The Structure and Operation of Organized Crime in America* (New York: Harper and Row, 1969), 250-51.

37. Reprinted from William J. Chambliss, *On the Take: From Petty Crooks to Presidents* (Bloomington: Indiana University Press, 1978), 1-2. © 1978 by William J. Chambliss. Reprinted by permission of Indiana University Press.

38. Benson, 33. Reprinted by permission of the publisher, from *Political Corruption in America*, by George C. S. Benson (Lexington, MA: Lexington Books, D. C. Heath and Company), Copyright 1978, D. C. Heath and Company.

39. This account of the Tweed Ring is taken basically from three sources: Benson, 37-43; Allen Weinstein and R. Jackson Wilson, *Freedom and Crisis* (New York: Random House, 1974), 530; and Gustavus Myers, *The History of Tammany Hall*, rev. ed. (New York: Burt Franklin, 1917), Chapter 13.

40. Benson, 39. Reprinted by permission of the publisher, Copyright 1978, D. C. Heath and Company.

41. Weinstein and Wilson, 530.

42. Jack Newfield and Paul DuBrul, *The Abuse of Power: The Permanent Government and the Fall of New York* (New York: Penguin Books, 1978), 84-85. Copyright © 1977 by Jack Newfield and Paul DuBrul. Reprinted by permission of Viking Penguin Inc. For an elaboration of this thesis of a national power elite, see the following: C. Wright Mills, *The Power Elite* (New York: Oxford University Press, 1956); G. William Domhoff, *Who Rules America?* (Englewood Cliffs, NJ: Prentice-Hall, 1967); and Michael Parenti, *Democracy for the Few*, 2nd ed. (New York: St. Martin's Press, 1977).

43. This material is from Newfield and DuBrul, 75-108.

44. Newfield and DuBrul, 76. Copyright © 1977 by Jack Newfield and Paul DuBrul. Reprinted by permission of Viking Penguin Inc.

45. See Robert Caro, *The Power Broker: Robert Moses and the Fall of New York* (New York: Vintage, 1975).

46. Newfield and DuBrul, 118-19.

47. For an elaboration of this thesis, see Charles Beard, *An Economic Interpretation of the Constitution of the United States* (New York: MacMillan, 1919).

48. Max Ferrand, ed., *Records of the Federal Convention* (New Haven: Yale University Press, 1927), quoted in Parenti, 53.

49. Quoted in Parenti, 56.

50. C. B. Macpherson, *The Real World of Democracy* (New York: Oxford University Press, 1972), Chapter 1.

51. Parenti, 56.

52. Parenti, 57-58,

53. Weinstein and Wilson, 430.

54. Parenti, 51.

55. Cited in Matthew Josephson, *The Robber Barons: The Great American Capitalists, 1861-1901* (New York: Harcourt, Brace and World, 1962), 352.

56. The following is taken from V. O. Key, Jr., *Southern Politics* (New York: Vintage, 1949), Chapter 26.

57. Howard Ball, "Mississippi's Voting Wrongs," *Washington Post,* 26 January 1982, p. A-19.

58. Benson, 171.

59. Victor Lasky, *It Didn't Start with Watergate* (New York: Dial Press, 1977), 122.

60. Benson, 172 (originally appeared in *Los Angeles Times,* 8 August 1976, pp. 1, 24).

61. Lasky, 199-23.

62. "More Mississippi Mud," *Newsweek,* 30 January 1984, 32. For historical examples of the use of slander in political campaigns, see John S. Lang, "Political Invective: It's Not What It Use to Be," *U.S. News and World Report,* 16 July 1984, 86-87.

63. See Frank H. Jonas, ed., *Political Dynamiting* (Salt Lake City: University of Utah Press, 1970).

64. These examples are from Frank Mankiewicz, *Perfectly Clear: Nixon from Whittier to Watergate* (New York: Quadrangle, 1973), 39, 45, 51-52.

65. Mankiewicz, 52-53.

66. Mankiewicz, 54-55.

67. Cited in David W. Adamany and George E. Agree, *Political Money* (Baltimore: Johns Hopkins, 1975), 4.

68. Stu Bishop and Bert Knorr, "The Moneymen," in *Big Brother and the Holding Company: The World Behind Watergate,* ed. Steve Weissman (Palo Alto, CA: Ramparts Press, 1974), 211-12.

69. Benson, 177; CBS News, "The Best Congress Money Can Buy."

70. Benson, 179.

71. Benson, 181-83. Reprinted by permission of the publisher, Copyright 1978, D. C. Heath and Company.

72. The following sources elaborate on the reform of the campaign contributions problem: Adamany and Agree: Herbert E. Alexander, ed., *Campaign Money* (New York: Macmillan, 1976); Herbert E. Alexander, *Money in Politics* (Washington, D.C.: Public Affairs Press, 1972); and George Thayer, *Who Shakes the Money Tree? American Campaign Financing Practices from 1789 to the Present* (New York: Simon and Schuster, 1973).

73. This section on Watergate is taken from D. Stanley Eitzen, *Social Problems* (Boston: Allyn and Bacon, 1980), Chapter 2.

74. David Wise, *The Politics of Lying* (New York: Vintage, 1973), x-xi.

75. See also Wise, xi-xiv; "The Tangled Web They Wove," *Newsweek,* 2 December 1974, 32-37; "Four Key Convictions in the Watergate

Affair," *U.S. News and World Report,* 13 January 1975, 15-17; William A. Dobrovir, Joseph D. Gebhardt, Samuel J. Buffone, and Andra N. Oakes, *The Offenses of Richard Nixon* (New York: Quadrangle, 1973); Theodore H. White, *Breach of Faith: The Fall of Richard Nixon* (New York: Atheneum, 1975); and John Dean, *Blind Ambition* (New York: Simon and Schuster, 1976). For a sociological analysis of Watergate, see Jack D. Douglas, "Watergate: Harbinger of the American Prince," in *Official Deviance,* ed. Jack D. Douglas and John M. Johnson (Philadelphia: J. B. Lippincott, 1977), 112-20.

76. Benson, 3. Reprinted by permission of the publisher, Copyright 1978, D. C. Heath and Company.

CHAPTER 7

Political Deviance

Criminologists interested in political crimes have traditionally concentrated on acts by individuals and organizations against the government--namely, attempts to change the political system through violating the law. While these political acts are important to understand, this exclusive focus neglects those crimes perpetrated by the government against the people. Again, in this chapter, we will attempt to right this imbalance by focusing on the deviance of the political elite (see also Chapter 6).[1]

Political deviance is an omnibus concept, including a number of practices. Under this rubric are the myriad forms of political corruption noted in Chapter 6, as well as the consequences of the government's bias toward business that negatively impacts the powerless.

This chapter will catalogue additional political acts that are deviant. Specifically, we will examine deviance in the domestic and foreign spheres. On the domestic level, we will consider (1) the secrecy and deception used by government officials to manipulate public opinion; (2) the abuse of power by government officials and agencies; (3) political prisoners; and (4) official violence, as manifested in police brutality and the use of citizens as unwilling guinea pigs. On the international level, we will focus on two illegal warlike acts: clandestine intervention and war crimes.

DOMESTIC POLITICAL DEVIANCE

Secrecy, Lying, and Deception

The hallmark of any democracy is consent of the governed based on a reliable flow of information from the government. Unfortunately, a number of mechanisms serve to thwart this principle in U.S. society.[2] One common technique used to withhold information is the presidential exercise of *executive privilege*. The doctrine of executive privilege is the constitutionally questionable belief that the president and his staff cannot be forced to testify and that presidential documents cannot be examined without the president's permission. The argument given for such immunity is that such information might compromise national security. However, the more realistic effect is that executive privilege allows the *executive branch of government to withhold information from the Courts* and Congress, not to mention the general public.

Executive privilege has been used several times in recent U.S. history.[3]

Item: President Truman refused to turn over to the House Un-American Activities Committee an FBI report on a government scientist.

Item: In 1963, General Maxwell Taylor declined to appear before the House Subcommittee on Defense Appropriations to discuss the Bay of Pigs invasion.

Item: In 1972, the Securities Exchange Commission refused to give certain information to the House Interstate and Foreign Commerce Subcommittee concerning its investigation of ITT.

Item: In 1973, President Nixon refused to surrender the White House tape recordings to Special Prosecutor Archibald Cox.

Another method used to stonewall is to designate information as *classified.* The classification of documents is based on the necessity of safeguarding sensitive military and foreign policy information in the national interest. However, one problem with classifying documents as secret is defining the category. Thus, while some material is warranted as classified, too much ends up as secret.

In 1972, the Chairman of the House Foreign Operations and Government Information Subcommittee described the magnitude of this problem:

> There are 55,000 arms pumping up and down in Government offices stamping "confidential" on stacks of Government documents; more than 18,000 Government employees are wielding "secret" stamps, and a censorship elite of nearly 3,000 bureaucrats have authority to stamp "top secret" on public records.
>
> These are not wild estimates. These numbers were provided by the Government agencies, themselves. But even this huge number of Government censors is just the top of the secrecy iceberg.[4]

The classification of sensitive materials can also be used as a ploy to hide those materials embarrassing to government officials. An apt example is the attempt by the Nixon White House to suppress publication of the Pentagon Papers, which revealed how U.S. involvement in Vietnam had been shaped during several administrations while being shielded from the public. In early 1965, before President Johnson had sent combat troops to Vietnam, the goals of the United States, as stated in a secret memorandum from Assistant Secretary of Defense Daniel McNaughton to Secretary Robert McNamara were:

> 70 percent to avoid a humiliating U.S. defeat (to our reputation as a guarantor),
>
> 20 percent to keep South Vietnam (and the adjacent territory) from Chinese hands,
>
> 10 percent to permit the people of South Vietnam a better, freer way of life.[5]

What would've happened had these goals been made public?

Would Congress have authorized a major war and more than 50,000 U.S. combat deaths for these goals? Would the American people have supported a war for these goals? And if not, was an American President justified in going to war for them anyway? More importantly, was an American President justified in concealing these goals and our own acts of provocation while he was, in fact, making a unilateral decision to go to war?[6]

Most likely, the people would not have supported the war if they had known about the government's goals. Realizing this, President Nixon (who broadened the war from Johnson's policies) attempted to suppress publication of the Pentagon Papers, which would have revealed the United States' true intentions and behaviors. In addition, the weight of the government's force was brought to the prosecution of those who had leaked the Pentagon Papers (Daniel Ellsberg and Anthony Russo). The government even went so far as to offer the judge in that case the directorship of the FBI while the case was being heard.[7]

Officials can also deceive the public by the "you-did-not-ask-me-the-right-question,-so-I-did-not-give-you-the-right-answer" game.[8] As an example, when Richard Helms was director of the CIA, he was asked before Congress if his agency had been involved in Watergate. His reply was "no." Much later, when it became known that the CIA had lent equipment to the Watergate burglars and concealed the laundering of checks used in the coverup, Helms was reminded of his previous answer. He explained that he had not been asked the right questions, for he had assumed that the original question meant involvement in the actual break-in at Democratic headquarters.

Although all of the above tactics work to deceive the public, none is more onerous than outright lying by government officials, which has occurred more than once in recent U.S. history.[9]

Item: In 1954, Secretary of State John Foster Dulles said that Americans were not involved in the coup in Guatemala to depose the regime of leftist President Guzman, even though the operation was financed, organized, and run by the CIA.

Item: In 1960, a U.S. spy plane, flown by a CIA pilot, was shot down over the Soviet Union. Although the United States had been using U-2 planes to spy on the Soviets for the preceding four years, officials denied the incident, saying we had not violated Soviet air space.

Item: In 1961, the CIA, under President Kennedy, organized an invasion of Cuba at the Bay of Pigs. Yet when the Cubans charged in the United Nations that the United States was behind the operation, Ambassador Adlai Stevenson responded that no U.S. personnel or government planes were involved.

Item: In 1963, the United States supported but officially denied its involvement in the coup against South Vietnam President Ngo Dinh Diem.

Item: In 1964, President Johnson used an incident where U.S. ships were allegedly shot at in the Tonkin Gulf to give him a free hand to escalate the war in Vietnam. Congress was deliberately misled by the official representation of the facts.[10]

Item: President Johnson praised our Asian allies for sending supposed
volunteers to fight in Vietnam when, in fact, our government had
paid Thailand and the Philippines $200 million each to make this
gesture.

Item: President Nixon and his advisors told the U.S. public that the
neutrality of Cambodia had not been violated when we had
already conducted 3,600 bombing missions in that country over a
five-year period. To carry out this deception, the U.S. government falsified the death certificates of Americans who died in
Cambodia.

Item: U.S. military and government officials in the Vietnam War deliberately underestimated enemy troop strength to provide the
illusion of our military progress.[11]

In addition to these examples, we must remember coverups of the
CIA involvement in the takeover of the Allende government in Chile, the
attempted whitewashing of the sheep deaths in Utah because of an
unintended release of chemicals used in biological warfare, the denial by
Attorney General Mitchell that ITT had offered $400,000 to underwrite
the 1972 Republican National Convention, and so on.

Coverups, lies, and secrecy by the government certainly run
counter to our long-standing philosophical commitment to an open system
in which the public is included in the decision-making process. Thomas
Emerson, Yale law professor, alleges that secrecy in a democratic society
is a source of illegitimate power, for several reasons:

1. When the people are assumed to be the masters and the
government, the servant, it makes no sense that the master should be
denied the information upon which to direct the activities of the servants;

2. Each branch of government has its constitutional role to
play--for one branch to withhold information from another undermines
the whole principle of checks and balances; and

3. Secrecy denies the individual due process. Due process
demands that the citizen be furnished all the information upon which his
destiny rests.[12]

Of course, at times, the public must be kept in the dark. The
question, though, is when secrecy is legitimate. The burden of proof lies
with those imposing the secrecy. The key is whether the intentional
tampering with the free flow of public information is more beneficial to
the public interest than disclosure.[13] This principle is difficult to
operationalize, however, since one can argue that the public interest
always is paramount, regardless of the situation. For example, most
Americans believed the actions of Daniel Ellsberg were wrong when he
disclosed the secrets of the Pentagon Papers. Thus, the secretleaker was
deemed guilty while the secretkeepers were innocent because the public
interest required secrecy in these militarily sensitive matters. Others, in
contrast, perceived Ellsberg as a hero, one with courage enough to reveal
the errors of the establishment. In this view, the secretkeepers were
guilty and the secretleaker was honored because public policy in Vietnam
was against the public's interest.

David Wise has bluntly summarized the secrecy problem:

With its control over information supported by an official system of secrecy and classification, the government has almost unlimited power to misinform the public. It does so for various reasons. The government lies to manipulate public opinion, to generate public support for its policies, and to silence its critics. Ultimately, it lies to stay in power.[14]

Abuse of Power by Government Agencies

Watergate revealed that the United States' highest leaders had conspired, among other things, to win an election by using such illegal means as dirty tricks, burglary of opponents, and soliciting of campaign funds by threats and bribes. But these White House transgressions (which we examined earlier in some detail) are only one expression of illicit government intervention. In this section, we will focus on the deviant actions of government agencies in several key areas.

Many government abuses have occurred under the guise of internal security. Domestic surveillance is one example. Government agencies have a long history of surveilling citizens.[15] The pace quickened in the 1930s and increased further with the communist threat in the 1950s. Surveillance reached its peak during the height of antiwar and civil rights protests during the late 1960s and early 1970s. The FBI's concern with internal security, for example, dates back to 1936 when President Roosevelt asked Director J. Edgar Hoover to investigate domestic communist and fascist organizations in the United States.[16] In 1939, as World War II began in Europe, President Roosevelt issued a proclamation that the FBI would be in charge of investigating subversive activities, espionage, sabotage, and that all law enforcement offices should give the FBI any relevant information on suspected activities. These directives began a pattern followed by the FBI under the administrations of Presidents Truman, Eisenhower, Kennedy, Johnson, Nixon, Ford, Carter, and Reagan.

The scope of these abuses by the FBI and other government agencies, including the CIA, the National Security Agency, and the Internal Revenue Service, is incredible. Indeed, many questionable acts against U.S. citizens have been performed in the name of national security.

Item: From 1967 to 1973, the NSA (National Security Agency) monitored the overseas telephone calls and cables of approximately 1,650 U.S. citizens and organizations, as well as almost 6,000 foreign nationals and groups.[17]

Item: Between 1953 and 1973, the CIA opened and photographed nearly 250,000 first-class letters in the United States.

Item: As director of the CIA, William Colby acknowledged to Congress that his organization had opened the mail of private citizens and accumulated secret files on more than 10,000 Americans.[18]

Item: Over the years, the FBI has conducted about 1,500 break-ins of foreign embassies and missions, mob hangouts, and the headquarters of such organizations as the Ku Klux Klan and the American Communist Party.[19]

Item: The FBI confessed to the Senate Intelligence Committee that, during a twenty-six-year period ending in 1968, it had committed 238 burglaries against fourteen domestic organizations.[20]

Item: Between 1959 and 1971, the FBI collected over 500,000 dossiers on communists, black leaders, student radicals, and feminists.[21]

Item: The husband of an officer in ACTION, a St. Louis civil rights organization, received a handwritten note that said, "Look man, I guess your old lady doesn't get enough at home or she wouldn't be shucking and jiving with our black men in ACTION, you dig? Like, all she wants to integrate is the bedroom and we black sisters ain't gonna take no second best from our men. So lay it on her man or get her the hell off Newstead (Street)." The couple soon separated and the local FBI officer wrote to headquarters, "This matrimonial stress and strain should cause her to function much less effectively in ACTION."[22]

Item: In 1972, the FBI paid 7,402 ghetto informants to provide information about racial extremists.[23]

Item: In 1970, actress Jean Seberg helped raise money for a militant organization, the Black Panthers. According to documents released by the FBI in 1979, after the suicide of Ms. Seberg, the FBI tried to discredit the actress by planting the rumor that the father of her baby was a prominent Black Panther leader. This false story led to a miscarriage and psychotic behavior, and possibly her suicide, as well.[24]

   These are but a few examples of government abuses against its citizens. To make the point clearer, we will describe in greater detail two nefarious (but representative) government campaigns: (1) the FBI's vendetta against Martin Luther King, Jr.; and (2) the FBI's campaign to nullify the effectiveness of the Socialist Workers Party.

   The FBI campaigned to destroy civil rights groups. The most infamous example was the attempt to negate the power of Martin Luther King, Jr. King had been openly critical of the Bureau's ineffectual enforcement of civil rights laws. This apparently led the director, J. Edgar Hoover, to label King "the most notorious liar in the U.S." and to launch a vendetta against him.[25]   From 1957, when King became prominent in the Montgomery Bus Boycott, the FBI monitored King's activities under its vague authority to investigate subversives. The more powerful King became, the more the FBI pursued him. King was indexed in the files as a communist; as a result, he was to be imprisoned in the event of a national emergency. This charge against King was based on the allegation that two of his associates in the Southern Christian Leadership Conference were communists.

   Because Hoover had convinced Attorney General Robert Kennedy of the possible link between King and the communists, Kennedy authorized wiretaps of King's phones, which continued for the next two years. Kennedy did not know, however, that the FBI planned to use the wiretaps to discredit King.

   The FBI's efforts to neutralize or even destroy King were intensified with King's increasing popularity, as exemplified by his "I Have a Dream" speech before 250,000 in Washington, D.C., in August 1963. King was thus characterized in an FBI memo:

He stands head and shoulders over all other Negro leaders put together when it comes to influencing great masses of Negroes. *We must mark him now . . . as the most* dangerous Negro of the future of this Nation from the standpoint of Communism, the Negro and national security.[26]

The efforts now escalated to include physical and photographic surveillance and the placement of illegal bugs in his living quarters. Tapes of conversations in a Washington hotel were used by the FBI to imply that King engaged in extramarital sexual activities. The FBI used these tapes, which may or may not have been altered, to dishonor King. At the very time King was receiving great honors—including the Nobel Peace Prize, *Time* magazine's "Man of the Year," and numerous honorary degrees—the FBI countered with briefings, distribution of the tapes to newspeople and columnists, and congressional testimony about King's supposed communist activities and questionable private behavior. The FBI even briefed officials of the National Council of Churches and other church bodies about King's alleged deviance.

The smear campaign against King reached its zenith when the FBI mailed the tapes to the SCLC (Southern Christian Leadership Conference) offices in Atlanta with a covering letter suggesting that he commit suicide or face humiliation when the tapes were made public on the eve of the Nobel Award ceremonies in Sweden.

Summing up the sordid affair, Halperin and his associates have editorialized:

> The FBI had turned its arsenal of surveillance and disruption techniques on Martin Luther King and the civil rights movement. It was concerned not with Soviet agents nor with criminal activity, but with the political and personal activities of a man and a movement committed to nonviolence and democracy. King was not the first such target, nor the last. In the end we are all victims, as our political life is distorted and constricted by the FBI, a law enforcement agency now policing politics.[27]

This comment is critical of the FBI, and justifiably so. Quite clearly, the FBI's tactics were illegal, whether King was a communist or not. And that is a moot point, because King was not a communist. In testimony before a Senate committee, the FBI's assistant deputy director, James Adams, was asked by Senator Frank Church if the FBI ever found that King was a communist. Replied Adams, "No, we did not."[28]

Another example of an FBI vendetta against a nonexistent threat involved the Socialist Workers Party, a small, peaceful, and legal political group. This party became the target of FBI abuses because it supported Castro's Cuba and worked for racial integration in the South. For these transgressions, the FBI kept the SWP under surveillance for thirty-four years. FBI documents have revealed that, in one six-and-a-half-year period in the early 1960s, the agency burglarized the offices of the party in ninety-four raids, often with the complicity of the New York City police department. Over this period, FBI agents photographed 8,700 pages of party files and compiled dossiers totalling eight million pages.

The FBI tried to destroy the party by sending anonymous letters to members' employers, working to keep the party's candidates off the ballot, and by otherwise sabotaging political campaigns. Informants were also used to collect information about the political views of the organization.

Several points need to be made about these FBI activities. Obviously, they were a thorough waste of time and money. As one observer put it, "If they had devoted tens of thousands of man-hours to pursuing true criminals--say, those involved in organized crime--they might have served the public interest as they were meant to."[30] Most important, the FBI's tactics were not only illegal but were directed at an organization that was working legally *within* the system.

> Just as the FBI's illegal assumption of the authority to investigate subversive activities led to illegal methods, the failure of those methods to produce evidence that could be used to take legal action against radical and liberal political movements led to further lawlessness: active efforts to destroy them. In October, 1961, for example, the FBI put into operation its "S.W.P. Disruption Program." The grounds for this program, as a confidential Bureau memorandum described them, were that the Socialist Workers Party had been "openly espousing its line on a local and national basis through running candidates for public office. . . ." The memorandum is astonishingly revealing about the political sophistication of the FBI. If these Socialists were openly espousing their line by running candidates for public office, including the Presidency, these activities weren't illegal. And if their support for the civil-rights movement was subversive, then so was that of many millions of Americans.[31]

Some justice was finally served, as the SWP sued the FBI for violation of civil rights. This, too, was accomplished by working legally within the system.

Finally, it is important to recognize that the governments' violation of the rights of its citizens was not just on aberration of the Nixon years. For instance, illegal wiretaps were commonplace during the Roosevelt and Truman years. Although bugging declined during the Eisenhower administration, it rose sharply during the Kennedy and Nixon presidencies. And under President Reagan, illegal wiretaps have reached an all-time high.[32]

Political Prisoners

In 1978, when he was ambassador to the United Nations, Andrew Young commented publicly that the United States was guilty, as were other nations, of having political prisoners. Young's accusation was widely denounced by politicians and editorial writers, many of whom saw such wild statements as reason enough for the ambassador's ouster. Andrew Young, however, was correct.

Exactly what is meant by *political prisoner*? The key is that a political prisoner is prosecuted by the criminal justice system because of his or her political activities.[33] McConnell has described this concept:

Socrates, Charles I and Patty Hearst, despite their widely varied times, circumstances and beliefs, shared the common characteristic that at a certain time in their lives they were placed on trial because of behavior found reprehensible by the political elite of their day, for activities thought highly prejudicial to the welfare of the state, and tried in legal proceedings from which a large political element and an inflamed public opinion could not be severed. And they were tried, moreover, by bodies seeking to foster official values or notions of public policy which the victims repudiated.[34]

Three factors are central to our distinction of political prisoners. First, political repression begins with the assumption that the law serves the interests of those with the power to make and enforce it. The law, therefore, is a tool by which the powerful retain their advantages. They do this by legally punishing those who threaten the status quo.

Second, while political criminals and other criminals may both pose a threat, the former are considered a direct threat to established political power.[35]

If the members of a ruling elite believe a particular individual or group to be imminently hostile to the prevailing pattern of value distribution, and if they activate the criminal process against him (or them) for that reason, what results is a political trial. Additionally, if members of the ruling elite feel someone seriously intends to alter the *way* in which the government distributes those values, and if the elite activates the criminal process against them for that reason--that, too, constitutes a political trial.[36]

Third, the political criminal does not perceive himself/herself as a criminal but as one who has violated the law out of a set of convictions to create a better society. Thus, they see the system and its agents as the criminals and the enemy.

Of course, according to our view of political prisoners, acts such as assassination, treason, mutiny, and conspiracy to overthrow the government are examples of dissent by perpetrators who will be punished by the legal system.

Throughout U.S. history, groups that were oppressed resorted to various illegitimate means to secure the rights and privileges they believed were justly theirs. The revolutionary colonists used acts of civil disobedience and finally eight years of war to accomplish their goals. Native Americans have fought the intrusions of white settlers and systematic suppression by the U.S. government. And other groups such as farmers, slaveholders, WASP supremacists, ethnic and racial minorities, and laborers have at times broken the law in efforts to change what they considered an unfair system.[37] While these are extremely important, we will concentrate here on the efforts by dissenters during the Vietnam War to change the government's course, as well as the governmental efforts to silence these critics.

The Vietnam War was never formally declared by Congress.[38] It escalated from presidential decisions and commitments that were camouflaged from the public. In effect, the United States had taken a side in an

Asian civil war without the consent of the people. Even if this consent had been given, it would have been achieved through the manipulation of events and information by our leaders, as we know now. Because of the uniqueness of our involvement in this war, many young men refused to serve. Some became fugitives from the law by hiding in the United States or by fleeing to other countries. Others accepted imprisonment. Some 20,000 Americans of all ages refused to pay all or a part of their taxes because the money would support a war they considered illegal, immoral, and unjust. As a result, they risked harassment by the Internal Revenue Service and possible imprisonment.

At one demonstration before the Oakland induction center in 1965, one David Miller set fire to his draft card, saying, "I believe the napalming of villages to be an immoral act. I hope this will be a significant political act, so here goes."[39] He was arrested and later sentenced to two and one-half years in prison. This started a rash of similar protests that the establishment considered a threat to their power. At one rally, the Reverend Sloane Coffin, Dr. Benjamin Spock, and two others announced that they would henceforth counsel young men to refuse to serve in the armed forces as long as the Vietnam War continued. They were arrested for conspiracy, convicted, and sentenced to two years imprisonment for treason.

One of the most infamous political trials of this era involved the Chicago Eight.[40] In 1968, a year of ghetto riots and the assassinations of Martin Luther King, Jr., and Robert Kennedy, Congress passed the so-called Rap Brown Amendment (Brown was chairperson of the Student Nonviolent Coordinating Committee--SNCC--at the time), which nearly outlawed interstate travel by political activists. In the summer of that year, the Democratic National Convention was held in Chicago. Because Hubert Humphrey, a hawk on Vietnam, was the leading nominee, thousands of youths flooded Chicago bent on protesting the war and venting their anger against what they perceived as an unresponsive political leadership. They protested and the police reacted violently, adding to the volatility of the situation.

Months later, when Richard Nixon took office and John Mitchell became attorney general, the federal government issued indictments against individuals felt to be the leaders of the Chicago riots--David Dellinger, Rennie Davis, Tom Hayden, Abbie Hoffman, Jerry Rubin, Lee Weiner, John Froines, and Bobby Seales--soon to be known collectively as the Chicago Eight. These persons were charged with conspiracy to cross state lines with intent to cause a riot (violating the Rap Brown law). Together, they represented various kinds of dissent, such as radical pacifism, the New Left, political hippies, academic dissent, and black militance. The case was heard in the U.S. District Court in Chicago, Judge Julius Hoffman presiding.

Many knowledgeable observers--including former Attorney General Ramsey Clark--felt that the trial was a political gesture by the new Nixon administration to demonstrate a no-nonsense policy against dissent. The conspiracy charge made little sense because the actions of the defendants and their constituencies were uncoordinated. Moreover, Bobby Seales, an alleged coconspirator, knew only one of the other defendants.

The Chicago Eight trial was a symbolic showcase for the defendants, as well. Because of their disrespect for the system, the defendants refused to accept the traditional role.[41] Instead of allowing the system to keep them quiet while the long judicial process wound down, the defendants acted so that their actions would be headline news. Thus, they continually challenged the judiciary's legitimacy. Sternberg has characterized their rationale:

> The argument that the court is illegitimate rests on the defendants' analysis and condemnation of the existing situation in the United States. They see themselves as political prisoners trapped by a power structure of laws created by societal groups hostile to their interests. The court is both an agent for these groups and institutions—most significantly, monopoly capitalism, racism, colonialism, the military-industrial complex, and incipient fascism—and also an oppressive power group in its own right. Although defendants may vary somewhat in the rank or order of their targets, all are in agreement that the criminal court's allegiances are squarely with the oppressor groups and directly hostile to the powerless classes in American society.[42]

As a result of their disrespectful behavior toward the court, Judge Hoffman found the defendants and their lawyers guilty of 159 contempt citations and sentenced them to jail for terms ranging from sixty-eight days to four years and thirteen days. In addition, each defendant was found guilty of inciting a riot, receiving a sentence of five years in prison and a $5,000 fine. However, all were acquitted of conspiracy. Before the sentences were passed, each defendant was allowed to make a final statement. The speech by Tom Hayden captured the essence of the problem from the perspective of the accused:

> Our intention in coming to Chicago was not to incite a riot. . . . (It) was to see to it that certain things, that is, the right of every human being, the right to assemble, the right to protest, can be carried out even where the Government chooses to suspend those rights. It was because we chose to exercise those rights to Chicago. . .that we are here today. . . . We would hardly be notorious characters if they had left us alone in the streets of Chicago last year. . . . It would have been testimony to our failure as organizers. But instead we became the architects, the master minds, and the geniuses of a conspiracy to overthrow the government. We were invented. We were chosen by the government to serve as scapegoats for all that they wanted to prevent happening in the 1970's.[43]

Daniel Berrigan, himself a political prisoner, has discussed his concern for the direction of the government and the need for dissent:

> Indeed it cannot be thought that men and women like ourselves will continue, as though we were automated heroes, to rush for redress from the King of the Blind. The King will have to listen to other voices, over which neither he nor we will indefinitely have control: voices of public violence and chaos. For you cannot set up a court in the Kingdom of the Blind, to condemn those who see; a court presided over by those who would pluck out the eyes of men and call it rehabilitation.[44]

More recently, the so-called sanctuary movement has raised the issue of political prisoners, highlighting the conflict between law and morality.   This movement is composed of liberal religious groups who provide shelter, transportation, and other aid to illegal immigrants who have fled to the United States to escape tyranny in their native countries of El Salvador and Guatemala.   The U.S. government prosecutes those persons who aid these refugees, because they disobey the law by harboring an illegal immigrant.   These individuals argue that they are simply showing humanitarian concern for the suffering. Moreover, they argue, if they were providing shelter to those fleeing communist countries (e.g., Cuba or Nicaragua), the government would treat them as heroes.   But since they give sanctuary to those fleeing governments that are friendly to the United States (but nonetheless repressive), they are treated as criminals. Hence, these individuals are political prisoners.

Official Violence

We do not usually think of government actions as violent. Most often, violence is viewed as injury to persons or property. We make this distinction because the powerful--through the law-making process and control of communication--actually define what behavior is violent.

In this section, we will examine instances of what we have called *official violence*, including those overt acts by the government and those subtle ways the system operates to do harm.

Consider, for example, the violence perpetrated against minorities throughout U.S. history according to official government policy. The government supported slavery. The government took land forcibly from the Indians and for a time had an official policy to exterminate them. During World War II, Japanese-Americans were relocated in detention camps, causing them great losses of property and wealth.

The law itself has helped cause violence against minority groups. A study of sentences for rape in Florida between 1940 and 1964 found that none of the whites found guilty of raping a black woman was sentenced to death, but fifty-four percent of the blacks found guilty of raping white women were.[45]   The system of supposed justice works a tremendous hardship on minorities, as seen in the statistics on capital punishment provided by former Attorney General Ramsey Clark:

> Racial discrimination is manifest from the bare statistics of capital punishment. Since we began keeping records in 1930, there have been 2,066 Negroes and only 1,751 white persons put to death. Hundreds of thousands of rapes have occurred in America since 1930, yet only 455 men have been executed for rape--and 405 of them were Negroes. There can be no rationalization or justification of such clear discrimination. It is outrageous public murder, illuminating our darkest racism.[46]

The system also injures when reforms that would adequately house, clothe, feed, and provide medical attention are not instituted. Carmichael and Hamilton describe how this phenomenon does violence to minority members.

When white terrorists bomb a black church and kill five black children, that is an act of individual racism, widely deplored by most segments of the society. But when in that same city--Birmingham, Alabama--five hundred black babies die each year because of the lack of proper food, shelter and medical facilities, and thousands more are destroyed and maimed physically, emotionally, and intellectually because of conditions of poverty and discrimination in the black community, that is a function of institutional racism.[47]

Of the many forms of official violence, we will consider two in some detail--police brutality and the use of citizens as unknowing guinea pigs.

Police brutality. What is or is not classified as police brutality depends on one's placement in the hierarchy of power. An act is perceived as violent if it challenges existing arrangements. Thus, what a victimized group may perceive as police brutality is viewed by those in power as the legitimate enforcement of law and order.[48]

Police are legally permitted to carry weapons and use them against citizens. This unique power results occasionally in citizens being killed by their law enforcement officers. Five times as many citizens as police are killed in these shootouts.[49] Also, the killings appear to be selective by the social characteristics of the victims. For example, research has shown that very few women are killed by police (.8 percent), while a disproportionately large proportion of nonwhite males are killed (49.6 percent of all males killed).[50] Put another way, statistically, the shooting deaths of blacks and Chicanos by police is ten to thirteen times higher per 100,000 population than of whites.[51] These data support the charge of police brutality that is so often heard from minority communities.

The use of deadly force by police varies greatly from community to community. For instance, recent data show that each year more than two persons per 100,000 die at the hands of the police in New Orleans, a rate nearly twenty-seven times as high as that in Sacramento, California.[52]

Three of the most publicized instances of police brutality in recent years are the Chicago police's treatment of civil rights demonstrators at the 1968 Democratic convention, the Ohio National Guard's firing of sixty-one shots that killed four college students and wounded nine at Kent State University in 1970, and the killing of forty-three inmates at Attica Prison in 1971. Let's examine the Attica incident.

The Attica case is noteworthy because the prisoner revolt at Attica was a result, in part, of a raised consciousness among the prisoners that they were in jail for political reasons.[53] They tended to think of themselves as political prisoners--as victims rather than criminals--for two reasons:

1. As members of largely black or Spanish ghettos, they were acutely aware of the inequities of society; and

2. They were especially aware of the ways the criminal justice system singled them out unfairly.

Many factors caused the inmates' rage but one was particularly symbolic: The corrections staff did not include one black or Puerto Rican. The primary concern of the all-white staff from rural western New York state was that the inmates "knew their place." This typical attitude clashed with the inmates' view that they were victims rather than criminals, which resulted in a rising level of tension as inmates increasingly refused to adhere to the demands of the corrections officers.

Under these conditions, a spontaneous riot occurred after an incident, with 1,281 inmates eventually controlling four cellblocks and forty hostages. Negotiations took place over a four-day period with the prisoners demanding twenty-eight prison reforms and amnesty for the uprising. Governor Nelson Rockefeller was convinced that the revolt was led by revolutionaries and he refused to negotiate. As he told the Commission investigating the Attica incident:

> One of the most recent and widely used techniques of modern-day revolutionaries has been the taking of political hostages and using the threat to kill them as blackmail to achieve unconditional demands and to gain wide public attention to further their revolutionary ends. ... If tolerated, they pose a serious threat to the ability of free government to preserve order and to protect the security of the individual citizens.
>
> Therefore, I firmly believe that a duly elected official sworn to defend the Constitution and the laws of the state and nation would be betraying his trust to the people he serves if he were to sanction or condone such criminal acts by negotiating under such circumstances.[54]

Thus came the decision to retake the prison by force. The time had come to reassert the sovereignty and power of the state over the rebels. A full-scale assault was launched and in fifteen minutes, the State Police had retaken the prison at a cost of thirty-nine deaths and eighty wounded--the bloodiest one-day encounter between Americans since the Civil War, with the exception of the Indian massacres of the late nineteenth century.

Although the charge of police brutality is often made, it is seldom punished. Few of the officers involved in fatal cases of brutality have ever been indicted for murder. Some have been suspended from the force, while others have been tried for lesser crimes (such as justifiable homicide or manslaughter) and then been acquitted or given light sentences.[55]

The use of citizens as guinea pigs. Nazi Germany is often cited as a horrible example of a government's disregard for human life. Among the Nazi's crimes was medical experimentation on human subjects. For example, Josef Mengele, the infamous Nazi doctor known as "the angel of death," conducted a variety of inhumane experiments using the Auschwitz inmates as subjects. Included in Mengele's so-called medical experiments were sewing together three-year-old twins, back to back, and injecting dye into infants' eyeballs.

The United States has also used unwilling and unknowing subjects in potentially dangerous medical experiments. One case that clearly rivals Nazi Germany for its contempt for the human subjects was conducted by the U.S. Public Health Service. Beginning in 1932, doctors under the auspices of the Public Health Service began observing 400 black male syphilis patients in Macon County, Alabama. The patients did not know they had syphilis; rather, they were told that they had "bad blood." The purpose of the study was to assess the consequences of not treating the disease. So, during the forty years of the experiment, the men were not treated; their pain was not even alleviated. When the men's wives contracted syphilis, again, they were not treated. And when their children were born with congenital syphilis, they, too, were not treated.[56]

Also consider this example: From 1946 to 1963, between 250,000 and 300,000 soldiers and civilians were exposed to radiation during 192 nuclear bomb tests. Among the tests conducted by the Army was one that assessed the resultant psychological effects on soldiers who observed an atomic blast four times the size of the bomb dropped on Hiroshima from a distance of two miles. The Army wanted to determine whether or not soldiers could perform battlefield assignments after being exposed to such an explosion. These exposed soldiers suffered severe, long-term negative effects from this experiment, yet the government has been unwilling to accept blame for the higher than usual incidence of leukemia and cancer. Instead, the government has tried to suppress scientific research findings linking low-level radiation exposure to medical problems. In addition, many of the medical records of the men exposed have mysteriously disappeared.[57]

In the late 1970s, a declassification of government documents revealed that the U.S. people had been subjects in 239 open-air bacteriological tests conducted by the Army between 1949 and 1969. The objectives of these tests were to investigate the offensive possibilities of biological warfare, to understand the magnitude of defensing against biological warfare, and to gain data on the behavior of biological agents as they are borne downwind. During one of these tests, San Francisco was blanketed with poisonous bacteria known as serratia, which causes a type of pneumonia that can be fatal. One hospital treated twelve persons for serratia pneumonia, and one victim died.[58]

Another example of the exposure of Americans to potentially dangerous chemicals without their knowledge or consent was the behavioral-control experiments conducted by the government after World War II.[59] For thirty-five years, various government agencies have used tens of thousands of individuals to test several mind control techniques: hypnosis, electronic brain stimulation, aversive and other behavior-modification therapies, and drugs. Many of the subjects in these experiments were volunteers, but many were not.

Throughout U.S. history, one government agency in particular has proven its disregard for the rights of citizens in its quest for national security--the CIA.

Item: Documents revealed in the 1950s under the Freedom of Information Act show that, during the height of the Cold War, the CIA developed knockout substances and incapacitating agents. The pool of subjects used to develop these compounds consisted of terminal cancer patients, who had no idea they were being used as guinea pigs.[60]

Item: In 1953, a CIA scientist slipped LSD into the after-dinner drinks of scientists from the Army Chemical Corps. The drug had an especially adverse effect on one of these persons. He experienced psychotic confusion and two days later leapt to his death from a hotel window. The CIA withheld these facts from the victim's family for twenty-two years.[61]

Item: The CIA hired prostitutes in San Francisco to give their customers drugs. The behavior of the victims was then observed through two-way mirrors and heard through hidden microphones.

Item: The CIA administered LSD to the borderline underworld--"prostitutes, drug addicts, and other small timers who would be powerless to seek any sort of revenge if they ever found out what the CIA had done to them."[62]

Agents working on the project would randomly choose a victim at a bar or off the street and, with no prior consent or medical pre-screening, would take the individual back to a safe house and administer the drug. For many of the unsuspecting victims, the result was days or even weeks of hospitalization and mental stress.[63]

These examples demonstrate the arrogance of the CIA, an agency of government, which is willing to victimize some of its citizens to accomplish an edge in its battle against the country's enemies. Some would argue that this behavior, so contrary to life in a free society, is more characteristic of the enemy.

The present policy, at least overtly, is not to use human subjects. However, the risk is always present that this practice may again occur. It is important to note, in this regard, that President Reagan's 1983 budget for chemical and biological warfare was just over half a billion dollars--up from $157 million in 1980.

INTERNATIONAL CRIMES

Crimes by the government are not limited to those directed at its citizens. War is an obvious example of one government's willful attempt to harm citizens of another country. Other government acts short of war are also harmful to others, including trade embargos, arms sales, colonial arrangements, and the like. In this section, we will discuss two other types of crimes perpetrated by the U.S. government against others--intervention in domestic affairs and war crimes.

American Intervention
in the Domestic Affairs of Other Nations

How would the United States respond if foreigners assassinated the president? What if foreign agents tried to influence the outcome of an election? Or what if a foreign power supported one side in a domestic dispute with money and weapons? Obviously, we would not tolerate these attempts by outsiders to affect our domestic affairs. Such acts would be interpreted as imperialistic acts of war. The irony, of course, is that we have and continue to perpetrate such acts on other countries as part of U.S. foreign policy.

The number of clandestine acts of intervention by the U.S. government is legion. Evidence from Senate investigating committees has shown, for example, that, over a twenty-year period, one government agency--the CIA--was involved in over 900 foreign interventions, including paramilitary operations, surreptitious manipulation of foreign governments, and assassinations.[64] We will limit our discussion here to several of the more well-known cases of CIA involvement in the domestic affairs of other nations.

Chile. The United States, primarily through the CIA, has been actively involved in orchestrating the internal politics of Chile.[65] The government's concern was to protect U.S. business interests, primarily those of ITT. ITT feared the rise of revolutionary parties because they would likely expropriate foreign holdings. In 1966, an election was held and the United States gave the moderate candidate, Eduardo Frei, $20 million in direct campaign contributions. After Frei's victory, Chile expanded its telephone system, giving the contract to ITT, even though a Swedish company had a lower bid.

In the 1970 presidential elections, the CIA and ITT feared the election of the socialist candidate, Salvador Allende, because he had pledged to seize the company's $150 million Chilean property. The CIA spent some $13 million to block Allende's election, including $350,000 to bribe members of the Chilean Congress, who cast electoral votes, to vote against Allende. The extent of ITT's involvement in the election has not been made public because the government has refused to prosecute, fearing that such a trial would expose CIA secrets. Despite these efforts, Allende was elected. At that point, the CIA plotted his overthrow. The strategy was to create economic chaos in the country, which would lead the Chilean army to pull a coup. To achieve this chaos, several tactics were used:

1. The CIA spent $8 million on economic sabotage;
2. U.S. banks boycotted Chile;
3. Rumors were spread that Chile's copper supplies were far greater than they were in reality in a deliberate campaign to weaken the price of copper, Chile's major product;
4. U.S. companies refused to supply repair parts for machines owned and used in Chile; and
5. The United States played an important role in the creation of an extensive black market in goods and dollars.

These efforts were successful, as Allende was assassinated in 1973 amidst right-wing violence and a military takeover.

The ruling military regime that followed Allende completely changed domestic and foreign policy. Most important to ITT and the United States was the adoption of a program of unconditional support for U.S. policies and business interests in Chile.

Iran. The United States has had a long-term special interest in Iran because of that country's vast supplies of oil and its proximity to the Soviet Union. U.S. involvement in the internal affairs of Iran began in the early 1950s, when Prime Minister Mohammed Mossadegh moved to nationalize U.S. oil companies, as we noted in Chapter 5. The CIA engineered a coup that ousted Mossadegh and restored the Shah to power. Over the next twenty-five years, the United States supported the Shah's government, especially with military aid, despite evidence that the Shah's rule was becoming more and more repressive. The Shah, in turn, acted as a trusted ally, faithfully supporting U.S. interests in the Persian Gulf area, supplying oil, and remaining staunchly anticommunist.[66]

Nicaragua. The United States also has a long history of intervention in the affairs of Nicaragua, and, of course, the other nations of Latin America, as well. In 1912, for example, the United States sent Marines to Nicaragua to settle a local dispute; they stayed in that country intermittently for the next twenty years.[67] Before the Marines left in 1932, they established a national guard under the leadership of Anastasio Somoza Garcia to oppose the popular Nicaraguan leader, Augusta Cesar Sandino. Sandino was assassinated by the National Guard and Somoza became dictator of Nicaragua, with the blessing of the United States.

Somoza and his two sons ruled Nicaragua for forty years. The family became very wealthy and their regime was notorious for its intolerance and brutality. But the Somoza dictatorship was friendly to the United States and supported the interests of U.S. businesses in Central America. As President Franklin Roosevelt said, "Somoza may be a son-of-a-bitch, but he is *our* son-of-a-bitch."[68]

In 1961, the Sandinista Front for National Liberation (named after the early popular leader, Sandino) was founded to overthrow the Somoza regime and institute a socialist government. After nearly twenty years, the Sandinistas finally triumphed in 1979. However, their victory was perceived by political conservatives in the United States as a direct threat to U.S. business, political, and defense interests. Foremost, it was perceived as another communist foothold in Latin America, a possible launching pad for additional communist takeovers in this hemisphere, and a direct threat to U.S. multinational corporations in the region.

To counter this threat, the Reagan administration has aimed--through both official and covert policy--to overthrow the Sandinista government. To accomplish this goal, several means have been employed:

1. Promised economic aid has been cut back.

2. Economic and military support have been provided to anti-Sandinista elements within Nicaragua and in neighboring countries.

3. A network of bases in Honduras, El Salvador, and Costa Rica has been set up to stage overt and covert operations. Moreover, these bases have been staffed with CIA and Special Forces personnel to train soldiers for combat and other insurgency measures.[69]

4. Nicaraguan harbors have been mined to attempt a blockade. The Sandinista government took this action to the World Court, claiming that it constitutes a flagrant act of war. In response, the United States declared itself exempt from any World Court decision on the matter.[70]

5. The CIA admitted to supplying a booklet entitled "Psychological Operations in Guerrilla Warfare" to the Nicaraguan *contras*

seeking to overthrow the Sandinistas. This booklet recommended "selective violence" to "neutralize" Sandinista public officials. In effect, this booklet was a primer on assassination. As such, it violated President Reagan's 1981 Executive Order prohibiting even indirect U.S. participation in assassinations.[71]

CIA murder plots. In 1975, the Senate Select Committee on Intelligence reported on the activities of the CIA over a thirteen-year period. The publication of this report occurred over the objections of President Ford and CIA Director William Colby. The reason for their fears was obvious: The government was embarrassed for citizens to find out that the CIA was actively involved in assassination plots and coups against foreign governments.[72]

Item: Between 1960 and 1965, the CIA initiated at least eight plots to assassinate Fidel Castro, Prime Minister of Cuba. The unsuccessful attempts included applying instantly lethal botulinium toxin to a box of Castro's cigars, hiring the Mafia to poison him, and presenting him a gift of a wet suit (for skin diving) treated with a fungus.

Item: In 1975, the Senate Select Committee on Intelligence found strong evidence that CIA officials had planned the assassination of Congolese (Zaire) leader Patrice Lumumba and that President Eisenhower had ordered his death.

Item: The United States was implicated in the assassination of Dominican dictator Rafael Trujillo, South Vietnam's President Ngo Dinh Diem, and General Rene Schneider of Chile.

The CIA's actions are contrary to U.S. principles in fundamental ways. Aside from supporting regimes notorious for their violation of human rights (see Chapter 5), the United States--which achieved its independence claiming the people's right to self-determination--is now actively involved in manipulating foreign governments to achieve its own will. The infusion of money in foreign elections, the use of propaganda, assassination attempts, and the like are all contrary to the guiding principle of the Monroe Doctrine--the self-determination of peoples-- which we invoke readily when other nations intrude in the affairs of state in any Western Hemisphere nation.

War Crimes

War crimes can be interpreted in three ways. According to the first view, crimes in war are illogical--war is hell, anything goes. The only crime, from this position, is to lose.

A second view is that war crimes are acts for which the victors punish the losers. The winners denounce the atrocities committed by the enemy, while justifying their own conduct. Thus, the Germans and Japanese were tried for war crimes at the conclusion of World War II, but the United States was not, even though it had used atomic bombs to destroy two cities and kill most of their inhabitants. For even if one assumes that the bombing of Hiroshima was necessary to bring an early end to the war (a debatable assumption), the bombing of Nagasaki two days later was clearly an unnecessary waste of life.

A third view of war crimes is one that applies a standard of morality to war, applicable to winners and losers alike. The Chief U.S. Prosecutor at Nuremberg, Robert Jackson, summarizes this interpretation:

> If certain acts in violation of treaties are crimes, they are crimes whether the United States does them or whether Germany does them, and we are not prepared to lay down a rule of criminal conduct against others which we would be unwilling to have invoked against us.[73]

We will use this last view in our examination of war crimes. And in doing so, we will see that nations throughout history have been guilty of war crimes, including the United States (examples are the conquering of the Indians, and our 1900 counterinsurgency campaign in the Philippines).[74] Since the government, the media, and the schools traditionally remind us of the heinous acts of our enemies throughout history, we will focus on the war crimes perpetrated by the United States, limiting the discussion to the Vietnam experience. The principle we will apply is the definition of war crimes established by the Nuremberg tribunal (Principle VI, b):

> Violations of the laws of customs of war which include, but are not limited to, murder, ill-treatment or deportation to slave-labor or for any other purpose of civilian population of or in occupied territory, murder or ill-treatment of prisoners of war or persons on the seas, killing of hostages, plunder of public or private property, wanton destruction of cities, towns, or villages, or devastation not justified by military necessity.[75]

The Vietnam War provides many examples of U.S. actions in clear violation of this principle.

Indiscriminate shelling and bombing of civilians. The enemy in the Vietnam War, the National Liberation Front, was difficult to fight because it was everywhere. We often could not distinguish allies from enemies. Thus, in strategic terms, the entire geographical area of Vietnam was the enemy. As Roebuck and Weeber have observed, "In order to 'save' Vietnam from Communism, it was therefore necessary to destroy the entire country."[76]

As a result, civilian villages were bombed in the enemy region of North Vietnam and in South Vietnam, as well. The amount of firepower was unparalleled in history.

> From 315,000 tons of air ordnance dropped in Southeast Asia in 1965, the quantity by January-October, 1969, the peak year of the war, reached 1,388,000 tons. Over that period, 4,580,000 tons were dropped on Southeast Asia, or six and one-half times that employed in Korea. To this we must add ground munitions, which rose from 577,000 tons in 1966 to 1,278,000 tons in the first eleven months of 1969.[77]

Perhaps the most significant (and certainly the most infamous) bomb used by the United States was napalm, a jellylike, inflammable mixture packed into canisters and dropped from aircraft. This mixture of benzene, gasoline, and polystyrene is a highly incendiary fluid that clings. It is an antipersonnel weapon that causes deep and persistent burning.

> Napalm is probably the most horrible anti-personnel weapon ever invented. The point of a weapon in war is to put an enemy out of action, and that is most readily and permanently accomplished by killing him; but civilized nations have tried not to induce more suffering than is necessary to accomplish this end. Napalm, in its means of action, in its capacity to maim permanently and to induce slow death, is a particularly horrifying weapon. That its use in Vietnam has involved many civilians--peasant families in undefended villages--has magnified the horror.[78]

Ground attacks on villages and civilians. The most celebrated and infamous incident of the war was the March 1968 massacre at Song My (also known as My Lai). Under orders from their superiors, U.S. soldiers slaughtered over 500 civilians.[79] The troops had been told to destroy all structures and render the place uninhabitable. They killed every inhabitant, regardless of age or sex, encountering no opposition or hostile behavior.

In Operation Cedar Falls, 30,000 U.S. troops were assigned the task of destroying all villages in a forty-square-mile area. In this and other operations, groups of soldiers known as "Zippo squads" burned village after village.

> The intensely cultivated flat lands south of the Vaico Oriental River about 20 miles from Saigon are prime "scorched earth" targets. U.S. paratroopers from the 173rd Airborne Brigade began operating there last weekend.
> They burned to the ground every hut they saw. Sampans were sunk and bullock carts were smashed. The 173rd laid their base camp among the blackened frames of burned houses. Within two miles of the camp not a house was left standing. . . .
> Every house found by the 173rd was burned to the ground. Every cooking utensil was smashed, every banana tree severed, every mattress slashed. . . . Thousands of ducks and chickens were slaughtered. . . . Dozens of pigs, water buffalo and cows were destroyed. A twenty-mile stretch along the Vaico Oriental was left scorched and barren.[80]

Ecocide. A variation on the scorched-earth policy just noted was the use of anticrop chemicals. The Air Force sprayed defoliants on 100,000 acres in 1964 and 1,500,000 acres in 1969. Herbicides were used to destroy foliage that hid the enemy, as well as the crops that fed the Vietcong soldiers and their civilian supporters. The results of this campaign were devastating in a number of ways:

1. Timber, a major crop in South Vietnam, was destroyed and replaced by bamboo, generally considered a nuisance;

2. The mangroves in swamp lands were killed, negatively affecting shellfish and migratory fish, major sources of protein for the Vietnamese;

3. Vast areas of soil eroded; and

4. Toxic substances such as 2,4,5T were ingested by humans and animals, which may lead to birth abnormalities.[81]

Gaston has summarized this catastrophe of U.S. war strategy:

> After the end of World War II, and as a result of the Nuremberg trials, we justly condemned the willful destruction of an entire people and its culture, calling this crime against humanity *genocide*. It seems to me that the willful and permanent destruction of environment in which a people can live in a manner of their own choosing ought similarly to be designated as a crime against humanity, to be designated by the term *ecocide*. . . . At the present time, the United States stands alone as possibly having committed ecocide against another country, Vietnam, through its massive use of chemical defoliants and herbicides.[82]

In addition to ecocide, U.S. conduct in Vietnam killed a sizable portion of the population. Entire villages of people were killed. Thousands more were killed in bombings. The enormous tragedy of this is seen in data supplied by the Senate Subcommittee on Refugees, which estimated that, from 1965 to 1969, over a million refugees were killed and two million were wounded by the U.S. Armed Services.[83]

In sum, U.S. strategy in the Vietnam civil war served to shatter the whole society, from its ecology to village life, and to life itself. Daniel Ellsberg has called this violent destruction of a patterned society *sociocide*.[84] Most certainly, that qualifies as the ultimate war crime.

CONCLUSION

In this chapter, we have catalogued many overt and horrifying forms of political deviance. We have also observed the ultimate irony: The United States, a country that takes pride in calling itself a free and open society, sponsors repressive government organizations that, in the name of national security, operate to make society anything but free and open. Thus, it seems that to protect the national interest means to punish dissent and manipulate foreign governments. Somehow, the FBI, the CIA, and other such agencies have come to believe that it is necessary to break the law in order to protect the system. In so doing, their actions reap the very results they wish to abolish. Supreme Court Justice Louis Brandeis summarizes this, saying, "For to break some laws in order to enforce other laws is not to fight anarchy and terrorism but to create them."[85] Harris concurs:

> In a government of laws, existence of the government will be imperiled if it fails to observe the law scrupulously. . . . Our government is the potent, the omnipresent teacher. For good or

for ill, it teaches the whole people by its example. Crime is contagious. If the government becomes a lawbreaker, it breeds contempt for the law; it invites every man to become a law unto himself; it invites anarchy. To declare that in the administration of the criminal law the end justifies the means--to declare that the government may commit crimes in order to secure the conviction of a private criminal--would bring terrible retribution.[86]

NOTES

1. For other sources emphasizing government deviance, consult the following: Julian Roebuck and Stanley C. Weeber, *Political Crime in the United States: Analyzing Crime by and against Government* (New York: Praeger, 1978); Alan Wolfe, *The Seamy Side of Democracy: Repression in America,* 2nd ed. (New York: Longman, 1978); David Wise, *The American Police State: The Government against the People* (New York: Vintage, 1978); Charles E. Reasons, *The Criminologist: Crime and the Criminal* (Pacific Palisades, CA: Goodyear, 1974); Amitai Etzioni, *Capital Corruption* (New York: Harcourt, Brace, Jovanovich, 1984); and James W. Coleman, *The Criminal Elite* (New York: St. Martin's Press, 1985).

2. Our discussion here is limited to the federal government, especially the executive branch. However, attempts to deceive the public are found at all levels of government. For examples of coverups, secrecy, and the like at other levels, see: Seymour M. Hersh, *Cover-Up* (New York: Random House, 1972); Peter K. Manning, "The Police: Mandate, Strategies, and Appearances," in *Criminal Justice in America: A Critical Understanding,* ed. Richard Quinney, 170-200 (Boston: Little, Brown, 1974); and Mike Royko, *Boss: Richard J. Daley of Chicago* (New York: E. P. Dutton, 1971).

3. Norman Dorsen and John H. F. Shattuck, "Executive Privilege: The President Won't Tell," in *None of Your Business: Government Secrecy in America,* ed. Norman Dorsen and Stephen Gillers, 27-60 (New York: Viking, 1974).

4. Cited in William G. Phillips, "The Government's Classification System," in *None of Your Business: Government Secrecy in America,* ed. Norman Dorsen and Stephen Gillers (New York: Viking, 1974), 71.

5. Cited in Paul N. McCloskey, Jr., *Truth and Untruth: Political Deceit in America* (New York: Simon and Schuster, 1972), 54.

6. McCloskey, 54.

7. Michael Parenti, *Democracy for the Few,* 3rd ed. (New York: St. Martin's Press, 1980), 157.

8. Anthony Lewis, "Introduction," in *None of Your Business: Government Secrecy in America,* ed. Norman Dorsen and Stephen Gillers, 3-24 (New York: Viking, 1974).

9. The examples in this section are taken from David Wise, *The Politics of Lying: Government Deception, Secrecy, and Power* (New York: Random House Vintage Books, 1973).

10. See also "The 'Phantom Battle' that Led to War," *U.S. News and World Report,* 23 July 1984, 56-67.

11. Walter Schneir and Miriam Schneir, "How the Military Cooked the Books," *The Nation,* 12 May 1984, 570-76.

12. Thomas I. Emerson, "The Danger of State Secrecy," *The Nation,* 30 March 1974, 395-99. See also Arthur S. Miller, "Watergate and Beyond: The Issue of Secrecy," *The Progressive* 37 (December 1973), 15-19.

13. Itzhak Galnoor, "The Politics of Public Information," *Society* 16 (May/June 1979), 20-30.

14. Wise, 40.

15. For a history of the government's monitoring of its citizens, see Alan Wolfe, "Political Repression and the Liberal Democratic State," *Monthly Review* 23 (December 1971), 18-38; Donald B. Davis, "Internal Security in Historical Perspective: From the Revolution to World War II," in *Surveillance and Espionage in a Free Society,* ed. Richard H. Blum, 3-19 (New York: Praeger, 1972); "It's Official: Government Snooping Has Been Going On for 50 Years," *U.S. News and World Report,* 24 May 1976, 65; and U.S. Senate, Select Committee to Study Governmental Operations with Respect to Intelligence Activities, *Intelligence Activities and the Rights of Americans: Book II* Report 94-755 (26 April 1976 pp. 1-20), in *Corporate and Governmental Deviance,* ed. M. David Ermann and Richard J. Lundman, 151-73 (New York: Oxford University Press, 1978).

16. This brief history of the FBI is taken from Richard Harris, "Crime in the FBI," *The New Yorker,* 8 August 1977, 30-42.

17. "Project Minaret," *Newsweek,* 10 November 1975, 31-32.

18. U.S. Senate, Select Committee to Study Governmental Operations with Respect to Intelligence Activities, *Intelligence Activities, Book II,* 156. See also "Who's Chipping Away at Your Privacy," *U.S. News and World Report,* 31 March 1975, 18.

19. "The FBI's 'Black-Bag Boys,'" *Newsweek,* 28 July 1975, 18, 21.

20. Associated Press release, 29 March 1979.

21. United Press International release, 19 November 1975.

22. "Tales of the FBI," *Newsweek,* 1 December 1975, 36.

23. "Curbing the Spooks," *The Progressive* 42 (November 1978), 10-11.

24. "The FBI vs. Jean Seberg," *Time,* 24 September 1979, 25.

25. The following account is taken from several sources: Morton H. Halperin et al., *The Lawless State: The Crimes of the U.S. Intelligence Agencies* (New York: Penguin, 1976), 61-89; "The Truth about Hoover," *Time,* 22 December 1975, 14-21; "Tales of the FBI;" and "The Crusade to Topple King," *Time,* 1 December 1975, 11-12.

26. U.S. Senate, Final Report of the Select Committee to Study Governmental Operations with Respect to Intelligence Activities, "Dr. Martin Luther King, Jr., Case Study," in *Intelligence Activities and the Rights of Americans: Book III,* 107-98 (Washington, D.C.: U.S. Government Printing Office, 1976), cited in Halperin et al., 78.

27. Halperin et al., 89.

28. Quoted in "The Crusade to Topple King," 11.

29. The evidence presented on the FBI's campaign against the SWP is taken from Harris; Associated Press release, 29 March 1976; and "Monitoring Repression," *The Progressive* 41 (January 1977), 7.

30. Harris, 40.

31. Harris, 40.

32. Ronald J. Ostrow, "Electronic Surveillance Hits New Highs in War on Crime," *Los Angeles Times*, 18 December 1983, p. I-4. See also James W. Coleman, *The Criminal Elite* (New York: St. Martin's Press, 1985), 59-60.

33. Charles Goodell, *Political Prisoners in America* (New York: Random House, 1973), 3-13.

34. W. H. McConnell, "Political Trials East and West," in *The Sociology of Law: A Conflict Perspective*, ed. Charles E. Reasons and Robert M. Rich (Toronto: Butterworth, 1978), 333.

35. We will consider political crimes only in the narrow sense of crimes against the establishment. We are sympathetic, however, with the view expressed by Alexander Liazos:

> Only now are we beginning to realize that most prisoners are *political prisoners*--that their criminal actions (whether against individuals, such as robbing, or conscious political acts against the state) result largely from current social and political conditions, and not the work of "disturbed" and "psychotic" personalities. (p. 108)

In this view, then all prisoners are political in the sense that they became criminals as a result of struggling against the inequities of society.   See Alexander Liazos, "The Poverty of the Sociology of Deviance: Nuts, Sluts, and Preverts," *Social Problems* 20 (Summer 1972).

36. Theodore Becker, ed., *Political Trials* (Indianapolis: Bobbs-Merrill, 1971), xi-xii.

37. See D. Stanley Eitzen, *In Conflict and Order: Understanding Society* (Boston: Allyn and Bacon, 1978), 62-66; Richard E. Rubenstein, *Rebels in Eden: Mass Political Violence in the United States* (Boston: Little, Brown, 1970); and Goodell.

38. Much of this account is taken from Goodell, 126-59.

39. Quoted in Goodell, 130.

40. The following account is taken primarily from David J. Danelski, "The Chicago Conspiracy Trial," in *Political Trials*, ed. Theodore Becker, 134-80 (Indianapolis: Bobbs-Merrill, 1971).   We have taken this case as representative of many others from the same time period. For other illustrations of the existence of political trials and political prisoners, see the following trial accounts: the vendetta against the Black Panthers, Tom Hayden, *Trial* (New York: Holt, Rinehart and Winston, 1970); the trials of the Berrigans, Daniel Berrigan, *The Trial of the Catonsville Nine* (Boston: Beacon Press, 1970); and the trial of the Wilmington 10, Jack Anderson, "U.S. is Cited for Human Rights Violations," *Rocky Mountain News*, 11 December 1978, 61.   For general statements on political criminals, see: Judith Frutig, "Political Trials: What Impact on America?" *Christian Science Monitor*, 27 August 1976, 16-17; Goodell; and Becker.

41. See David Sternberg, "The New Radical-Criminal Trials: A Step Toward a Class-for-Itself in the American Proletariat?" in *Criminal Justice in America: A Critical Understanding*, ed. Richard Quinney, 274-94 (Boston: Little, Brown, 1974).

42. Sternberg, 281.

43. Quoted in Danelski, 177.

44. Berrigan, x-xii.

45. Florida Civil Liberties Union, *Rape: Selective Electrocution Based on Race* (Miami: Florida Civil Liberties Union, 1964).

46. Ramsey Clark, *Crime in America: Observations on Its Nature, Causes, Prevention and Control* (New York: Simon and Schuster, 1970), 335.

47. Stokely Carmichael and Charles V. Hamilton, *Black Power: The Politics of Liberation in America* (New York: Random House, 1967), 4.

48. See Jerome Skolnick, *The Politics of Protest* (New York: Ballantine Books, 1969), 3-8.

49. Arthur L. Kobler, "Police Homicide in a Democracy," *The Journal of Social Issues* 31 (Winter 1975), 163-84.

50. U.S. Public Health Service data, quoted in Kobler, 164.

51. Paul T. Takagi, "Abuse of Authority Is a Very Explosive Situation," *U.S. News and World Report*, 27 August 1979, 29.

52. Reported in David A. Wiessler, "When Police Officers Use Deadly Force," *U.S. News and World Report*, 10 January 1983, 59.

53. The following is taken from the New York State Special Commission on Attica, *Attica: The Official Report* (New York: Bantam, 1972), excerpted in *Official Deviance*, ed. Jack D. Douglas and John M. Johnson (Philadelphia: J. B. Lippincott, 1977), 186-94.

54. Quoted in New York State Special Commission on Attica, 193.

55. Michael Parenti, *Democracy for the Few*, 4th ed. (New York: St. Martin's Press, 1983), 154.

56. J. H. Jones, *Bad Blood* (New York: Free Press, 1981).

57. H. L. Rosenberg, "The Guinea Pigs at Camp Desert Rock," *The Progressive* 40 (June 1976), 37-43.

58. Norman Cousins, "How the U.S. Used Its Citizens as Guinea Pigs, *Saturday Review*, 10 November 1979, 10. See also United Press International release, 4 December 1979.

59. See W. H. Bowart, *Operation Mind Control: Our Government's War against Its Own People* (New York: Dell, 1978); and John Marks, "Sex, Drugs, and the CIA," *Saturday Review*, 3 February 1979, 12-16.

60. M. A. Lee, "CIA: Carcinogen," *The Nation*, 5 June 1982, 675.

61. Bowart, 87-91.

62. Marks, 12-16.

63. Halperin et al., 52.

64. Roebuck and Weeber, 82.

65. Discussion of CIA involvement in Chile is based on several accounts: Roebuck and Weeber, 83-86; Adam Schesch and Patricia Garrett, "The Case of Chile," in *Uncloaking the CIA*, ed. Howard Frazier, 36-54 (New York: The Free Press, 1978); Hortensia Bussi de Allende, "The Facts about Chile," also in Frazier, 55-68; Jack Anderson, "Evidence Strong CIA, ITT Behind Chile Coup," *Rocky Mountain News* 27 September 1974, 66; Associated Press release, 8 March 1979; Thomas Powers, "Inside the Department of Dirty Tricks," *The Atlantic*, August 1979, 45-57; and James F. Petras, "Chile: Crime, Class Consciousness and the Bourgeosie," in *The Sociology of Law: A Conflict Perspective*, ed. Charles E. Reasons and Robert M. Rich, 413-27 (Toronto: Butterworth, 1978).

66. Parenti, 174.

67. For brief histories of U.S. involvement in Nicaragua, see Tom Barry, Beth Wood, and Deb Preusch, *Dollars and Dictators* (New York:

Grove Press, 1983); and Richard Alan White, *The Morass: United States Intervention in Central America* (New York: Harper/Colophon, 1984).

68. Quoted in Barry, Wood, and Preusch, 216.

69. Peter H. Stone, "The Special Forces in 'Covert Action,'" *The Nation*, 7-14 July 1984, 8-12.

70. Steven Strasser, "The CIA's Harbor Warfare," *Newsweek*, 16 April 1984, 45; and "The Debate: Those CIA Mines," *USA Today*, 11 April 1984, p. 8-A.

71. Evan Thomas, "How to 'Neutralize' the Enemy," *Time*, 29 October 1984, 35; and Margaret Shapiro, "House Committee Rules CIA Manual was Illegal," *Denver Post*, 6 December 1984, p. 14-A.

72. The following list is taken from "CIA Murder Plots--Weighing the Damage to U.S.," *U.S. News and World Report*, 1 December 1975, 13-15; and "The CIA's Hit List," *Newsweek*, 1 December 1975, 28-32.

73. Quoted in Erwin Knoll and Judith Nies McFadden, eds., *War Crimes and the American Conscience* (New York: Holt, Rinehart and Winston, 1970), 1.

74. For information regarding U.S. treatment of Native Americans, see: Bruce Johansen and Roberto Maestas, *Wasi'chu: The Continuing Indian Wars* (New York: Monthly Review Press, 1979); and Dee Brown, *Bury My Heart at Wounded Knee: An Indian History of the American West* (New York: Bantam, 1972). For information regarding U.S. involvement in the Philippines, see Stuart C. Miller, "Our My Lai of 1900: Americans in the Philippine Insurrection," *Trans-action* 7 (September 1970), 19-28; and Telford Taylor, *Nuremberg and Vietnam: An American Tragedy* (New York: Bantam, 1971), 173-74.

75. Cited in Knoll and McFadden, 193. See also William Thomas Mallison, "Political Crimes in the International Law of War: Concepts and Consequences," in *Crime and the International Scene: An Inter-American Focus*, ed. Freda Adler and G. O. W. Mueller, 96-107 (San Juan, Puerto Rico: North-South Center Press, 1972).

76. Roebuck and Weeber, 70.

77. Gabriel Kolko, quoted in Knoll and McFadden, 57.

78. George Wald, in Knoll and McFadden, 73.

79. See Taylor, 122-53; and Richard A. Falk, "Song My: War Crimes and Individual Responsibility," *Trans-action* 7 (January 1970), 33-40.

80. Associated Press release, quoted in Edward S. Herman, *Atrocities in Vietnam: Myths and Realities* (Philadelphia: Pilgrim Press, 1970), 84.

81. Arthur W. Gaston, quoted in Knoll and McFadden, 69-72.

82. Knoll and McFadden, 71.

83. Roebuck and Weeber, 71.

84. Quoted in Knoll and McFadden, 82.

85. Harris, 35.

86. Harris, 35.

CHAPTER 8

Understanding
Elite Deviance

In 1941, I. G. Farben, the largest chemical company in Germany, voluntarily cooperated with the Nazi government to build synthetic oil and rubber factories at a location in Selesia, Poland.[1] One of Farben's chemists was dispatched to select a site for the new plants. The location chosen was four miles from the Auschwitz concentration camp, which would soon become infamous for the torture and systematic extermination of hundreds of thousands of Jews and other so-called problem populations.

The site near Auschwitz was selected because the head of the Nazi SS (secret police), Heinrich Himmler, personally guaranteed I. G. Farben's top executives a labor supply of 10,000 concentration camp inmates per day for use in building the new factories. The SS also arranged to provide supervisory bosses, or Capos. These men were largely composed of professional criminals and sadists; they were transferred to Auschwitz expressly for the purpose of participating in the Farben projects. In return, Farben agreed to pay the SS three reichsmarks per day for each unskilled inmate and four reichsmarks per day for each unskilled inmate laborer.

Not surprisingly, the work proceeded slowly. The slave laborers were in such a weakened condition that the cement blocks they were forced to lift frequently outweighed them. Moreover, they travelled the eight miles to and from the factory site on foot, every day. Nonetheless, dissatisfied, the Capos beat and tortured many of the slower workers.

By 1942, Farben's board members agreed that the work was proceeding much too slowly and voted to establish the company's own concentration camp near the factory site. An agreement was reached with the SS by which I. G. Farben would provide food, housing, and health care facilities for the laborers, while the SS would provide security. To facilitate production, Farben's board members voted to exploit the slave laborers "to the fullest extent possible at the lowest conceivable degree of expenditure."[2]

Each day, between five and one hundred workers died on the job at the Farben site. Those prisoners who became too weak or ill to work were marched by SS troops to the gas chambers at Auschwitz, where they were killed with Zyklon B, a compound used to kill insects. (Not coincidentally, Farben owned 42.5 percent of the company that produced Zyklon B.)

When the war ended in 1945, 300,000 workers had passed through the I. G. Farben sites on their way to Auschwitz. Some 25,000 of those workers died working for Farben. In addition, Farben contracted with the Nazis to utilize 150 inmate women as subjects in an experiment involving a new soporific (sleep inducing) drug. The firm paid the SS 170 reichsmarks for each subject. All of the women involved in the experiment died.[3]

In addition to these costs in human lives, I. G. Farben spent the equivalent of $250 million dollars on the factory projects. In the end, only a very small amount of synthetic fuel and no synthetic rubber were ever produced.

How could I. G. Farben rationalize these atrocities?

[B]y adapting the theory and practice of Nazi morality, [Farben] was able to depart from the conventional economics of slave labor in which slaves are traditionally treated as capital equipment to be maintained and serviced for optimum use and depreciated over a normal life span. Instead, I. G. reduced slave labor to consumable raw material. . . . When no usable energy remained, the living dross (waste matter) was shipped to the gassing chambers and cremation furnaces . . . where the SS re-cycled it for the German war economy--gold teeth for the Reichsbank, hair for mattresses, and fat for soap.[4]

Soon after World War II, twelve I. G. Farben executives were tried, convicted, and imprisoned for participating in "the enslave-ment, . . . mistreatment, . . . torture, and murder of enslaved persons."[5] At the trial, the Farben defense attorney argued that the executives were doing what businesspersons the world over were attempting: to make a profit by whatever means necessary. It was also argued that, if the Farben managers had not participated in the plans for building the synthetic chemical plants, Hitler would have had them shot. Still another rationale maintained that Farben's support of Hitler's regime represented a testimony to anticommunism, a common interest shared with business-persons in the United States. This defense was designed to impress representatives of the United States, who had just begun a Cold War with the Soviets.

The Farben executives were convicted and sentenced to minor jail terms, ranging from one and one-half to eight years. In addition, as part of the punishment, the convicted executives were forbidden to ever serve on the boards of the newly created chemical companies. Once Allied control loosened somewhat, however, a number of the convicted execu-tives were elected to the boards of Hoechst and Bayer (formerly Farben), two as board chairs.[6]

WHY ELITE DEVIANCE?

The I. G. Farben case represents an extreme but nonetheless characteristic example of elite deviance. In particular, it clearly differentiates elite deviance from so-called white-collar or corporate crime. We will explore this difference in detail throughout the following sections.

Elite Deviance as Exploitation

In this book, we have examined how society's most wealthy and powerful organizations and individuals inflict harm on less-powerful consumers, stockholders, taxpayers, citizens, and, in some cases, the general public. In our example, the Farben case, the largest chemical firm in Germany was responsible for the deaths of at least 25,000 slave laborers, who it literally worked to death. However, at the time, the employment of slave labor was not against the law.

As we have argued throughout, legality does not necessarily characterize elite deviance. Deviant acts may be either illegal or legal. The determining factor is that they are viewed as immoral or unethical because they cause demonstrable harm. Whether or not the harm done is deliberate does not matter. Certainly, knowledge that harm is being done is clearly deviant; however, the crucial issue is not intent but harm itself.

Today, in the United States, we can find many cases in which activities are not against the law yet work to exploit the less powerful, causing them great harm. This harm may be physical, causing death or injury, or it may be financial, as money or property are seized via concealment, manipulation, or guile, but without use of force. Most certainly, such deviance brings moral harm as the public trust in governmental and business institutions is damaged, if not destroyed.[7] Several examples will illustrate this point.

The consumption of alcohol figures in some 100,000 deaths per year and costs the United States some $120 billion in lost work days, medical expenditures, and other social costs. Yet the Busch, Miller, and Coors brewing firms now employ students on some 550 U.S. college campuses to distribute everything from free beer to bumper stickers and hats with company logos in order to encourage alcohol consumption among the young. Groups such as the Center for Science in the Public Interest are convinced that the activities of these campus "booze merchants" are predatory and actually do create drinkers, thus increasing the harm caused by alcohol consumption.[8]

Similarly, tobacco use in the United States figures in nearly 350,000 deaths due to heart disease, lung cancer, and a host of additional ailments. Moreover, tobacco use results in costs of some $50 billion a year in missed work days, medical bills, and other expenses, far exceeding all profits and taxes on tobacco items. Yet the tobacco industry has never acknowledged that any harmful effects may result from smoking, despite overwhelming evidence to the contrary. There is some evidence that tobacco companies have even sought to keep information regarding the harmful effects of smoking from becoming public knowledge.[9]

Taken together, these two legal drugs, tobacco and alcohol, are responsible for more deaths and financial loss than all illegal drugs (e.g., marijuana, heroin, and cocaine) combined.

Corporate crime alone accounts for an estimated $200 billion a year in avoidable loss. This huge loss is larger than that of all other types of crime combined, plus the cost of running the entire U.S. criminal justice system.[10]

In addition to these tangible losses, elite deviance causes another harm, as it damages public trust. Societal elites serve as role models after whom nonelites and even other elites base their ethical and legal conduct. We have seen how the I. G. Farben executives willingly adopted Nazi morality by exploiting slave labor. Such emulation is not uncommon. It is widely held that the perception of immoral behavior by elites has caused much deviance by nonelites (e.g., income tax cheating and employee theft), as well as such phenomena as political alienation (e.g., nonvoting).[11]

The perception of public trust is usually analyzed as it relates to the level of elite crime: more crime, less trust. However, we believe that many unethical or immoral elite acts (e.g., defense cost overruns and corporate dumping of goods in the Third World) also contribute to the public's alienation. Studies in recent years by Francis Cullen and his associates have demonstrated that the public perceives white-collar or corporate crime--in particular, violence that causes injury or death and price fixing--as being more serious today than just seven years earlier.[12] Moreover, the public tends to believe that white-collar criminals "have been treated too leniently and that they deserve to be punished and incarcerated just as severely as regular street criminals."[13]

Such studies are clearly useful in demonstrating that the public is not indifferent to elite crime. However, our point is that unethical and immoral acts, as well as criminal acts, contribute to public distrust in major societal institutions.

Elite Deviance as Cooperation

Elite deviance is, in a number of respects, interorganizational in nature. That is, it often requires the explicit coordination of a number of bureaucratic institutions in order to be planned and executed yet remain undetected and unpunished. Thus, the Farben case required the participation of the Nazi government in order for slave labor to be utilized in the building of synthetic chemical plants. Similarly, throughout this book, we have cited numerous additional examples, illustrating how elite deviance involved interorganizational cooperation.

Item: In 1975, Lockheed asked the CIA to check with the Indonesian government concerning the reputation of the businessman Lockheed had hired to deliver bribes to Indonesian officials.

Item: The Ford Motor Company asked the Federal National Highway Traffic and Safety Administration to estimate the monetary cost of a human life before Ford decided on the profitability of replacing the Pinto's lethal gas tank.

Item: For years, government and business groups have employed organized crime to perform illegal and unethical acts. In the early 1960s, the CIA hired Mafia members to assassinate Fidel Castro. Mafia-generated drug money is routinely laundered through banks in Miami, often with the bankers' full knowledge.[14] In Seattle, in the early 1960s, a crime cabal consisting of bankers, businessmen, journalists, politicians, judges, and law enforcement officials were involved in a scheme whereby Mafia members were invited into the city to operate an illegal gambling and prostitution operation. In New Jersey, a number of firms have hired Mafia-run companies to dispose of toxic waste illegally .[15]

These examples show that elite deviance often involves links between business, government, and organized crime. And because of these interorganizational ties, elite deviance has a great chance of going undetected and unpunished (or at least lightly punished). As we have discussed, economic elites regularly participate in political processes involving candidate selection, monetary contributions to candidates and parties, and lobbying. This means that elites have great influence over the content and character of the law. As a result, many acts that might otherwise become crimes are prevented from becoming illegal in the first place. Thus, Hoffman-LaRoche, a drug company, successfully kept amphetamines out of federal control by paying a Washington law firm three times the amount of the annual budget of the Senate subcommittee seeking legislation for tighter controls.

Moreover, when elite deviance is made illegal, it is often treated quite differently than nonelite deviance. For instance, a number of the environmental protection laws require corporations to monitor the pollution levels at their own factories. Other laws only address breaking regulations per se; what happens as a result of the infraction is ignored. For example, in England, a company was found to be responsible for an accident that resulted in the deaths of five workers. The firm was prosecuted for not properly maintaining or inspecting the equipment; it was not charged with the deaths of the workers.

Such laws focus on intention in order to substantiate guilt, which makes it virtually impossible to prove fault in the case of worker injury or fatality.[16] Under these circumstances, it is little wonder that many acts of elite deviance constitute violations of civil or administrative law, rather than criminal law. Moreover, the penalties for such violations-- barring a serious public outcry or a request by elites themselves for government regulation--tend to remain relatively lenient.

LINKS BETWEEN ELITE DEVIANCE AND NONELITE DEVIANCE

Another critical aspect of elite deviance often overlooked when the subject is confined to so-called corporate criminality or political deviance involves the mutually dependent (symbiotic) relationship between certain types of elite and nonelite deviance. This symbiotic alliance exists on two levels: tangible (involving money, products, and/or services); and symbolic (involving the construction of ideological and social structural variables).[17]

Tangible Links

The tangible links between elite and nonelite deviance are represented in Figure 8-1. As the figure shows, the great bridge between elite and nonelite deviance is organized crime. Profits from the activities of organized criminal syndicates are made from various types of street crime, including prostitution, illegal gambling, and selling drugs, which includes monies obtained by burglars and robbers who need to support drug habits. Such proceeds, totalling some $150 billion in annual gross revenues, generate an estimated $50 billion in net profits, profits that

Figure 8-1
Links among Tangible Forms of Deviance

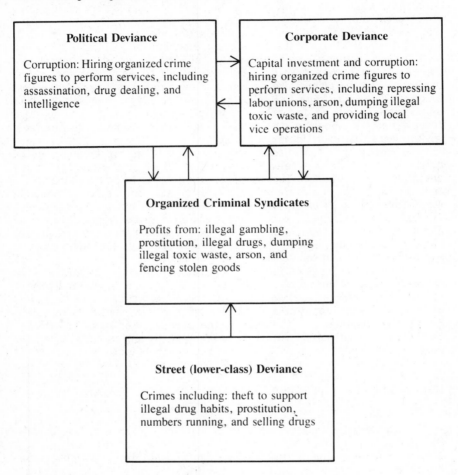

must be reinvested in order to grow.[18]   At times, such profits have been invested in partnership ventures with legitimate corporations, as when Pan Am and Mafia interests opened gambling resorts in the Caribbean following Castro's expulsion of the Mafia from Cuban casinos.

Likewise, business dealings between organized crime and legitimate corporations include the use of racketeers to suppress labor unions and the laundering of Mafia drug funds through banks and other legal enterprises.   In addition, there are numerous financial links between organized criminal syndicates and the government, from campaign donations of Mafia monies to outright bribery of politicians (not to mention the infamous activities of the CIA).

Finally, as mentioned above, numerous legitimate and illegitimate financial links exist between political and economic elites: political lobby groups, government contracts, bribery, and corporate efforts to influence governmental behavior overseas. This is not to say that all legitimate corporations working with legitimate politicians are also automatically linked to organized criminal syndicates. It is merely to say that such three-way links do exist. And, obviously, many of the links between legitimate corporations and Mafia-owned businesses are of a customer-retailer nature. This includes phone calls made by bookies using AT&T lines, Mafia-owned automobile dealerships, syndicate influence in the legitimate gambling industry (i.e., Las Vegas and Atlantic City), and relationships between the Mafia-dominated Teamsters Union, legitimate corporations, and politicians.

Symbolic Links

As discussed in Chapters 1 and 2, the United States' most powerful elites have access to the nation's great socializing institutions, especially the mass media and the schools. Such access has been utilized, in part, to create an ideological view of deviance. This view holds that the U.S. crime problem is the fault of a supposedly dangerous lower class that is criminal in nature, deserving of its poverty and moral inferiority, and in need of increased social control measures by the state. Such deviants are typically viewed as the products of certain individual pathologies (e.g., "evil" subculture of poverty). The notion that justice is blind in its fairness--ignoring race, class, and power--is completely overlooked.

Because many people in the United States are convinced that the deviance of the powerless is a greater harm to society than that of elites, both moral indignation and financial resources are focused there. This further serves to convince elites of their own moral superiority, reaffirming that their acts do not constitute the real deviance of common criminals. Thus, the official (elite) ideology of deviance serves to convince elites of the rightness of their own conduct, even if unethical or illegal. It also serves to keep the attention of lawmakers and enforcers diverted from the deviance of elites, focusing instead on the apprehension, processing, and punishing of so-called street criminals.

Finally, the official ideology of deviance gives rise to a situation in which the deviance of the powerless reinforces the inequality between the powerless (nonelites) and powerful (elites). This occurs, in part, because the victims of nonelite street criminals are disproportionately members of the same powerless lower class. Such deviance tends to keep the lower class divided within itself, destroying any sense of community that might result in a united lower-class movement for social change.

For its part, the deviance of elites has both direct and indirect impacts on the deviance of nonelites. First, elites, under certain circumstances, may order relatively powerless people to commit deviant acts. We observed this in the Farben case, where the cruel Capos were ordered to oversee the slave-labor inmates of Nazi concentration camps. Second, as we have already noted, elite deviance often has a trickle-down effect, providing a standard of ethics and behavior by which nonelites can justify their own deviant acts. Finally, elite deviance often victimizes nonelites financially and in other ways. Such exploitation serves to reinforce the inequalities of power and wealth that are, in large measure, responsible for this symbiotic relationship between elite and nonelite deviance. To understand the causes of elite deviance, one must first understand the symbolic and symbiotic dimensions of the structure of wealth and power, in U.S. society and elsewhere.

ELITE DEVIANCE
AND THE STRUCTURE OF POWER

Modern Corporate Organizations

Throughout this book, we have described and analyzed the nature of the contemporary capitalist system. One of the central problems of this economic system, which is based on the private ownership of property, is the tendency for firms to eliminate competition in order to gain larger shares of a given market. In the United States, a few large firms have historically dominated markets, providing oligopolies in manufacturing, transportation, insurance, communication, and banking (see Chapters 1, 3, and 4). This oligopolistic control of markets functions to produce certainty in an uncertain environment.

To maintain an environment of certainty, corporate organizations seek to exert influence in the political environment via techniques such as lobbying, offering private-sector posts to persons serving in government, and making sizable campaign contributions. This penetration of the political system by economic elites, coupled with the tendency of many governmental elites to enter or return to the ranks of business upon leaving government, has created an interlinked, elite power structure in U.S. society (see Chapter 1).

Despite its influence, the corporate elite remains unable to establish a completely predictable environment in which to amass profits and secure suitable investment outlets. Thus, when the need for a predictable, safe, profit-generating environment contradicts with the legal and moral/ethical requirements of that environment, corporate entities seek alternative, rational solutions to these problems. It is important to note that these solutions are considered to be rational by corporate actors (executives) to the extent that they entail large rewards (profits) and small risks of apprehension and punishment. Such business philosophy provides the ideal scenario for elite deviance.

Rational solutions to problems with other corporate competitors may lie in price fixing, industrial espionage, or arson (again, often with the aid of organized criminal syndicates). Solutions to problems with government may involve bribery, making illegal campaign contributions, or providing false information to governmental agencies. Regarding employees, rational solutions may entail refusing to provide a safe working environment (due to high costs) and the illegal harassment of labor unions (with the aid of organized criminal syndicates). Consumers may also be the victims of corporate rationality via advertising fraud, price fixing, and the manufacture of dangerous products. Finally, business solutions may cause the public at large to suffer the effects of air and water pollution, tax evasion by corporations, and the illegal dumping of toxic waste.

Governmental Organizations

Like corporations, governmental organizations are also goal-oriented bureaucracies. As such, they always possess the potential for deviant behavior.[19] In the case of political and military organizations, goals relate to the maintenance and enhancement of power, authority, and responsibility. Like corporate organizations, governmental entities also seek to create an environment that is predictable, one that allows them to maintain or increase their responsibilities and resources (i.e., budgetary allocations and number of staff employees).

When dealing with rival political organizations, political parties may engage in election fraud and dirty campaign tricks. When dealing with businesses, political organizations may engage in extorting political contributions, accepting bribes/kickbacks on government contracts, and other forms of graft. Presidential administrations may also be motivated to act against government employees by extorting political contributions and violating civil liberties in attempts to squash leaks of embarrassing information. When dealing with its citizens, governments may violate civil liberties by illegally spying, censuring communications, or infiltrating and breaking up supposedly threatening organizations. When dealing with consumers, government organizations may commit deviant acts by failing to enforce laws related to product safety and the environment, usually in exchange for corporate contributions. Finally, governmental elites may victimize the public and the world at large via support for corrupt and repressive dictatorships, by allowing corporations to sell dangerous and domestically banned products abroad, by practicing a form of genocide against its own people (as the Nazis did), by engaging in war crimes against civilians and prisoners of war, and by participating in an all-out arms race that is likely to result in a war of nuclear annihilation.

Thus, like corporate organizations, governmental entities may commit acts that result in great physical, financial, and moral harm on a national and even a world scale.

The Nature of Evil in Organizations

Throughout this book, we have described many examples of illegal and immoral acts, some of them unbelievably cruel and unjust. Does this mean, then, that organizations themselves are inherently evil entities?

C. Wright Mills argued that "moral men cannot be developed in an immoral society, [and] . . . a moral society cannot be developed without moral men."[20] This was not a chicken-and-egg dilemma, Mills argued, merely a social process in which the social character of people is formed by institutions, which are also modified and created by people.

While we agree with Mills that, to a great extent, modern organizations form social character, his arguments concerning clear-cut moralities and immoralities on the parts of either actors or organizations are much less convincing. Indeed, because they are so goal oriented, most organizations are neither inherently moral nor inherently immoral; rather they are inherently amoral. Freed from moral restraints, organizations can act at will "with equal success for benevolent or inhumane purposes."[21]   What determines whether such organizations will use their power for good or ill is largely controlled by a series of factors both internal and external to the organizational environment.

This also means that the deviance of organizations cannot be explained adequately by the personalities of the individuals involved therein.   As we have noted in the I. G. Farben case, people playing organizational roles often behave differently than they do as private individuals. Thus, executives who were viewed as pillars of the German business community engaged in atrocities within the Nazi-created immoral environment. Moreover, as individuals, Farben's executives could not have forced 25,000 people to work themselves to death or committed 150 women to participate in lethal drug experiments. Killing on such a massive scale requires the power to coordinate centrally the skills, efforts, and talents of large numbers of specialists, as well as absolute obedience from such roleplayers, particularly when the task at hand is an evil one. Much of the deviance of organizations can be explained by analyzing how such tasks are coordinated and how such conformity is produced and maintained.

THE CHARACTERISTICS OF BUREAUCRATIC STRUCTURES

We agree with Braithwaite and others that elite deviance is explained by examining the nature of the actors' roles within an organization, as well as the bureaucratic structures (characteristics) that shape such roles.[22]   Bureaucracy, as a form of social organization, possesses certain structural characteristics that account for both its amoral ethical nature and potential to generate acts of great harm.

Modern bureaucracies are characterized by several things, including these central qualities: (1) centralization of authority; (2) creation of specialized vocabularies and ideologies; and (3) fragmentation and routinization of tasks. Each of these characteristics, in turn, often produces a number of social and psychological processes, all of which help create the environment for elite deviance.

Centralization of Authority

Obedience to elite authority is of central importance to the study of organizations and to the deviance they commit. Orders, decisions, and plans that are unethical or illegal are often carried out by underlings, in part, because they feel they have no choice; they feel powerless to disobey, regardless of the intent of the order. Examples of such cases are numerous, including the massacre at My Lai, Watergate, and the General Electric price-fixing case of 1961.

Surprisingly, those who seem most powerless include both those "far removed from the centers of power and . . . those relatively close."[23]

Thus, while such perceived powerlessness is usually characteristic of the lower-middle and lower classes, Kelman found a striking degree of such conformity among high-level military officers and bureaucratic functionaries, as well. Kanter and Kanter and Stein have discussed the existence of widespread feelings of powerlessness at both top and middle levels of organizations.[24] However, the empirical study of such powerlessness and its relationship to organizational and interorganizational deviance remains understudied. We do know that conformity among those in the higher circles of the power elite results for a variety of reasons.

One important structural condition that perpetuates elite deviance is the massive centralization of power in the hands of the elite themselves. Such centralization tends to guarantee the conformity of underling bureaucrats, either corporate or governmental, for two reasons. Because they possess such overwhelming power, elites can often secure nonelite cooperation by giving direct orders to engage in deviant acts. Refusal to conform to such directives may result in severe sanctions for potential dissidents, including being fired, court-martialled, blacklisted, demoted, or not promoted. Still other sanctions might include transfer to a less-desirable assignment or geographic location or forced early retirement.[25]

Thus, the distinction often made between those deviant acts committed by workers for their personal enrichment versus those committed on behalf of their employer is misleading.[26] That is, given the centralization of power in organizations, acts committed on behalf of an organization often involve personal rewards for nonelites, as well as the threat of sanctions for noncompliance with elite directives.

Moreover, people who occupy positions in bureaucratic organizations play roles for which they have been trained. As such, they are acutely aware that, as people, they are replaceable, interchangeable parts, mere occupants of bureaucratic positions.[27] This is certainly a dehumanizing realization for the individuals involved. Nonetheless, such conformity is the rule rather than exception.

Quite clearly, much conformity is due to feelings of powerlessness. On the other hand, no organization operates by the threat of sanction alone. Elite authority--especially that of a national president or an upper corporate manager--is obeyed in large measure because it is recognized as legitimate. Such authority is seldom questioned. This legitimacy is part of another aspect of elite deviance, the higher immorality.

As we discussed in Chapter 2, the higher immorality includes many forms of deviance that are not considered to be particularly wrong by the elites who engage in them (e.g., antitrust violations). A number of social-psychological factors account for elite approval of such deviance.

Specialized Vocabularies and Ideologies

From a social-psychological perspective, the higher immorality consists of a subculture that forms at the top of the bureaucratic organizations. A small group of powerholders tends to develop precepts and customs delicately balanced between conventional and criminal (deviant) behavior, as well as objectives that may be obtained through both deviant and nondeviant means.   Part of this subculture of elite behavior consists of norms and sentiments that make deviance permissible. That is, deviant acts are filtered through a sanitizing, ideological prism, which gives them the appearance of not being criminal or deviant.[28]

Part of this sanitizing ideology involves the adoption of special vocabularies of motive. According to Mills, "It is an hypothesis worthy of test that typical vocabularies of motive for different situations are significant determinants of conduct."[29] A number of recent case studies of elite deviance report the construction of an elaborate vocabulary designed to provide both motive and neutralization of guilt.[30] Janis made this observation of the Johnson administration's Vietnam policy group:

> The members of the group adopted a special vocabulary for describing the Vietnam war, using such terms as body count, armed reconnaissance, and surgical strikes, which they picked up from their military colleagues. The Vietnam policy makers, by using this professional military vocabulary, were able to avoid in their discussions with each other all direct references to human suffering and thus to form an attitude of detachment similar to that of surgeons.[31]

Likewise, the Nazi SS, in their extermination of the Jews, adopted such a vocabulary in dealing with "the Jewish problem." Special language rules were adopted. Terms like "final solution," "evacuation," "special treatment," and "clearing up fundamental problems" were utilized as euphemisms for mass murder.[32] Moreover, such vocabularies are symptomatic of the alienation, stereotyping, and dehumanization involved in elite deviance (also see section below).

A final aspect of the vocabulary of motives involves a series of mechanisms specifically designed to neutralize guilt. While such mechanisms are found in virtually all deviant subcultures, in the case of the elite, their adoption is more direct and absolute, since the elite themselves have generated and established the ideology of deviance, as discussed above. When applied to elite deviance, the general ideology of deviance becomes interlaced with a number of guilt-reducing rationalizations.

1. Denying responsibility: The rationalization here is that what went wrong was not the organization's fault. Mechanical malfunctions in the workplace resulting in employee deaths are termed "accidents." Likewise, consumers are blamed for their ignorance in "misusing" products that cause harm.   Or blame may be shifted to other officials or organizations, as when businesses blame a problem on a lack of government regulations.

2. Denying victimization/dehumanization: This guilt-neutralizing mechanism functions to convince interested parties that no real person was or is being victimized. Such denials usually take one of two forms. The first may be termed *object-directed dehumanization;* it involves the perception of others as statistics or commodities in a vast numbers game. People are no longer perceived as human beings but as a portion of a less-than-human collectivity (e.g., the enemy, the market, the competition, or the government).

Janis has described the presence of a second denial mechanism at work in elite circles. Termed *groupthink*, it refers to "a mode of thinking that people engage in where they are deeply involved in a cohesive in-group, where the member's striving for unanimity override their motivations to realistically appraise alternative courses of action."[33] Groupthink reduces individual capacity for moral judgment, enhancing the formation of stereotyped thought by in-group members. Thus, during the Vietnam era, members of the Johnson inner circle of policymakers created stereotypes, portraying the poor of the world as wanting to take from the rich and espousing the Asian disregard for human life. The Vietnamese were also the subjects of racial stereotypes developed by U.S. troops, who used terms like "mooks," "gooks," "slopes," and "dinks," and described the people as barbaric and uncivilized, deserving of ruthless slaughter.

3. Authorization/higher loyalties: Another rationalization technique, termed *authorization*, stems directly from the legitimacy of elite power. Authorization is an ideological device involving the creation of some transcendent mission whereby elites stake claim to supposedly higher purposes that are clearly outside legal and ethical boundaries. In the case of government, such purposes usually relate to the national interest, executive privilege, fighting the Communist menace, or other foreign threats. In the case of corporate deviance, such notions usually involve meeting profit targets or protecting the interests of the stockholders. Such amoral justifications have been propagated for decades by conservative social critics. Milton Friedman, for example, has long argued that businesses possess virtually no social responsibility for their acts.

> [T]here is one and only one social responsibility of business—to use its resources and engage in activities designed to increase its profits so long as it stays within the rules of the game . . . [and] engages in open and free competition, without deception or fraud. . . . Few trends could so thoroughly undermine the very foundations of our free society as the acceptance by corporate officials of a social responsibility other than to make as much money for their stockholders as possible. This is a fundamentally subversive doctrine. If businessmen do have a social responsibility other than making maximum profits, how are they to know what it is?[34]

Such statements can easily be interpreted to mean that any profit-making behavior in which businesses engage is morally acceptable, as long as no laws are broken.

4. Condemning condemners: This mechanism is used to handle critics of deviant behavior. Namely, attention is diverted away from the real issue and focused on another topic or even the critics themselves. For instance, corporations often attack proposals involving further governmental regulation as being opposed to free enterprise. Governments, in turn, often view critics of civil rights abuses or war crimes as "Communist sympathizers."

These neutralization techniques, along with an official ideology of deviance accepted by general society, ensure that elites may commit deviant acts without guilt or damage to their respectable self-images.

Moreover, underlings will come to share these ideological visions and adopt the Adolf Eichmann excuse of elite authorization (i.e., "only following orders").

Finally, these ideological constructions allow elites to attribute real deviance and crime to the lower classes, thus mystifying themselves as to their own deviance and misdirecting perceptions of the distribution of societal harm in general. The dimensions of such harm are even greater when committed by organizations because of the nature of modern organizational life.

Fragmentation and Routinization

Decisions to commit deviant acts—even murder—are carried out within established routines. Such routines not only involve filling out forms, reports, and schedules. Indeed, a number of scholars maintain that the large, complex nature of modern organizations encourages deviance, for two reasons: (1) specialized tasks involve the same routines, whether they are deviant or legitimate; and (2) elites both discourage being informed of scandals within organizations by lower functionaries and also hide acts of elite deviance from functionaries and the public.[35]

Related to the specialization of tasks found in modern organizations is alienation, which denotes "a mode of experience in which the person experiences him/herself and [and other people] as alien."[36] Within bureaucratic organizations, alienation is manifested partially through distance. For example, workers engaged in producing dioxin never witnessed the effects of the chemical on the residents of Love Canal in Niagara Falls. Similarly, pilots serving in the Vietnam War convinced themselves that they were bombing geographic targets on maps, not killing civilians in their homes. In modern society, technology has produced a world of such extreme distances that victimization becomes impersonal.

ELITE DEVIANCE:
IMAGE CONSTRUCTION AND INAUTHENTICITY

The centralization of power and fragmentation of tasks in large organizations creates still another important aspect of elite deviance: a world of image construction that masks acts of deviance behind a smokescreen of *front activities*.

A number of scholars have commented on the subject of front activities involved in elite deviance.[37] Yet the term is vague and has come to include everything from making deceptive or false statements about a deviant act (or series of acts) to creating pseudoevents and phony crises by news media, public relations firms, and governmental agencies.[38] Quite simply and directly, front activities may be described as management via image manipulation.

During the Watergate era, for example, a number of commentators observed that the White House staff felt the basic problem was successfully managing public opinion.[39] And during the Carter era, White House staffers commonly complained that the confidence gap between the

White House and the public was due to an image problem.

Front activities to camouflage deviance is a common and accepted practice of virtually all types of bureaucratic entities. Turk believes that lying within governmental security agencies is "a routine tactic" and that its use is limited only by expediency.[40] Such lying is accompanied by many front activities: (1) providing only the information requested by investigating officials or citizens; (2) destroying or conveniently misfiling incriminating items before they have to be produced; (3) fragmenting information so it appears incomplete and out of sequence; and (4) depicting deviant acts as the work of bad apples or even past leaders. Another common ploy is to deny access to information on the basis of "need to know," "national security," or other justifications to hide embarrassing secrets.[41]

The discussion in this chapter has centered around the structural causes of elite deviance. A central portion of this discussion has emphasized that the causes and consequences of elite deviance are hidden, even mystified, from both elites and nonelites, from victimizers, as well as victims.

This mystification of elite deviance via an official ideology and a host of guilt-neutralizing techniques and front activities has serious implications for those who occupy positions in bureaucratic hierarchies. The alienation and dehumanization that characterizes elite deviance produces a condition that has been described as *inauthentic*. This condition is so important that it merits further discussion.

Inauthenticity

Although the concept of inauthenticity has been used in several senses, unifying themes do exist.[42] Namely, there are two dominant yet opposing trends in alienation studies: (1) alienation as an objective social condition versus (2) alienation as a psychological, subjective state.[43]

As an objective social condition, inauthenticity refers to maintaining overt positive appearances, despite the presence of negative underlying realities. Within powerful organizations, inauthenticity is indicated by the amount of resources spent on various front activities, as the organization tries to convince workers, clients, and the general public of its positive attributes in the face of negative, often tightly held secrets.

As a psychological, subjective state, inauthenticity produces a number of negative emotional consequences. Because negative underlying conditions are often masked by the smokescreen of front activities and guilt-reducing rationalizations, bad feelings resulting from acts of elite deviance may also be masked. As a result, those individuals involved are likely to suffer from a vague feeling that something is wrong, producing diffuse, unfocused, bottled-up aggression.[44] Such repressed anger may lead to major personal problems, including psychosomatic diseases, drug and alcohol abuse, and even suicide. At the very least, inauthenticity involves an element of self-deception, as the individual fails to understand or may even deny his or her own experiences.

For example, psychiatrist Robert Lifton studied inauthenticity in relation to combat troops in Vietnam. Soldiers involved in killing innocent civilians and other combat situations came to view virtually all Vietnamese as the enemy.   However, this ideology was based on self-delusion. Underneath it all, many of those who fought actually stopped believing in the usefulness of the war.   In addition, many of the troops felt that they had been "victimized and betrayed by their country."   Lifton predicted that such feelings would cause a variety of disturbances in Vietnam veterans, ranging from "mild withdrawal to periodic depression to severe psychosomatic disorders to disabling psychosis."[45]

This evidence suggests that, when morality is reduced to being an exercise in public relations, those involved in the inauthenticity are not necessarily comfortable with their conformity.   In fact, the evidence gathered thus far indicates that those elites and underlings who engage in elite deviance tend to suffer from major personal problems, as mentioned above.

Presthus has noted that one type of social character is particularly successful in making it to the top of bureaucratic organizations.[46]   Such an individual exudes charisma via a superficial sense of warmth and charm.   He or she is able to make decisions easily, because matters are viewed in black-and-white terms.   This requires the ability to categorize and thus dehumanize humans as nonhuman entities for the purposes of making decisions concerning layoffs, firings, plant closings, and advertising campaigns.

Clinard's study of managers of large corporations found that those executives likely to engage in acts of organizational deviance were often recruited from outside the companies they administered.[47]   These executives were interested in getting publicity in financial journals, showing quick increases in profits, and moving on to higher positions within two years.

Recent studies of work alienation demonstrate that people with such high extrinsic needs also tend to be workaholics, displaying what are called type-A personality characteristics.   Such traits involve "free-floating hostility, competitiveness, a high need for socially approved success, unbridled ambitions, aggressiveness, impatience, and polyphasic thought and action" (i.e., trying to do two things at once).[48]   Such persons also frequently exhibit the lowest scores on mental health measures in such studies.   Thus, victimizers in elite deviance often turn into victims, in a sense, dehumanizing both their victims and themselves.

Finally, there is evidence that, within single organizational hierarchies, many of the same people who execute deviance on behalf of the organization also commit acts against it for their own personal gain.   In a Canadian study, Reasons noted that supervisory personnel accounted for approximately two-thirds of the business dishonesty over the last decade.[49]   Furthermore, within the organizations that commit deviant acts, those individuals who participated were likely to engage in acts of deviance for personal gain against their employers.   This may be true because such employees resent being asked to engage in deviant acts and thus strike out against their employers in revenge.   Or perhaps, having demonstrated their corrupt moral nature to their employees, such organizations invite acts of deviance against them by providing an untrustworthy role model.

Again, we come to a similar conclusion regarding conformity within bureaucratic organizations: It is often rendered in a reluctant, incomplete, and psychologically stressful manner.   Moreover, such conformity is related to a number of types of more personal deviance, even among elites themselves. This is especially true when front activities fail and organizations are implicated in deviant acts. For instance, Eli Black, chairman of United Brands, committed suicide when it was revealed that his company was involved in a bribery scandal designed to hold down taxes on bananas. Similarly, Japanese executive Mitsushiro Shimada killed himself when his company was proven to be involved in the Grumman bribery scandal.[50] We can conclude, then, that if official ideologies of deviance were fully accepted, embarrassed organizational elites would probably not resort to such desperate acts.

CONSTRUCTIONIST AND OBJECTIVIST POSITIONS ON ELITE DEVIANCE

Throughout this book, we have presented a view of elite deviance that is admittedly controversial. Rather than taking a safe position, involving only white-collar criminal acts, we have argued for a definition that encompasses both illegal and immoral acts. But, one may ask, whose morality is to be used as a basis in deciding what may be termed elite deviance?

In general, two answers may be offered to this question. First, we have the constructionist position, which views all deviance as acts occurring in a particular context: a given historical period, a specific culture, and even an isolated situation within a specific culture.[51] Thus, a murder committed during peacetime may become an heroic act in war. But not all societies condone all wars or even war, in general.

In this chapter, we have stressed the importance of reality as a social construction in our discussion of the official, elite ideology of deviance. This official ideology has several negative effects: (1) it blinds both elites and nonelites to the greater harms generated by elite deviance; (2) it focuses attention and resources on the less-harmful deviance of the powerless; and (3) it serves as a basis for guilt-reducing rationalizations used by powerful individuals engaged in deviance. We have also examined the question of who possesses the power to construct such definitions, or, conversely, to prevent competing definitions of deviance from being constructed. Finally, we have assessed the harmful consequences that follow from defining deviance in this way.

A central problem with the constructionist position is that it treats all moral positions as relative, denying the existence of any absolutes. Ideologically, the constructionist position is safe because it easily excuses one from taking sides and advocating solutions, which leads to the implicit acceptance of the dominant ideology concerning social problems, including various forms of deviance. Thus, the constructionist position supports the stance that nothing matters, which, for us, is unacceptable.

An alternate position is that of the objectivists, which holds that there are moral absolutes regarding social problems.

[T]here are [social] structures that induce material or psychic suffering for certain segments of the population; there are structures that ensure the maldistribution of resources within and across societies; . . . there are corporate and political organizations that waste valuable resources, that pollute the environment, that are imperialistic, and that increase the gap between the 'haves' and 'have nots' globally and societally.[52]

The objectivist (or normative) approach, unlike that of social constructionism, argues for the adoption of moral imperatives and human needs that are universal and ahistorical. Violation of these norms by elites constitutes "wrongs," "deviance," or "social problems" is merely to state such universals using another label. Stated in the positive, such universals provide a coherent view of basic human needs that may serve as a foundation for policies designed to address the causes and consequences of the types of deviance we have described in this book. Among these basic needs are essential physical requirements (food, clothing, shelter, and medical care), as well as a host of nonmaterial needs, including the basic human rights discussed in Chapter 5. (Others are discussed in the Epilogue.)

Criticism of Positions

More important, however, is the realization that dangers are involved with adopting any set of basic "rights," "wrongs," and "shoulds," or causes and solutions. Objections can be offered to any position, as seen in the following examples:

1. *The only reason most of the examples that make up this book are here is because they constitute what Simon and Eitzen believe to be deviance. They're just being self-righteous.*
To this charge, we answer profoundly untrue! The examples in this book constitute a case-by-case series of deviant acts that have offended the sensibilities of many leading social critics, muckrakers, and social scientists. Our ethical foundation rests on the same moral principle on which the Judao-Christian, as well as many other non-Western ethical systems, are founded: namely, the Golden Rule, which holds that one should treat others as he or she would like to be treated. We are unaware of any society that would sanction the behavior related in our examples. Even I. G. Farben's use of slave labor would have been disapproved of by the mass of the German people, had they known about it and been free to render a judgment.
2. *How dare you speak of the three-martini lunch, salaries of corporate executives, war crimes, antitrust violations, and pollution as if they all constitute equal wrongs? All you do is open up a Pandora's Box! Now virtually anything elites do can be considered deviant by someone writing on the subject. As a result, the issue of criminal elite deviance is lost in the process.*
Such an argument forgets that we have introduced a standard by which to measure deviance: harm, including physical loss (death and injury), financial loss, and the destruction of public trust. Our argument is not that all deviant acts cause the same kind and degree of harm. Instead, we find that such acts--whether technically criminal or not--are harmful in some way. For instance, the three-martini lunch and other

special privileges given the elite executives cause harm by furthering massive federal deficits, as wealthy individuals and corporations legally evade paying taxes.   In addition, citizens lose faith in taxation, thus destroying public trust.   Those $3,000-per-day executive salaries and perks further contribute to many social inequalities, which are, in turn, related to many social ills, including crime at all societal levels. So, yes, not all of the wrongs we discuss are of equal dimension.   Nonetheless, they are still wrongs and are symbolic and symptomatic of still greater problems.

3. *Calling some practices "deviant" when they are not considered to be so by those who commit them is irrational.   Practices such as corporate dumping, even if dangerous, are still legal and justified by those individuals involved.   They have their reasons.   Your approach completely rules out any understanding of the people involved.*

Yes, and juvenile delinquents, Nazis, I. G. Farben executives, rapists, and all other criminals have their reasons, too.   Deviant individuals erect ideologies and rationalizations to reduce the guilt they feel. Further, they feel that what they do is quite rational, according to their own value system.

Still, just because corporate dumping in foreign countries is profitable and legal does not make the harm it causes any less serious for those who lose their lives to pesticide poisoning or suffer birth defects due to faulty contraceptives.   And the fact that they are not Americans should not matter--they are still human beings.   Calling such behavior "rational" misses the point.   The harm is intrinsically real and empirically measurable, as this book documents.

Moreover, the rational pursuit of profit may not be as rational as we sometimes think.   Practices like corporate bribery actually have very negative consequences for many of the companies and officials involved. Therefore, in the long run, they may be viewed as irrational.

It is impossible to account for every individual rationale when trying to define elite deviance. So, instead, should we limit our definition to include only criminal acts?   Doing so would be unfortunate.   Many great harms would go neglected, harms that, if properly understood, would aid in our knowledge of how and why elite deviance works.

CONCLUSION

Our discussion in this chapter has analyzed how rationalizations for elite deviance are constructed and maintained through the use of front activities and fail due to the emergence of scandal and opposing beliefs. Based on this analysis, we conclude that elite deviance is understandable from the deviant's perspective.

In addition, we feel that elite deviance is empirically testable.   To establish such empiricism, the following hypotheses must be verified:

1. Hypothesis: *Public trust and alienation are increased by elite acts that are considered to be immoral/unethical, as well as by those that are clearly illegal.*

2. Hypothesis: *Major corporations involved in scandals (like pollution or dangerous working conditions) are likely to suffer from*

distrust among their employees, the result of which will be deviance: stealing from the workplace, absenteeism, and perhaps drug and alcohol abuse.

    3. Hypothesis: Employees asked to participate directly in acts of organizational deviance may comply with such directives. But in some cases, especially when scandal occurs, intense psychological strain will result in acts of personal deviance (e.g., drug addiction, mental illness, suicide) and resentment against the organization (causing white-collar crime).

    Each of these hypotheses may be tested via interviews, as a number of recent studies attest.[53] Thus, we see little incompatibility between our so-called ideological stance and the canons of empirical science. This factor--that elite deviance is empirically testable--is one of the major strengths of our view of deviance.

    Our discussion in this chapter has illustrated the complexity of our subject, elite deviance. It is quite clearly a product of our complex society, as a number of forces work together to provide the motive, the opportunity, and the structure necessary for deviance to occur (see Figure 8-2).

Figure 8-2
Interrelated Causes of Elite Deviance

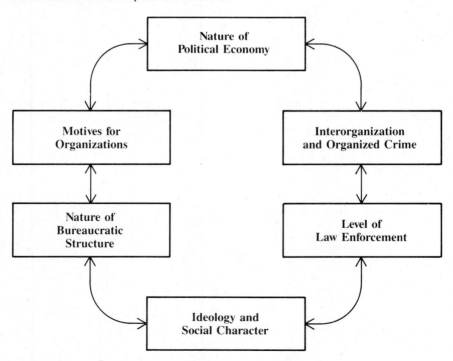

Perhaps the most basic cause of elite deviance is the structure and interworkings of the contemporary political economy. Assigning structural causes requires one to examine solutions that are structural, as well. Not to include solutions in a text such as this does little more than contribute to the feelings of powerlessness and alienation that already plague U.S. society, not to mention much of social science. Not to propose such changes would be, we feel, intellectually dishonest.

Unfortunately, we find that a double standard operates in this area. When so-called objective social scientists offer reformist solutions to the problems plaguing society, their work is labeled as "policy study," "social policy," "foreign policy," or some other pseudoscientific label. Most important, it is believed to be unbiased, scientific, and value free. On the other hand, when anyone proposes change that involves the basic distribution of wealth, power, and private property, their work is labeled as "utopian," "unscientific," "social criticism," or even "subversive."

To this arbitrary approach to social problems we suggest that the time for labels is past. To avoid making proposals leaves students with a sense of hopelessness and fatalism that merely serves to perpetuate such problems. To label our approach as being more ideologically biased than reformist in nature is to deny the pluralistic nature of the U.S. political and intellectual landscape. However, to criticize our beliefs as being utopian does us great honor, for we, with Kenneth Keniston, hold that positive utopian visions are essential as a source of hope in an increasingly cynical, alienated, and negative world.

NOTES

1. This discussion of the I. G. Farben pharmaceutical company's involvement with the Nazis is taken from J. Borkin, *The Crime and Punishment of I. G. Farben* (New York: Free Press, 1978).

2. Borkin, 121.

3. J. Braithwaite, *Corporate Crime in the Pharmaceutical Industry* (London: Routledge and Kegan Paul, 1984), 5.

4. Borkin, 126.

5. Borkin, 138.

6. Braithwaite, 5.

7. For more discussion on the concept of harm, see R. Kramer, "Corporate Criminality: the Development of an Idea," in *Corporations as Criminals,* ed. E. Hochstedler, 13-37 (Beverly Hills: Sage, 1984). In addition, we wish to thank William Kornhauser, University of California, Berkeley Department of Sociology, for suggesting exploitation as a definition of elite deviance.

8. See Coleman McCarthy in *Oakland Tribune,* 12 October 1983.

9. *New York Times,* 12 January 1977, p. A-14; *New York Times,* 23 February 1982, p. 1; and E. Eckholm, "Four Billion Cigarettes," *The Progressive* 42 (July 1978), 27.

10. For further discussion, see Steven Box, *Crime, Power, and Mystification* (London: Travistock, 1983), 13-17.

11. See Kramer, 21; R. Meier and J. F. Short, "The Consequences of White-Collar Crime," in *White-Collar Crime: An Agenda for Research,* ed. H. Edelhertz and T. D. Overcast, 23-50 (Lexington, MA:

D. C. Heath, 1982); A. Thio, *Deviant Behavior,* 2nd ed. (Boston: Houghton Mifflin), 90-92; and L. S. Schrager and J. F. Short, "Toward a Sociology of Organizational Crime," *Social Problems 25* (February 1978), 407-19.

12. See F. Cullen et al., "The Seriousness of Crime Revisited," *Criminology 20* (May 1982), 83-102.

13. F. Cullen et al., "Public Support for Punishing White-Collar Crime," *Journal of Criminal Justice 11* (Winter 1983), 481-93. Our sincere thanks to Frank Cullen for providing us with an early copy of this piece.

14. See, for example, P. Lernoux, "The Miami Connection," *The Nation,* 18 February 1984, 186-98; and P. Lernoux, *In Banks We Trust* (New York: Anchor/Doubleday Press, 1984).

15. See, for example, William Chambliss, *On the Take: From Petty Crooks to Presidents* (Bloomington: Indiana University Press, 1978).

16. Box, 58-60.

17. See Thio, 88-96; and Box, Chapter 1.

18. This argument is based primarily on Box, Chapter 2. For a related perspective, consult the following: D. C. Smith, "White Collar Crime, Organized Crime, and the Business Establishment: Resolving a Crisis in Criminological Theory," in *White-Collar and Economic Crime,* ed. P. Wickman and T. Dailey, 23-38 (Lexington, MA: D. C. Heath, 1982): D. C. Smith, "Paragons, Pariahs, and Pirates: A Spectrum Based Theory of Enterprise," *Crime and Delinquency 26* (January 1980), 358-86; and S. Terreberry, "The Evolution of Organizational Environments," *Administrative Science Quarterly 12* (March 1968), 590-613. For estimates, see J. Cook, "The Invisible Enterprise," *Forbes,* 29 September 1980, 60-71.

19. E. Gross argues that organizations are inherently crimenogenic. See Gross, "Organizations as Criminal Actors," in *Two Faces of Deviance,* ed. P. R. Wilson and J. Braithwaite (Queensland, Australia: University of Queensland Press, 1978), 199.

20. C. Wright Mills, "A Diagnosis of Our Moral Uneasiness," in *Power, Politics, and People,* ed. I. L. Horowitz, 330-38 (New York: Oxford University Press, 1963). For a view that holds that profit making via the ability to commit illegal acts and receive the large payoffs are much admired by judges, see also E. Stotland, "White Collar Criminals," *Journal of Social Issues 34* (Fall 1977), 79-96.

21. L. Coser et al., *An Introduction to Sociology* (New York: Harcourt, Brace, Jovanovich, 1983), 150.

22. Braithwaite, 26.

23. H. Kelman, "The Social-Psychological Context of Watergate, *Psychiatry 39* (Winter 1976), 308; and H. Kelman, "Violence Without Moral Restraint: Reflections on the Dehumanization of Victims and Victimizers," *Journal of Social Issues 29* (Fall 1973), 25-61.

24. R. M. Kanter, *Men and Women of the Corporation* (New York: Basic Books, 1977), 189-205; and R. M. Kanter and B. A. Stein, eds., *Life in Organizations* (New York: Basic Books, 1979), 80-96.

25. On this point, see J. Glass, "Organizations in Action," *Journal of Contemporary Business,* Autumn 1976, 91-111.

26. H. Edelhertz et al., *The Investigation of White-Collar Crime* (Washington, D.C.: U.S. Government Printing Office, 1977), 7.

27. M. D. Ermann and R. J. Lundman, eds., *Corporate and Governmental Deviance: Problems of Organizational Behavior in Contemporary*

Society, 2nd ed. (New York: Oxford University Press, 1982), Chapter 1; and M. MacCoby, *The Gamesman* (New York: Simon and Schuster, 1976), 230.

28. Based on Box, 54-57.

29. C. Wright Mills, in Horowitz, 445.

30. G. Sykes and D. Matza, "Techniques of Neutralization: A Theory of Delinquency," *American Sociological Review* 22 (May 1957), 664-70.

31. I. Janis, "Groupthink Among Policy Makers," in *Sanctions for Evil,* ed. N. Sanford and C. Comstock (San Francisco: Jossey-Bass, 1971), 73.

32. H. Arendt, *Eichmann in Jerusalem: A Report on the Banality of Evil* (New York: Viking, 1964).

33. I. Janis, *Victims of Groupthink* (Boston: Houghton Mifflin, 1972), 9. For more on dehumanization, see V. Bernard et al., "Dehumanization," in *Sanctions for Evil,* ed. N. Sanford and C. Comstock, 102-24 (San Francisco: Jossey-Bass, 1971); and T. Duster, "Conditions for Guilt Free Massacre," also in Sanford and Comstock, 25-36.

34. Milton Friedman, *Capitalism and Freedom* (Chicago: University of Chicago Press, 1972), 133. For an interesting elaboration, see James W. McKie, ed., *Social Responsibility and the Business Relationship* (Washington, D.C.: Brookings, 1974).

35. See M. Silver and D. Geller, "On the Irrelevance of Evil: The Organization and Individual Action," *Journal of Social Issues* 34 (Fall 1978),125-36; D. Vaughn, "Crime Between Organizations: Implications for Victimology," in *White-Collar Crime: Theory and Research,* ed. G Geis and E. Stotland (Beverly Hills: Sage, 1980), 87; R. C. Kramer, "Corporate Crime: An Organizational Perspective," in *White-Collar and Economic Crime,* ed. P. Wickman and T. Dailey, 75-94 (Lexington, MA: D. C. Heath, 1982); and E. Smigel, "Public Attitudes toward Stealing in Relationship to the Size of the Victim Organization," *American Sociological Review* 21 (February 1956), 320-47.

36. E. Fromm, *The Sane Society* (New York: Holt, Rinehart, and Winston, 1955), 111.

37. R. Barnet, *The Roots of War* (Baltimore: Penguin, 1972); C. Wright Mills, *The Power Elite* (New York: Oxford University Press, 1956), 354-56.

38. D. Boorstin, *The Image: A Guide to Pseudo-Events in America* (New York: Harper and Row, 1961).

39. For an analysis of conservative, liberal, and socialist reactions to Watergate, see D. R. Simon, "Watergate as a Social Problem," paper presented at the Meeting of the Society for the Study of Social Problems, August 1978.

40. A. Turk, "Organizational Deviance and Political Policing," *Criminology* 19 (February 1981), 231-50.

41. B. Bernstein, "The Road to Watergate and Beyond: The Growth and Abuse of Executive Authority Since 1940," *Law and Contemporary Problems* 40 (Spring 1976), 57-86.

42. M. Seeman, "Status and Identity: The Problem of Inauthenticity," *Pacific Sociological Review* 9 (Fall 1966), 67-73; B. Baxter, *Alienation and Inauthenticity* (London: Routledge, Kegan Paul, 1982); A. Etzioni, "Basic Human Needs, Alienation, and Inauthenticity," *American Sociological Review* 33 (December 1968),870-84; and A. Etzioni, "Man and

Society: The Inauthentic Condition," *Human Relations* 22 (Spring 1969), 325-32.

43. W. Plasek, "Marxist and Sociological Concepts of Alienation: Implications for Social Problems Theory," *Social Problems* 21 (February 1974), 316-28; and D. Schweitzer, "Contemporary Alienation Theory and Research," in *Sociology, The State of the Art,* ed. T. Bottomore et al. (Beverly Hills: Sage, 1982), 68.

44. A. Etzioni, "Basic Human Needs, Alienation, and Inauthenticity," 881.

45. R. J. Lifton, "Existential Evil," in *Sanctions for Evil,* ed. N. Sanford and C. Comstock (San Francisco: Jossey-Bass, 1971), 48.

46. R. Presthus, *The Organizational Society,* rev. ed. (New York: St. Martin's Press, 1978).

47. M. B. Clinard, *Corporate Ethics and Crime: The Role of Middle Management* (Beverly Hills: Sage, 1983), 136-38.

48. R. N. Kanungo, *Work Alienation: An Integrated Approach* (New York: Praeger, 1982), 157.

49. C. Reasons, "Crime and the Abuse of Power: Offenses Beyond the Reach of the Law," in *White-Collar and Economic Crime,* ed. P. Wickman and T. Dailey, 59-72 (Lexington, MA: D. C. Heath, 1982), 60-61.

50. B. Fisse and J. Braithwaite, *The Impact of Publicity on Corporate Crime* (Albany: SUNY Press, 1983), 240.

51. The following discussion is based, in part, on D. Stanley Eitzen, "Teaching Social Problems: Implications of the Objectivist-Subjectivist Debate," paper presented at the 1984 Meeting of the Society for the Study of Social Problems, San Antonio, Texas, 23-26 August 1984.

52. Eitzen, 7.

53. Clinard, 136-38; and Fisse and Braithwaite, 240.

54. See Kenneth Keniston, *The Uncommitted* (New York: Dell, 1965), Chapter 2.

The Economy and Elite Deviance: A Proposal to Transform Society

As long as there are social problems in U.S. society, we cannot be content with the status quo. The dominant theme of this book is that the source of these problems is the structure of society. It follows, then, that any real solution must require that the system change fundamentally. We believe that changing the basis of the existing system--the capitalist economy--is the key.

The economy must be changed so that people, rather than profit, are paramount. And the economy must be changed to achieve a reasonably equitable distribution of goods and services. While absolute equality is utopian, the economic system can be changed to eliminate the upside-down effect, where the few benefit at the expense of the many, and where jobs for all are guaranteed with a reasonable wage along with the assurance of adequate housing, food, and medical care. There is no excuse for a society such as ours to allow some of its citizens to live in squalor, to be poorly fed, to have inadequate medical attention, and to be the objects of contempt from other citizens. A final change needed for our economic system is greater regulation of business activity in accord with central planning to achieve societal objectives and meet the needs of a future characterized by shortages, ecological threats, and worldwide population pressures.

In this Epilogue, we propose an economic system that makes the most sense to us--economic democracy. We will outline the assumptions and programmatic details of this economic form as a way to generate dialogue and debate about alternatives to the present system. Other proposals may also help to solve the problems endemic to the contemporary United States. We should, however, be aware that all social systems, regardless of their economic and political underpinnings, will have social problems. Utopia literally means nowhere. Thus, we do not assume that this system will be perfect. There will be unanticipated problems. But the fear of unknown problems should not deter our willingness to work for social change to reduce or even eradicate current problems. Also, we reject the proposition that, just because utopia is impossible to attain, we should not try to approximate perfection.

We believe that the call to change society to eliminate current problems is the most important call any patriot can answer. What follows is our plan for change. We challenge you to work your way through it, find the flaws, and propose alternative planks to the platform or entire new schemes to achieve the goal of "a more perfect Union."

ECONOMIC DEMOCRACY

Basic Assumptions

Let's begin by enumerating the assumptions that must guide our search for a possible solution to the elite deviance that plagues contemporary U.S. society.

Foremost is the assumption that these problems will be alleviated only through altering the social structure, not altering so-called problem persons. This assumption does not deny that some individuals are pathological and need personal attention. But attending to these individuals only attacks the symptoms of the problem, not the disease itself. The basic premise is that elite deviance is endemic to our social system.[1]

A second guiding assumption in our search for a solution to elite deviance is that the system must be fundamentally changed. Cosmetic changes or even genuine reforms are likely to fail because they are based on the political-economic base that is the source of many social problems. As Parenti has observed, "As long as we look for solutions within the very system that causes the problems, we will continue to produce cosmetic, band-aid programs. The end result is shameful public poverty and shameless private wealth."[2]

In short, the U.S. economic system--state-supported capitalism--is the source for many of our elite-deviance problems. Capitalism and the government that accompanies it have no fundamental commitment to remedying social ills.[3] Instead of a commitment to a more equitable distribution of resources, capitalism promotes competition, with the victors widening the gap between themselves and the losers. Tax reforms are instituted to encourage profits rather than solve problems of unemployment and low wages. Inflation, rather than unemployment, is viewed as the culprit. Suburbanites may work in the city, but they do everything possible to avoid paying taxes that will help the city eliminate its fiscal woes. The current wave of reducing taxes, government services, and government intervention, while aimed at government waste, also reflects the lack of humane concern for those who are less fortunate, which characterizes capitalists.[4] For capitalism and the highly competitive individuals it engenders create a me-first mentality. According to Michael Parenti:

> Contrary to the view of liberal critics, the nation's immense social problems are not irrational offshoots of a basically rational system, to be solved by replacing the existing corporate and political decision-makers with persons who would be better intentioned and more socially aware. Rather, the problems are rational outcomes of a basically irrational system, a

system structured not for the satisfaction of human need but the multiplication of human greed.[5]

A third assumption is that the level of the United States' current social problems will only be magnified further by the conditions of the future, unless the politico-economic structure is changed significantly. International tensions in the future will be heightened by scarcity, pollution, and the ever-increasing gap between rich and poor nations. Domestically, the future holds similar problems, as well as increased unemployment, deeper economic cycles, urban blight, and problems of racism, ageism, and sexism. Will societies propelled by the profit motive increase or lessen these international and domestic problems?

While capitalism was instrumental in bringing the United States to its present level of affluence and power (at the expense of labor, minorities, and the Third World), the organization and needs of capitalism are not appropriate for a world of scarcity, overpopulation, ecological disasters, and vast inequities. The future does not hold promise unless competition gives way to cooperation; individual choice is superseded by the needs of society; uncoordinated efforts are supplanted by democratic (not bureaucratic) planning; and economic advantages are spread more evenly throughout society.

Our final assumption is that any attempt to make significant changes in society will be resisted by those in positions of power and wealth (the elite) in current society. Those who benefit by the present arrangement quite naturally favor stability, law and order, and other practices that guarantee their advantages. On the other side are those who favor change because they are disadvantaged by the existing system. Thus, the basic problem of implementing change is that "those who have the interest in fundamental change have not the power, while those who have the power have not the interest."[6]

We assume that change will only occur with the emergence of a mass political movement that is a coalition of the poor, the disadvantaged blue-collar worker, and the increasingly impoverished middle class. The formation becomes all the more probable as the current economy and polity become less effective at meeting contemporary problems, described in the following quote from Michael Harrington:

> The economy has become a sickening, uncontrollable roller coaster; cities rot, and the black, the Spanish-speaking, the poor, women, the young and the old are the special victims of our collective failures. The corporations arrogantly propose to deal with these crises by holding down wages, cutting social spending and legislating increased profits. The threat of nuclear war persists and the anti-environmentalists are on the offensive.[7]

General Principles

Given these assumptions, which we believe reflect reality, what is the best solution? As a prologue for further discussion and realizing that one cannot foresee all the possible angles, let us elaborate on the features of the political-economic form for U.S. society that would make the necessary structural changes to alleviate those problems that are part of the current politico-economic system--economic democracy (also called democratic socialism).

The form of socialism characterized here is the ideal--what socialism is supposed to be and how it is supposed to work. The closer we get to this ideal, the greater the promise of solving many of the problems native to capitalism.

The three fundamental themes of economic democracy are democratism, egalitarianism, and efficiency.[8] Authentic socialism must be democratic. Representatives must be answerable and responsive to the wishes of the public they serve, which means that public officials, whether in the political or economic spheres, must be accountable for their actions. Elite deviance is, above all, a problem of poor accountability.

> Unaccountability pervades American life--not merely the Presidency, not merely the rest of government, but all public and private institutions that exert substantial power over us and, inevitably, over future generations. ... Accountability, if it means anything, means that those who wield power have to answer in another place and give reasons for decisions that are taken.[9]

The problem for present-day U.S. society is that the democratic goal of the people having the ultimate power is not realized. As Parenti has charged, "'Democracy,' as it is practiced by institutional oligarchs, consists of allowing others the opportunity to *say* what they want while the oligarchs, commanding all institutional resources, continue to *do* what they want."[10]

The democratic socialism proposed here is not the socialism found in Cuba, China, Poland, or the Soviet Union. Those nations claim to be socialistic but are, in fact, totalitarian, and, therefore, run counter to this fundamental aspect of socialism. The key to differentiation between authentic and spurious socialism is to determine who is making the decisions and whose interests are being served.[11]

Democratic relations must also be found throughout the social structure: in government, at work, at school, and in the community. Along with the election of officials responsive to public opinion and the disappearance of authoritarian relations, democracy entails the full extension of civic freedoms to protect individuals and groups from the arbitrariness of officials.

The second principle of democratic socialism is egalitarianism. The goal is equality: equality of opportunity for the self-fulfillment of all; equality rather than hierachy in making decisions; and equality in sharing the benefits of society. Thus, socialism requires a fundamental commitment to achieving a rough equality by leveling out the gross inequities in income, property, and opportunities. This means, of course, that arbitrary distinctions such as sex, age, race, and ethnicity no longer serve as criteria for oppression or for forcing certain categories of persons into limited opportunities.[12]

A major question for socialism is whether the goal is equality of opportunity or equality of outcomes. Equality of opportunity is a neccessity of socialism, while equality of outcome is probably impossible to attain in complex societies. The key is a leveling of the advantages so that all receive the necessities (food, clothing, medical care, living wages, sick pay, retirement benefits, and shelter). But an absolute equality of outcomes is very likely an unattainable goal given unequal endowments, motivations, and the like. Moreover, the efforts to approximate this goal would require the imposition of the tightest controls on society and thus in very likely destined to fail.

A third feature of democratic socialism is efficiency. This refers to the organization of the society to provide, at the least possible individual and collective cost, the best conditions to meet the material needs of the citizens. Production of necessary goods must be assured, as well as the distribution of the goods produced, and the services offered must be planned and managed. But this is true of all types of economies. The key method to accomplish economic efficiency for socialism is the substitution of public for private ownership of the means of production. The people own the basic industries, financial institutions, agriculture, utilities, transportation, and communication companies. The goal is to serve the public, not to make profit, as is the case in capitalism. Socialism, compared to capitalism, will likely have lower prices, greater availability of necessary goods and services, better coordination of economic endeavors, and better central planning to achieve societal goals, such as protecting the environment, combating pollution, saving natural resources, and developing new technologies.

A proposal by former President Gerald Ford, former Vice-President Nelson Rockefeller, and Senator Henry Jackson illustrates a fundamental difference between the present state-supported capitalism and socialism. This group proposed that taxpayers subsidize the huge development costs of new energy technologies (e.g., refining of shale oil, gasification of coal) and then, once perfected, turn over the benefits of these technologies to private corporations. This tactic allows the public to take all the risks while private corporations wait for the right time to take over the enterprise for their own profit, at the expense of the public. If the socialist principle were applied, the people would collectively take the risks but then reap the benefits, too.[13]

A fundamental argument of the socialist credo is that private corporations work in opposition to human needs. In the search for profit, private corporations have withheld supplies to contrive shortages, colluded with competitors to keep prices abnormally high, encouraged extraordinary and wasteful military expenditures, polluted the environment, and encouraged wasteful consumptive patterns. Moreover, capitalism encourages unemployment. As Harrington has argued, "Sustained full employment is a threat to corporations. For when there is full employment, the labor market tightens up, unions become more combative, and wages tend to rise at the expense of profits."[14]

To summarize, democratic socialism or economic democracy is a politico-economic form of organization dedicated to full human equality, cooperation, participatory democracy, and meeting human needs. Admittedly, these goals are idealistic. But the closer U.S. society approaches them, the more social problems such as poverty, racism, sexism, exploitation, unemployment, and human misery will be minimized. To the degree that they are achieved, elite deviance is reduced.

The Planks of a Democratic-Socialist Platform

A number of fundamental changes must be made to bring about democratic socialism. Let's begin with the central problem of capitalism--corporate control of the economy for private gain.

Reorganizing large corporations to meet public needs. The major corporations present the primary obstacles to social justice. The primacy of profit means that these huge organizations resist social goals. They are not concerned with their role in unemployment, pollution, and the perpetuation of poverty. The curbing of pollution reduces profits. High labor costs at home force the company officials to move their operations overseas or to another part of the country, where costs are lower. Supposedly competing corporations in a shared monopoly continue to raise prices, even during economic downturns, which contributes to the problem of stagflation. The greed of corporate officials and owners inclines them to use and abuse natural resources without regard for conservation. This greed also encourages them to produce and market unsafe and unhealthy products.

At one time, economic activity was the result of many decisions made by individual entrepreneurs and the heads of small businesses. But now, a handful of corporations have virtual control over the marketplace. The decisions made by the boards of directors and the management personnel of these huge corporations--determined solely by the profit motive--affect employment and production, consumption patterns, wages and prices, the extent of foreign trade, the rate of natural resource depletion, and the like.

Economic democracy requires that the decisions made by corporations be in the public interest. However, the public's interest will not be primary unless there is democracy within these corporations and the boards of directors are composed of owners and representatives of the workers and the public. Representatives of the workers are important to democratize the workplace and improve the morale and material conditions of the workers. The public must also be represented on the boards so that the decisions of the organizations will take into account the larger public issues of pollution, use of natural resources, plant location, prices, and product safety. These moves from economic oligarchy to industrial democracy represent a monumental shift from the present arrangement.

Economic democracy can be achieved in a number of ways. First, all major corporations could be required to have a certain proportion of public and employee representatives on their boards of directors as a condition for doing business in interstate commerce.[15] Another procedure would be that, every year, the corporation would add a number of worker and public representatives, depending on the profits of the previous year. This would mean, in effect, that, after fifteen or twenty years, the corporation would be controlled by the workers and public representatives. A final example of how industrial democracy could be accomplished would be for the government to insist that, with each subsidy given to the company, a proportion of the company's stock be given to the workers and the public. Thus, in return for tax breaks, low-interest loans, loan guarantees, and the like, the owners of the corporation would lose some of their control. As an example, in 1980, the government agreed to prop up the ailing Chrysler Corporation with loan guarantees of $1.5 billion. Under a plan to bring about democratic socialism, the government could have agreed to this proposal in return for a percentage of Chrysler's stock, say 30 percent. Such a plan would give the public a return for its risk capital.

The goal of all these proposals is the social management of the corporations for the public good. Interesting evidence indicates that the U.S. public is in favor of such measures. A poll by Hart Research Associates of 1,209 U.S. adults, during the week of July 25, 1975 (commissioned by the Peoples' Bicentennial Commission), revealed the following related alternatives to our present economic system:

> 66% of the American public feel that it would do "more good than harm" to develop a program in which employees own a majority of the company's stock, while only 25% feel that it would do "more harm than good."
>
> 74% of the public feel that it would do "more good than harm" to institute a plan whereby consumers in local communities are represented on the boards of companies that operate in their local region, while only 17% feel that it would do "more harm than good."
>
> 50% of the public feel that employee owned and con-trolled companies--ones where the people who work in the company select the management, set policies and share in the profits--would improve the condition of the economy. 14% say that such an arrangement would worsen the economy's condition. 29% feel the institution of employee ownership and control of companies would not make much difference in terms of the country's economic condition.
>
> 44% of the public believes there is "a great possibility" or "some possibility" that our country will have employee owned and controlled companies within the next 10 years, while 49% feel there is "little possibility" or "no possibility."
>
> 56% of the public would "probably support" or "definitely support" a candidate for President who favored employee owner-ship and control of U.S. companies, while only 26% said they would "probably not support" or "definitely not support" such a candidate. 18% volunteered that their presidential decision would be based on other factors or were not sure.
>
> 67% of the public feel there has been "too little discus-sion" about employee ownership and control of U.S. companies, while only 10% feel there has been "too much," and just 9% feel that there has been "about the right amount."[16]

These data indicate that a majority of the U.S. public favors the basic structure of economic democracy and would support a mass democratic movement designed to move the United States in this direction.

One question raised about socialism involves individualism, as we know it. A socialist society is generally perceived as one in which the group smothers the individual personality, prohibiting the use of individual initiative to start businesses. Neither assumption needs be true. One plan to promote individualism is to nationalize only those companies that possess, or are soon likely to possess, a great amount of assets (e.g., $100 million). Small companies could still be owned by groups or individuals. Similarly, large apartment complexes, supermarkets, and department stores could be purchased by government and run cooperatively by local community groups.

Establishing government ownership of certain industries. We propose that the utilities, owners and processors of natural resources, transportation, banks, and credit institutions should be nationalized to ensure the adequacy of services, to plan for the social good, and to minimize business cycles.

The irony of the capitalist system stems, in part, from its bouts with economic crises: inflation, unemployment, depression, and the like. In order to end the vicious swings of business cycles and to provide rationally for the needs of all, economic planning is necessary. Community needs, regional needs, and national needs would all be balanced against each other at succeeding levels of government. But this planning, like all other decisions in this regard, would be done democratically by boards of elected representatives at each governmental level. Many such bodies already exist today, but their roles are largely advisory. Thus, we do not see ourselves merely adding another layer of bureaucracy with this proposal. Rather, we propose to provide a democratic mechanism that would make the most humane and rational use of human and natural resources.

Such planning would also apply to wages, prices, monetary supplies, and interest rates. Presently, these decisions are already made by business-dominated groups such as the Federal Reserve Board. The question of economic planning, in the estimation of many, is not if it will be done, but who will do it--big business or the people? For people to have a democratic voice in economic matters requires a democratization of banking and credit, as well as production.

Finally, we would nationalize all major defense contractors whose prime client is the government. These companies are currently subsidized by the government; they take no risks but make enormous profits. The nationalization of these companies would reduce Pentagon waste significantly, increase efficiency, and eliminate the current sham of government subsidies to profit-making businesses.[17]

Maintaining a democratic government. Government control, governmental planning, and the nationalization of industries will not accomplish socialist goals unless accompanied by true democracy.

> Where the government owns or directs the means of production, the crucial question is: Who owns the government? There is only one way for the majority to "own" the government: through a political democracy which allows them to change its policies and personnel and which assures minorities, not only civil liberties to try and become a majority, but technical and financial means to exercise that liberty as well. So democracy is thus not simply central to the political structure of socialism; it is the guarantee, the only guarantee, of the people's economic and social power.[18]

This quote makes two important points. First, the lack of democracy found in the communist countries means that they are not socialist. Second, if democracy at the national level is missing under socialism, then we will likely repeat a fundamental problem of contemporary U.S. society--collusion between the government and the economic elite.

Legislating a progressive income tax, without loopholes. One of the perennial issues in U.S. politics is the structure of the income-tax laws. In the 1976 election, President Carter termed such laws "a disgrace to the human race." We have examined many of the loopholes that make for this disgrace, but little has been done to correct this situation. We believe that little will ever be done until a mass democratic movement brings about change in such laws. Again, the tax system is a key mechanism by which the rich retain their wealth. Numerous studies reveal that the middle class and the poor pay a higher percentage of their incomes in taxes than do the rich.[19]

The problem socialists face concerning tax reform is that the average person is taught that socialist reforms mean heavier taxes for the nonwealthy, but this need not necessarily be the case. What is being proposed here is no less than a truly progressive income tax, one that would require those with the highest income to pay the highest percentage in taxes. Thus, 100 percent of the money over a certain amount (to be determined democratically) would be taxed. Under the current system, a number of millionaires pay no income taxes. Under the proposed system, such people would still be comfortable yet pay their fair share.

Legislating an inheritance tax with sufficient controls. We have seen that the power and wealth of elites rests, in part, on the special tax advantages they have been granted. The heart of these advantages is the ability to transfer wealth from one generation to the next via inheritance and tax-exempt foundations. Our proposal would not end inheritance altogether, but it would prohibit the amassing of huge fortunes, which makes elite rule possible. One recent study shows that 50 percent of U.S. families would have less than $3,000 dollars to leave to their children if they had to pay all their debts at once.[20] On the other hand, we have upper-class families with a net worth of $100 million! Certainly, this contrast illustrates the necessity of this provision.

The amount a given individual or family would be allowed to inherit would have to be determined democratically. The monies raised by the imposition of such taxes would go to pay for the various social projects and programs deemed necessary for a universal decent standard of living. Such standards are already regularly set by the federal government and are not difficult to determine.

Implementing a program of progressive income redistribution. The goal of this plank is to eliminate misery associated with poverty. All citizens would, under this proposal, be provided with cradle-to-grave insurance, paid for entirely from income and inheritance taxes. In addition, everyone would be guaranteed adequate housing, an acceptable standard of health care, and a sufficient standard of living. As the Democratic Socialist Organizing Committee has stated, "Socialist democracy, we believe, would make it increasingly possible for the free provision of the necessities of life. That should be done as soon as possible with medicine; eventually, it should extend to housing, food and clothing."[21]

This program would also guarantee full employment for its workers. The societal commitment to full employment is crucial. The typical criticism of full employment concerns the incentive to work. Socialists are often accused of favoring measures that would reward people for not working, but this proposal might not be for the able-bodied who refused to work. This proposal would be coupled with one that legally required U.S. society to provide full employment. The wages and programs mentioned above would go to those unable to work, as well as to all who did work. Not everyone would earn the same amount of money, but the great inequalities of income that plague this society would be reduced.

In addition, this program would guarantee annual income approximately equivalent to trade-union wages. Thus, there would be no need for welfare from the state to those who were unemployed, because there would be no unemployment. As for those who refused to work, we believe that there are very few such people in society. Studies demonstrate that the number of those people on welfare yet able to work constitutes less than 25 percent of welfare recipients. The studies done concerning various groups of poor show that they are virtually unanimous in demonstrating a willingness and need to engage in useful labor.[22] The problem with capitalism is that it has always required a pool of cheap labor to exploit, and it has created unemployment during economic crises. We believe that a decent wage and fringe benefits, together with full employment, are the most rational and humane ways of guaranteeing a decent standard of living at all.

Implementing an expanded program of social construction. In providing full employment, there are always questions about the kind of work people will do. Will such jobs be meaningful, and will they be undertaken voluntarily? We believe that there is a great deal of work that urgently needs to be done but has a low priority due to the profit motive that dominates U.S. capitalism. For instance, the need for low-cost housing is immense, with inflation placing the cost of homes beyond even families at the median income level. Moreover, four out of ten U.S. families live in apartments. Many people, especially those of modest means, would like a house but cannot afford one. Aside from housing, there are energy needs that can be urgently met by converting to power from the sun, wind, and tides, a step that would provide millions of new jobs.[23] Employment in construction and related trades is often erratic because of weather and market conditions. This industry contains many who would prefer steady work at a decent standard of living. We believe that in providing full employment, there are enough unmet and important needs in this nation to provide everyone who wants one a freely chosen position.

Aside from social construction, we envision more teachers for special education and a reduction in class sizes at all levels of education. We also foresee the creation of many jobs for people who wish to represent community interests at all levels of government.

Implementing national indicator planning.   Unlike the current system, where private, profit-maximizing corporations are the planners of the economy, we propose a system where the primary goal of economic activity is the public good.   National indicator planning would use monetary, import, resource allocation, and other controls to direct production into more useful channels, redistributing income and wealth in favor of the lower classes. The present system requires that government policy making benefits the corporations.   These trickle-down solutions disproportionately benefit the elite and are therefore not only unfair but inefficient.[24] For example, the government is faced periodically with the problem of finding a way to stimulate the economy during an economic downturn. The socialist solution would be to spend federal monies through unemployment insurance, government jobs, and housing subsidies. In this way, the funds go directly to those most hurt by shortages, unemployment, inadequate housing, and the like. The capitalist response, on the other hand, is to advocate subsidies directly to business, which, they claim, will help the economy by encouraging companies to hire more workers, add to their inventories, and build new plants.   To provide subsidies to businesses rather than directly to needy individuals is based on the (faulty, we contend) assumption that private profit maximizes the public good.

Developing a national ecological plan compatible with the overall economic plan.   As discussed earlier, we live in an age in which the environment is threatened daily by hazardous chemicals, nuclear waste, and a host of air and water pollutants.   We believe that decisions concerning nuclear power and the dumping of hazardous materials should be made by the people who will be most affected by such events. We have provided ample evidence that the pollution problem in the United States is primarily a problem involving the priorities of capitalism--namely, profit. We believe that only a system that does not depend on profit, economic growth, and the continuous use and depletion of resources can practice conservation. Such conservation, we feel, must be carefully planned in a way that balances human needs with environmental quality.   Again, we feel that this is best accomplished through the widest democratic participation.

Michael Lerner has written about the economic and ecological planning in a democratic socialist state. He envisions each home being equipped with a voting device that is attached to the phone or television set.[25]   After issues have been debated in the media and at community meetings, the wishes of the public could be recorded and presented to elected public officials at local, regional, and national levels (each of whom would face a recall election anytime 10 percent of the registered voters signed a petition to that effect). In addition, groups would also have the power to put a given issue on the political agenda:

> Signatures of 1 percent of the voting population in the relevant area would give the group the right to (1) write its own proposal to be put directly to the people, and (2) air its views on the media (it would be given more time than any single position normally is, on the grounds that its view had not previously been given exposure in the usual debates on relevant issues).[26]

Lerner has further suggested that there would be an elected executive branch at all levels, but their decisions could easily be put to the voters for approval. In Lerner's scheme, the planning required for production and ecology, while complex, would be democratic:

> Each work unit and each consumer entity would submit its ideas and desires to a community board which would try to adjust them into a coherent whole, then resubmit the adjustments back to the populace for approval. Thereafter, they would be submitted to a regional board that took all the ideas and tried to develop a regional plan, which itself would be sent to a national board, which would try to adjust the regional plans. The last step would be to send the plan back to everyone for approval.[27]

Lerner has argued that equally complex planning is already done by the Department of Defense and other governmental units. However, the people consulted now are the heads of corporate boards, not working-class people. The decisions made by such boards reflect, of course, the wishes of the decision makers.

Lerner has also argued that it would be necessary to vote on the components as well as the totality of plans, and that one aspect of any plan would be the economy of the local community in which it is generated.

> Every community must have enough resources to experiment with education, housing, creativity, etc. The regional and national plans should deal with the minimum necessary number of issues: e.g., where to build new cities, how to solve general ecological problems, how to arrange transportation between localities, foreign trade, taxation, and long-term financing. The regional and national plans would have as one key task the allocation and redistribution of resources in such a way as to guarantee that no one area suffers because it does not have adequate natural resources or because a main source of its economic strength (e.g., car manufacturing or mining) is shut down for reasons of preserving the ecology. But since the idea of giving each community a large sum initially for discretionary planning is key to this conception, the national plan is likely to be less complicated than the present federal budget in an unplanned economy, because so much that is now decided nationally will be decided at the local level.[28]

Such planning would be oriented toward overcoming some of the root causes of certain types of elite deviance. Instead of being based on planned obsolescence, all goods would be designed to last as long as possible. This would eliminate much waste and pollution and would save energy, as well.

Implementing a tax policy that would discourage private overseas investment and development of multinational corporations. We suggest that the United States does not need a multinational empire. Rather, its best hope lies in the promotion of a peaceful, stable, and prosperous world. This is best accomplished by policies designed to end the poverty, famine, and political instability in the Third World. Such humane policies would also end the unpopular opinion concerning "ugly American" and "Yankee imperialism" in much of the Third World. In addition, these policies will return many jobs to the United States that have been exported by multinationals in recent years. To accomplish these goals, stringent measures should be provided to curb and then liquidate the great multinational corporations. Moreover, private investment by U.S. corporations overseas should be discouraged through an appropriate tax policy. These things cannot be accomplished overnight and will require a transition period to minimize the disruption of the U.S. economy. We do, however, believe such a conversion is both possible and prudent.

The Implementation of Economic Democracy

Now that we have characterized how economic democracy ought to work, let's deal with some of the practical problems and questions that always seem to arise in any serious discussion of how it might be implemented.

To begin, the essence of socialism is a cooperative spirit among the people. Yet, for some reason, it is commonly believed that people are naturally sinful, aggressive, and self-seeking. In this perspective, competition is natural and long-range cooperation is impossible. If this postulate is accurate, then the goal of socialism will always elude human societies. The question, then, is whether human beings in groups are capable of long-range cooperative relationships in which the needs of the group supersede the needs of the individual.

The U.S. experience is so competitive that we easily assume such competition is natural. Virtually all aspects of American life involve competition, whether in school or on the job, in organizations, or in activities such as sports, music, and dating. However, there is ample evidence from anthropological studies to show that societies like the Zuni have individuals who are group centered. The members of these societies never attempt to outdo anyone in their society, and they accept the sacrifice for the accomplishment of group goals as natural.[29] The conclusion derived from studies like this is that people in societies can be taught to be competitive or cooperative. There is no necessary obstacle to the possibility that Americans could be taught from infancy to work for group goals, rather than strive for individual achievement at the expense of others. In short, human nature is really social nature shaped by the society in which the individual lives.

In a related issue, it is often argued that socialism runs contrary to human nature, because one's needs are met by society, whether he or she works or not. The assumption is that massive inequalities are necessary to motivate citizens to work and avoid a class of lazy welfare recipients. Motivation in socialist countries could be achieved in several ways, without using the repressive tactics of a totalitarian regime. The first is to socialize citizens to work for the good of the community. Evidence from many experiments with communes shows that the successful ones developed an ideology that the members of the community shared. In a group sharing a common ideology, informal sanctions can be used to achieve conformity among potential deviants.

All societies have members who vary in talent, achievement, and motivation. The problem for a socialist society is how to reward excellence. This could be done through nonmaterial satisfactions, such as honors, responsible community functions, or some extra material benefits. The extra material benefits must be kept in check within a socialist economy, however, so that the private accumulation of wealth is confined within tolerable limits. The permissible maximum, for example, could be twice the median income with the guaranteed minimum being one-half the median income. Such a plan would allow everyone the necessities and the personal choice to work for some additional benefits.[30]

Another motivational problem is how to get people to do society's dirty work. After all, if all of one's basic needs are met, why should he or she do dangerous or menial jobs? Capitalist countries solve this problem of job allocation by paying extra monies in the case of hazardous jobs, or, in the case of demeaning work, having an underclass (usually minorities) whose opportunities are so limited that they have little choice but to cooperate. A socialist country could see that these necessary tasks were done by either appealing to persons on ideological grounds to give a period of time for these societal duties or by conscripting youth to do the necessary work of society as a kind of societal tax that they owe as citizens. Just as in the time of war, able-bodied persons (male and female) would owe, say, two years of service to their society.

A problem that plagues all existing socialist systems (but is not limited to them) is massive bureaucratization. The more the economy is controlled by the government, the greater the problem of inflated statism, which translates into the twin problems of centralized power and inefficiency. The problem of inefficiency can be addressed through the constant monitoring of procedures and administrators, with the people affected having the power to redress grievances and change inadequate procedures.

The other problem emanating from excessive bureaucratization--centralized power--is especially crucial, for if it is not solved, then the goal of democratic socialism is unachievable. This is the problem of the so-called socialist countries with totalitarian regimes. The group that gains power tends to stay in power and sees its goals as those needed by the society. This illustrates the strong organizational tendency labeled the "Iron Law of Oligarchy" by Robert Michels.[31]

While this probability plagues social organizations, under certain conditions, it does not occur--namely, where democracy prevails.[32] By definition, a democracy exists where at least two political parties regularly compete for office, and control alternates periodically. The changes of this happening are maximized when: (1) the citizens have a strong interest, concern, and commitment to the society; (2) the subunits (communities, states) are relatively autonomous units forming a federation; (3) the leaders get few special prerequisites of office, making them little different from the masses in material rewards; and (4) dissent and innovation are allowed.[33] Admittedly, the problem of the emergence of a self-serving power elite is an especially dangerous issue for socialist countries. Therefore, these societies must institutionalize forms of democratic control at all levels, using the insights provided above. The key is to control power, making it both concentrated and dispersed. The citizens must be ever diligent to counter oligarchic tendencies, and there must be constitutional avenues for the control of the controllers.

Another practical problem facing any socialist society is the high cost of providing minimal benefits to all members. The semisocialist countries of Western Europe have extremely high taxes to level material differences and provide the necessary services. Also, it is charged, societies will experience ruinous inflation if they increase expenditures for social services.

In the United States, there are at least two basic ways that money could be raised for increasing social programs without too great an adjustment. One source of money would come from paring the inflated military budget. The question is how much the $250 billion budget could be reduced without endangering the safety of the society. This question quickly divides liberals and conservatives. Nonetheless, we believe that it is safe to say that, if objective observers (i.e., those outside the military, those in business without military contracts, and those public officials outside districts with huge military expenditures) examined military expenditures carefully, they would find numerous military bases that should be closed, redundancy in weapons systems, too many highly paid officers, and a too-expensive pension system. Obviously, if the appropriate cuts in the military budget were made, the savings could be deployed elsewhere to meet social needs.

A second and even more lucrative source of monies to finance increased social programs would be to eliminate tax expenditures (about $330 billion dollars in 1984). These are monies that the government could collect but chooses not to. Most of these tax breaks go to the upper-middle and upper classes. "There are enormous savings to be made in these areas simply by following in fact the principle we now honor in the breech: that those best able to pay should bear their share of the tax burden."[34]

Finally, there is the question upon which all else hinges: How could an economic democracy develop in U.S. society? If the corporate rich are the powerful and control the governmental apparatus (including the ability to repress dissent, the media, and the universities), how are the fundamental changes in the structure necessary for democratic socialism to occur? And who will be included in a social movement bent on making these social changes?

The obvious candidates are those most oppressed by capitalism--the poor, minorities, women, the aged, and the working class (including white- and blue-collar workers). These categories, however, have historically failed to cooperate in a common venture to change the system. They have not developed the class consciousness Marx envisioned because of racial antipathies and other prejudices, because of their own self-doubt, and because they believe in the viability of the current politico-economic system. They tend to believe that the opportunities available in society will eventually pay off for them or their children. They believe that capitalism is responsible for our greatness and will meet the challenges of the future successfully. In short, persons in these social categories have not seen that they are oppressed. Ironically, they accept the system that works to their disadvantage. Thus, they adhere to beliefs damaging to their interests, or what Marx termed *false consciousness*.

Elite Deviance and Economic Democracy

Most certainly, there are those who view these proposals for economic democracy as being "too radical," fearing that such change would undermine the very capitalist system that has given U.S. society the wealth and power that has, in the minds of many Americans, proven the United States' superiority in the world. For such critics, the nature of capitalism is not the issue at hand. Such critics accept the distribution of power and wealth as given and believe that the solutions to the problems of elite deviance (defined by them as "white-collar crime") merely require a series of legal reforms designed to fine tune an otherwise useful and just social order.

In the past few years, a multitude of schemes have been put forth, designed to deal with corporate crime. In fact, so many of these schemes have been proposed that only a brief summary can be given here. Basically, such proposals say more about the faults of the current system than they do about the chances of accomplishing meaningful inroads against the problem of corporate crime. Fisse and Braithwaite have recently devoted an entire volume to the impact of publicity on corporate offenders.[35]   After examining thirteen of the most celebrated cases of corporate crime in the last fifteen years or so, the authors conclude that the only adverse impact such publicity had was nonfinancial, including the loss of individual and corporate prestige, declining morale, distraction from job goals, and humiliation in the witness box for corporate executives. At times, reforms within corporations were instituted following the revelation of scandal. However, according to the authors, these reforms were initiated largely to convince the government not to prosecute offending companies.

What is truly needed, claim these researchers, are more effective means of publicizing corporate wrongdoing. A host of recommendations have been made, including:

• Using qui tam suits by consumer groups, which would allow for private prosecution and securing of funds from imposed fines on corporate offenders.
• Relaxing of contempt laws to allow good-faith press comments on matters pertinent to trials.
• Providing immunity from prosecution for voluntary corporate disclosure.
• Requiring official, governmental inquiries into corporate reactions to scandal, particularly those concerning changes in corporate policies.
• Requiring mandatory corporate disclosure of risks of serious harms.
• Promoting international exposure of irresponsible corporate practices, including international consumer information networks, investigative journalism, and an international complaint forum.
• Using publicity paid for by corporations as part of the punishment inflicted on offending corporations.
• Using formal publicity following trials to convey information to the public concerning corporate offenses and the consequences of noncompliance with the judgments laid down.

• Initiating presentence or probation orders against offending corporations, requiring disclosure of organizational reforms and disciplinary action undertaken as a result of the offenses in question.[36]

Aside from the use of publicity, other reform-oriented students of corporate deviance have advocated such measures as:

• Declaring occupational disqualification for corporate offenders.[37]
• Using fines, imprisonment, and rehabilitation more extensively in punishing convicted corporate executives.
• Appointing certain members of boards of directors of convicted companies to represent the public interest by a Federal Corporation Commission. Their task would be to assure that laws are being complied with, to oversee the environmental impact of future actions by convicted corporations, to oversee mandated reforms, and to implement judgments against the corporation.
• Denying insurance coverage to companies lacking adequate systems of information concerning internal wrongdoing.
• Designating a specific corporate official to be charged with the preparation of all raw data concerning violations and disclosure thereof.
• Providing inspectors to oversee enforcement of federal regulations.
• Offering protection and rewards to so-called whistle blowers.
• Establishing an exchange program between officials in both business and government.[38]

Conklin has also developed a scheme of corporate criminal law reforms.[39] These reforms fall into two broad categories: (1) those that deal specifically with laws and practices relating to crimes committed by corporations; and (2) those that deal specifically with the corporation's internal structure of decision making and rewards.

In many ways, the proposals for corporate criminal law reforms amount to a get-tough policy regarding corporations who commit crimes. Such proposals include but are by no means limited to the following:

1. The consolidation of existing consumer protection agencies and/or the sharing of information among such agencies. This would make obtaining evidence of fraud easier than it is now. Gilbert Geis has proposed that such agencies infiltrate corporations suspected of committing crimes for delicate undercover work.[40]
2. A mandatory replacement or refund system should be established, through which consumer loss resulting from merchant or corporate dishonesty would be reimbursed from tax revenues.
3. An annual report of business crimes by government, like the FBI Uniform Crime Reports, should be developed. Perhaps, suggests Geis, we should establish a list of the ten most-wanted white-collar criminals.
4. Agencies that are designed to regulate corporate practices should either have administrators who are given fixed terms (perhaps coinciding with that of the president) or be removed from the control of the executive branch and made responsible to either Congress or the federal courts.

5. Those companies and executives found guilty of wrong doing should be required to make a public confession, which is done in countries such as Germany.

6. Corporate accountability to both stockholders and the public should be increased, perhaps through the practice of federal chartering. Under this proposal:

a. Corporations whose gross assets (including those of subsidiaries) exceeded $100,000 would be required to obtain a federal license to engage in interstate business.

b. Detailed information on the financial affairs of the corporation, including dealings with foreign firms, would have to be supplied periodically to the FTC.

c. Diversification "incidental to the business in which it is authorized to engage," as well as ownership of the stock in other companies, would be forbidden (this rule would be prospective only, leaving existing relationships unchanged).

d. Any proposal altering the existing rights of shareholders, as well as any financial dealings between the corporation and the officers and directors, would have to be fully disclosed to the shareholders.

e. Directors could not be employed by or have a financial interest in a competitor, but would have to have a financial interest in their own corporation.

f. Any corporation in violation of the antitrust laws, or one which discriminated by sex, employed child labor, or refused to bargain collectively, could lose its federal license and hence its right to do interstate business.

g. Penalties would range from nominal fines for a thirty-day period during a violation of the license, to 1 percent of the book value of the capital stock or assets per month, to actual revocation of the license following hearings by the FTC and an action instituted by the Attorney General in any district court.[41]

Walter Adams proposes extending federal chartering regulations to include any industry with assets in excess of $250 million or any corporation that ranks among the eight top producers in an industry where eight firms control 70 percent of more of a market. Under Adams' plan, chartered firms would be prohibited from:

1. acquiring the stock, assets, or property of another company;

2. granting or receiving any discrimination in price, service, or allowances, except where such discrimination can be demonstrated to be justified by savings in cost;

3. engaging in any tie-in arrangements or exclusive dealerships; and

4. participating in any scheme of interlocking control over any other corporation.[42]

In addition, such firms would be obligated to:

1. perform the duties of a common carrier by serving all customers on reasonable and nondiscriminatory terms;

2. license patents and know-how to other firms on a reasonable royalty basis;

3. pursue pricing and product policies, calculated to achieve capacity production and full employment;[43]

4. allow those who blow the whistle on corporate crime to keep as reward up to one-half of the fine(s) levied in court against the corporation reported. The 1899 Rivers and Harbors Act already contains such so-called qui tam action clauses; they could be extended to include other types of corporate criminality;[44]

5. eliminate the nolo contendere plea and pass reforms that clearly specify the extent of liability of both corporate executives and the corporations for which they work in various situations;

6. prohibit executives from working in their profession following conviction of wrongdoing and release from prison;

7. encourage business to develop better internal controls through the use of audits and accounting procedures that make it more difficult to conduct secret and illegal financial transactions.

The other major thrust of liberal reform concerns changing the corporate structure itself. The following proposals take modest steps toward socialism. However, as Andrew Hacker has commented:

> None . . . call for so drastic a transformation as proposed by Marx and Engels (The Communist Manifesto). . . . [T]he implications inhering in these essays should not be minimized. Put very simply, they will be fought at every stage by organizations having the skills, resources, and experiences for this kind of struggle.[45]

Thus, some liberals are not hopeful about even modest reforms concerning corporate conduct and corporate structure. Still, critics like John Flynn do have some interesting suggestions:

1. The corporation's constituency should be redefined. Under this plan, employees would be given a voice in the running of the corporation's affairs. (See Lens' proposals in Chapter 1 for a socialist view of this proposal.) Workers would provide a check-and-power balance against corporate management.

2. The Kelso Plan should be implemented to give workers a second income. Under this plan, corporate capital formation would take place via the purchase of stock to an Employee Stock Ownership Trust, which is paid credit on future corporate dividends. The plan requires the corporation to pay dividends based on net earnings to the employee stockholders. The goal here is to redistribute the wealth in part, as well as to give employees a shareholder's status in the company for which they work.

3. Finally, measures should be provided to end the influence of large amounts of corporate funds in political financing; corporate disclosure of ownership; antitrust actions to break up both vertical (within one industry) and horizontal (across different industries) monopolies by huge corporations (without nationalization).[46]

Thus, liberal proposals to remedy the ills of corporate crime employ a combination of criminal justice reform and further democratization of the corporation itself.

In part, these proposals assume that democracy, when extended to the corporation and the workplace, will work to overcome the undemocratic effects of the maldistribution of wealth and political power. Liberals believe that it is possible to do this using nonsocialistic reforms.

There are a number of problems with these suggestions. First, each in its own way represents a tacit acknowledgment that corporate crime is out of control. This conclusion is understandable, considering the secrecy that surrounds corporate crime (hence the need for publicity), the lack of punishment that results (hence the need for experimental techniques such as occupational disqualification), and the lack of resources that are committed to fight it (hence the suggestion for more government inspectors). Many of these reforms are compatible with the framework for economic democracy incorporated above. But by themselves, none of them aims at the root cause of corporate crime: the system of political economy that makes crime both profitable and even necessary.

There is a fundamental distinction between the liberal, reformist approach to white-collar crime and our own. Liberal students of the subject view corporate criminality as a function of bad apples, including supposedly criminogenic industries, amoral managers, and unethical companies.[47] Such students are careful to point out that the fault is not that of the system of corporate capitalism itself. In defense, they assume that there are large corporations and entire industries in which corporate deviance is either rare or virtually nonexistent. Thus, it is not the business system that is at fault, but a few of its bad apples.

We feel that this argument is based on very unreliable evidence; no such assumption is warranted. First, the bad-apple theory is based almost solely on official statistics concerning corporations that are charged with and convicted of criminal wrongdoing. However, this is misrepresentative, since it does not count those corporations that victimize workers, consumers, or the public at large yet never get caught. There are no victimization surveys that estimate the actual rate of corporate offenses. We do not study the incidence of corporate crime like we study street crime. Therefore, we cannot accept at face value any theory based on unreliable evidence.

Second, as mentioned in Chapter 1, between 1970 and 1979, 11 percent of the largest 1,000 U.S. corporations were convicted of at least one illegal act (and this estimate is low). Imagine for a moment that, between 1970 and 1979, 11 percent of the adult population of the United States had been convicted of some illegal offense and sentenced to prison. As a result, approximately 12 million people would be placed in a prison system that is overcrowded with a mere one-half million inmates. At such a point, liberals and conservatives alike would call crime an epidemic--an institutionalized phenomena in U.S. society. However, when the same level of corporate crime is discussed, the problem is not considered to be as serious.

There is, of course, the question of just how much deviant behavior has to occur before it is considered to be an institutionalized practice. We can find no simple answer. If one examines both the illegal and unethical practices we have described in this book, there is plenty of evidence to indicate that virtually all sectors of the corporate economy and federal government engage regularly in deviant behavior. At the very least, a great deal more research needs to be done. For the moment, we reiterate that we find no credible evidence whatsoever in support of the bad-apple view of white-collar criminality.

Second, the reforms mentioned above deal only with corporate criminality. Barely, if ever, do reforms address the interdependent nature of corporate, political, and organized criminal deviance (as discussed in Chapter 8). While corporate crime is a major factor in elite deviance, it is certainly not the only problem in need of resolution. Elite deviance is deviance between and within organizations. No matter how many corporate executives, politicians, and organized crime leaders are sent to jail, the organizations of which they were a part continue on.

Third, reformist suggestions fail to deal with many of the social problems created by the organizational society in which we live: environmental pollution, the threat of nuclear war, inflation, unemployment, poverty, economic development in the Third World, racism, sexism, the decay of the United States' economic infrastructure, government deficits, alienation in the work place, street crime, and cost overruns in defense weapons systems contracting. None of these problems is dealt with when the focus is placed on corporate criminality alone.[48]

Finally, elite deviance includes more than just criminal acts. Ethical values and moral principles are created, shaped, and accepted as part of ideologies precisely because of the great power and wealth held by elites. We stand with the National Conference of Catholic Bishops in asserting that "the time has come for ... [an] ... experiment in economic democracy: the creation of an order that guarantees the minimum conditions of human dignity for in the economic sphere for every person."[49]

We believe that corporate morality flies in the face of such dignity, and that such dignity is achievable only through a fundamental democratic restructuring of society.

SUGGESTED READINGS
ON NEW DIRECTIONS FOR U.S. SOCIETY

Alperovitz, Gar, and Jeff Faux. *Rebuilding America: A Blueprint for the New Economy.* New York: Pantheon, 1984.

Bowles, Samuel, David M. Gordon, and Thomas E. Weisskopf. *Beyond the Waste Land: A Democratic Alternative to Economic Decline.* Garden City, NY: Doubleday/Anchor, 1984.

Carnoy, Martin, and Derek Schearer. *Economic Democracy: The Challenge of 1980's.* Armonk, NY: M. E. Sharpe, 1980.

Cohen, Joshua, and Joel Rogers. *On Democracy: Toward a Transformation of American Society.* Baltimore: Penguin, 1983.

Green, Mark. *Winning Back America.* New York: Bantam, 1982.

Harrington, Michael. *The New American Poverty.* New York: Holt, Rinehart and Winston, 1984.

------. "A Case for Democratic Planning." In *Alternatives: Proposals for America from the Democratic Left*, edited by Irving Howe. New York: Pantheon, 1984.

Hayden, Tom. *The American Future: New Visions Beyond Old Frontiers.* Boston: South End Press, 1980.

"The New Populism." *The Progressive* 48 (June 1984): entire issue.

NOTES

1. For elaboration on this point, see the following: James M. Henslin, "Social Problems and Systemic Origins," in *Social Problems in American Society*, 2nd ed., ed. James M. Henslin and Larry T. Reynolds, 375-81 (Boston: Holbrook, 1976); William Ryan, *Blaming the Victim*, 2nd ed. (New York: Pantheon, 1977); and Michael Parenti, *Power and the Powerless* (New York: St. Martin's Press, 1978).
2. Michael Parenti, *Democracy for the Few*, 3rd ed. (New York: St. Martin's Press, 1980), 314.
3. Parenti, *Democracy for the Few*, 3rd ed., 314.
4. Also see Vernon E. Jordan, Jr., "The New Minimalism," *Newsweek*, 14 August 1978, 13.
5. Parenti, *Democracy for the Few*, 3rd ed., 314.
6. Parenti, *Democracy for the Few*, 3rd ed., 312.
7. Michael Harrington, cited in "We Are Socialists of the Democratic Left," a statement of principles by the Democratic Socialist Organizing Committee (1978), 2. For more on this theme, see Michael Harrington, *Decade of Decision* (New York: Simon and Schuster, 1980).
8. Ralph Miliband, "The Future of Socialism in England," in *The Socialist Register 1977*, 38-50 (London: Merlin, 1977). See also Samuel Bowles and Herbert Gintis, *Schooling in Capitalist America: Educational Reforms and the Contradictions of Economic Life* (New York: Basic Books, 1976), Chapter 11.
9. M. Mintz and J. Cohen, *Power Inc.* (New York: Viking, 1976), iii.
10. Parenti, *Power and the Powerless*, 203.
11. Michael Harrington, *Socialism* (New York: Saturday Review Press, 1979), 8-9.
12. Richard C. Edwards, Michael Reich, and Thomas E. Weisskopf, eds., *The Capitalist System*, 2nd ed. (Englewood Cliffs, NJ: Prentice-Hall, 1978), 517.
13. Miliband, 42-43.
14. Michael Harrington, "How to Reshape America's Economy," *Dissent* 23 (Spring 1976), 122.
15. Harrington, "How to Reshape America's Economy," 122.
16. John Woodmansee et al., *The World of a Giant Corporation* (Seattle: North Country Press, 1975), 70-71. Used with permission of People's Business Commission.
17. Harrington, "How to Reshape America's Economy," 22.
18. Harrington, "We Are Socialists of the Democratic Left," 3.

19. See, for example, R. Parker, *The Myth of the Middle Class* (New York: Liveright, 1972); Phillip Stern, *The Rape of the Taxpayer* (New York: Random House, 1973); J. Turner and C. Starnes, *Inequality: Privilege and Power in America* (Pacific Palisades, CA: Goodyear, 1976).

20. M. Zeitlin, "Who Runs America? The Same Old Gang," *The Progressive* 26 (June 1978), 14-19.

21. Harrington, "We Are Socialists of the Democratic Left," 2.

22. For a detailed review of such studies, see C. H. Anderson and J. R. Gibson, *Toward a New Sociology*, 3rd ed. (Homewood, IL: Dorsey Press, 1978), 170-76.

23. See the so-called program for economic conversion designed to shift the United States toward a peacetime economy, available from SANE, Washington, D.C.

24. Michael Harrington, "The Socialist Case," *The Center Magazine*, July/August 1976.

25. Cable television in Columbus, Ohio, currently provides an interactive system where individuals can instantaneously record their preferences in a central computer.

26. Michael Lerner, cited in M. Edwards et al., eds., *The Capitalist System*, 2nd ed. (Englewood Cliffs, NJ: Prentice-Hall, 1978), 535. For more complete information, see Lerner, *The New Socialist Revolution* (New York: Dell, 1973).

27. Edwards et al., 536.

28. Edwards et al., 536.

29. See Ruth Benedict, *Patterns of Culture* (New York: Mentor Books, 1934).

30. See Henry Pachter, "Freedom, Authority, Participation," *Dissent* 25 (Summer 1978), 296.

31. Robert Michels, *Political Parties*, trans. Eden and Cedar Paul (New York: Free Press, 1966). See also Max Weber, *The Theory of Social and Economic Organization* (Glencoe, IL: Free Press, 1947).

32. See Seymour Martin Lipset, Martin Trow, and James C. Coleman, *Union Democracy: The Internal Politics of the International Typographers Union* (Garden City, NY: Doubleday Anchor, 1962).

33. Anthony M. Orum, *Introduction to Political Sociology: The Social Anatomy of the Body Politic* (Englewood Cliffs, NJ: Prentice-Hall, 1978), 259-60.

34. Harrington, "How to Reshape America's Economy," 122. See also Robert M. Brandon et al., *Tax Politics* (New York: Pantheon, 1976).

35. B. Fisse and J. Braithwaite, *The Impact of Publicity on Corporate Offenders* (Albany: SUNY Press, 1983).

36. Fisse and Braithwaite, 243, 312.

37. M. F. McDermott, "Occupational Disqualification of Corporate Executives: An Innovative Condition of Probation," *Journal of Criminal Law and Criminology* 73 (Summer 1982), 604-41.

38. C. D. Stone, *Where the Law Ends* (New York: Harper and Row, 1975), 133-60.

39. J. Conklin, *Illegal But Not Criminal: Business Crime in America* (Englewood Cliffs, NJ: Prentice-Hall, 1977), 104-following.

40. G. Geis, "Upper World Crime," in *Current Perspectives on Criminal Behavior: Original Essays in Criminology*, ed. A. Blumberg, 130-following (New York: Knopf, 1984).

41. R. Nader, "The Case for Federal Chartering," in *Taming the Giant Corporation*, ed. R. Nader and M. Green (New York: Grossman, 1973).

42. W. Adams, "The Antitrust Alternative," in *Taming the Giant Corporation*, ed. R. Nader and M. Green, 130–50 (New York: Grossman, 1973).

43. A. S. Miller, "The Courts and Corporate Accountability," in *Taming the Giant Corporation*, ed. R. Nader and M. Green, 198–214 (New York: Grossman, 1973).

44. Miller, 146–47.

45. A. Hacker, "Citizen Counteraction, in *Taming the Giant Corporation*, ed. R. Nader and M. Green, 182–97 (New York: Grossman, 1973), 182.

46. J. Flynn, "Corporate Democracy: Nice Work if You Can Get It," in *Taming the Giant Corporation*, ed. R. Nader and M. Green, 94–111 (New York: Grossman, 1973).

47. See, for example, M. B. Clinard and M. Yeager, *Corporate Crime* (New York: Macmillan, 1980); and M. B. Clinard, *Corporate Ethics and Crime: The Role of Middle Management* (Beverly Hills: Sage, 1983).

48. For an excellent discussion of how the alienating nature of capitalism itself relates to many of these conditions, see J. Wildeman, *Social Problems in America: Alienation and Discontinuity* (New York: Irvington, 1983).

49. *New York Times*, 12 November 1984, p. B-10.

Subject Index

Name Index